ALLEGORY

The Theory of a Symbolic Mode

ALLEGORY

The Theory
of a Symbolic Mode

By ANGUS FLETCHER
Columbia University

'Tis no disparagement to be a stranger,
or so irksome to be an exile. The rain is
a stranger to the earth, rivers to the Sea,
Jupiter in Egypt, the Sun to us all. The
Soul is an alien to the Body, a Nightingale
to the air, a Swallow in an house, and
Ganymede in Heaven, an Elephant at
Rome, a Phoenix in India; and such things
commonly please us best which are most
strange, and come farthest off.

—*The Anatomy of Melancholy*

Cornell Paperbacks
CORNELL UNIVERSITY PRESS
Ithaca and London

CORNELL UNIVERSITY PRESS

First published 1964
Second printing 1965
Third printing 1967
First printing, Cornell Paperbacks, 1970

International Standard Book Number 0-8014-9106-1
Library of Congress Catalog Card Number 64-11415

PRINTED IN THE UNITED STATES OF AMERICA
BY VAIL-BALLOU PRESS, INC.
ILLUSTRATIONS BY THE MERIDEN GRAVURE CO.
BOUND BY VAIL-BALLOU PRESS, INC.

IN MEMORIAM

Angus Somerville Fletcher

Nancy Erickson

Acknowledgments

IN the preparation of this book I have received help and encouragement of many kinds. The list of works cited gives some idea of my indebtedness to other authors, a number of whom, Northrop Frye, Mircea Eliade, I. A. Richards, Kenneth Burke, William Empson, and above all, Freud, have been guiding influences on almost every aspect of my research. I find that my thoughts on allegory go back several years to discussions with former teachers and colleagues. At Yale, Professor John Pope's graduate seminar in Spenser introduced me to the subject of allegory, while before that, in undergraduate courses with Professors J. T. Curtiss and L. P. Curtis, I became interested in the history of ideas. Later at Harvard I again took up my study of allegory, beginning first with some short essays for Professor Archibald MacLeish, then continuing it in a doctoral dissertation written under the direction of Professors I. A. Richards and Reuben Brower. To these three men I would like to express my thanks, especially for their patience in letting my thoughts take shape rather slowly. I particularly recall Professor Brower in the midst of heavy academic and administrative duties finding the time to give a careful and detailed reading to the manuscript of my thesis. One further debt from my years as a graduate student needs to be acknowledged. Professor W. J. Bate was an inspiration to all who studied the work of Johnson with him, and he also trained us in literary criticism; his influence here too remains deep and pervasive.

ACKNOWLEDGMENTS

I would like to thank my friends and colleagues at Cornell University for their kindness in giving technical advice and general encouragement. At no specific point, but throughout the evolution of this book, Professor Ephim Fogel was a source of information, and I would like to acknowledge his willingness to put at my disposal his broad knowledge of Continental as well as of English letters. Professor Robert M. Adams has likewise exercised over my thinking a leavening influence, his wit and learning always being at the service of critical debate. Professor William R. Keast arranged for me to receive financial aid from the Cornell English Department's Grant-in-Aid Fund, for which I am most grateful.

My thanks are due also to the Dean of the Faculty of Columbia University for arranging a grant from Columbia University so that an enlarged section of illustrations could be included in this book.

I have incurred a lasting obligation to the Library of Cornell University; its cooperative staff, particularly its Director of Circulation, Mr. Arthur Kulp, facilitated my research in many ways.

A number of friends have in a sense been the second authors of this book. Professor Taylor Stoehr read and reread large parts of the manuscript, correcting, evaluating, and suggesting many valuable changes. I would like to thank him for all his criticisms. Professor Calvin Edwards put at my disposal his encyclopedic knowledge of Spenserian poetics and Renaissance mythography, and in the course of innumerable conversations with him I have no doubt simply assimilated ideas without thinking that they were his. There is no way to state the extent of my indebtedness to him. Finally, I would like to thank my friend Professor Howard Flock. His expert counsel on psychological theory, his advice in the selection of illustrations, and his numerous general criticisms have played a continuing role in the development of this book. It is an especial pleasure to record this debt of gratitude.

ANGUS FLETCHER

New York City
January 1964

viii

Contents

Illustrations

ALLEGORY

The Theory of a Symbolic Mode

Introduction

ALLEGORY is a protean device, omnipresent in Western literature from the earliest times to the modern era. No comprehensive historical treatment of it exists or would be possible in a single volume, nor is it my aim to fill even a part of this gap. Hoping instead to get at the essence of the mode, I have outlined a theoretical, mainly nonhistorical analysis of literary elements.

Whereas a full-scale history would entail numberless small observations of changing literary convention, a theoretical treatment of allegory will succeed by opposite means: it must keep to a plane of generality. We have to account for an even wider variety of materials than with categories like "satire," "tragedy," or "comedy." Only the broadest notions, for example the modal concepts of "irony" or "mimesis," embrace so many different kinds of literature. Given this range of reference, no narrowly exclusive stipulated definition will be useful, however desirable it might seem, while formal precision may at present even be misleading to the student of the subject. What I have attempted, therefore, is to balance the claims of general theory and simple induction: what follows is a preliminary description intended to yield a model of allegory. I have gone through some initial mapping stages of criticism and have asked, in a spirit of theoretical discussion, what sort of characters are called allegorical heroes, what sort of things they typically do, what their style of behavior is, what sort of images are used to portray their actions and

Questions

1

character. In brief, I have asked what is the mode of an allegorical
fiction.

In the simplest terms, allegory says one thing and means another.
It destroys the normal expectation we have about language, that
our words "mean what they say." When we predicate quality *x* of
person Y, Y really is what our predication says he is (or we assume
so); but allegory would turn Y into something other (*allos*) than
what the open and direct statement tells the reader.[1] Pushed to an
extreme, this ironic usage would subvert language itself, turning
everything into an Orwellian newspeak.[2] In this sense we see how

[1] *Allegory* from *allos* + *agoreuein* (*other* + *speak openly, speak in the assembly or market*). *Agoreuein* connotes public, open, declarative speech. This
sense is inverted by the prefix *allos.* Thus allegory is often called "inversion."
E.g., ed. Thomas Cooper, in Thomas Elyot, *Bibliotheca Eliotae: Eliotes Dictionarie* (London, 1559): "*Allegoria*—a figure called inversion, where it is
one in woordes, and an other in sentence or meaning"; Edward Phillips, in
The New World of English Words (4th ed., London, 1678): "*Allegory*—
Inversion or changing: In Rhetorick it is a mysterious saying, wherein there
is couched something that is different from the literal sense." Sometimes the
term *inversio* may be taken in its original sense of *translation,* while *translatio*
is but the Latin equivalent of the Greek *metaphor.* On translation as an exegetical device, see R. M. Grant, *The Letter and the Spirit* (London, 1957), 34.
Jules Pépin, in *Mythe et allégorie* (Paris, 1958), 87–88, finds Plutarch the first
critic to use the word "allegory" instead of its older Greek equivalent *hyponoia,* also the first to use the verb "to allegorize." The political overtones
of the verb *agoreuein* need always to be emphasized, insofar as censorship may
produce devious, ironical ways of speaking.

[2] Thucydides, *The Peloponnesian War,* tr. Rex Warner (Penguin ed., 1954),
III, ch. vi, provides the first major discussion of newspeak in Western history.
Describing the revolution in Corcyra, Thucydides shows that "the love of
power, operating through greed and through personal ambition," created a
new linguistic climate in which language itself was corrupted, as by a plague,
the same plague which is a synecdoche, or perhaps a metonymy, for all the
ills of the Peloponnesian war. Such was the inauguration of the Big Lie. "So
revolutions broke out in city after city. . . . To fit in with the change of
events, words, too, had to change their usual meanings. What used to be
described as a thoughtless act of aggression was now regarded as the courage
one would expect to find in a party member; to think of the future and wait
was merely another way of saying one was a coward; any idea of moderation
was just an attempt to disguise one's unmanly character; ability to understand

allegory is properly considered a mode: it is a fundamental process of encoding our speech. For the very reason that it is a radical linguistic procedure, it can appear in all sorts of different works, many of which fall far short of the confusing doubleness that made Orwell's newspeak such an effective brainwashing device.

An allegorical mode of expression characterizes a quite extraordinary variety of literary kinds: chivalric or picaresque romances and their modern equivalent, the "western," utopian political satires, quasi-philosophical anatomies, personal attacks in epigrammatic form, pastorals of all sorts, apocalyptic visions, encyclopedic epics containing *summas* of true and false learning, naturalistic muckraking novels whose aim is to propagandize social change, imaginary voyages like Lucian's *The True History*, Swift's *Gulliver's Travels*, Verne's *A Journey to the Center of the Earth*, or Henri Michaux's *Voyage en Grande Garabagne*, detective stories in both the genteel whodunit and the hard-boiled Hammett-Chandler styles, fairy tales (many of which are "cautionary tales"),[3] debate poems like the anonymous medieval "The Owl and the Nightingale" and Yeats's

---

a question from all sides meant that one was totally unfitted for action. Fanatical enthusiasm was the mark of a real man, and to plot against an enemy behind his back was perfectly legitimate self-defence. . . . These parties were not formed to enjoy the benefits of the established laws, but to acquire power by overthrowing the existing regime; and the members of these parties felt confidence in each other not because of any fellowship in a religious communion, but because they were partners in crime. If an opponent made a reasonable speech, the party in power, so far from giving it a generous reception, took every precaution to see that it had no practical effect" (*Peloponnesian War*, 209). Since Thucydides' semifictional speeches present the ideology of the Greek city-states, this passage gives us a theory of political revolution; he is making the same point Orwell made in his essay "Politics and the English language." With almost religious belief in the truth-value of individual words and phrases, Orwell asserted that "the present political chaos [at the end of the Second World War] is connected with the decay of language, and . . . one can probably bring about some improvement by starting at the verbal end." *Homage to Catalonia* attacks the press for causing this verbal corruption.

[3] See Karel Čapek, "Towards a Theory of Fairy Tales," *In Praise of Newspapers*, tr. M. and R. Weatherall (New York, 1951), 49–89.

ALLEGORY

"Dialogue of Self and Soul," complaints like Alain de Lille's *De Planctu Naturae* and Allen Ginsberg's "Howl" (incongruous as the juxtaposition may seem). All these and more, with one genre sometimes merging into another, may be termed allegorical or partly allegorical works—by which we mean primarily that as they go along they are usually saying one thing in order to mean something beyond that one thing. There is no reason why allegories should not be written entirely in prose, entirely in verse, or in a mixture of the two, as in the *Consolation of Philosophy*, a typical anatomy.[4] There is no reason why allegory must always be narrated; it can be used in the drama, whether ancient (*Prometheus Bound*), medieval (the moralities), Renaissance (the *autos sacramentales*[5] and the masques), or modern (the surrealist drama of Ionesco or Beckett, the "epic theatre" of Brecht). Besides drama and narrative fiction, lyrical poetry is available to convey the "extended metaphor," as for example in certain Imagist poems (Pound's "Papyrus,"[6] Stevens' "Thirteen Ways of Looking at a Blackbird"),[7] and more familiarly in the conceits of Metaphysical verse, above all through its excesses (Clevelandism).

This variety is an advantage for the theorist, as well as a challenge, since he can be checked by many other readers, all of whom have special areas of interest and many of whom will have particular com-

[4] "Boethius' *Consolation of Philosophy*, with its dialogue form, its verse interludes and its pervading tone of contemplative irony, is a pure anatomy, a fact of considerable importance for the understanding of its vast influence" (Northrop Frye, *Anatomy of Criticism: Four Essays* [Princeton, 1957], 312). See Frye, 308–314, on the genre in general.

[5] On the *autos* of Calderón, see Frye's *Anatomy*, 282–284; also A. L. Constandse, *Le Baroque espagnol et Calderón de la Barca* (Amsterdam, 1951), *passim*; A. A. Parker, *The Allegorical Drama of Calderón* (London, 1943); Ernst Curtius, *European Literature and the Latin Middle Ages*, tr. W. R. Trask (New York, 1953), 205, 244. Edwin Honig has especially interested himself in Calderón. See his article, "Calderón's Strange Mercy Play," *Massachusetts Review*, III (Autumn 1961), 80–107; his translation of and introduction to *Four Plays* (New York, 1961).

[6] In Ezra Pound, *Personae* (New York, 1926), 112.

[7] Wallace Stevens, *Collected Poems* (New York, 1954), 92–95.

4

petence in genres the theorist can know only superficially. Frequently we can refer a theory of allegory to works we read for entertainment—the western romance, the imaginary voyage of science fiction, the melodrama based on fictional "case histories"—all of which are direct descendants of a more sober ancient tradition. The reader is often perhaps not aware that these works, mainly romances, are at least partially allegorical. In the middle ages, we can guess, the priest's homily did not strike his hearers as a blank, abstract, boring exordium, perhaps not even as particularly symbolic.[8] The listeners, however, could return home from church to meditate systematically on the hidden meaning of the parable, if they chose, and doubtless in times of plague and civil strife they did precisely that. While allegory in the middle ages came to the people from the pulpit, it comes to the modern reader in secular, but no less popular, form. The modern romance and the detective story with its solution also carry double meanings that are no less important to the completion of their plots than is the *moralitas* to the preacher's parable.

The older iconographic languages of religious parable now need a good deal of interpretation,[9] because their worlds are remote from

---

[8] See G. R. Owst, *Literature and Pulpit in Medieval England* (Cambridge, 1933), chs. i, iv–vii. The interpretation of Holy Writ was continually enlivened by "vivid illustration, lively anecdote, homely portraiture, witty and ruthless satire" (55). Satire, as in *Joseph Andrews* and *Tristram Shandy*, was later turned against the purely routine publication of any and all sermons. With the sermons of Donne exegesis becomes a structural device for the development of dramatic, sometimes even forensic, speech.

[9] Besides the formal obscurity that inheres in enigma, there is also a historical barrier between modern and medieval contexts. Thus James Hastings, *Encyclopedia of Religion and Ethics* (New York, 1916), I, 327b: "Allegory is almost always a relative, not an absolute conception, which has nothing to do with the actual truth of the matter, and for the most part springs from the natural desire to conserve some idea which, owing to its age, has come to be regarded as sacred." Also Roger Hinks, *Myth and Allegory in Ancient Art* (London, 1939), 16–17: "It is the mark of allegory that its *dramatis personae* are abstract concepts; they have no separate existence or legend, such as the characters of myth enjoy; and as a rule they are created *ad hoc*, to suit a particular occasion." The occasion gone, the symbolism loses its meaning. On

our world, which would explain why medieval allegory seems so obviously allegorical to us, while modern allegories (if I am right in so extending the class) may not be read as fables. The degree of familiarity with the old and new iconographies is the varying factor.[10] Even though the twentieth-century reader has no actual experience with detectives and murderers, he understands the world of the "private eye," and the same holds for other kinds of stereotype. The lack of a similar familiarity with medieval religious symbolism makes the modern reader think that what he reads for pleasure and what the preacher preached must be different in kind. But the whodunit demands a solution to a riddle, making it a member of that oldest allegorical type, the *aenigma*.[11] The western of Zane Grey has a different affinity: instead of the allegorical riddle, a surface texture of sublime scenic description is the carrier of thematic meaning. The western scenery in Grey is always more than a tacked-up backdrop. It is a *paysage moralisé*,[12] and Grey's heroes act in

Christian and Philonic exegesis, see R. P. C. Hanson, *Allegory and Event* (London, 1959), where the central subject is Origen; Grant, *The Letter and the Spirit;* H. A. Wolfson, *The Philosophy of the Church Fathers* (Cambridge, Mass., 1956); Wolfson, *Philo* (Cambridge, Mass., 1947); Pépin, *Mythe et allégorie;* Jean Daniélou, *Philon d'Alexandre* (Paris, 1958). These are among the texts which have been useful to me; the literature on the subject is of course extensive.

[10] On the term "iconography," see Erwin Panofsky, "Iconography and Iconology: An Introduction to the Study of Renaissance Art," in *Meaning in the Visual Arts* (New York, 1955), first published in *Studies in Iconology: Humanistic Themes in the Art of the Renaissance* (New York, 1939).

[11] See W. H. Auden, "The Guilty Vicarage: Notes on the Detective Story, by an Addict," in *The Critical Performance*, ed. S. E. Hyman (New York, 1956): "The interest in the thriller is the ethical and eristic conflict between good and evil, between Us and Them. The interest in the study of the murderer is the observation, by the innocent many, of the sufferings of the guilty one. The interest in the detective story is the dialectic of innocence and guilt" (302). Auden intends a slightly mocking tone.

[12] Auden has a major poem to which he gave this title, *Paysage Moralisé*, in *The Collected Poetry of W. H. Auden* (New York, 1945), 47–48. See the discussion of this poem in J. W. Beach's *Obsessive Images: Symbolism in Poetry of the 1930's and 1940's* (Minneapolis, 1960), 104–113.

harmony with or in violent opposition to that scenic tapestry.[13] Furthermore, the conflicts of the cowboy hero and the bandit villain, as in the detective thriller, are drawn according to a dualism of good and evil—a defining characteristic of the mode from the earliest period of Occidental literature. It is with fictions of this familiar, popular, unassuming sort that we can equip ourselves in determining whether any particular theory of allegory is adequate. Whatever applies to our favorite romances will apply with even greater force to the major examples of tradition, let us say, *The Faerie Queene* and *The Pilgrim's Progress*.

An objection needs to be met here, namely that all romances are not necessarily allegorical. A good adventure story, the reader will say, needs no interpolated secondary meaning in order to be significant and entertaining. But that objection does not concern the true criterion for allegory. The whole point of allegory is that it does not *need* to be read exegetically; it often has a literal level that makes good enough sense all by itself. But somehow this literal surface suggests a peculiar doubleness of intention, and while it can, as it were, get along without interpretation, it becomes much richer and more interesting if given interpretation. Even the most deliberate fables, if read naïvely or carelessly, may seem mere stories, but what counts in our discussion is a structure that lends itself to a secondary reading, or rather, one that becomes stronger when given a secondary meaning as well as a primary meaning.

Nevertheless, we must avoid the notion that all people must see

---

[13] *Black Mesa*, ch. ix: "The Desert of Bitter Seeps, all stone and baked earth, retained the heat into the fall. Each succeeding day grew drier, hotter, fiercer. . . . Paul, too, was wearing to a disastrous break. He realized it, but could not check the overpowering forces of the place, the time, and whatever terrible climax seemed imminent. . . . Belmont, too, was plotting. His deep and gloomy thought resembled the brooding of the wasteland. The subtle, almost imperceptible change of the last few weeks now stood out palpably, Belmont was under a tremendous strain, the havoc of which he did not suspect. His greed and lust and love of the bottle seemed to have united with the disintegrating influence of Bitter Seeps."

the double meaning, for the work to be rightly called allegory. At least one branch of allegory, the ironic *aenigma*,[14] serves political and social purposes by the very fact that a reigning authority (as in a police state) does not see the secondary meaning of the "Aesoplanguage." [15] But someone does see that meaning, and, once seen, it is felt strongly to be the final intention behind the primary meaning. Perhaps naïve readers do not see the erotic allegory under the surface action of a Zane Grey romance, but then in discussing allegory we are not much concerned with naïve readers. We are talking about sophisticated readers and what they read *into* literature. There is on the other hand no harm in admitting that stories can move the reader by sheer plot, action, and surprise. But these stories are much rarer than one would expect. It is commoner to find a veneer of action laid over a moralizing intent. Finally, whether one thinks there is such a thing as pure storytelling, or only degrees of abstract thematic structure (Aristotle's *dianoia*) underlying every fiction, the main point is surely that in discussing literature generally we must be ready to discern in almost any work at least a small degree of allegory. All literature, as Northrop Frye has observed, is from the point of view of commentary more or less allegorical, while no "pure allegory" will ever be found.[16] There is therefore no harm in draw-

[14] Henry Peacham, *The Garden of Eloquence* (London, 1593; reprinted Gainesville, Fla., 1954): "Aenigma: a kind of Allegorie, differing only in obscuritie, for Aenigma is a sentence or forme of speech, which for the darknesse, the sense may hardly be gathered" (27). This figure is usually identified with *riddle*, e.g., George Puttenham, *The Arte of English Poesie*, ed. Gladys Willcock and Alice Walker (London, 1589; reprinted Cambridge, 1936): "We dissemble againe under covert and darke speaches, when we speake by way of riddle (*Enigma*) of which the sence can hardly be picked out, but by the parties owne assoile" (188). See below, chapter 7, on the political uses of allegory.

[15] See Alan Paton's article "The South African Treason Trial," *Atlantic Monthly*, CCV (Jan. 1960); also, more general, E. S. Hobsbawm, *Social Bandits and Primitive Rebels* (Glencoe, Ill., 1959), ch. ix, "Ritual in Social Movements."

[16] For dramatic proof that commentary, especially when carried to an extreme, is perforce allegorical we have nothing better than certain parodies, e.g., Theodore Spencer's "new critical" reading of "Thirty Days Hath Sep-

ing instances from borderline cases. Even *The Divine Comedy*, which most readers would assume to be the greatest Western example of allegory, seemed to Coleridge, and has more recently been

---

tember" (*New Republic*, Dec. 6, 1943). Spencer showed that the New Criticism, while it attacked allegory in theory, still used the mode in practice, by conscientiously overreading the text.

Equally revealing are some entries in a *Church Times* contest for absurdly serious interpretations. The contest was entitled "Hidden Meaning." The readings were to be based on the children's stories of Beatrix Potter. I give five of these parodies, in part or in full.

On Beatrix Potter's *Tale of Johnny Town Mouse*: "The resignation of both the principals to their own lot, and their half-hearted sampling of each other's, mark this as a sharp study in organized social frustration, of the little man subject to gigantic and compulsive forces. Consider the hamper. . . . The little man may choose to move by it from one pattern of frustration to another: by boarding it he *votes*—here we may note that the hamper 'goes to the country': thereafter he is the prisoner of his decision, taking no part in shaping events until the next arbitrary decision to send the hamper to him. . . ."

Another Beatrix Potter fable for children, concerning Jeremy Fisher, is called "a deeply mystical allegory which, reduced to its simplest terms, resolves itself into an arresting tract against reliance upon the material. The dominant motif concerns obsession with a physical element, and for Freudians it is significant that this recalls the environment of the embryo."

An even more scholastic reading was made of *The Tale of Mr. Jeremy Fisher*: "It reflects sadly on modern scholarship that the true anthropological significance of this work should not have been more widely recognized. To those attuned to the overtones of narrative, this is clearly yet another restatement of the myth of the Fisher King, whose immolation and subsequent rebirth restores fertility to an otherwise waste land; the processes of sacrifice and renewal being here represented by ingestion and regurgitation.

"In the close web of allusion and cultural cross-reference that forms the fabric of the text, the names even of the guests at the final dinner (a thinly-disguised vegetation ceremony) have deep symbolic significance. 'Sir Isaac Newton' sets the myth in its proper context of the space-time continuum; while Mr. Alderman Ptolemy Tortoise, in his predilection for salad, is a clear link with Ancient Egyptian fertility rites.

"Serious students would do well to consult the recently published *Der Weltschmerz und die Frau Potter*, by Professor Ludwig Schwartz-Metterklume (Leipzig: 1905). . . ."

On *The Tale of Jemima Puddle-Duck*: "The focal point in *The Tale of Jemima Puddle-Duck* is the Woodshed, which, as all psychologists know, is

shown by Auerbach, to be a quasi-allegorical work.[17] With such a major example in mind one cannot help wondering if borderline cases are not going to be the norm.

the universally accepted symbol of the Fascination of Evil. With a few deft strokes the authoress sets the scene, and almost at once the dreadful Woodshed begins to exert its magnetic spell. The Primrose Path, while not directly mentioned in the text, is delicately suggested in the superb illustrations. Half unaware, the heroine is drawn onward at an accelerating pace, which develops from an initial waddle, through a run, into precipitate flight. This is true insight.

"So much for the dynamic angle. From the static angle, the approach to the Woodshed is handled with equal mastery. Always by the Woodshed is the Fox (Deception, the invariable concomitant of Evil), and concealing the Fox are the beautiful Fox-gloves. As the Bard said, 'O, what a goodly outside Falsehood hath!' "

On *The Tale of Peter Rabbit*: "This poignant allegory pinpoints the tragic dilemma of adolescence. Youth emerges from its safe childhood (the underground burrow) to choose between dull respectability and the mysterious forbidden territory, the unlawful El Dorado—Mr. McGregor's garden!

"By a brilliant stroke Miss Potter epitomises her hero's descent into crime, as he squeezes *under* the gate. At first the rewards come easily, and lettuce-gorged Youth sheds his inhibitions (coat and shoes), until he comes face to face with his great Foe, the destroyer of his father and the enemy of all his tribe.

"Dramatically the atmosphere changes. The fatal Garden, easy to enter, is hard to escape from. An undercurrent of sadism suggested earlier in the sinister "made into a pie," becomes explicit in the terrors of the rake, the sieve and the waiting cat.

"While certainly not light reading, this grim book with its ruthless message can be recommended to readers over twenty-one."

[17] Coleridge, *Miscellaneous Criticism*, ed. T. M. Raysor (London, 1936), 151: "The Divina Commedia is a system of moral, political, and theological truths, with arbitrary personal exemplifications, which are not, in my opinion, allegorical. I do not even feel convinced that the punishments in the Inferno are strictly allegorical. I rather take them to have been in Dante's mind quasi-allegorical, or conceived in analogy to pure allegory." The *Miscellaneous Criticism* is sprinkled with commentary on the nature of allegory, not only with respect to major allegorists like Bunyan, Dante, and Spenser, but also with borderline authors like Rabelais, Sterne, and Defoe. Coleridge's "quasi-allegorical" reading is confirmed by Erich Auerbach, *Dante: Poet of the Secular World*, tr. Ralph Manheim (Chicago, 1961).

Besides the scope of the literature involved, certain areas of critical disagreement may be mentioned, because they suggest the main trouble we have to contend with: our psychological and linguistic uncertainty as to what is going on when language is used figuratively. Figurative language is not understood at the present time in any final way. The tortuous subtlety of William Empson and Kenneth Burke, both of them major critics, suggests that no simple formulas are possible, given our limited knowledge of the psychology of speech.[18] Terms like "tenor" and "vehicle" have been helpful, but are only labels.[19] I. A. Richards' recent interest in communication theory and in scientific pedagogy has not carried his revolutionary notions of metaphor much beyond the earlier position reached in *Practical Criticism* and *The Philosophy of Rhetoric*. Another important treatise, Rosemond Tuve's *Elizabethan and Metaphysical Imagery*, gave the study of rhetoric a close historical analysis, but in spite of references to certain modern poets, Tuve remained essentially concerned with a single period, the Renaissance.[20] In his *Fearful Symmetry* Northrop Frye displayed what may be the most brilliant exercise of allegorical interpretation on record, but about this particular

[18] Empson would place allegory in his third type, in *Seven Types of Ambiguity* (London, 1930; reprinted New York, 1955). Kenneth Burke's discussions of allegory are mainly concerned with its political uses, e.g., in Part III of *A Rhetoric of Motives* (New York, 1950), entitled "Order." Like Empson, Burke is interested in "symbolic action" as a means of coping with social and political tensions.

[19] "Tenor" and "vehicle" were introduced by I. A. Richards in his lectures, *The Philosophy of Rhetoric* (London, 1936). See his recent *Speculative Instruments* (Chicago, 1955), for examples of his interest in pedagogic, communication problems (translation, for example). See Max Black on Richards' Terminology: *Models and Metaphors: Studies in Language and Philosophy* (Ithaca, 1962), ch. iii, "Metaphor."

[20] Miss Tuve's *casus belli* was the misunderstanding in twentieth-century criticism of the rhetorical techniques presupposed by poets like Donne, Drayton, and Herbert. Her chief object of study was "Renaissance Poetics," revealed in both the theory and practice of the Elizabethan and Jacobean period.

procedure his theoretical views were not, I think, greatly advanced in the even more remarkable *Anatomy of Criticism*.[21] There Frye observed that allegory is a type of thematic "counterpoint," encountered most often in romances, and that a high degree of thematic content in any piece of literature probably implies allegorical techniques at work.[22] Given this rather broad conception of the term, theory would have been left in an impressionist stage, had not Edwin Honig's general treatise, *Dark Conceit*, laid down some of the major lines of inquiry.[23] This book is to my knowledge the pioneer work on the subject in modern times. My own disagreements with it are a matter of some detail, and where they are large-scale disagreements, I prefer to leave them to a more objective comparison than my own. I had the pleasure of attending Mr. Honig's lectures on the subject of allegory given during the evolution of *Dark Conceit*, and I was doubtless influenced by them in ways that I cannot now see. Honig's book seems to me to be concerned chiefly with accounting for the *creative* aspects of allegory. Honig wants to show how allegory comes into being, what are the cultural determinants *from without*. My own approach, despite the chapter I devote to the psycho-

---

[21] Frye, on allegory: *Fearful Symmetry: A Study of William Blake* (Princeton, 1947), 115–117 and the final chapter, "The Valley of Vision"; also *Anatomy of Criticism*, 89–92; "The Typology of *Paradise Regained*," *Modern Philology*, LIII, 227–238; "Notes for a Commentary on *Milton*," in *The Divine Vision*, ed. V. de Sola Pinto (London, 1957).

[22] Frye, *Anatomy*, 90. The summary treatment of the whole range of allegory, pp. 89–92, is a marvel of compactness, and perhaps therefore criticism is unfair.

[23] Honig, *Dark Conceit: The Making of Allegory* (Evanston, 1959). I have been unable to consult Abraham Bezankis, "An Introduction to the Problem of Allegory in Literary Criticism" (Ph.D. dissertation, University of Michigan, 1955). Among briefer general accounts, see "The Allegorical Method," in Rex Warner, *The Cult of Power* (London, 1946); Edward Bloom, "The Allegorical Principle," *Journal of English Literary History* (hereafter abbreviated as *ELH*), XVIII (1951), 163–190. C. S. Lewis devotes a chapter to this general subject in *The Allegory of Love* (Oxford, 1936), 44–111, where he emphasizes the *psychomachia*. Lewis is himself the author of several fables, *That Hideous Strength, Perelandra, Out of the Silent Planet, The Screwtape Letters, The Chronicles of Narcion*.

analytic theory of allegory, is less genetic, and more formal. I am not so much concerned with individual authors or individual periods as with the form that any given allegory will be likely to present to a sophisticated reader, regardless of the ways by which it came into being. In that sense I am attempting an account rather unlike *Dark Conceit.*

While there is still need for an analysis of the figurative nature of allegory in rhetorical terms, there are certain special historical confusions that can be avoided if we formulate a theory cutting across historical lines. The first of these is the controversy over the difference between "allegory" and "symbol." This unhappy controversy, which begins with Goethe's distinction between the two terms, has had its fair share of critical attention.[24] It is a primarily historical matter, since it concerns romantic conceptions of the mind, and of "imagination" in particular. The psychology of the imagination would have to be dealt with in any full historical treatment of the development of allegorical literature. Goethe's concern with the allegory-symbol distinction has especial value in the light of his evolving attitudes toward the Faust legend, and yet, though such origins of modern critical theory have historical interest, they rather lead us to reconsider the means we shall take to describe allegory for present-day students of literature. As critics, we of the twentieth century come out of a climate, well described by M. H. Abrams in *The Mirror and the Lamp,* in which there is a gradual sophistication of the psychological part of critical theory.[25] We live in an age of

---

[24] René Wellek, *A History of Modern Criticism* (New Haven, 1955), I, 200; also Honig, *Dark Conceit,* 39-50. Goethe, *Maximen,* as tr. by Wellek (I, 211), says: "There is a great difference, whether the poet seeks the particular for the general or sees the general in the particular. From the first procedure arises allegory, where the particular serves only as an example of the general; the second procedure, however, is really the nature of poetry: it expresses something particular, without thinking of the general or pointing to it."
"True symbolism is where the particular represents the more general, not as a dream or a shadow, but as a living momentary revelation of the Inscrutable."

[25] With the development of psychology into the fields of Gestalt, behaviorist, and psychoanalytic theory, the concept of "imagination" has been overlaid by

psychological and psychoanalytic speculation, and we need to return periodically to earlier stages of that speculation, where perhaps we can find the starting point for both our more profitable and our more dubious explorings. Perhaps a closer attention to the history of nineteenth-century criticism would prevent unfortunate oversimplifications such as are likely when we speak loosely of concepts like the "romantic imagination" or the *"symbolisme"* of the French poets. The word "symbol" in particular has become a banner for confusion, since it lends itself to a falsely evaluative function whenever it is used to mean "good" ("symbolic") poetry as opposed to "bad" ("allegorical") poetry, and in this way it clouds distinctions that are already difficult enough to make.

The same objection against a leveling critical language may be made against a more recent tendency to praise "myth" at the expense of allegory. Thus, a critic may say of *The Castle* or *The Trial* or *The Metamorphosis* that they are "mythic," and then proceed to read them, perhaps employing Freudian symbols, as the purest sort of allegory. The basis of "myth criticism" is a search for certain recurrent archetypal patterns (e.g., the dragon-slaying myth) at the heart of stories which would present a more complex appearance to another critic who did not think in terms of archetypes.[26] The arche-

---

complicating factors. I. A. Richards is the chief theorist to follow Coleridgean leads; M. H. Abrams' *The Mirror and the Lamp: Romantic Theory and the Critical Tradition* (New York, 1953) is chiefly historical.

[26] See W. K. Wimsatt and Cleanth Brooks, *Literary Criticism: A Short History* (New York, 1957). There is to be a chapter on "myth criticism" in Wellek's forthcoming sequel to Volume II of his *A History of Modern Criticism*. The major influence on these critics is Carl Jung, whose theory of archetypes may be found summarized in Jolande Jacobi, *Complex/Archetype/Symbol*, tr. Ralph Manheim (New York, 1959). Typical Jungian studies are Jung, "The Archetypes of the Collective Unconscious," in *Collected Works*, IX (New York, 1952–1961); "The Paradigm of the Unicorn," *ibid.*, XII; with Karl Kerenyi, *Essays on a Science of Mythology*, tr. R. F. C. Hull (New York, 1949). Also, Erich Neumann, *The Great Mother: An Analysis of the Archetype* (New York, 1955), and *The Origins and History of Consciousness* (New York, 1954); Joseph Campbell, *The Hero with a Thousand Faces* (New York, 1949). These works lean away from literary criticism, toward anthro-

typal pattern is the form in which the deepest psychic significance of the hero or heroine's action is expressed. Probably such irreducible patterns are present in storytelling of all kinds.[27] But a curious development takes place in "myth criticism." What began as unprejudiced description in terms of archetypes becomes a valuation of only those works where the archetypes are clearly discernible. When the critic uses the word "mythic" to describe Kafka or Faulkner, we need to be sure it is not a covert term of praise. It seems to be descriptive, but in fact it often evaluates. The term "myth," when used in this way, seems to be the heir of "symbol" in the older controversy over allegory and symbol. It has simply become richer in connotations, owing to its significance for cultural anthropology. What was localized in time and space as a pregnant moment, under the Goethean rubric of Symbol, may now be universalized as a manifestation of a supposed "collective unconscious." We have indeed to go back one stage before the advent of Myth on the critical scene.

Coleridge makes a natural starting point for an analysis of allegorical practice, since he is at the center of the disputation which has so obscured the problem.

For Coleridge the definition of allegory was an important matter because it allowed him once again to make the distinction between "organic" and "mechanic" form,[28] and to provide a major instance

---

pology. They tend to collapse literary distinctions, but are extremely suggestive for the study of allegory as well as myth. Less psychoanalytic, more clearly literary in emphasis is Maud Bodkin's *Archetypal Patterns in Poetry: Psychological Studies of Imagination* (London, 1934; reprinted New York, 1958).

[27] See *Myth: A Symposium*, ed. T. A. Seboek (Bloomington, 1958), chapters by Claude Lévi-Strauss, Lord Raglan, Stanley Edgar Hyman, and Stith Thompson, on mythic patterns. Also the pioneer work of Lord Raglan, *The Hero* (London, 1936; reprinted New York, 1956); and Vladimir Propp, *The Morphology of the Folktale*, ed. Svatava Pirkova-Jacobson, tr. Laurence Scott (Bloomington, 1958). The latter is a classic of Russian "formalist" criticism.

[28] Coleridge, "Lectures on Shakespeare," "Recapitulation, and Summary of the Characteristics of Shakespeare's Dramas," in S. T. Coleridge, *Essays and Lectures on Shakespeare and Some Other Old Poets and Dramatists* (Every-

of literature created out of a compromising relationship between the imagination and the logical powers of the reason.[29] Such a compromise could not give rise to the highest art, but it was precisely what was required for that mixture of theme and image we call allegory. Coleridge made his criticism of allegory implicit in his distinction between symbol and allegory, as well as in his definition of allegory. To take the distinction first:

The Symbolical cannot perhaps be better defined in distinction from the Allegorical, than that it is always itself a part of that, of the whole of which it is representative.—"Here comes a sail,"—(that is a ship) is a

---

man ed., London, 1907), 46: "The form is mechanic, when on any given material we impress a pre-determined form, not necessarily arising out of the properties of the material;—as when to a mass of wet clay we give whatever shape we wish it to retain when hardened. The organic form, on the other hand, is innate; it shapes, as it develops, itself from within, and the fulness of its development is one and the same with the perfection of its outward form. Such as the life is, such is the form." What Coleridge says of mechanic form is also implied by the theory of *figura* and *impresa*. Erich Auerbach, *"Figura,"* in *Scenes from the Drama of European Literature: Six Essays* (New York, 1959), 13: "It should be borne in mind that Varro, like all Latin authors who were not specialists in philosophy endowed with an exact terminology, used *figura* and *forma* interchangeably, in the general sense of form. Strictly speaking, *forma* meant 'mold,' French *'moule,'* and was related to *figura* as the hollow form to the plastic shape that issues from it." On *impresa*, see Mario Praz, *Studies in Seventeenth Century Imagery* (London, 1939), I, ch. i, "Emblem, Device, Epigram, Conceit," and the Appendix, "Emblems and Devices in Literature."

[29] "Now an allegory is but a translation of abstract notions into a picture-language, which is itself nothing but an abstraction from objects of the senses; the principal being more worthless even than its phantom proxy, both alike unsubstantial, and the former shapeless to boot. On the other hand a symbol . . . is characterized by a translucence of the special in the individual, or of the general in the special, or of the universal in the general; above all by the translucence of the eternal through and in the temporal. It always partakes of the reality which it renders intelligible; and while it enunciates the whole, abides itself as a living part in that unity of which it is the representative. The other are but empty echoes which the fancy arbitrarily associates with apparitions of matter, less beautiful but not less shadowy than the sloping orchard or hill-side pasture seen in the transparent lake below" (Coleridge, *The Statesman's Manual*, ed. W. G. T. Shedd [New York, 1875], 437-438).

symbolical expression. "Behold our lion!" when we speak of some gallant soldier, is allegorical. Of most importance to our present subject is this point, that the latter (allegory) cannot be other than spoken consciously; —whereas in the former (the symbol) it is very possible that the general truth may be unconsciously in the writer's mind during the construction of the symbol; and it proves itself by being produced out of his own mind,—as the Don Quixote out of the perfectly sane mind of Cervantes, and not by outward observation or historically. The advantage of symbolic writing over allegory is, that it presumes no disjunction of faculties, but simple dominance.[30]

By identifying Symbol with synecdoche, Coleridge is assuming a sort of *participation mystique* [31] of the Symbol with the idea

[30] *Misc. Crit.*, 29. Coleridge here echoes the Goethean maxim: "True symbolism is where the particular represents the more general, not as a dream or a shadow, but as a living momentary revelation of the Inscrutable" (quoted by Wellek, *History*, I, 211). Coleridge likewise follows the Goethean distinction between allegory and symbol: "Allegory changes a phenomenon into a concept, a concept into an image, but in such a way that the concept is still limited and completely kept and held in the image and expressed by it (whereas symbolism) changes the phenomenon into the idea, the idea into the Image, in such a way that the idea remains always infinitely active and unapproachable in the image, and will remain inexpressible even though expressed in all languages." The final point here made is that allegory is a kind of translatable jargon, whereas symbol is a universal language impervious to local limitations. One cannot, in Goethe's sense, "translate" the Cross, since by itself this symbol is supralinguistic.

[31] The term, now somewhat questioned by anthropologists, is Lévy-Bruhl's. See his *L'Ame primitive* (Paris, 1927); also his *Les Fonctions mentales dans les sociétés inférieures* (Paris, 1910). Johan Huizinga, *The Waning of the Middle Ages*, tr. F. Hopman (New York, 1954), 205: "All realism, in the medieval sense, leads to anthropomorphism. Having attributed a real existence to an idea, the mind wants to see this idea alive, and can only effect this by personifying it. In this way allegory is born. It is not the same thing as symbolism. Symbolism expresses a mysterious connection between two ideas, allegory gives a visible form to the conception of such a connection. Symbolism is a very profound function of the mind, allegory is a superficial one. It aids symbolic thought to express itself, but endangers it at the same time by substituting a figure for a living idea. The force of the symbol is easily lost in the allegory. So allegory in itself implies from the outset normalizing, projecting on a surface, crystallizing."

symbolized. The Symbol is furthermore given directly in the act of perceiving the ship. With Symbol the mind perceives the rational order of things directly, by an "unmediated vision," [32] without any logical extrapolation from the phenomena of our material world, whereas in allegory there is always (as Coleridge sees it) an attempt to categorize logical orders first, and fit them to convenient phenomena second, to set forth ideal systems first, and illustrate them second. This latter Platonic idea-image relationship can exist only when one is conscious of the philosophic status of the ideas one is conceiving. One need not necessarily be aware of one's own private motives in constructing such ideal systems, but one does need to have a conscious, highly organized view of the interrelationships that bind the system into a unity. Coleridge emphasized the unconsciousness of the Symbolic process in a way that tempts a Freudian reinterpretation of his view.[33] Without actually saying that Symbol is an expression of the Freudian *Unconscious*—and therefore equivalent to dream symbol—we could speculate about Coleridge's idea of the "disjunction of the faculties," since in allegory there is clearly a disjunction of meanings. *Allegoria* manifestly has two or more levels of meaning, and the apprehension of these must require at least two attitudes of mind. When, for example, one witnessed a court masque with decor by Inigo Jones, one no doubt lavished considerable attention on the mere ornament of the play, on the costumes, the decor, the dancing, the music, and so on, and to shift from this kind of sensuous world to the world of ideas must have engaged a secondary train of thought. Yet Coleridgean theory goes only so far, and modern approaches will eventually replace it. Whether duplicity of meaning in all allegory follows necessarily from a splitting of *reason* and *imagination* is not a question that modern psychology would pose in Coleridgean terms.

[32] See Geoffrey Hartman, *The Unmediated Vision: An Interpretation of Wordsworth, Hopkins, Rilke and Valéry* (New Haven, 1954).

[33] M. H. Abrams has shown striking anticipations of Freud in both Hazlitt and John Keble. He quotes Hazlitt: "The imagination, by thus embodying and turning them to shape, gives an obvious relief to the indistinct and importunate cravings of the will" (*Mirror and the Lamp*, 143).

However, Coleridge defined allegory in such a way as to make possible a double approach, a double attention to the surface of works and to their psychic effects and significance, by a rigid adherence to both psychological and rhetorical theories.

We may then safely define allegorical writing as the employment of one set of agents and images with actions and accompaniments correspondent, so as to convey, while in disguise, either moral qualities or conceptions of the mind that are not in themselves objects of the senses, or other images, agents, actions, fortunes, and circumstances so that the difference is everywhere presented to the eye or imagination, while the likeness is suggested to the mind; and this connectedly, so that the parts combine to form a consistent whole.[34]

Although in every case the terms are elaborated, and sometimes redefined, each chapter of the following discussion is devoted to a major element mentioned in this definition. Chapter 1 considers the central focus of narrative and drama, their agents, the people they show in movement. Chapter 2 considers the textural aspect of allegory, its tapestried surface of images. The vocabulary employed in these and subsequent chapters comes from various sources. The notion of the agent as daemon comes from comparative religion and from the history of Christianity.[35] (Frye has recently written of daemonic agency in his *Anatomy of Criticism*.) [36] The notion of

[34] Coleridge, *Misc. Crit.*, 30. We have on record two statements of this definition, the one quoted and another which accounts less well for the presumed mechanical effect of allegory, since it reverses the functions of mind and imagination ("with a likeness to the imagination but with a difference to the understanding").

[35] On Defoe's fabulous, daemonic style, see Coleridge, *Misc. Crit.*, 194. Coleridge regarded both *Gargantua and Pantagruel* and *Tristram Shandy* as partially if not mainly allegorical ("All Rabelais' personages are phantasmagoric allegories, but Panurge above all"). He saw a tendency of certain narratives to become less allegorical as their agents became "too strongly individualized." "This is often felt in the Pilgrim's Progress where the characters are real persons with nick names" (*Misc. Crit.*, 33).

[36] See Frye, *Anatomy*, 147–150, on "demonic imagery." Frye takes "demonic" in its standard, late-Christian sense of "diabolic." I prefer a neutral definition, to include angelic powers.

kosmos, used for the allegorical image, does not come from the history of science, but from ancient rhetoric; I have tried to restore its original, very useful meaning. The term has not been much used for practical criticism, but it would form a bridge between anthropology (e.g., Mircea Eliade) and criticism (the New Critics or the historical scholarship of Rosemond Tuve). Chapter 3 considers action under the aspect of ritual, a concept validated chiefly in comparative religion and, rather differently, in psychoanalysis. Both views of ritual are relevant, and are employed. Further, ritual as a term for a "symbolic action" has become established in the criticism of Kenneth Burke. Since all stories are unified on some basis of probability or necessity, that is, according to some type of causal system, Chapter 4 takes up this problem and employs the Frazerian anthropological concept of contagious and sympathetic magic to explain the causal sequences underlying events in allegories. Finally, to describe the thematic dualism of levels that Coleridge referred to as a "disguise," Chapter 5 invokes the psychoanalytic concept of ambivalence. But to approach this concept more easily I have related the "disjunction of the faculties" to that conflict of mind which Schiller and Kant found inherent in the sublime. Chapter 6 uses psychoanalytic theory to show the mental basis of allegory. Chapter 7 broaches the ultimate problem of aesthetic value and suggests both the limitations and the advantages of the mode. It shows how allegorists flex an inherently rigid control of intention, how by means of irony and digressive commentary they alleviate the burden of pure ritual, and we get what might be called a "good" literature.

The terms of my description may suggest that allegory is closely identified with religious ritual and symbolism. This is not an accident. As C. S. Lewis has remarked, "it would appear that all allegories whatever are likely to seem Catholic to the general reader, and this phenomenon is worth investigation." [37] Precisely this investigation

---

[37] *Allegory of Love,* 322. My subsequent argument will show precisely why this is so, on the grounds that allegory makes an excess of a behavior frequent enough in Catholic piety: "When Catholicism goes bad it becomes the world-

has been one of my aims. Even without taking a psychoanalytic view, one can show the truth of Lewis' assertion; but psychoanalysis gives a strong reinforcement to it, in that we can show the close similarity between allegorical forms and so-called "compulsive rituals," [38] and these rituals in turn are analogues to religious rituals. The various analogies that can be drawn between religious, literary, and psychoanalytically observed phenomena all point to the oldest idea about allegory, that it is a human reconstitution of divinely inspired messages, a revealed transcendental language which tries to preserve the remoteness of a properly veiled godhead.[39] To reach this traditional conclusion, however, a nonmetaphysical line of argument seems the best initial course, and that is the course I have followed. I have stayed away from the metaphysics of the subject. I have also stayed away from the history and theory of biblical exegesis because, in the words of a friend, "Biblical exegesis has as its aim and basis of argument the historical and theological defense of the Bible as the revealed word of God—in other words, a concern that is tangential to the scope of the present investigation." This is not to say that traditional readings of the prophetic books of the Old Testament and of the Book of Revelation are not relevant to the study of poems

---

old, world-wide *religio* of amulets and holy places and priestcraft" (Lewis, *Allegory*, 323).

[38] See below, Chapter 6, *passim.*

[39] The intermediaries in this process of divine revelation were spirits, the good and bad daemons who led or misled—Sir Thomas Browne, *Religio Medici*, ed. J. J. Denonain (Cambridge, 1955), sec. 31, 42: "I doe thinke that many mysteries ascribed to our owne inventions have beene the courteous revelations of Spirits; for those noble essences in heaven beare a friendly regard unto their fellow natures on earth; and therefore beleeve that those many prodigies and ominous prognostickes, which forerun the ruines of States, Princes, and private persons, are the charitable premonitions of good Angels, which more carelesse enquiries terme but the effects of chance and nature." On the doctrine of inspiration, see also R. P. C. Hanson, *Allegory and Event* (London, 1959), ch. vii; also, H. W. Robinson, *Inspiration and Revelation in the Old Testament* (Oxford, 1946), 160–198; John Skinner, *Prophecy and Religion: Studies in the Life of Jeremiah* (1922; reprinted Cambridge, 1961), ch. x.

like *The Divine Comedy* or *Piers Plowman* or *The Faerie Queene;* [40]
indeed the conclusion of my remarks on value and function will
dwell on the apocalyptic, visionary moments into which "mere allegory" sometimes emerges. The reader may, however, ask how often
this emergence occurs. When an allegory becomes purely visionary,
when for example *The Pilgrim's Progress* shows us the Heavenly
City, it does so *after* a struggle to reach that goal. The stage prior to
final vision seems to be qualitatively unlike that final vision; the latter
is a moment of liberation. The former is a sequence of difficult
labors, often taking the form of the hero's enslavement to a fatal
destiny. The *psychomachia* and the progress are narrative images of
this struggle. They are battles for, and journeys toward, the final
liberation of the hero. If a temporary liberation occurs along the
way, it is but the precursor of one final victory. If the poet wishes
to show evil triumphing, he can take a totally ironic attitude toward
good and evil; if the hero is a Jonathan Wild, he also journeys toward
an apocalypse, but of death instead of rebirth.

Considered also as a nonmetaphysical semantic device, whether
leading to apocalypse or not, allegory likewise appears to express
conflict between rival authorities, as in times of political oppression
we may get "Aesop-language" to avoid censorship of dissident
thought. At the heart of any allegory will be found this conflict of
authorities. One ideal will be pitted against another, its opposite:
thus the familiar propagandist function of the mode, thus the conservative satirical function, thus the didactic function. The mode
is hierarchical in essence, owing not only to its use of traditional
imageries which are arranged in systems of "correspondences," but

[40] Bishop Hurd, whose criticism of Spenser attempts to justify his "Gothic"
forms, is also author of *An Introduction to the Study of the Prophecies concerning the Christian Church, and, in Particular, concerning the Church of
Papal Rome, in Twelve Sermons* (2d ed., London, 1772). This series of sermons
not only sets forth the theological presumptions on which true prophecy is
based, but in Sermons IX–XI gives a description of the "prophetic style." Here,
as with Spenserian criticism, Hurd is a somewhat romantic theorist, in that his
remarks would sanction authors like Blake, Young, and Shelley.

furthermore because all hierarchies imply a chain of command, of *order* in the secondary sense that is meant when we say "the general *ordered* his officers to command their *subordinates*." Hierarchy is never simply a system giving people their "proper place"; it goes further and tells them what their legitimate *powers* are. Any hierarchy is bound to elicit sharp emotive responses toward these powers. We are therefore able to describe the mode from a dynamic point of view. Allegories are far less often the dull systems that they are reputed to be than they are symbolic power struggles. If they are often rigid, muscle-bound structures, that follows from their involvement with authoritarian conflict. If they are abstract, harsh, mechanistic, and remote from everyday life, that may sometimes answer a genuine need. When a people is being lulled into inaction by the routine of daily life, so as to forget all higher aspirations, an author perhaps does well to present behavior in a grotesque, abstract caricature. In such a way he may arouse a general self-criticism, and the method will be justified.

Both this satirical criticism and the apocalyptical escape into an infinite space and time tend toward high human goals. In both cases allegory is serving major social and spiritual needs. When we add to these the functions of education (the didactic strain) and entertainment (the riddling or romantic strains), we have a modality of symbolism which we must respect. Allegory, as I have tried to define it, seems to be a many-sided phenomenon. Its overall purposes are capable of many minor variations. I have tried to bring out these overall purposes, yet without damaging the minor subtleties. What follows is therefore in the nature of a mapping expedition, for which I have, in my notes, kept a running journal or sketchbook of the day's events. The notes are not absolutely necessary to the overall map, but they will, I hope, usefully complement it with references to old and new scholarly works.

I

The Daemonic Agent

COLERIDGE treated allegory as if it were always narrative or drama and therefore always had "agents." In many cases this seems the best assumption to make, especially when we are talking about longer works. Yet there is a large body of emblematic poems where not much action occurs.[1] The poet describes a lady holding a bal-

---

[1] See Rosemary Freeman, *English Emblem Books* (London, 1948). Also Erwin Panofsky, *Meaning in the Visual Arts*, ch. i, "Iconography and Iconology: An Introduction to the Study of Renaissance Art"; and ch. iv, "Titian's *Allegory of Prudence:* A Postscript"; finally, Emile Durkheim, *The Elementary Forms of the Religious Life*, tr. J. W. Swain (Glencoe, Ill., 1947), Bk. II, ch. i, "The Totem as Name and as Emblem," and ch. vii, "The Origin of the Notion of Emblem." Writing of Dürer, Panofsky thus defines emblems: "images which refuse to be accepted as representations of mere things but demand to be interpreted as vehicles of concepts; they are tolerated by most modern critics, as a rule, only if incorporated in a work so rich in 'atmosphere' that it can, after all, be 'accepted' without a detailed explanation (as in Dürer's engraving of *Melencolia I*)" (*Albrecht Dürer* [Princeton, 1948], 173). Elsewhere Panofsky gives a more detailed description of the emblem. It is partly (1) symbol, (2) puzzle, (3) apothegm, (4) proverb—yet with these crucial differences, emblem is (1) particular, not universal, (2) not so difficult, (3) visual, not verbal, (4) erudite, not commonplace. See *Meaning in the Visual Arts*, 148.

ance, and we call her Justice, or a blindfold child managing a bow and arrow, whom we call Love, though these hints at movement do little more than convey the fixed, conventional ideas of just balance and erotic attachment. Not much is left of the action of weighing relative merits or of passion's sudden, violent onset. Even so, the remnants of an action are there, while more frequently the poet's fable sets forth a true sequence of events. Unless he is a pure emblematist, the poet is likely to complicate his poem, so that the just weighing of merits becomes a process with several moments and the lover's infatuation a process of gradual involvement. The poet makes what Spenser called "a pleasing analysis of all," [2] and in the course of this analysis an action unfolds, with agents to carry it.

Personification and topical allusion. The agency here is of two sorts: the agents are intended either to represent abstract ideas or to represent actual, historical persons. The former will be our chief concern, since they are essential to the mode and are more problematic and permanently important (because less topical) than agents representing contemporary or historical persons. Personified abstractions are probably the most obviously allegorical agents, whether virtues and vices in a *psychomachia* [3] or chivalric ideals in a medieval

[2] Spenser's "Letter to Raleigh" makes it clear that he distinguished this "analysis" from the historian's chronological method: "For the methode of a poet historical [we should call him an epic poet] is not such as of an historiographer. For an historiographer discourseth of affayres orderly as they were donne, accounting as well the times as the actions; but a poet thrusteth into the middest, even where it most concerneth him, and there recoursing to the thinges forepaste, and divining of thinges to come, maketh a pleasing analysis of all." See Spenser's *Faerie Queene*, ed. J. C. Smith (Oxford, 1909), II, 486. Poetry thus allows of great temporal freedom, even so far as to indulge in prophecy. Coleridge, *Misc. Crit.*, 36, comments on "the marvellous independence and true imaginative absence of all particular space or time in the Faery Queene. It is in the domains neither of history or geography; it is ignorant of all artificial boundary, all material obstacles; it is truly in land of Faery, that is, of mental space." *Prosopopoeia* is, from the point of view of action, timeless. See George Puttenham, *The Arte of English Poesie*, 239, and Peacham, *Garden*, 136, on actions using personified abstractions, i.e., *prosopopoeia*.

[3] Thomas Warton, "Of Spenser's Allegorical Character" (*Observations on*

romance or magic agencies in a romantic epic.[4] Whatever area the abstract ideas come from, these agents give a sort of life to intellectual conceptions; they may not actually create a personality before our eyes, but they do create a semblance of personality.[5] This personify-

The Fairy Queen *of Spenser*, 2d ed., 1762, sec. 10), in *Spenser's Critics*, ed. William Mueller (Syracuse, 1959), 60: "We should remember, that in this age, allegory was applied as the subject and foundation of public shews and spectacles, which were exhibited with a magnificence superior to that of former times. The virtues and vices, distinguished by their respective emblematical types, were frequently personified, and represented by living actors. These figures bore a chief part in furnishing what they called PAGEAUNTS; which were then the principal species of entertainment, and were shewn, not only in private, or upon the stage, but very often in the open streets for solemnising public occasion, or celebrating any grand event." Jacob Burckhardt, *The Civilization of the Renaissance in Italy*, ed. B. Nelson and N. Trinkhaus (New York, 1958), gives a vivid description of these pageants; Gabriel Mourey, *Le Livre des fêtes françaises* (Paris, 1930), gives illustrations showing the devices of pageantry; see also Jean Jacquot, ed., *Les Fêtes de la Renaissance* (Paris, 1956).

[4] Bishop Hurd, in his *Letters on Chivalry and Romance* (1762) praised Tasso's *Jerusalem Delivered* for its "world of magic and enchantments" and applied a "gothic" standard of decorum to Spenser. On Tasso's magical incidents, see C. M. Bowra, *From Virgil to Milton* (London, 1948), 139 ff., and especially 163 and 171. Thomas Warton associated enchantment and allegory as the elements of the romantic epic; e.g., he says "the practice of Ariosto, was to consist of allegories, enchantments, and romantic expeditions, conducted by knights, giants, magicians, and fictitious beings"; see Warton, "Of the Plan and Conduct of the *Fairy Queen*" (1762), in *Spenser's Critics*, ed. Mueller (Syracuse, 1959), 45.

[5] See I. A. Richards, *Practical Criticism* (New York, 1956), 190-192 and Pt. III, ch. ii, *passim*, on relation of metaphor and personification. On animism and "mythic personification," cf. E. B. Tylor, *Origins of Culture* (1871; reprinted New York, 1958), I, 287.

Freud, *Totem and Taboo*, in *Basic Writings* (Mod. Lib. ed., New York, 1938), 857: "In the foregoing case the mechanism of projection is used to settle an emotional conflict; it serves the same purpose in a large number of psychic situations which lead to neuroses. But projection is not specially created for the purpose of defence, it also comes into being where there are no conflicts. The projection of inner perceptions to the outside is a primitive mechanism which, for instance, also influences our sense-perceptions, so that it normally has the greatest share in shaping our outer world. Under conditions that have not yet been sufficiently determined even inner perceptions of ideational and emo-

ing process has a reverse type, in which the poet treats real people in a formulaic way so that they become walking Ideas. When they are historical persons taking part in God's providential structuring of time, as in Dante, the procedure is called *figura* or typology.[6]

The typical "pure" allegory would be a poem like "The Phoenix and the Turtle," where we find the following lines:

> Propertie was thus appalled,
> That the selfe was not the same:
> Single Natures double name,
> Neither two nor one was called.
>
> Reason in itselfe confounded,
> Saw Division grow together,
> To themselves yet either neither,
> Simple were so well compounded.

---

tional processes are projected outwardly, like sense perceptions, and are used to shape the outer world, whereas they ought to remain in the inner world. This is perhaps genetically connected with the fact that the function of attention was originally directed not towards the inner world, but to the stimuli streaming in from the outer world, and only received reports of pleasure and pain from the endopsychic processes. Only with the development of the language of abstract thought through the association of sensory remnants of word representations with inner processes, did the latter gradually become capable of perception. Before this took place primitive man had developed a picture of the outer world through the outward projection of inner projections, which we, with our reinforced conscious perception, must now translate back into psychology." See the Strachey translation of *Totem and Taboo* (Standard ed.), XIII.

[6] Auerbach's classic essay, *"Figura,"* has been reprinted in *Scenes from the Drama of European Literature,* 11–76. This volume also includes the exegetical essay, "St. Francis of Assisi in Dante's 'Commedia,'" 79–100. *Figura* is, strictly speaking, to be distinguished from allegory, in that it is based on a special, nonallegoric view of history. "Since in figural interpretation one thing stands for another, since one thing represents and signifies the other, figural interpretation is 'allegorical' in the widest sense. But it differs from most of the allegorical forms known to us by the historicity both of the sign and what it signifies" (*Scenes,* 54). This distinction is also made by R. P. C. Hanson, *Allegory and Event,* 7, where *figura* is understood by the equally common term "typology."

That it cried, how true a twaine,
Seemeth this concordant one,
Love hath reason, Reason none,
If what parts, can so remaine.[7]

Throughout these stanzas Shakespeare has ascribed a degree of logical interaction to the ideas of property, nature, reason, division, and love. Even though they may not be given personality, these ideas are partially personified and can be said to operate within a dynamic system.[8] They all modify each other in some way. The concept, Property, according to which the two lovers ought to have remained two distinct selves, appears by the death of one to have suffered an almost human loss; it is appalled in the sense of "taken aback," as well as in the punning sense of "dressed in the death-shroud." In either case Property is given a characteristic which normally a philosophical abstraction would lack, namely feeling. While this and the other "Ideas" of the poem are interrelated in a complex syllogistic

---

[7] I have followed the text as reprinted in *The Phoenix and Turtle: By William Shakespeare, John Marston, George Chapman, Ben Jonson, and Others,* ed. Bernard Newdigate (Oxford, 1937). This reprint gives us a clear picture of the constellated positioning of Shakespeare's poem: it was only one among several memorial pieces, and derived its gloss from the interplay between it and those pieces. The *aenigma* was preserved throughout.

[8] See Bertrand Bronson, "Personification Reconsidered," *ELH,* XIV (1947), 163–177; R. W. Frank, "The Art of Reading Medieval Personification Allegory," *ELH,* XX (1953), 237–250; C. F. Chapin, *Personification in Eighteenth-Century English Poetry* (New York, 1955). The theory of allegorical abstraction has been much clouded by the failure of critics to consider the *dynamic* meaning of abstraction. Allegory is usually said to be "abstract" because it uses "personified abstractions." But allegory is much more profoundly abstract than in the mere use of animated philosophic terms. It is abstract in Whitehead's sense, when he says that abstraction is "the omission of part of the truth." It is abstract in the sense of suppressing part of the conditions relevant to its subjects and objects. An allegory of Justice, for example, will omit the contingencies that make a nonrepressive, tolerant justice so difficult to achieve. It omits the human detail, which the mimetic mode, and its highly condensed form, the mythical mode, do not omit. "Abstraction" in allegory also has the meaning of "abstracted behavior"—behavior that lacks the full breadth and excitement of human involvement. Allegory often has "an abstracted air."

system, each one preserves its identity with a sharpness no humanized portraiture would allow. The Ideas remain philosophically distinct (they seem not to dare touch each other), almost in inverse proportion to the degree of interaction they exhibit.[9] The very paradox of Property's gainful loss depends upon a rigid separation of each Idea from every other. This means that along with a complicating movement there goes a simplifying movement. While the overall effect is one of syllogism and system, the particular effect at any given moment is one of discrete particularity: the Ideas are presented, each one in turn, as entities capable of the most refined and narrow delineation. The reader has a strong sense of the barriers between ideas. There is nothing like the feeling one gets of a common humanity binding together the characters of a mimetic drama. This lack of a common humanity is, we shall see, not always a characteristic of allegory—witness the Seven Deadly Sins in Langland's satire—but it is more frequent than its opposite.

Even when the ideas of "The Phoenix and the Turtle" are complex, they remain closely circumscribed by their function in the overall syllogistic structure of the poem. Much the same compartmentalizing of a complex notion occurs in the following lines from Marvell's "Definition of Love."

> My Love is of a birth so rare
> As 'tis, for object, strange and high;
> It was begotten by Despair,
> Upon Impossibility.

[9] "The Idea does not pertain to the changeable and perishable objects of sense experience, but to thrones beyond them in 'splendid isolation.'" Thus Richard Kroner, on Platonic theory, in *Speculation in Pre-Christian Philosophy* (Philadelphia, 1956). On the other hand, cf. a less hackneyed and perhaps more correct view, G. M. A. Grube, *Plato's Thought* (London, 1935; reprinted Boston, 1958), 41: "The stranger thus makes clear that the Ideas cannot exist in absolute isolation from one another. We have already seen in the *Phaedo* that particulars can participate in several Ideas at the same time. The question is now asked about the Ideas themselves. How far can they intermingle?" This is, from a metaphysical point of view, the cardinal question raised by allegory.

Magnanimous Despair alone
Could show me so divine a thing,
Where feeble hope could ne'er have flown,
But vainly flapped its tinsel wing.

In this reworking of Plato's *Symposium*, despair seems to be the very opposite of its normal self and its "magnanimity" is ironic and paradoxical. This would suggest a humanizing of the speaker's state of mind, since it is the nature of human states of mind to be complex and mixed.[10] Allegorically strict relations pertain, however, between Despair and Impossibility, and later in the poem between these and the concept of Fate. The effect is only one remove from dialectic analysis; that one remove is achieved by irony, while aside from the natural subtlety that arises when such irony is employed, there is little enough about these personifications to suggest human character, although "personality" in the caricaturist's sense might be thus represented. Since the Metaphysical poet is likely to stress the relations within a logical system, he may draw the reader's attention away from a mimetic criterion; the reader may never ask if it is strange to be shown ideas in action. Modern readers do, however, ask just this question when they meet the personifications, many of them daemonic and preternatural, which comprise the main device of the eighteenth-century allegorical ode. We perhaps object to "rosy-bosom'd Hours," "Contemplation's sober eye," "Gay Hope," "black Misfortune," "The vultures of the mind,/Disdainful Anger, pallid

[10] Cf. Johan Huizinga, *The Waning of the Middle Ages,* 114: "Here, then, in the *Roman de la Rose,* the sexual motif is again placed in the centre of erotic poetry, but enveloped by symbolism and mystery and presented in the guise of saintliness. It is impossible to imagine a more deliberate defiance of the Christian ideal. The dream of love had taken a form as artistic as it was passionate. The profusion of allegory satisfied all the requirements of medieval imagination. These personifications were indispensable for expressing the finer shades of sentiments. Erotic terminology, to be understood, could not dispense with these graceful puppets. People used these figures of Danger, Evil Mouth, etc., as the accepted terms of a scientific psychology. The passionate character of the central motif prevented tediousness and pedantry."

Fear,/And Shame that skulks behind." These picturesque features of Thomas Gray's grand style lack any ironical perspective, it would seem. As a result, they are almost monstrous.

Such personified agents are of course intended to represent ideas, not real people; they could not, like the characters in a young author's first novel, be traced to their particular "originals." This point can be easily misunderstood—allegorical agents are *real enough*, however ideal their referents may be, however "unlike ourselves" they may appear. They have what might be called an "adequate representational power." Note, for example, the trouble and questionable usefulness of trying to decide which is most real: the statue of Hermione in *The Winter's Tale*, or the idea we get of the "real" Hermione in Acts I–III, or Hermione revived, when the statue is brought to life. Too many philosophic questions are raised: What constitutes reality? Is it accuracy of representation? Then what constitutes accuracy? Or representation? Questions like these concern the ontological issues defined by Shakespeare's play: they do not define the type of play it is. Such questions are somewhat too radical, somewhat too philosophical, for my purposes in literary theorizing.[11] The main point here is that we should make no automatic assumptions about the "unreality" of allegorical personifications.

The typical personified agent can "act" only in consort with other similar agents, a combination which limits each work to a given problem or set of problems. The highly controlled interaction of ideas requires a corresponding definition of the limits of each. "Thus Fame tells a tale and Victory hovers over a general or perches on a standard; but Fame and Victory can do no more." [12] Each of the

[11] This problem is fully discussed in H. A. Myers, *Systematic Pluralism* (Ithaca, 1961), 48, 125–129.

[12] From the discussion of Milton's Sin and Death, in Samuel Johnson, "The Life of Milton," *Works*, ed. Arthur Murphy (New York, 1843), II, 44. Here Johnson also attacks Aeschylus, on the grounds that the interaction of personified ideas is an absurdity: "What I cannot for a moment believe, I cannot for a moment behold with interest or anxiety." Wellek sums up the Johnsonian prejudice: for Johnson, "all allegories which are active agents are absurd: they

fabled birds in "The Phoenix and the Turtle" has one meaning, and as each is brought into the funeral procession it presents that meaning to us, while passing in review. Such strong control of "message" may be thought of as a narrowing, a constriction, a compartmentalizing of meaning. Even when the allegory is more naturalistic, when it appropriates the language of documentary journalism, it bottles up concepts in the form of caricatures. The typical case would be a figure of eighteenth-century burlesque or a minor character in Dickens,[13] and the indication of narrowness is the fact that the names of these characters have supplied bywords for narrow conceptions: Malapropism for a verbal eccentricity, Pecksniffery for hypocrisy, Micawberism for ne'er-do-well poverty. Even supposing that caricature evinces a delight in exaggeration of *real* characteristics,[14] it still transforms what is purportedly real into an abstraction, as Gogol transforms the Inspector's nose into the idea of a nose, by actually removing it from the man's face.[15] A caricaturist gets much of his

---

are only approved if they are mere figurative discourse, pleasing vehicles of instruction, such as Johnson himself composed for the *Rambler* and *Idler* in dull profusion" (*History of Modern Criticism*, I, 82).

[13] See Fielding's Preface to *Joseph Andrews*. Also, Coleridge on the nature of "humour," in *Misc. Crit.*, 118: "In ridiculous positions laughed at by the vulgar, there is a subtle personification going on, something symbolical. Hence the imperfect and awkward effect of comic stories of animals: the *understanding* is satisfied with the allegory; but the *senses* are not." In Coleridge's definition of allegory the same disjunction of aesthetic effect is stressed.

[14] *Caricature*, from *caricare*, "to overload." This suggests the Freudian term, "overdetermined." Caricature might be defined as humorous mannerism.

[15] In Gogol the nose becomes the main agent of the story, "The Nose," as, in a sense, the overcoat becomes the main agent in "The Overcoat." In *Tristram Shandy* the discourse on noses serves a similar function on a more cosmic scale, since, along with other images of parts of the body and along with the imagery of fortifications and bridges, they suggest the problem of impotence, which is so much the heart of the book. (Sterne therein follows Rabelais, II, ch. xv.) Coleridge emphasizes disproportion, and the sense of the absurd overdevelopment of some "humour," in his discussion of Sterne. He is very much aware of the problem of impotence: "Humorous writers, therefore, as Sterne in particular, delight to end in nothing, or a direct contradiction" (*Misc. Crit.*, 118).

vivacity from the powerful elimination of any complicating features in the drawing of his characters, and if the elimination requires complete excision then, as the example of Gogol and others will show, he willingly goes as far as that. I would argue that caricature, as I have described it, is allegorical in essence, since it strives for the simplification of character in terms of single, predominant traits. The traits thus isolated are the iconographic "meanings" of each agent.

What holds true for the more obvious artificial devices of personification, holds true also for the allegorical hero, who is immediately a more plausible agent. When during the middle ages Odysseus and Aeneas and Hercules were used in a representative fashion to convey ideals of Christian knowledge and imperial power, no assumption was made that depth of significance implied human character, with all its variability.[16] Aeneas is the "type" of single-mindedness, and for this reason he lends himself to medieval exegesis. His single-minded acts lend themselves to single-track interpretations, which, though they may have differed from reader to reader, never departed from the guiding notion that Aeneas is a predestined, fated agent.[17]

When writers wish to see a more complex moral world, however, we may ask how restricted the hero will be. Are Dante's self-image, his Virgil, his Beatrice, single in meaning? Is any main protagonist

[16] See Jean Seznec, *The Survival of the Pagan Gods*, tr. Barbara Sessions (New York, 1953), ch. iii, *passim*. For discussions of Hercules as a Christianized figure see also Curtius, *European Literature*, 170–175, 203–207; Marcel Simon, *Hercule et le Christianisme* (Paris, 1955); on his appearance in the Renaissance English drama, E. M. Waith, *The Herculean Hero in Marlowe, Chapman, Shakespeare and Dryden* (New York, 1962).

[17] "If, however, the *Aeneid* has in addition the character of a national epic, it is because Vergil perceives that to build a civilization requires something more than effort, and that is organization. . . . Aeneas is thus the pilgrim father of antiquity; his followers the *Mayflower* company of the Ancient World; while the organized society of the empire is the Graeco-Roman counterpart to the New England Kingdom of the Saints" (C. N. Cochrane, *Christianity and Classical Culture: A Study of Thought and Action from Augustus to Augustine* [New York, 1957], 64–65). See R. W. Cruttwell, *Virgil's Mind at Work* (Oxford, 1946), ch. vi, on the relationship between Aeneas and Hercules.

of *The Faerie Queene* restricted to a single virtue? Is Bunyan's Christian one-sided in character? Surely these all add up to complex figures, which would suggest that allegories may have very human agents. In some sense, especially with Bunyan, major allegorical heroes can have a range of human weakness and strength. They may live through many adventures, in which different trials occur. But is not the nature of such heroes comparable to the nature of a whole poem like "The Phoenix and the Turtle," where the whole was a complex system of interrelated terms, each of which was circumscribed? Putting the matter another way, for allegorical heroes life has a segmented character,[18] and as each event occurs a new discrete characteristic of the hero is revealed, almost as if it had no connection with prior events or with other tied-in characteristics. The allegorical hero is not so much a real person as he is a generator of other secondary personalities, which are partial aspects of himself.

The conceptual hero: his generation of subcharacters. A systematically complicated character will generate a large number of other protagonists who react against or with him in a syllogistic manner. I say "generate," because the heroes in Dante and Spenser and Bunyan seem to create the worlds about them. They are like those people in real life who "project," ascribing fictitious personalities to those whom they meet and live with. By analyzing the projections, we determine what is going on in the mind of the highly imaginative projector. By the same token, if the reader wants a sketch of the character of Redcrosse in Spenser, he lists the series of adventures and tests undergone by Redcrosse, not so much for the

---

[18] "One thing at a time" does not imply that *as an organization of agents* the fable fails to have interest. The sum of all single steps may be extremely complex, as in a mosaic. Curtius, *European Literature*, 174, argues this for Aeneas: "It is possible to find Aeneas a lifeless character. But the great theme of the *Aeneid* is not Aeneas, but the destiny of Rome. And, embedded in this richly allusive poem of history and destiny, is the journey to the otherworld (in Book VI), which raises us above everything earthly and is the greatest beauty of the poem. Its later influence was most significant. To it we owe Dante's *Commedia*."

35

pleasure of seeing *how* Redcrosse reacts in each case, as to see, literally, what aspects of the hero have been displayed by the poet. Redcrosse imagines Sansfoi and his brothers; Sir Guyon imagines Mammon and his cave; Sir Calidore imagines the Blatant Beast—in this sense the subcharacters, the most numerous agents of an allegory, may be generated by the main protagonists, and the finest hero will then be the one who most naturally seems to generate subcharacters—aspects of himself—who become the means by which he is revealed, facet by facet. This generative function accounts for the frequency with which an ascetic like St. Anthony is made the allegorical subject of both painting and literature.[19] Ascetic habits induce visions of daemons, which are projected needs, desires, and hates. This is psychologically a valid image of the Saint, because the state of asceticism with its physical debility induces extremely varied, abundant fantasies.[20] Another natural hero for allegory is the traveler, because on his journey he is plausibly led into numerous fresh situa-

[19] The fountainhead of this tradition: St. Athanasius' *Life of St. Anthony*, tr. Robert T. Meyer (Westminster, Md., 1950).

[20] "Allegory's natural theme is temptation," as Lewis says. A major aim of Christian asceticism is the freeing of the believer from "the tyranny of the passions," on which see Jean Daniélou, *Platonisme et théologie mystique* (Paris, 1944), 76 ff. On the passions which are represented symbolically by animals, monsters, and the like, 78: "[Gregory's *Life of Moses* employs the figure of the charioteer to indicate the higher, good passions, while it uses the equally Platonic image of the steeds for the lower passions, the bad passions.] It is to this second category that we must address ourselves. This is the type against which the soul must defend itself if it is to arrive at the state of apathy (*apatheia*). We shall study the different symbols by which Gregory describes for us this world of passion, which is the world of the deadly sins. These images belong to five categories: the passions are represented first of all as animal life and are symbolized by various beasts; . . . next they are considered as tyrants who keep the mind (*nous*) enslaved; thirdly they are envisaged as a kind of contamination: mud, rust, etc.; finally they are presented as agitation and illusion. To each of these aspects is opposed a contrary aspect: *apatheia* to animality" (my translation). The monsters associated with the Temptation of St. Anthony are beasts of the kind that only an ascetic "apathy" could destroy, yet it is clear that his temptation necessitates the creation of these very monsters. Temptation creates a grotesque symbolic vocabulary similar to that of the Bestiaries.

tions, where it seems likely that new aspects of himself may be turned up.[21] Dante's journey is on one level a refraction of himself as Everyman, while Swift's Gulliver meets not one, but a hundred alter egos, and characteristically himself gives us the key to his involvement with these alter egos when he says "I too was a projector once." [22] Bunyan's Christian suffers extreme and constant anxiety, and we are reminded of Bunyan's own story, how in *Grace Abounding to the Chief of Sinners* he chronicles the fantasies that arose during his own periods of spiritual despair and anxiety. What was true of the man Bunyan was equally true of his creations, and is true of the heroes in Melville and Hawthorne, in Kafka and Orwell, authors whose anxieties are close to the surface of their works. Anxiety is not a necessary ingredient of allegory, but it is the most fertile ground from which allegorical abstractions appear, like the Wood of Dunsinane, before the hero.

Besides subcharacters arising in opposition to the hero, possessing thereby a semblance, if only a semblance, of human personality, we have subcharacters who arise to help the hero, like the servant Sancho Panza,[23] or the Dwarf in Book I, the Palmer in Book II, and

[21] The travels described in Marjorie Nicolson's *Voyages to the Moon* (New York, 1960) are chiefly symbolic of intellectual discoveries. Geometry provides Bacon with another similar metaphor for the process of intellectual discovery, the invasion; *Advancement of Learning*, ch. xiii: "We, like augurs, only measure countries in our mind, and know not how to invade them."

[22] "Projector" here does not have a Freudian sense, but the parallels with that modern sense are remarkable. Swift regarded utopian schemes as projections of the mind, particularly as "the mechanical operation of the spirit" in which the variability of nature was denied. Swift's travesty, *A Modest Proposal*, dramatizes the daemonic inspiration of the typical "projector" and shows the extent to which such thought is obsessive.

[23] Thus Franz Kafka, in "The Truth about Sancho Panza," *Parables*, tr. Willa and Edwin Muir (New York, 1947), 125: "Without making any boast of it Sancho Panza succeeded in the course of years, by devouring a great number of romances of chivalry and adventure in the evening and night hours, in so diverting from him his demon, whom he later called Don Quixote, that his demon thereupon set out in perfect freedom on the maddest exploits, which, however, for the lack of a preordained object, which should have been Sancho Panza himself, harmed nobody. A free man, Sancho Panza

Talus in Book V of *The Faerie Queene*.[24] Here the process of fractionating personality is no less at work. By splitting off these chips of composite character, the author is able to treat them as pure, isolated, personified ideas, and they lend themselves better, as a result, to the overall aim of system and "consistency." This splitting is very clear with a subcharacter like Talus, who is the agent of violence, acting for Artegall in such a way that Artegall himself never has to dirty his hands in the violence of law enforcement. That such crude violence is not directly part of Artegall's own function is evidence, not of any particular soft-heartedness in Spenser's image of Lord Grey, but of Spenser's poetic control over an embarrassingly unmagnanimous characteristic. The poet can control Talus far better than he could control fits of rage and savage vengefulness in his titular hero. Further, the poet controls the meaning, or meanings, his hero is intended to carry. But as a result of this procedure, the poet denies true human character to that hero.

Daemonic constriction in thematic actions. The criterion of increasing constriction of meaning, by which we recognize the iconographic significance of the agent, can be translated into more precise terms. Narrowness, constriction, singleness of meaning are not self-evident semantic notions, nor do they at first sight suggest a proper term for the allegorical agent.[25] To find the proper term we have to analyze the "constricted meaning" in an almost psychological way. The hero is either a personified abstraction or a representative type, which amount to much the same thing, and in either case what is felt as a narrowed iconographic meaning is known to us the readers through the hero's characteristic way of acting, which is severely limited in variety. We must return to the allegorical hero's behavior

---

philosophically followed Don Quixote on his crusades, perhaps out of a sense of responsibility, and had of them a great and edifying entertainment to the end of his days." Reprinted by permission of Schocken Books Inc. from *Parables and Paradoxes* by Franz Kafka; copyright 1936, 1937, by Heinr. Mercer Sohn, Prague; copyright 1946, 1947, 1948, 1953, 1954, 1958, by Schocken Books Inc.

[24] Cf. B. E. C. Davis, *Edmund Spenser: A Critical Study* (Cambridge, 1933), 122–126.

[25] Terms like *figura* and *paradeigma* suggest abstract outlines, schematic

for our answer. We find that he conforms to the type of behavior manifested by people who are thought (however unscientifically) to be possessed by a daemon.[26] This notion may be hard to accept, but only because the present common idea of a daemon is of a wild, unkempt, bestial, monstrous, diabolic creature,[27] whereas ancient

---

shapes, or stylized masks. Profile and façade seem to be related concepts.

[26] Drayton, in the Preface to his *Heroical Epistles*, gives to his heroes the status of demigods, i.e., *daimoniai:* "And tho' Heroical be properly understood of Demigods, as of Hercules and Aeneas, whose parents were said to be, the one celestial, the other mortal; yet it is also transferred to them who for the greatness of mind come near to Gods. For to be born of a celestial Incubus, is nothing else, but to have a great and mighty spirit, far above the earthly weakness of men; in which sense Ovid (whose imitator I partly profess to be) doth also use Heroical." See "To the Reader," *Works,* ed. J. W. Hebel (Oxford, 1931), II, 130.

On demonology I have used Edward Langton, *Essentials of Demonology* (London, 1949); Martin P. Nilsson, *Greek Piety,* tr. H. J. Rose (Oxford, 1948), especially ch. i, sec. 7, and iii, sec. 10; E. R. Dodds, *The Greeks and the Irrational* (Berkeley, 1951); F. M. Cornford, *From Religion to Philosophy* (1912; reprinted New York, 1957); M. P. Nilsson, *Greek Folk Religion,* ed. A. D. Nock (1940; reprinted New York, 1961), especially 10 ff. and 101 ff.; Franz Cumont, *After Life in Roman Paganism,* tr. H. D. Irvine (1922; reprinted New York, 1959), especially ch. vi, "The Journey to the Beyond"; Cumont, *Astrology and Religion among the Greeks and Romans,* tr. J. B. Baker (1912; reprinted New York, 1960), 61–63 especially, for the allegorical representation of astral deities; Guy Soury, *La Démonologie de Plutarque* (Paris, 1942); Emil Schneweis, *Angels and Demons according to Lactantius* (Washington, 1944), which has a useful general bibliography.

[27] The proper place for these picturesquely deformed creatures is the anti-masque, where they act as foils to the higher angels. Thus Bacon, in his essay *Of Masques and Triumphs:* "Let anti-masques not be long; they have been commonly of fools, satyrs, baboons, wild-men, antics, beasts, sprites, witches, Ethiops, pigmies, turquets, nymphs, rustics, Cupids, statua's moving, and the like. As for angels, it is not comical enough to put them in anti-masques; and any thing that is hideous, as devils, giants, is on the other side as unfit." Bacon asks that the chariots proper to tourneys be drawn "with strange beasts: as lions, bears, camels, and the like." Such allegories could be problematical. Canon Raven reports that James I decided to preach to his courtiers "a sermon of warning in the shape of an acted fable. Aesop had related how the King of Beasts had dealt as judge and executioner with a refractory subject, the Bear. There was in the menagerie of the Tower a magnificent lion sent to him by the Sultan of Morocco: there was also a bear that had broken loose from the bear-pit at Southwark and killed a child. James ordered a cage to be

myth and religion recognized many mild and beneficent daemons, the *eudaimoniai*. Between the extremely good and the extremely bad daemons there are all the intermediate stages of good and evil,[28] so there is no shortage of patterns for any and all allegorical types, at least on the score of moral or spiritual status.

Daemons, as I shall define them, share this major characteristic of allegorical agents, the fact that they compartmentalize function. If we were to meet an allegorical character in real life, we would say of him that he was obsessed with only one idea, or that he had an absolutely one-track mind, or that his life was patterned according to absolutely rigid habits from which he never allowed himself to vary. It would seem that he was driven by some hidden, private force;[29] or, viewing him from another angle, it would appear that he

built on Tower Green in the shape of a law-court, and round it thrones for himself and seats for his troublesome nobles. The scene was set; the lion was placed in the judgment-seat; then the bear was admitted to the dock. But at that point Aesop proved unreliable: the lion fled whimpering to a corner of the cage; the bear, inured to mastiffs, saw no reason to pick a quarrel; and the intended demonstration of royal justice developed into a farce" (*Natural Religion and Christian Theology* [Cambridge, 1953], I, 56. On King James's menagerie see J. E. Egerton, "King James's Beasts," *History Today*, XII (June 1962), 405–415.

[28] Plutarch, in his essay "On the Cessation of Oracles," sec. x, in Plutarch's *Morals*, tr. C. W. King (London, 1903), speaks of a "family of *Daemons*, intermediate between gods and men, and after a certain fashion bringing together and uniting in one the society of both." Since the oracles were thought to be inspired and voiced by daemons (through their agents the priests), this Plutarch essay is concerned entirely with the doctrine of daemonic inspiration. The same essay appears in the Loeb Classics edition of Plutarch's complete *Works*.

[29] "The daemonic character appears in its most dreadful form when it stands out dominatingly in some *men*. Such are not always the most remarkable men, either in spiritual quality or natural talents, and they seldom have any goodness of heart to recommend them. [Fn.: They are merely *numinous*, not *holy* men.] But an incredible force goes forth from them and they exercise an incredible power over all creatures, nay, perhaps even over the elements. And who can say how far such an influence may not extend?" (Goethe's *Dichtung und Wahrheit*, as quoted by Rudolph Otto, *The Idea of the Holy*, tr. J. W. Harvey [New York, 1958], 152; see also 122).

did not control his own destiny, but appeared to be controlled by some foreign force, something outside the sphere of his own ego.

Take moral allegory, for example. It is concerned chiefly with virtue, and one might assume that virtues were a sort of habit of good; one might assume that they transcend differences in relative power. Virtue might be conceived without regard to the original sense of *virtus* (Ital. *virtù*), meaning "manliness" or "power." [30] If moral allegory is the narrative or dramatic rendition of contests between virtues and vices, however, it will inevitably be a contest between warring powers. By equating daemonic and allegorical agency, I believe we shall be able to explain the relationship between virtue in its Christian sense of "purity" and in its original pagan sense of "strength." We can also easily enough describe non-Christian allegory.

Daemons: good and evil agency. The notion of the daemonic is complex, as a result of the different religious cultures in which it arises.[31] The common Christian idea presents a daemon with horns

[30] Otto, *Idea*, 118: "the daemonic, a character ascribed to certain definite operations of force, be they strong or weak, extraordinary or quite trivial, the work of a soul or a 'non-soul.' The quality can be only suggested through that unique element of feeling, the feeling of 'uncanniness' . . . whose positive content cannot be defined conceptually, and can only be indicated by that mental response to it which we called 'shuddering.'" With this feeling of awe and fear Boethius asks, "Are riches valuable for their own nature, or on account of your and other men's natures? Which is the more valuable, the gold itself or the power of the stored-up money?" *The Consolation of Philosophy* would appear at first to be entirely pragmatic about the corruption of avarice, but gradually a deeper concern over the freedom of the possessor becomes apparent, a freedom from daemonic control. Power is conferred by wealth, and wealth in turn becomes a daemonic agency, Mammon. On the daemonic as occult source of power, see Nilsson, *Greek Piety*, 103–110, "Power." Our word "virtuoso" retains the old sense, and furthermore connotes the *awe-inspiring*, and the *sublime* (cf. Otto, *Idea*, 150–151).

[31] One of the richest commentaries on the development of daemonology is that contained in Ralph Cudworth's *The True Intellectual System of the Universe* (1678), in the London edition of 1845, to which are added notes and dissertations of Dr. J. L. Mosheim, translated by John Harrison. Since for the Cambridge Platonists there is a cardinal dispute over what are called

and a pitchfork, a devil, but that is the simplest stereotype, arising from equating daemons with the Fallen Angels. This equivalence shows that the daemonic and the angelic are closely related and shows that in Hebrew religious myth, as well as in Greek myth, the daemons could be either good or evil spirits.

Etymologically, the word demon is usually derived from δαίομαι (*daiomai*) meaning to distribute or to divide. The demon is a distributor,

---

"incorporeal substances," and daemons fill this position, we naturally have extended discussion and annotation on daemonology. See especially I, 114–119, II, 342 ff. Cudworth calls the Pythagorean daemons "beings superior to men, commonly called by the Greeks demons (which Philo tells us are the same with angels amongst the Jews, and accordingly are those words, demons and angels, by Hierocles and Simplicius, and other of the latter pagan writers, sometimes used indifferently, as synonymous) viz. that these demons or angels are not pure, abstract, incorporeal substances, devoid of vital union with any matter; but that they consist of something incorporeal and something corporeal, joined together. . . . 'They have a superior and an inferior part in them; and their superior part is an incorporeal substance; their inferior corporeal'" (342–343). Mosheim says that Cudworth "plainly and openly approves of the opinion of those who like the Platonists of former times maintain that all genii and demons are endowed with a natural body" (fn., 345). On Cudworth's position, see Basil Willey, *The Seventeenth Century Background* (1934; reprinted New York, 1953), ch. viii.

To the extent that Christianity is syncretic, it tolerates daemonology. Hobbes, for example, concluding his *Leviathan* with a treatise on the daemonic, blamed the Greeks and the Church Fathers for thereby encouraging superstition: "For men being generally possessed before the time of our Saviour, by contagion of the demonology of the Greeks, of an opinion that the souls of men were substances distinct from their bodies, and therefore that when the body was dead, the soul of every man, whether godly or wicked, must subsist somewhere by virtue of its own nature, without acknowledging therein any supernatural gift of God; the doctors of the Church doubted a long time, what was the place which they were to abide in, till they should be reunited to their bodies in the resurrection; supposing for awhile, they lay under the altars; but afterwards the Church of Rome found it more profitable to build for them this place of purgatory; which by some other Churches in this latter age has been demolished" (*Leviathan*, XLIV, quoted by Willey, 110–111). On this basis the classic location of allegorical narratives would be a purgatory; the most clearly and simply allegorical section of *The Divine Comedy* would be the "Purgatory."

usually of destinies. Lactantius recalls the opinion of Plato, that demon might come from δαήμονας (daēmonas) meaning one who is skilled and learned, because, he says, "Grammarians say demons were gods by reason of their skill and their knowledge." Very early in history the term demon had a religious and a spiritual signification, and was referred to the other-world. In its religious signification it was used in a three-fold sense in pagan antiquity, namely: for gods, for intermediaries, and for the souls of the dead without any direct connection with intermediaries. These three senses are further developed into a very intricate and complex maze of meanings.[32]

The most interesting sense, from our point of view, is the second. As intermediaries, part man, part god, the daemons were often considered in both pagan and Christian antiquity to be the guardians of the human species.[33] Each man would be guided by his guardian

[32] Schneweis, *Angels and Demons*, 82–83. Langton agrees with this traditional etymology (*Essentials*, 84), but further qualifies the term, in the direction required by my own argument, that there is an intimate relation between the daemonic and the ornamental: "The etymology of the *daimon* is rather uncertain. It is generally derived from the root *daio*, meaning 'to divide,' 'part out,' or 'distribute.' By some scholars it is therefore understood to denote God as the Alotter or Distributor—He who apportions to man his lot on earth. Welcker, however, points out that 'to divide' is also 'to order' and 'to know,' and suggests that the word may also mean 'He who knows,' a signification that is peculiarly appropriate to the Greeks. Ramsay remarks that Fick derives the word from the root *das*, 'to teach,' and identifies it with the Sanskrit *dasmant* ('wise'); whilst Pauly-Wissowa allows that the etymology is uncertain." The term is often loosely synonymous with *theos* (god).

[33] On the daemon as intermediary, see A. D. Nock, *Conversion: The Old and the New in Religion from Alexander the Great to Augustine of Hippo* (London, 1933), 222–224. Nock notes that the daemon need not have any "evil colouring." A familiar instance, in antiquity and in the Renaissance, would be the description of Eros in the *Symposium*, where Diotima says, "He is a great spirit [daimon], and like all spirits he is intermediate between the divine and the mortal." "And what," I said, "is his power?" "He interprets," she replied, "between gods and men, conveying and taking across to the gods the prayers and sacrifices of men, and to men the commands and replies of the gods; he is the mediator who spans the chasm which divides them, and therefore in him all is bound together, and through him the arts of the prophet and the priest, their sacrifices and charms, and all prophecy and incantation, find their way. . . . Now these spirits or intermediate powers are many and di-

angel, in this case, a *daimon*—the most celebrated of all cases being Socrates' *daimon,* the "voice" that spoke to him.[34] This voice not only informed Socrates of the right path, but enforced virtue upon him, in that he never departed from its dictates. The daemonic "advice" is of such authority that one would not willingly go against it, and would probably never even question one's *daimon.* A voice that cannot be questioned, or an oracle (since the daemons were given charge of the oracular revelation of the deity's will),[35] have

verse, and one of them is Love." (Franz Kafka rewrote this mythology ironically in his parable, "Couriers.")

The intermediate function appears also in Neoplatonic imagery in the Renaissance: "From Ficino's numerous expositions of demonology the following general outline can be gathered. Demons are primarily planetary, though there are also supercelestial and elemental ones. They have souls and aetheric or aerial bodies, according to their status; these bodies are of a like nature to the human spirit. Planetary demons, then, are like men without earthly bodies who live in the heavenly spheres; they perform the function of transmitting celestial influences; they can, being both soul and spirit, act both on man's spirit and his soul. The Neoplatonic hierarchy of demons is identified with the Christian hierarchy of angels. [Fn.: The starting point of this is, of course, Ps.—Dionysius; but the distribution of the Dionysian angelic hierarchies among the celestial spheres seems to begin with Dante.] A guardian angel is the same as a familiar planetary demon. There are bad demons, of a low status and with aerial bodies, who trouble men's spirits and imagination" (D. P. Walker, *Spiritual and Demonic Magic from Ficino to Campanella* [London, 1958], 46).

[34] See Soury, *Démonologie*, ch. viii, "Le Démon de Socrate." One associates "voices" with the *poltergeist* and witchcraft, but in ancient times the oracles were all, in effect, "voices." Shakespeare makes much of this in his *Coriolanus,* dramatizing a ceremony by which the populace accords its "voice" to the tribune. In another context *The Tempest* also presents daemonic speech directly.

[35] Plutarch's "On the Cessation of Oracles," sec. xiii: "Let us, then neither listen to people saying that oracles are not divinely inspired, or that certain ceremonies and wild rites are unheeded by the gods; nor, on the other hand, let us imagine that the Deity goes up and down, and is present at, and assists in, things of the sort; but as is right and proper, let us assign these operations to *agents,* or as it were, servants and clerks of the gods, and believe in daemons, presiding over the performers in the divine rites and mysteries, whilst others go about as punishers of the proud and mighty sinners."

Cf. also *Paradise Regained*, I, 406-464, on the cessation of the Pagan Oracles at the birth of Christ. These oracles had been associated with pagan demons,

more than a perfection worthy of respect and worship. They have the power to govern man's life, down to the finest detail. Roman religion shows a marked increase in the number of petty gods, all of them properly speaking daemons, and they are endowed with specific functions, many of them so minute as to seem ridiculously overcontrolled as a result.[36] When a daemon has charge of one's eyes, one's hair, one's knife, one's hat, one's book, one's mirror, the proliferation has reached an extreme.[37] Such a wealth of daemonic

---

or with the Devil, and at the purifying birth of Christ they ceased to foretell the future accurately. One aspect of predetermination is prediction, and magic makes use of many devices besides the Oracle to achieve this purpose. For example, the fortune-teller uses the Tarot cards, and in modern poetry Eliot revives this device as a specifically magical one, making us aware that Mme. Sosostris is a wicked woman with the cards, while he then personifies these cards, making them actors in his symbolic drama. The Tarot cards are a perfect instance of true emblems; they have a dynamic as well as ideal meaning. On Tarot see Grillot de Givry, *A Pictorial Anthology of Witchcraft, Magic, and Alchemy*, tr. J. C. Locke (New Hyde Park, 1958), Bk. II, ch. viii, "Cartomancy and the Tarot." Charles Williams employs the Tarot symbolism in his romance, *The Greater Trumps* (New York, 1950).

[36] For a brief characterization of Roman religion see Ernst Cassirer, *An Essay on Man* (New York, 1953), ch. vii, "Myth and Religion," 113, 128–130.

[37] Nilsson, *Greek Piety*, 60: "The application of the word *daimon* to the great gods was restricted, and it was principally employed in reference to lesser gods and indefinite supernatural powers. In the Attic orators we note a manifest tendency to ascribe ill fortune to a daimon; they hesitated to make the gods responsible for it. This is the beginning of the deterioration of the word which finally led to its getting the meaning which 'demon' has in our language." See also A. H. Krappe, *La Genèse des mythes* (Paris, 1952), 55: "These 'special divinities' (*sondergötter*) are all those divinities dedicated to a special activity, a particular duty." An amusing instance would be the petty divinities which Sir John Harington saw presiding over the Elizabethans' privies, "for they [the ancients] that had gods and goddesses for all the necessaries of our life, from our cradles to our graves; viz., 1. for sucking, 2. for swathing, 3. for eating, 4. for drinking, 5. for sleeping . . . etc., etc., I say, you must not think they would commit such an oversight, to omit such a necessary, as in all languages hath the name of necessity, or ease; wherefore they had both a god and a goddess, that had the charge of the whole business: the god was called *Stercutius*. . . . But the goddess was much more especially, and properly assigned to this business, whose name was *Dea Cloacina;* her statue was erected by *Titus Tatius,* he that reigned with *Romulus,* in a goodly

agencies controlling the citizen's daily life suggests that in fact religion is no longer involved, and instead the place of religion has been usurped by magic, thaumaturgy,[38] theurgy,[39] spiritualism, and superstition, which is precisely the accusation often leveled against ancient Roman religion.[40] When the development of daemonic agency is checked by Christianity, this check takes the form of a dualistic division of spirits into the good angels and the evil demons (e.g., in Lactantius); the number of daemons does not decrease; they merely fall into two groups more sharply divided than in pagan religious practice. But even pagan Near Eastern Zoroastrian thought allows this division into good and evil spirits, and to the extent that Christianity is dualistic it reflects this Near Eastern influence.[41] The restriction of daemonic agency into two classes does not in any way alter its essential nature, which is, the

---

large house of office (a fit shrine for such a saint), which *Lodovicus Vives* cites out of *Lactantius*" (in *The Metamorphosis of Ajax* [reprinted at Chiswick, 1814], 28-29; new ed. by E. S. Donno [New York, 1962]). Cloacina is a patroness of satire, where scatology is an extreme type of cursing and profanation.

[38] Nilsson, *Greek Piety*, 138-150.

[39] Dodds, *The Greeks and the Irrational*, App. II, "Theurgy."

[40] For example, in Tertullian's attack on the belief in many daemons, "On Idolatry," sec. 9, where he attacks astrology, by which "men are led to think that they need not call on God, on the assumption that we are driven by the immutable will of the stars" (in *The Library of Christian Classics*, V, tr. and ed. S. L. Greenslade [London, 1956]).

[41] Krappe, *Genèse des mythes*, 64, speaks of "the formation, by means of abstraction, of the concept of an Evil Demon, presiding over all the forces that are harmful and hostile to man. This concept is opposed naturally to the concept of a father-god such as we have noticed, and leads thus to the genesis of a dualist system. . . . At a later stage of development, it is supposed that the two demons, good and bad, are two brothers, often two twin brothers, on the old assumption that twins are bound to be mortal enemies. This is the origin of the Egyptian myth of Osiris and Set, of the Persian myth of Ahura Mazda and Ahriman, but also of the Iroquois myth of Haweyn and Hanegoasegeh. Iranian dualism no doubt influenced slavic mythology, where we find, in the Middle Ages, Bielbog and Czernibog, the 'white god' and the 'black god'" (my translation). See Hans Jonas, *The Gnostic Religion: The Message of the Alien God and the Beginnings of Christianity* (Boston, 1958), 48-97, on the dualistic iconography of Gnosticism.

embodiment of powers in quasi-divine agencies. J. B. Beer has very helpfully reduced this concept of the embodied power to a concept of energy.[42] Speaking of the "daemonic ambivalence" whereby we get both good and bad, agathodaemons and cacodaemons, he says:

> The ambiguity can be resolved, however, if one thinks of daemons in terms, not of their influence on human beings but of their inward power. For good or evil, they are characterized by their peculiar supernatural energies, like Milton's Satan—and may indeed be equated with fallen angels. Like Boehme's fire, they have lost an essential part of their angelic nature, and the residue, which should normally be the basis of that nature, is now available as energy for either good or evil.[43]

It may help, in the case of moral allegory, to think of each virtue, acquired or lacking, as a kind of moral energy, not, as Aristotle's *Ethics* would define virtue, a state of being, but an equivalent in the moral world of a tuned-up muscle in the physical world. And similarly with other skills. A magian character may exhibit a purely intellectual power,[44] the kind of strength that made the grammarians

---

[42] *Coleridge the Visionary* (London, 1959), 114. In this analysis of the Osiris myth in Coleridge, Osiris is the masculine, energizing deity, Isis the "passive, recipient, feminine Nature."

[43] *Ibid.*, 124 ff. This chapter, "The Daemonic Sublime," would make a helpful gloss on Book V of *The Faerie Queene*, since it is centrally concerned with Osiris as an ambivalent mythic figure. "This 'daemonic ambivalence' can be traced," says Beer, "in a good deal of the mythology concerning serpents, where the serpent appears sometimes as a good figure, sometimes as a bad." This fits perfectly the situation in the Temple of Isis, in Book V, since the crocodile is both fawning and threatening, both amorous and hostile. Cf. Torgny Säve-Söderbergh, *Pharaohs and Mortals*, tr. R. E. Oldenburg (Indianapolis, 1961), the chapter "The Friendly Crocodile"; Joseph Fontenrose, *Python: A Study of Delphic Myth and Its Origins* (Berkeley and Los Angeles, 1959), especially chs. iii, vi, x.

[44] See P. F. Fisher, "Blake's Attacks on the Classical Tradition," *Philological Quarterly*, XL (Jan. 1961), 14–15. Fisher quotes Blake's *Vision of the Last Judgment:* "Allegories are things that Relate to Moral Virtues. Moral Virtues do not Exist; they are Allegories and dissimulations." Fisher comments: "The correction of the natural self or 'Spectre' by conformity to a scheme of moral ideals or virtues was the counsel of Greek rationalism and the Deists. The difficulty about these moral ideals was that they could never be realized but

equate learning and rhetorical technique with daemonic power.[45]

Daemonic possession. It follows, if one wishes to equate allegorical agents with daemons, that a certain adjustment has to be made, on the grounds that a man may be possessed by a daemon without actually becoming that daemon. This objection is not a serious one, however. We can say either that the man is possessed by *his* daemon or that he is completely identified with the dictates of his daemon, so that there is no apparent difference between his character and the daemonic force governing it. In common parlance we have no hesitation about saying, "He is a demon," implying that daemonic influence so limits and simplifies character that character in the normal sense no longer exists, and the possessed man plays a role constricted in the very manner we have already discussed.[46] I shall

---

only simulated, since they were either prohibitions which negated the springs of life or abstractions which had lost their reference to concrete experience. There was an inevitable air of hypocrisy about a classical moralist like Seneca, for his platitudes lacked any real contact with man's actual plight. His moral virtues were either allegories derived from the vision of the seer—but lifted clear of their original context—or they were abstractions derived from generalizations on behavior. They were either the product of what Blake called 'Allegoric Fable' or what he called 'Experimental Theory.' "

[45] Thus Hercules becomes the defender of the Seven Liberal Arts, and Martianus Capella writes the *Marriage of Mercury and Philology*, in which, as Curtius remarks (*European Literature*, 38–39): "Not only all sorts of demons and demigods, but also the antique poets and philosophers (78, 9 ff.), are included. As her wedding present the bride receives the seven liberal arts. To each of them Capella devotes one book of his work. In accordance with the taste of the period, they are personified as women, and distinguished by their clothing, implements, and the manner in which their hair is worn. Thus, Grammar appears as a gray-haired woman of advanced age, who boasts that she descends from the Egyptian king Osiris."

[46] The later Shakespeare plays afford instances of this "decomposition" (the term is Ernest Jones's, from his study of *Hamlet*, on which see note 68 below). Thus Bradley noted the allegorical nature of Shakespeare's later dramas: "We seem to trace the tendency of imagination to analyse and abstract, to decompose human nature into its constituent factors, and then to construct beings in whom one or more of these factors is absent or atrophied or only incipient. This, of course, is a tendency which produces symbols, allegories, personifications, of qualities and abstract ideas. . . . While it would

therefore use the word daemon for any person possessed by a daemon, or even acting *as if* possessed by a daemon, since by definition
if a man is possessed by an influence that excludes all other influences while it is operating on him, then he clearly has no life outside an exclusive sphere of action.[47]

Malbecco, in Spenser, is possessed by jealousy and is left in a state
of total enslavement to this passion. The characterization here moves
toward allegory, away from realism and mimesis: Malbecco appears
first in the role of a jealous, petty-minded husband, and in that role
he is eminently real and natural and comic. But Spenser gradually
shifts this mimetic characterization away from the world of the
Italian *novella* toward the abstract world of personified virtues and
vices, and Malbecco becomes more and more deeply obsessed, more
absolutely possessed by his daemon, jealousy. The increase of daemonic control over the character amounts to an intensification of
the allegory. It is striking that this progress in abstraction is accompanied by an increased importance given to the name of the par-

---

be going too far to suggest that he was employing conscious symbolism or
allegory in *King Lear*, it does appear to disclose a mode of imagination not so
very far removed from the mode which, we must remember, Shakespeare was
familiar with in Morality plays and in *The Faerie Queene*" (from *Shakespearian
Tragedy*, 263–265, quoted by W. B. C. Watkins, *Shakespeare and Spenser*
(Princeton, 1950), 98. De Quincey's "On the Knocking at the Gate in Macbeth" (1823) anticipates both Bradley's and Jones's ideas of decomposition
and furthermore shows how the feelings of Macbeth, the daemonic hero, are
"caught chiefly by contagion" from his wife.

[47] Such a process occurs in one of the eighteenth-century acting versions of
Shakespeare's *Coriolanus*. The following lines, interpolated into the text,
appear in *Bell's Shakespeare* (London, 1773), II, 62:

> 2 *Cit.* Have our Tribunes done all this?
> 3 *Cit.* The Furies break their Necks for it.
> 4 *Cit.* What need we trouble the damn'd Neighbours for what we can do
> ourselves. We are the Furies.
> *All Cit.* Ay, we are the Furies, we are the Furies. To the Rock, to the Rock
> with them.

This makes explicit what is merely latent in the original. Here the Furies become the Citizens; possession leads to total identification.

ticular vice involved. Finally Spenser points out that Malbecco is called "Jealousy" ("and Gealosie is hight"), according to a process that can be found working throughout *The Faerie Queene*. It appears that to name a person is to fix his function irrevocably. This fact can be explained in terms of daemonology.[48] The daemon could only be invoked by recourse to his particular name, and when the daemons controlled the oracles, as they were thought to do, their names became the *Open sesame!* for the divinely inspired oracular message. The emblematic name could even serve as a substitute for the daemonic agency; to cast a spell over an enemy, using the name of one's own protective daemon would work as well as meeting the man in battle and then calling one's daemon to strengthen one's arm.

Daemonic heroes.[49] A rich variety of allegorical works have heroes

[48] On the properties of bodies, i.e., mere *names*, Cudworth (*Intellectual System*, I, 114-115) says: "As there is some use of those abstract names, so the abuse of them has been also very great; forasmuch as, though they be really the names of nothing, since the essence of this and that man is not any thing without the man, nor is an accident any thing without its substance, yet men have been led into a gross mistake by them, to imagine them to be realities existing by themselves. Which infatuation hath chiefly proceeded from scholastics." Names, given a daemonic world-view, are endowed with *mana* and are adequate substitutes for simple everyday material bodies and substances. One result of such beliefs is the multiplication of synonyms for each daemonic agent—i.e., *paronomasia*. On this subject, see Leo Spitzer, *Linguistics and Literary History* (Princeton, 1948), the chapter entitled "Linguistic Perspectivism in Don Quixote," 41-87. Spitzer shows that Cervantes allows "an instability and variety of the names given to certain characters." This instability is analogous to the "liking for indeterminateness" which appears in compulsive speech, on which see below, Chapter 6.

[49] Frye has systematized the concept of a hero by elaborating on Aristotle's notion that a hero always has a certain degree of power, greater, equal to, or less than ours. The range from high to low: (1) gods, (2) heroes of romance, (3) heroes of high mimetic literature (most epic and tragedy), (4) heroes of low mimetic literature (most comedy and realistic fiction), and (5) heroes of ironic literature (satire, travesty, the absurd). Frye's definition of the second rank, heroes of romance, accords precisely with the notion of a daemonic hero, or daimon. "If superior in *degree* to other men and to his environment, the hero is the typical hero of *romance*, whose actions are marvellous but who is himself identified as a human being. The hero of romance moves in a world in which the ordinary laws of nature are slightly suspended: prodigies of courage and endurance, unnatural to us, are natural to him, and enchanted weapons,

of the most obviously daemonic nature, works like *The Divine
Comedy*, where the daemons are chiefly of the third type noted by
Lactantius, the souls of those who have passed on, though there are
also in the "Purgatorio" and the "Paradiso" instances of the "intermediaries," the "powers" inhabiting the spiritual world above the
Mount of Purgatory. We need only point to the concept of "faerie
land" in Spenser, a concept that is in essence daemonic, since not
only are the knights and ladies inhabitants of a spirit-world, a world
of fairy princes and princesses, but they are all engaged in *fated
actions*, which happens to be the etymological implication of the
word "faerie." [50] Bunyan's daemons, in his *Grace Abounding* and
his fables, are well known. In the eighteenth century the term
"demon" is a common one for allegorical agency, and in neoclassic
odes and preromantic verse,[51] as well as in the gothic novel,[52] it is
openly accepted and understood for what it is, a means of develop-

---

talking animals, terrifying ogres and witches, and talismans of miraculous
power violate no rule of probability once the postulates of romance have been
established. Here we have moved from myth, properly so called, into legend,
folk tale, *märchen*, and their literary affiliates and derivatives." See *Anatomy*,
33–34.

[50] Frye, *Anatomy*, 147: "The demonic human world is a society held together
by a kind of molecular tension of egos, a loyalty of the group or the leader
which diminishes the individual, or, at best, contrasts his pleasure with his
duty or honor." On the intellectualizing function of demonic machines, see
Cassirer, *Language and Myth*, 58–59.

[51] For example, in James Thomson's *The Castle of Indolence*, Canto I, xxi, 1.
In the *Odes* of William Collins the "Thou" seems to me always a type of
daemon, most obviously so in the *Ode to Fear*. Collins usually seeks to define
his "Thou" in terms of ornamental dress.

[52] The predominant emotion of fear (or anxiety) gives the Gothic novel a
natural ground for daemonic imagery and agency. On the daemonic in the
Gothic revival, see A. O. Lovejoy, "The Chinese Origin of a Romanticism,"
in *Essays in the History of Ideas* (New York, 1960), 130; and "The First
Gothic Revival and the Return to Nature," *ibid.*, 145. The Gothic novel
abounds in daemonic agencies—statues bleeding and sweating, genii, magic
talismans, fantastic "doubles" (the *doppelgänger*). I would align this special
variety of agency with the notion of the sublime, which puts a high value on
all phenomena that suggest to man his own relative weakness. The uncanny,
for example, creates doubts about mere human powers.

ing romantic plots by giving miraculous power to heroes and heroines.[53] Thus Walpole noted in his first Preface that *The Castle of Otranto* was based on an idea of absolutely unremitting retribution, a fatal family destiny. His aim purported to be moralistic: "I could wish he [the author] had grounded his plan on a more useful moral than this; that *the sins of the fathers are visited on their children to the third and fourth generation.* I doubt whether, in his [the author's] time any more than at present, ambition curbed its appetite of dominion from the dread of so remote a punishment." The subject—ambition and its "appetite of dominion"—is perfectly fitted to the means of expression, since the daemonic world is one where supernatural energies and consuming appetites are the sole means to existence. The depiction of absolute power and its danger to the soul forms the basis likewise of Beckford's *Vathek*, where the caliph is "fired with the ambition of prescribing laws to the powers of darkness." [54]

[53] The Abbé Dubos attacks the absurdities of miracle and marvel which follow from the nature of allegory. Further, in his *Critical Reflections on Poetry, Painting and Music*, tr. Thomas Nugent (London, 1748), I, 171, he objects to the use of miraculous agents in allegorical painting, as being too awesome a subject for art: "These sacred truths, on which we should not even think without humility and terror, ought not to be painted with so much wit; nor represented under the emblem of an ingenious allegory." This has a Johnsonian ring to it.

[54] William Beckford, *Vathek* (1786), in *Shorter Novels*, ed. Philip Henderson (London, 1956), 268. Lewis' *The Monk* (1796) treats the theme of temptation in not entirely sensual terms. Ambrosio, who is patterned on the type of St. Anthony, suffers "the cravings of brutal appetite"; but he equally suffers a desire to *know*, to experience, to move outside of his "monastic seclusion" into the "great world." See *The Monk* (reprinted New York, 1952), 237 ff. This same hunger afflicts Maturin's hero; see William F. Axton's introduction to *Melmoth the Wanderer* (1820; reprinted Lincoln, 1961), xiv: "A figure reminiscent of the Wandering Jew or Milton's Satan, Melmoth is doomed to roam the face of the world in fruitless search of salvation, spiritually tortured by the isolation from the rest of humanity conferred by his immortality and the ironic punishment of being condemned to life. Self-damned, possessed of supernatural powers, and strangely sympathetic, Melmoth is an epitome of the Gothic hero-villain."

THE DAEMONIC AGENT

Turning to more realistic fables, it should be observed that Defoe is fascinated by the daemonic, and besides showing how Robinson Crusoe is plagued by weird mental aberrations that are a more sophisticated equivalent of the ancients' "daemonic possession," Defoe devoted at least three major works, *An Essay on the History and Reality of Apparitions, The Political History of the Devil,* and *A System of Magic,* to the analysis of daemonic agency. There is furthermore a close relation between the daemonic fantasies of *Robinson Crusoe* and the isolation of the hero, not only for symbolic reasons, as we shall see, but also because his physical isolation makes it plausible for Defoe to show Crusoe's actual weakness in contrast to the strength of his fantasies and hopes.[55] The theme of

[55] How modern Defoe is! In the *Serious Reflections of Robinson Crusoe with His Vision of the Angelic World* (London, 1790), ch. i, "Of Solitude," he has his hero say: "I have frequently looked back, you may be sure, and that with different thoughts, upon the notions of a long tedious life of solitude, which I have represented to the world, and of which you must have formed some ideas, from the life of a man in an island. . . . I have as much wondered, why it should be any grievance or affliction; seeing, upon the whole view of the stage of life which we act upon in this world, it seems to me, that life in general is, or ought to be, but one universal act of solitude. . . . The world, I say, is nothing to us, but as it is more or less to our relish: all reflection is carried home, and our dear self is, in one respect, the end of living. Hence man may be properly said to be *alone* in the midst of the crowds and hurry of men of business." From this observation Defoe's Crusoe argues that his life on the island was *not* solitude, in that while sometimes he filled his time with "the contemplation of sublime things," he failed to spend much of his time in this way—in short, the solitary is the true contemplative. By contemplation Crusoe can enjoy "much more solitude in the middle of the greatest collection of mankind in the world, I mean at London, than ever I could say I enjoyed in eight and twenty years confinement to a desolate island."

If we wonder why then did Crusoe not enjoy true solitude on his island, the answer is that "divine contemplations require a composure of soul, uninterrupted by any extraordinary motions or disorders of the passions; and this, I say, is much easier to be obtained and enjoyed in the ordinary course of life, than in monkish cells and forcible retreats" (7). Thus Defoe makes the hallucinations of Crusoe plausible—he is forcibly alone, not out of choice, and he has to populate his world with visions. Defoe herein attacks Catholic asceticism and suggests that the visions of a St. Anthony are to be expected, given such withdrawal from the controls of social intercourse. In fact *Robinson*

pride is again and again introduced in this context, because it comes into play naturally when an author is talking about the simple good reason for humility, namely physical weakness, as evinced in man's mortality.[56]

Pride, strength, and the struggle for power (or success, in the typical American "success story")[57] comprise a unity of concerns that frequently demonstrate in the clearest possible way the daemonic character of allegorical agency.[58] How many modern allegories take up the problem of political power directly: *The Plague, We, War with the Newts, R.U.R., 1984, Animal Farm, The Trial, A Country Doctor, The Castle, Mario and the Magician, Lord of the Flies,* to name only a few of the more striking instances. In none

---

Crusoe shows an increasing stress on the daemonic as it progresses. This is not only psychologically plausible; it is symbolically valid, in that it more and more demonstrates the religious isolation of Crusoe, as the island is increasingly populated by badmen.

[56] See Lovejoy, *Essays in the History of Ideas,* "Pride in Eighteenth Century Thought," 62–68. The Golden Chain is an endless circle (analogous to the Wheel of Fortune) which can be understood to revolve, besides suggesting movement upwards or downwards. The rise on the Wheel is likely, despite human pride, to be dashed downward as the cycle is completed. This rise and fall may involve a Faustian attempt to achieve universal knowledge, as well as to achieve any other kind of power. Such is the implication of Empson's ch. iv, "All in Milton," in *The Structure of Complex Words* (London, 1951).

[57] See Kenneth Lynn, *The Dream of Success* (Boston, 1955).

[58] John A. Wilson describes such an ethos in *Before Philosophy,* ed. Henri Frankfort (Penguin ed.), 110. In the Old Kingdom Egyptian values were attuned to an ideal of material success, and the result appears to have been a symbolic as well as actual bureaucracy: "A success visible to all men was the great good." Thorkild Jakobson, *Before Philosophy,* 151, says of the ancient Mesopotamian attitude toward the sky as a divine realm, that the sky inspires "the experience of greatness or even of the tremendous. There comes a keen realization of one's own insignificance, of unbridgeable remoteness. . . . Beyond all, however, the experience of majesty is the experience of power, of power bordering on the tremendous, but power at rest, not consciously imposing its will. The power behind majesty is so great that it need not exert itself." This awed reaction to sublime disproportion in God's relation to Man may perhaps, as Jakobson suggests, be traced to the "element of force and violence" that marks the Mesopotamian climate (see 138–140).

of these is the element of the miraculous far from the surface. They dramatize the tyrannical spellbinder's absolute hold over the common man. An unnatural Faustian energy drives their heroes and villains, and when, conversely, the hero is ironically reduced (i.e., weakened) to a K. or a Winston Smith he desperately tries to join hands with a tyrant, even though he may hate his oppressor.

Daemonic mechanism and allegorical "machines." Another aspect of the daemonic agent needs now to be introduced into the scheme we are developing. Constriction of meaning, when it is the limit put upon a personified force or power, causes that personification to act somewhat mechanistically. The perfect allegorical agent is not a man possessed by a daemon, but a robot, a Talus, and finally after certain prototypic creations, as in Mary Shelley's *Frankenstein*, this type of agent is fully exploited by a twentieth-century author, Karel Čapek, whose play *R.U.R.* makes robots out of creatures who look exactly like human beings.[59] Being indistinguishable, physically, from

[59] The robot of science fiction moves, but machinery of this kind is also present in the common form of a *deus ex machina*, a type of statuary, as in Gothic novels, where statues sweat or speak. Cf. Mozart's *Don Giovanni*—the statue of the Commendatore; *The Winter's Tale*—the statue of Hermione; the statue which Plutarch speaks of, but Shakespeare does not include, except by suggestive allusions, in his *Coriolanus*. The typically *static* nature of these machines suits their function as spectacle (*opsis*). Wonder likewise dictates the use of elaborate naturalistic stage sets in modern times; when in the twenties there was hot and cold running water coming from faucets on stage, this was a magical effect which was intended to awe, to overwhelm, to astound the audience, as Daguerre's dioramas had awed an earlier generation with apparently real outdoor scenes. Here, in the realm of the uncanny, the spectacular and the daemonic clearly meet.

Grant Jeffery's *Science and Technology Stocks* (New York, 1961), 11, gives a hint of the future robotization of man himself. Litton Industries, Jeffery observes, "is getting into amplification of the normal muscle power of soldiers, laborers, and amateur athletes. The firm's concept of an armored 'servo soldier' amounts to a one-man tank whose running, jumping, and lifting activities are electronically stepped up to rival the performance of a King Kong. For the construction market, Litton is working on an exoskeleton with dimensions twice those of an average worker, permitting the occupant of this hulking frame to take immense strides while handling a steel I-beam as easily as a base-ball bat."

the real human beings in the play, these robots come to seem just another kind of human being, which was exactly Čapek's satirical aim. The same implication that men are shadows of the robots they create occurs frequently in science fiction of a more popular kind, for these robots are represented as having been invented by scientists who take this outlet for their wildest ideas.[60] The machine may be mechanically so advanced in science fiction that, like Fred Hoyle's Black Cloud, it is more powerful than any of the most intelligent human agents in the story.[61] In this case the daemonic machine approaches the status and power of a god, and we are back at the first type of daemon recognized by the theologian Lactantius.

It has long been traditional to use the word "machine" in a technical sense, to mean the theatrical or rhetorical device by which daemonic agency was introduced onto the stage, so that the action could be resolved by fiat, by sheer force. The "god from the ma-

[60] Nicolson, *Voyages to the Moon*, gives numerous instances of such machinery, and reminds us that both Kepler and Huygens wrote narratives of cosmic voyage. The tradition traces back, in a literary way, to Lucian's *The True History* (the source for Swift's Flying Island), but Greek philosophy, trying to find metaphors for mental or spiritual travel, also recurs to the idea of the flying machine: e.g., Plato's *Phaedrus* (246a–256e), on which see Marignac, *Imagination et Dialectique* (Paris, 1951), 115, and earlier Parmenides, Fragment I (as in Burnet, *Early Greek Philosophy* [New York, 1957], 172): "The car that bears me carried me as far as ever my heart desired, when it had brought me and set me on the renowned way of the goddess, which leads the man who knows through all the towns. On that way was I borne along; for on it did the wise steeds carry me, drawing my car, and maidens showed the way. And the axle, glowing in the socket—for it was urged round by the whirling wheels at each end—gave further a sound as of a pipe, when the daughters of the Sun, hasting to convey me into the light, threw back their veils from their faces and left the abode of night." This periphrasis for "the sun" is an early instance of cosmological allegory.

[61] Fred Hoyle, *The Black Cloud* (New York, 1957). Hoyle is not an expert writer of fiction, but he introduces technology in a pleasant way. The Black Cloud requests that a Beethoven sonata be played a little faster by the heroine; the Cloud apparently knows, without being told, that Beethoven's absurdly fast metronome markings are "correct." On science fiction, see the brief, lively survey by Kingsley Amis, *New Maps of Hell* (New York, 1960).

chine" enters upon action blocked by an impasse and breaks this impasse in a manner beyond human strength.[62] The god's power is that of any perfect idea—perfect justice, perfect love, perfect skill —and its equivalent is introduced by writers of the eighteenth century in a much less dramatic form when they organize the so-called "sublime poem" according to a plan of allegorical agents which are often called "machines," or less frequently "engines." [63] In this sense the term "machine" does not, however, connote a scientific ordering of thought; the poet who thinks in terms of robots is not necessarily more a scientist than the man who finds them uninteresting or impracticable. It will be observed that while allegory employs "machinery," it is not an engineer's type of machinery at all.[64] It does not use up real fuels, does not transform such fuels into

[62] Cf. the article by Gwin J. Kolb, "Johnson's 'Dissertation on Flying' and John Wilkins' *Mathematical Magick*," *Modern Philology*, XLVII (1949), 24–31. Typically, Johnson rejects the optimism implied by space travel, and "in a single paragraph (of *Rasselas*)—the more forcible for its brevity—the flight begins and ends: the artist leaps into the air and drops into the lake. He is rescued—but Rasselas' hopes of seeing the world via wings is lost." The machine is a symbol of vanity and unbridled Daedalian imagination.

[63] Cf. Dryden's *Preface to the Fables,* and later Fielding's mockery of such machines in *Joseph Andrews*. With *Tristram Shandy,* where the fortifications of Uncle Toby are endowed with unconscious meanings (if interpreted psychoanalytically), there is a more complex satire against any use of machines.

[64] Even so, in stage designing actual mechanical devices are used. The construction manuals for Renaissance stage designers show most clearly the kind of daemonic magic that was intended to be suggested by the "machines." Thus, for example, Nicolo Sabbattini's *Manual for Constructing Theatrical Scenes and Machines (Practica di fabricar scene e machine ne' teatri,* Ravenna, 1638) discusses the following technical problems: "How to show the whole scene in flames"; "How to make a hell appear"; "How to make mountains and other objects rise from the stage"; "How to transform a man into a rock or a similar object"; "How to transform rocks or stones into men"; "How to make the sea rise, swell, get tempestuous or change color"; "How to make ships or galleys or other vessels seem to move over the sea"; "How to make dolphins and other marine monsters appear to spout water while they swim"; "How to make the Heavens in sections"; "How to make a cloud with people in it descend directly onto the stage from the Heavens." Such machinery abounds in heroic drama and in most classical, and some modern, ballet. The mode is synaesthetic alle-

usable real energy. Instead, it is a fantasied energy, like the fantasied power conferred on the shaman by his belief in daemons.[65] And the research of the science-fiction hero is a type of pseudoscience. Allegory is in no position to add to truly scientific knowledge, because its terms are never relativistic; they are always absolutes, rather like Plato's "eternal forms." [66] The best that can be said is that this fantastic art provides the prototypes of more serious empirical sciences—alchemy prefigures modern chemistry, but differs

---

gory. For Sabbattini and others, see *The Renaissance Stage: Documents of Serlio, Sabbattini, and Furttenbach*, tr. A. Nicoll, J. H. McDowell, and G. R. Kernodle, ed. B. Hewitt (Coral Gables, Fla., 1958).

A later borderline case would be the machines of Butler's *Erewhon*, chs. xxiii–xxv, where the *concept* of evolving bodies and organismic structure is turned into a *realization* of such a metamorphosis. Another instance, from the science fiction of Robert Sheckley: "The control board was covered with dials, switches, and gauges, which were made of metal, plastics, and quartz. Fleming, on the other hand, was flesh and blood and bone. It seemed too impossible that any relationship could exist between them, except the most perfunctory. Instead, Fleming seemed to merge into the control board. His eyes scanned the dials with mechanical precision, his fingers became extensions of the switches. The metal seemed to become pliable under his hands, and amenable to his will. The quartz gauges gleamed red, and Fleming's eyes shone red too, with a glow that didn't seem entirely reflection" ("Paradise II," in *Notions Unlimited* [New York, 1950], 103–104).

[65] Dodds, *The Greeks and the Irrational*, ch. v, "The Greek Shamans and the Origin of Puritanism," shows how *ascesis* and the production of "visions" can go hand in hand.

[66] One of the major theorists of this problem is Wilhelm Worringer, *Abstraction and Empathy*, tr. Michael Bullock (New York, 1953). The work dates from about 1913; it was followed by an equally important treatment of Gothic art. Worringer makes the important distinction between the "naturalization of a pure ornament, i.e., an abstract form" and the "stylization of a natural object" (60). The latter is what occurs in certain ultimately mimetic arts; the former in allegory of the "naturalist" sort. Worringer further shows (62–77) how "naturalism" turns originally abstract ideas and forms into the form of beast-personifications. We thence *appear* to have a mimetic art, but again, the imagery and agents are "purely the product of linear-abstract tendencies." Worringer reduces the function of such art finally to a stabilizing one; in a world of hardly controlled flux the mind seeks some point of repose and security, and finds it in abstract, linear, schematic, ornamental designs.

from it radically; phrenology prefigures a certain kind of modern psychology, the study of body types; a branch of astrology prefigures modern meteorology. In general it may be said that as a result of its daemonic agency, allegorical art can serve a protoscientific function.[67]

Cosmic systems governing personal fate. An almost analytic purpose, pseudoscientific if not protoscientific, follows from the very idea of daemon itself. Coming from the term that means "to divide," *daemon* implies an endless series of divisions of all important aspects of the world into separate elements for study and control.[68] The daemon of a man is his fate, his Moira, his fortune, his lot, whatever is specifically divided up and allotted to *him*.[69] Through the work-

[67] See Abrams, *Mirror and the Lamp*, ch. x, "The Criterion of Truth to Nature: Romance, Myth, and Metaphor," especially sec. iii, "The Poem as Heterocosm." The Swiss critic Bodmer is here shown to argue that poetry, through analogy with the primal act of creation, has a probability which is believable to the very extent that the Creator's power is great: "The poem of the marvellous is a second creation, and therefore not a replica nor even a reasonable facsimile of this world, but its own world, *sui generis*, subject only to its own laws, whose existence (it is suggested) is an end in itself" (278).

[68] Such a process recalls the process to which Jones gave the name "decomposition." "Decomposition . . . is the opposite of the 'condensation' so characteristic of dreams. Whereas in the latter process attributes of several individuals are fused together in the creation of one figure, much as in the production of a composite photograph, in the former process various attributes are invented, each endowed with one group of the original attributes" (*Hamlet and Oedipus* [New York, 1955], 149). It is true that Jones regarded this "decomposing" process as a property of mythology, but it depends on a belief in demons, and is, as he himself says, the *opposite* of the *dream*-process of condensation. This should mean that decomposition cannot occur in the dream. A contradiction in Jones? In the dream?

[69] See Cornford, *From Religion to Philosophy*, chs. i and ii, "Destiny and Law" and "The Origin of *Moira*," especially sec. 16, 37–39. "Behind the clearcut and highly differentiated personalities of the Olympians, it shows us older figures far less distinct and hardly personal. The proper term for them in Greek is not *theos*, but *daemon*. *Theos* always suggests individuality, whereas these daemons had as yet no 'figures,' and no peculiar functions or arts which differentiated one of them from another. We must give up the view, associated by Herodotus with his wrong derivation of *theos*, that these daemons 'set the universe in order.' They were not cosmic powers, but local spirits, good

ing of destiny he is narrowed to the function represented by his daemon. It follows that if nature is a composite system all parts and aspects of which are daemonically controlled,[70] and if man acts only within such a system, the allegorical agent—whose paradigm is daemonic man—is always a division of some larger power. It will be natural for him to have hieratic emblems associated with him, specific ornaments, specific garments, specific sacred names, and specific duties assigned to him, so there will be no mistake that a specific Idea possesses him and governs all he does.

Specificity in function is not, however, a matter of every man for himself, which the unwilled allotment of a Moira would suggest, but rather, as the ancient Greeks and Hebrews and even later European authors saw it, the specific daemonic control of the agent is a matter of a total cosmic organization. The world is not a random collection of people, things, and processes all going their own sweet way without regard to mutual interaction.[71] The Greeks thought of the cosmos in the image of a Body permeated with Mind.[72] They were

---

spirits, each rooted to the portion of earth inhabited and cultivated by his worshippers. This was his *moira,* and within it all dispensations (*nomai*) were in his hands." "This is a system of departments (*moirai*) clearly marked off from one another by boundaries of inviolable taboo, and each the seat of a potency which pervades that department, dispenses its power within it, and resists encroachment from without" (38). Thus, also, Nilsson, *Greek Piety,* 61, "*Daimon* also meant, occasionally, much the same as 'fate.'"

[70] Aristotle reports (*De Anima,* A.5) that Thales maintained, "All things are replete with gods (or demons)." Cf. Kroner, *Speculation in Pre-Christian Philosophy,* ch. iii, "The Rise of Cosmology," espec. 81.

[71] See Cornford, *From Religion to Philosophy,* 96–101, on the daemonic guardians of the divisions of tribal society, and of the divisions in the processes of nature.

[72] R. G. Collingwood, *The Idea of Nature* (1945; reprinted New York, 1960), Introd., sec. 2: "The world of nature is not only alive but intelligent; not only a vast animal with a 'soul' or life of its own, but a rational animal with a 'mind' of its own." All mind-bodies on the microcosmic scale participate in the great Body of the macrocosm. "The Greek view of nature as an intelligent organism was based on an analogy: an analogy between the world of nature and the individual human being, who begins by finding certain characteristics in himself as an individual, and goes on to think of nature as possessed of similar

able to structure their world picture with gods at the top of a hierarchy and men and animals at the bottom, and in this picture they placed daemons intermediate between man and god.[73] Daemonic forces thus became participants in the cosmic drama of man versus god, almost as if the daemons were the relationships, personified, of man to god. To the extent that he follows this intermediary pattern, the allegorical agent is not quite human, and not quite godlike, but shares something of both states. The absolute determination of an Ahab tracking his deadly enemy or a K. seeking his protector, or a Cavaliere Cipolla simultaneously obeying and commanding his victims, has something divinely simple about it, while in such cases the hero is helpless in a way no god could be; in such cases the hero has submitted to a curse which is identified with an overwhelming idea of either good or evil that has lodged itself in the brain.

It becomes a habit of mind for the man who believes in daemonic agency to see himself in such an intermediate position, and to emphasize the rank-order of everyone he deals with.[74] It is no wonder

---

characteristics. . . . The Renaissance view of nature as a machine is equally analogical in its origin, but it presupposes a quite different order of ideas. First, it is based on the Christian idea of a creative and omnipotent God. Secondly, it is based on the human experience of designing and constructing machines. The Greeks and Romans were not machine-users, except to a very small extent" (8). The body, however, is a kind of protomachine, and today we are getting back to that view, because mechanized extensions of the limbs and movements of the body are being developed industrially, and computers are sometimes modeled on the human brain.

On the nature/organism analogy, see Joseph A. Mazzeo, *Medieval Cultural Tradition in Dante's Comedy* (Ithaca, 1960), ch. iv, "The Analogy of Creation in Dante."

[73] Daemon and angel are thus paralleled, because both are messengers of a divine power. Kafka calls them "couriers" in his fable.

[74] Frye, "Notes for a Commentary on *Milton*," in *The Divine Vision*, 113: "In the demonic vision everything is hierarchic, leading up to an ego at the top, in contrast to the Christ who is a total form, and so self-evidently one." Frye has just remarked that in Blake's view "the divine world begins in the perception of a non-human power and will in nature, 'The Fairies, Nymphs, Gnomes, and Genii of the Four Elements' (M. 34:20). These spirits, with the

that the anti-Gnostic Tertullian (*ca.* 155–*ca.* 222) raged against the general infection by daemons of the pagan world, where he saw a vast corrupting fragmentation of experience, material and spiritual, resulting from the common people's belief in daemons.[75] He was arguing against *idées fixes* which would prevent the free influx of God's grace. He was arguing against a rigid cosmology, which, perhaps, he himself would have been only too happy to supplant by his own equally rigid pattern, a Christian ladder of perfection, in which all men were bound to their allotted rungs. Later,

---

advance of natural science, move further away, chiefly into the stars, and become gods. Such gods are conceived, on the analogy of the demonic human society, as inscrutable tyrants, jealous of their privileges, and while they do not exist, the results of believing in them do. One of them is usually in supreme control, asserting that he is 'God alone' and that 'There is no other' (M. 9:26)." The intermediate world of spirits is one in which man's fate is controlled arbitrarily: "The *spiritual* world is a society of self-righteous demons, who take possession of man to destroy him. They originate of course from the star-gods of a fatalistic view of divinity, and are usually represented in *Jerusalem* by the twelve sons of Albion, the number being Zodiacal."

[75] Tertullian, "On Idolatry," 95: This iconoclastic attack on art objects and images regards them as "unclean," a source of spiritual contagion. Tertullian believes in a "golden age" when there was no idolatry, but that when the devil created the makers of statues, the impulse toward profanation found this emblematic means of expression. The "idols" need not be effigies of human beings: "In Greek, *eidos* means form. It has a diminutive *eidolon*, like our *formula* from *form*. So every 'form' or 'formula' has a claim to be called 'idol.'" Speaking of impure followers of Christ, Tertullian says: "Small matter, maybe, if they receive from other hands something to contaminate. But they hand to others what they have contaminated, for idol-makers are accepted into the ranks of the clergy" (89). Cf. St. Cyprian, "That Idols Are Not Gods," ch. vi, in *The Fathers of the Church*, tr. and ed. R. J. Deferrari (New York, 1958), XXXVI; Gerhart B. Ladner, "Origin and Significance of the Byzantine Iconoclastic Controversy," *Medieval Studies* (New York and London, 1940), II, 127–149; Ladner, "The Concept of the Image in the Greek Fathers and the Byzantine Iconoclastic Controversy"; Paul J. Alexander, "The Iconoclastic Council of St. Sophia (815) and Its Definition (Horos)"; Francis Dvornik, "The Patriarch Photius and Iconoclasm"—all in *Dumbarton Oaks Papers*, Number 7 (Cambridge, 1953); Ernst Kitzinger, "The Cult of Images in the Age before Iconoclasm"; Milton V. Anastos, "The Ethical Theory of Images Formulated by the Iconoclasts in 754 and 815"—both in *Dumbarton Oaks Papers*, Number 8 (Cambridge, 1954).

after the cult of Fortune develops, this ladder is made into a circle, with obvious complications.[76] The "celestial hierarchy" of Pseudo-Dionysius the Areopagite, so perfect for the development of an allegoric vocabulary, submits all men and all human actions to a cosmic scale which places each person and personality intermediately between two other ranks, one higher and one lower.[77] This organization of the universe is given the military name, *taxis*.[78] To be an agent in such a scheme is to be not a free agent, but a fixed one. Even when Dante, who follows Pseudo-Dionysius, wants to show that the blessed spirits of the "Paradiso" are free to come and go as they wish, he also in fact shows them *fixed* to certain stages of the progress toward God. This, I think, is the case with all allegorical agents, and when an author is interested in what seem to be free metamorphoses and changes of state, he is in fact not showing his characters acting freely.[79] He is showing them changing, presto,

[76] H. R. Patch, *The Goddess Fortuna in Medieval Literature* (Cambridge, Mass., 1927); and Patch, *The Tradition of Boethius: A Study of His Importance in Medieval Culture* (New York, 1935), 99–113.

[77] On Dionysius, see René Roques, *L'Univers dionysien: Structure hiérarchique du monde selon le Pseudo-Denys* (Paris, 1954); and, a chapter indebted to Roques, in Mazzeo, *Medieval Cultural Tradition in Dante's Comedy*, "The Medieval Concept of Hierarchy." The notion of "calling" embodies this hierarchic conception of the world, on which see C. E. Raven, *Natural Religion and Christian Theology* (Cambridge, 1953), 76, and Ernst Troeltsch, *The Social Teaching of the Christian Churches*, tr. Olive Wyon (1911; reprinted New York, 1960), I, 293–296, on "Cosmos of Callings." Notice that the *ministerium* bears a resemblance to the function of the daimon who mediates between man and God.

[78] Burnet, *Early Greek Philosophy*, 9, takes the term "Kosmos" in the same way: "It meant originally the discipline of an army, and next the ordered constitution of a state." Perhaps, however, this was an error of derivation, and Burnet may have been thinking of *taxis*. The first chapter of Roques' *L'Univers dionysien* contains an admirable summary of the relevant meanings and cognates of *kosmos*. On *taxis* as a military ordering in the ornamentation of art, see below, the discussion of the picturesque.

[79] I am indebted here to J. S. Spink, "Form and Structure: Cyrano de Bergerac's Atomistic Conception of Metamorphosis," in *Literature and Science*, Proceedings of the Sixth Triennial Congress, Oxford, of the International Federation for Modern Languages and Literatures (Oxford, 1955), 144–150.

from one facet of a destiny to another. They remain bound to the Wheel of Fortune, though it turns, rising and falling to give them the illusion of a changed state. The chief metamorphic poet, Ovid, is naturally turned to exegetical use in the *Ovide Moralisé*, since he himself draws attention so often to the opposite of change, namely fixity. The idea that the hero undergoes a change as a result of a *psychomachia* in which he battles, or of an agony, a progress, a voyage to the moon, or whatever typical story we choose, should not blind us to the real lack of freedom in all these stories.[80] Picaresque romances, for example, submit their heroes to the workings of blind chance. These heroes do not choose, they do not "deliberate" but act on compulsion, continually demonstrating a lack of inner control.[81] This is most interesting in psychological allegory, in Spenser or in Kafka, for example, where the author shows over and over that men suffer from a primary illusion when they imagine they are in control of their own actions. This prideful imagination may be called a sin, but it is also a psychological fact, as common experience tells us.

If true change and true self-control are not possible, the quest will often be presented under the guise of an eternally unsatisfied search for perfection, a sort of Platonic quest for the truly worthy loved

[80] As in the picaresque form of *The Golden Ass of Apuleius*, on which see A. D. Nock, *Conversion* (London, 1933), ch. ix.

[81] Boethius, speaking of the human instinct and habits of reproduction: "Again, how great is nature's care, that they should all propagate themselves by the reproduction of their seed; they all, as is so well known, are like regular machines not merely for lasting a time, but for reproducing themselves for ever, and that by their own kinds" (*The Consolation of Philosophy* [Modern Library ed., New York, 1959], 67). He makes the point clear: "We are not now discussing the voluntary movements of a reasoning mind, but the natural instinct," which, by implication, is automatic, "for instance, we unwittingly digest the food we have eaten, and unconsciously breathe in sleep." The older daemonic world view specifies that these instinctual actions are controlled, absolutely, invariantly, by daemons who have particular circumscribed duties. A whole life of instinct would be a "humourous" life, in the Elizabethan sense, and in literature would lead to a drama of automatism, as with Ben Jonson, Molière, and their modern equivalent, the "Theatre of the Absurd."

object. The typical knight of *The Faerie Queene* has always a further trial ahead of him, and, as numerous critics have noticed, the reward for victory in one battle or progress is always a new challenge. There is no such thing as satisfaction in this world; daemonic agency implies a *manie de perfection*, an impossible desire to become one with an image of unchanging purity. The agent seeks to become isolated within himself, frozen into an eternally fixed form, an "idea" in the Platonic sense of the term.

Such a tendency has major consequences for the nature of allegory. The daemons all have their own ranks, and heroes or agents of the daemonic kind are similarly ranked and fixed, and finally pinned down at a particular level. Men are ranked according to spiritual and temporal powers, and thus, for example, the Pope or the King is always the first figure in the traditional Dance of Death, while the Fool or Antichrist is likely to be the last. Animals have their orders, with the lion as "king"; birds have theirs, and for them the eagle tops the hierarchy.[82] The same hierarchies can be established for all kinds of things in the universe, even stones, as the medieval lapidaries show.[83] As soon as all the several ladders of symbolic ascent are lined up "beside each other," it becomes apparent that instead of vertically parallel ladders, we have horizontally parallel "levels" of symbolism, according to which there are parallel species of things from many different realms—animals, images, stones, men—which can exist at the same relative level of purity or perfection. The line, "Let Gryll be Gryll, and have his hoggish mind," suggests that both the hog and the man who acts like a hog are at the same level of moral depravity.[84] The Stone of Scone is as

[82] This is the tradition of the bestiaries. See Emile Mâle, *The Gothic Image: Religious Art in France of the Thirteenth Century*, tr. Dora Nussey (1913; reprinted New York, 1958), 33-34. Also Louis Réau, *Iconographie de l'art chrétien* (Paris, 1955-1959). T. H. White has translated one of the twelfth-century bestiaries under the title *The Bestiary* (New York, 1954).

[83] See Mircea Eliade, *Traité d'histoire des religions* (Paris, 1949), ch. viii, on the hierarchies of plants, and ch. vi, on the hierarchies of magic stones and gems.

[84] H. W. Janson, in *Apes and Ape Lore in the Middle Ages and the Renais-

sacred as the king who is crowned over it. The eagle and the lion, though physically lower creatures than the king, are on the same symbolic level as he, in that they each rule their own kingdoms. Everywhere in this symbolic network there is a fixing of agents at single symbolic ranks.

From agent to image: static agency. This leaves us with a paradoxical situation. A fixed agent is tantamount to an image, as in reverse (for the iconoclasts) images were tantamount to daemonic agents. In a way we knew this all the time, since the agents of allegorical writing are often presented emblematically through visual icons. But we have come full circle to the point where we can explain why even in narration they are so often sheerly emblematic. Their hierarchic function forbids any other case. Fixation of sense follows from the need to obey narrow controls. As we usually understand human agency, we think that the psychologically or behaviorally natural sort of character type is that of a person who appears capable of making decisions (who "knows what he wants," can deliberate about means toward this end) and also, and this is equally important, who is capable of "growing." We perhaps do not ask ourselves what this change and growth might be, or even if it is possible, but if we did, I suspect we would answer that here change involves a movement in status and an ability to assimilate the new environment that goes with this new status. Growth then means "maturation." (This can be a quite private internal matter, and certainly need not involve social climbing or material changes of status.) The common criterion for good novels, that they show people growing, may not be capable of articulation into a clear theoretical statement, but it does point to our sense that realism of character is related to freedom of choice in action. The truly "real" character, the Pierre of *War and Peace*, does not necessarily change radically,

---

sance (London, 1952), presents a remarkably wide range of iconographic material. Ape lore is important because it presents a double image: The ape is wise, like man the imitative learner, and foul, like Satan. His double aspect parallels man's "high" and "lower" nature.

but he does have the power to change radically, if need be, and we are made to feel this potentiality. He can act according to probability, not solely according to fixed necessity, nor is he a victim of random chance. Suppose, on the contrary, that the hero is intended iconographically; in that case he obeys a strict causal necessity. He does not choose to do this or that, resist this temptation, embrace that ideal. His choices, if they can properly be so called, are made for him by his daemon.[85]

Aristotelian mimesis does not fit this pattern, since it is expected to show us characters deliberating about variable courses of action. Aristotle denounces "irrational" characters as subject matter for plays, on the grounds that they overdetermine the dramatic action. Once the mad king has been introduced, nothing is left for the courtiers but to kill him and rid the kingdom of its false destiny. The aim of mimetic art, in Aristotle's view, is to follow the variable course of nature, and if nature should, as in the case of an obsessional madman, turn out to be invariable the mimetic art will collapse in an excess of liveliness, by portraying that insane nature. Aristotle would perhaps say that for the standard subject matter of allegory mimesis presents too vivid an image, since the audience empathizes with whatever is imitated, and in that instance it would have to empathize with irrational, obsessional behavior. Instead of seeing a free agent on the stage, the audience would see a lively

---

[85] Aristotle discusses "choice" in *The Nicomachean Ethics*, III, 2 and 3. Note how little this kind of "deliberation" allows for the sort of compulsive teleology we have been ascribing to allegory: "A man is the originating cause of his actions; deliberation has for the sphere of its operation acts which are within his own power of doing them; all that we do is done with an eye to something else. It follows that when we deliberate it is about means and not ends. . . . Since, therefore, when we choose, we choose something within our reach which we desire as the result of deliberation, we may describe *proairesis* as 'the deliberate desire of something within our power' " J. A. K. Thomson, *The Ethics of Aristotle* (Penguin ed., 1958), 87. Aristotle elsewhere shows that one "deliberates" only about things that are variable, and never about absolutes, such as Plato's Eternal Ideas. Thus, deliberation again implies mimetic art, where probability, rather than necessity, is the rule.

idée fixe, which would induce the same fixated idea in the mind of the audience. By a process of identification the audience, like the allegorical agents, would itself tend to become fixed into stereotypes. This, of course, is precisely the aim of political propaganda art, and such a Platonic art evidently depends almost totally on allégorical agency. The victim of propaganda is allowed no other course but to empathize with scenes that are cast in highly organized, systematized, bureaucratized molds. Since this kind of order is often the aim of the political propagandist, he needs only to get his audience interested in the surface texture of the conformist action. By involving the audience in a syllogistic action, the propagandist gets a corresponding pattern of behavior from his audience when that audience leaves the theatre. At least that is what he hopes will happen. In getting this attention to the total action he depends, as we shall see, on imagery. The imagery of allegory is often glittering and excitingly rich, even wondrous.

Conclusion. The notion that allegorical protagonists are always daemonic has several consequences for criticism, some of which we have already seen, others of which will appear when we turn to the imagery, causal systems, rhythms, and thematic tendencies of the mode. We have seen that the protagonist will act as if possessed, and this implies more or less cosmic notions of fate and personal fortune. He will act part way between the human and divine spheres, touching on both, which suggests that he can be used for the model romantic hero, since romance allows its heroes both human interest and divine power. His essentially energic character will delight the reader with an appearance of unadulterated power. Like a Machiavellian prince, the allegorical hero can act free of the usual moral restraints, even when he is acting morally, since he is moral only in the interests of his power over other men. This sort of action has a crude fascination for us all; it impels us to read the detective story, the western, the saga of space exploration and interplanetary travel. But beyond the frequently superficial appeals that the daemonic agent thus can make to our need for unrestrained will and wish, allegory makes an appeal to an almost scientific curiosity about the order of things. The pilgrim's progress is a kind of research project, taking all life for its boundaries. With all the irrationality of daemonic agency per se, this is the very kind of agency necessary to discover a cosmic order. The hero is a conquistador; he arbitrates order over chaos by confronting a random collection of people and events, imposing his own fate upon that random collection. To a degree all the lesser protagonists also take part in this imposition of order. Each is like a willful personality asserting itself to produce a generalized system, a hierarchy of "thrones, dominations, powers, and princes." Allegory in this way allows its creator a maximum of will and wish-fulfillment with a maximum of restraint, a paradoxical combination that cannot fail to fascinate the reader. Finally, considered as a rhetorical device, allegory has the further capacity to provide narrative and dramatic equivalents of visual, geometric diagrams. We have noticed a tendency for the daemonic agent to become identified with a hierarchic position, thence with the name for that status, and thence even to become one with the name itself. By such a process agency becomes confused with imagery, and action becomes a diagram. The hypostatized agent is an emblem. Justice with the scales becomes an image; Cupid with his bow becomes an impresa—this suggests that allegorical agency is peculiarly fixated, and for this reason, conversely, as we turn to imagery we can perhaps ascribe to all allegorical images a kind of action, if only a symbolic one.

2

The Cosmic Image

THE traditional rhetoric set forth by Cicero, Quintilian, and the Renaissance rhetoricians asserts that allegory is a sequence of sub-metaphors which amount in aggregate to one single, continued, "extended" metaphor. This is formally correct, to the extent that the poet is giving us two large-scale meanings for one.

Part of the function of an allegory is to make you feel that two levels of being correspond to each other in detail and indeed that there is some underlying reality, something in the nature of things, which makes this happen. . . . But the effect of allegory is to keep the two levels of being very distinct in your mind though they interpenetrate each other in so many details.[1]

The poet who is thinking in this analytic manner presumably exploits something in the nature of things, not something figmented out of his own fantasy—unless Empson's description should be amended to read "something in the nature of our thoughts about things." In either case the poet is thinking analytically, "making a

[1] William Empson, *Structure of Complex Words*, 346–347.

pleasing analysis of all." He takes a grand, large-scale analogy and breaks it up into its elements, as for example Sin may be subdivided into at least seven aspects to which are applied specific iconographic labels. When each part of the human body is made to stand for a particular part of the body politic, the subdividing process shows the most obvious kind of unity in diversity; both bodies are being anatomized, and the parts of both are found to correspond isomorphically to each other. In a typical modern work, *The Plague*, by Camus, the analogy is drawn between a plague of rats carrying bubonic infection and the plague of an invading military occupation (the Nazi occupation of Oran) and its accompanying political diseases.

Traditional theory would describe this analogical symbolism as the gathering of many little metaphors into the scope of one larger unifying figure which is also a metaphor. Rosemond Tuve has amended this view slightly, and her description of Renaissance allegory ought also to be applicable to modern literature:

Allegoria does not use metaphor; it is one. By definition a continued metaphor, *allegoria* exhibits the normal relation of concretion to abstraction found in metaphor, in the shape of a series of particulars with further meanings. Each such concretion or sensuous detail is by virtue of its initial base *already* a metaphor.[2]

This view, which equates allegory directly with metaphor and assumes their effects are essentially the same, holds true as long as the term "metaphor" is understood loosely. If metaphor is to be the general name for any and all "transfers" of meaning, it will necessarily include allegory.

Objections to traditional theory. The difficulty here is that such a rhetorical terminology will obscure the very complications which are the interesting aspect of allegory. The detailed way in which Camus parallels the two kinds of plague makes us accept his fiction,

[2] Rosemond Tuve, *Elizabethan and Metaphysical Imagery* (Chicago, 1947), 105–106.

and by the same token we see how naïve or ironical Dr. Johnson was when he said of *Gulliver's Travels* that there was nothing to it once you knew there were "little people" and "big people." [3] Equating allegory with metaphor is likely to lead to a narrow, stultifying view of those works that are most interesting. Tuve concludes her remarks on *allegoria* by saying that, since "each such concretion or sensuous detail is by virtue of its initial base *already* a metaphor, . . . a poet desiring full comprehension will be chary of introducing double metaphors." [4] This advice can be found in numerous rhetoricians from the Renaissance through the eighteenth century. Tuve may not mean that all good allegory avoids obscurity, but although she makes no value judgment on this point, she hints that allegorists finally wish "full comprehension." Some critics might doubt the necessity of mechanical consistency in the fiction, by which an already metaphorical language is maintained on unmixed, uncrossed lines of secondary meaning. "What then happens to Dante's 'polysemous' meaning?" they will ask. Perhaps "mythical" literature is based on the kind of inconsistency and doubleness Tuve advises the allegorist to avoid. In any event the problem is complex, and my present concern is that we shall never lightly assume that clarity is an unclouded aim of most allegory.

[3] This is probably an instance of Johnson's attempt to counteract waves of unthinking public approbation. Remarking on the book's success, in the "Life of Swift," he says: "It was read by the high and low, the learned and the illiterate. Criticism was for a while lost in wonder: no rules of judgment were applied."

[4] Tuve, *Elizabethan and Metaphysical Imagery*, 106. Typical of the prejudice against obscure, mixed tropes is the comment of Joseph Priestley, in *A Course of Lectures on Oratory and Criticism* (London, 1777), 195: "It requires uncommon skill and caution to conduct a long allegory with propriety; because few things are analogous in many respects, at the same time that they are sufficiently different to make the analogy pleasing. Moreover, it is very difficult to make an allusion intelligible, and at the same time never name the thing we mean in direct terms, which we must by all means avoid; as it would introduce the greatest confusion into the metaphor." This common-sense prejudice seems fully established in eighteenth-century criticism; e.g., in Hugh Blair's typical *Lectures on Rhetoric and Belles Lettres* (Edinburgh, 1783), "Lecture XV," on metaphor.

The mode seems to aim at both clarity and obscurity together, each effect depending upon the other. Enigma, and not always decipherable enigma, appears to be allegory's most cherished function, and who will doubt that confusion in the symbolism will aid this function? It is furthermore probable that a writer can only with difficulty think of his image as "already a metaphor" when he uses it. Even though based on a traditional analogy, his metaphor (even on Tuve's own ground) could effectively be a metaphor only when he uses it, and its potential reference to traditional commonplace does not, of itself, limit the writer to a single metaphorical yield. The traditional point of reference (e.g., a traditional symbolism for the Christian year) indeed becomes the means by which the writer can allow himself a certain enriching confusion. Since the basic symbolism is highly articulated, he can increase the enigma with even private obscurities, while the allegory as a whole will not thereby disintegrate into nonsense.

"Full comprehension" of any allegory seems to be the consequence of the reader's sensing how many levels are involved. Even if there are ten levels and they are at odds with each other sometimes, this calculation can still theoretically be made and the allegory worked out. The process of explication, a gradual unfolding, is sequential in form. There is normally a gradual increase of comprehension, as the reader pursues the fable, and yet most allegories of major importance have ultimately very obscure images, and these are a source of their greatness.

There is another more serious objection to the traditional account: it asserts, I think somewhat uncritically, that allegory is metaphoric in a "normal" way. There is little enough consensus of opinion on the norms of metaphoric usage, while there is some difficulty in showing just what any metaphor does. We can nevertheless consult Aristotle and the rhetorical tradition following him. Here also, however, doubts arise.

A poem like "The Phoenix and the Turtle" may in fact use sub-metaphors, but they are of the most conventional, ponderous, thought-out, nonintuited sort; they do not flash with the "liveliness"

Aristotle so prized; they do not give us new perceptions of living experience. They are drawn from a scholarly account book of images and are combined in a rigid sequence. Shakespeare intended every bit of this inflexibility, and I doubt if we do this poetry a service in trying to bring it into line with the standard metaphoric usage of dramatic verse, a technique characterized by great freedom from iconographic pedantry. "The Phoenix and the Turtle" at least does not make use of metaphor as dramatic verse makes use of it, while the usages of mimetic drama would seem a possible norm for metaphoric language.

Cicero and Quintilian both however held the view that allegory is metaphor. Quintilian says that "continued metaphor develops into allegory," [5] a view deriving from the *Rhetorica ad Herennium* and from Cicero, who makes the point more clearly.

When there is a sequence of metaphors, the sense of the words is totally altered; thus, in this case when the Greeks speak of *allegoria* etymologically, this is correct; but logically, it would be better to follow Aristotle and range all these figures under the headings of metaphors.[6]

[5] Quintilian, *The Institutes of Oratory*, tr. H. E. Butler (Loeb Classics ed., London and Cambridge, Mass., 1953), VIII, vi, sec. 44, gives the initial definition: "*Allegory*, which is translated in Latin by *inversio*, either presents one thing in words and another in meaning, or else something absolutely opposed to the meaning of the words." Quintilian prefers a *mixed* use of the figure: "But far the most ornamental effect is provided by the artistic admixture of simile, metaphor and allegory" (sec. 49). He observes that allegory is not an especially recondite figure: "Allegory is often used by men of little ability and in the conversation of everyday life. For those hackneyed phrases of forensic pleading, 'to fight hand to hand,' 'to attack the throat,' or 'to let blood' are all of them allegorical, though they do not strike the attention" (sec. 51). Quintilian lays down the rule against mixing metaphors (from which we see that this prescription applies more to allegory than to metaphor per se): "It is all important to follow the principle illustrated . . . and never to mix your metaphors. But there are many who, after beginning with a tempest, will end with a fire or a falling house, with the result that they produce a hideously incongruous effect" (sec. 50).

[6] Cicero, *The Orator (De Oratore)*, ed. and tr. E. W. Sutton and H. Rackham (Loeb Classics, London, 1948), ch. xxvii, sec. 94.

Logically, allegory would have to be a type of metaphor for Aristotle, since he had laid down a fourth type of metaphor, which he called "proportional" (and which might better be called "analogical"),[7] to cover instances where the figure of speech set up a parallelism of *parts* as well as of the whole. An instance would be the line from *King Lear*, "As flies to wanton boys are we to the gods," to which Shakespeare added the explanatory key, "They kill us for their sport." We need to go beyond the logical description of this figure, a need reflected in the relatively infrequent use of Aristotelian metaphorics in modern times. The modern critic's equipment tends to be psychological rather than logical, and he finds it hard to see in Aristotle's discussion metaphors that we would call metaphorical. Aristotle, like a good linguist interested in the classifying function of the figure, draws his examples mainly from what we would call "dead metaphors."

Metaphor: the criterion of surprise. Metaphor would seem better exemplified by those striking images of twentieth-century verse, the "patient etherized upon a table," the "candy bride and groom," the "long-legged heart in his hand." Such phrases convey real transfers of meaning from a standard prose sense to an unusual poetic sense. The discussion in the *Poetics* does not consider images of that kind in any detail, though presumably they would fall under the heading of proportional metaphors.[8] Yet Aristotle did conceive metaphor

---

[7] Aristotle, *The Poetics* (*Works*, XI), ed. W. D. Ross, tr. Ingram Bywater (Oxford, 1924), 1457b. "Analogy or proportion is when the second term is to the first as the fourth is to the third. We may then use the fourth for the second, or the second for the fourth." Usually one or two of the terms are merely implicit. Aristotle gives the basis, incidentally, for what we now call "Symbol": "For some of the terms of the proportion there is at times no word in existence; still the metaphor may be used. For instance, to scatter seed is called sowing; but the action of the sun in scattering his rays is nameless" (1457b, 7).

[8] The closest thing in Aristotle are the analogical metaphors discussed in *The Poetics*, 1457b. Owen Barfield connects these analogical metaphors with what he calls "accidental metaphors," which in turn I would call "ornaments." These are "based on a *synthesis of ideas*, rather than on immediate cognition of reality." "In fact the accidental metaphor carries with it a suggestion of

75

psychologically as well as logically, and the Roman rhetoricians could look to a text other than the *Poetics*. In the *Rhetoric* (III, 12, 1412a) Aristotle spoke rather differently on the same subject.

Liveliness is specially conveyed by metaphor, and by the further power of surprising the hearer; because the hearer expected something different, his acquisition of the new idea impresses him all the more. His mind seems to say, "Yes, to be sure, I never thought of that." The liveliness of epigrammatic remarks is due to the meaning not being just what the words say; as in the saying of Stesichorus that "cicadas will chirp to themselves on the ground." Well constructed riddles are attractive for the same reason, a new idea is conveyed, and there is metaphorical expression. So with the "novelties" of Theodorus. In these the thought is startling, and, as Theodorus puts it, does not fit in with the ideas you already have. They are like the burlesque words that one finds in the comic writers. The effect produced even by jokes depending upon changes of the letter of a word, this too is a surprise.

This extremely important criterion of surprise should, I think, be weighed in the balance whenever we wish to call a figure metaphorical. The more metaphors, the more epigrams, the more "well constructed riddles," the greater the amount of liveliness.[9] This would normally be the case, since each new metaphor would introduce a

---

having been constructed upon a sort of framework of logic. This kind Aristotle calls *kata to analogon*, and the example he gives is 'the shield of Bacchus,' which describes a cup, because 'a cup is to Bacchus what a shield is to Ares.' . . . The distinction between true and false metaphor corresponds to the distinction between Myth and Allegory, allegory being a more or less conscious hypostatization of *ideas*, followed by a synthesis of them, and myth the true child of Meaning, begotten on Imagination. There is no doubt that, from a very early date, the Greek poets began to mix false metaphors with their original myths, just as the Greek philosophers began to contaminate them with allegory; so that in this case the form in which myths have come down to us is dual" (Barfield, *Poetic Diction* [London, 1952], 201).

[9] Cf. Quintilian, *Institutes*, VIII, iii, sec. 74: "For the more remote the simile is from the subject to which it is applied, the greater will be the impression of novelty and the unexpected which it produces." Quintilian tends to see liveliness in *all* figurative speech; he generalizes Aristotle's psychology of metaphor.

fresh perspective on a story or drama, especially because there would be no need for the metaphors to tie into each other. In Aristotle's view metaphor is normally a momentary dramatic device, not an organizing thematic principle. Usually the metaphor is a record of direct sense experience; Aristotle would say that Homer's metaphors let us "see" better. When metaphors are deliberately tied into each other, this situation alters. The addition of every new figure diminishes the surprise for the reader, and the whole is increasingly abstracted from sense experience.

A good case of this diminishing return would be the anonymous fifteenth-century poem, "The Ship of State," where the traditional analogy of ship to state is put through a sequence of divisions, stanza by stanza.[10] This quaint political poem deserves to be quoted in full,

[10] This is the commonplace first instanced by George Puttenham (*Arte of English Poesie*, III, xviii) to show what allegory is. A paradoxical relation of clarity to obscurity appears in the fact that Puttenham first stresses "dissimulation" (in very much our sense of the word) and then exemplifies allegory by a commonplace, hackneyed figure: "And ye shall know that we may dissemble, I mean speake otherwise then we thinke, in earnest as well as in sport, under covert and darke termes, and in learned and apparent speaches, in short sentences, and by long ambage and circumstance of wordes, and finally as well when we lye as when we tell the truth. To be short, every speach wrested from his owne naturall signification to another not altogether so naturall is a kinde of dissimulation, because the wordes beare contrary countenance to the intent. But properly and in his principall vertue *Allegoria* is when we do speake in sense translative and wrested from the owne [i.e., "proper"] signification, nevertheless applied to another not altogether contrary, but having much conveniencie with it as before we said of the metaphore: as for example if we should call the common wealth, a shipe; the Prince a Pilot, the Counsellors mariners, the stormes warres, the calme and (haven) peace, this is spoken all in allegorie: and because such inversion of sense in one single word is by the figure *Metaphore*, . . . and in this manner extending to whole and large speaches, it maketh the figure *allegorie* to be called a long and perpetuall Metaphore."

This particular figure can be traced at least as far back as Plato's *Republic*, where the parallel of ruler and *cybernetes*, "a pilot," is a continually used analogy ("governor" being derived from *cybernetes*, as also our modern science of control devices, cybernetics). The "ship of state" is a commonplace for Quintilian and reappears as a standard example in rhetoric texts, e.g.,

since it illustrates a number of peculiarly allegorical procedures, notably the use of topical reference, along with a number of typical weaknesses and strengths:

> Our ship is launched from the grounde,
> Blessed be god, both faire and sownde!
> Our maryners han the shypmen founde,
>   By there taklynge will a-byde.
> This noble shype made of good tree,
> Our souerayne lord, kynge henry.
> God gyde hym from aduersyte,
>   Where that he go or ryde.
>
> The shyp was charged with a mast;
> Crased it was, it myght not last.
> Now hath he one that wol not brest—
>   The old is leyde on syde.
> Thys fayre mast, this myghty yeard,
> Of whom fals shrewes be a-fered,
> hys name of ryght is prince Edward—
>   long myght he with vs a-byde.
>
> The ship hath closed hym a lyght
> To kepe her course in wey of ryght
> A fyre cressant that berneth bryght,
>   With fawte was neuer spyed.
> Thys good lyght, that is so clere,
> Call y the duke of exceter,

---

besides Puttenham, Thomas Wilson in *The Arte of Rhetorique* (1585), ed. G. H. Mair (Oxford, 1909) "An Allegorie is none other thing, but a Metaphore, used throughout a whole sentence, or Oration. As in speaking against a wicked offendour, I might say thus. Oh Lord, his nature was so evil, and his witte so wickedly bent, that he meant to bouge the ship, where he himself sailed: meaning that he purposed the destruction of his own countrey." A standard instance of the figure, in the tradition, would be the opening stanzas of Stephen Hawes's *The Pastime* [original: *Passtyme*] *of Pleasure*, ed. W. E. Mead (London, 1928) a late medieval compendium of standard devices. A late instance is Whitman's "O Captain! My Captain."

THE COSMIC IMAGE

Whos name in trouthe shyned clere;
   Hys worshyp spryngeth wyde.

Thys shyp hath a sterne full good,
hem to gyde in ebbe & flood,
A-geyne ther wawes both wild & wode
   That rynneth on euery syde.
The sterne that on the shype is sette
Ys the duke Somerset;
ffor ragged rokkes he woll not lette
   To sterre in ebbe and eke in tyde.

Ther is a sayle-yeard full good and sure,
To the shyp a grete tresour;
ffor alle stormes it wolle endure—
   It is trusty atte nede.
Now the sayle-yeard, y wolle reherse,
The Erle of Pembroke curtys and ferce;
A-cros the mast he hyeth travers,
   The good shyp for to lede.

The mast hath a welle good stay,
With shrowthes sure, y dare wel say,
In humble wyse hym to obey
   yf he to them hath nede.
The Duke of Bokyngham thys stay is he,
Thys shrowdes be sure in thare degre;
Devenshyre, & Grey, & becheham the free,
   And scales with them in tyde.

The shyp hath a well good sayle,
Of fyne canvas that woll not fayle,
With bonet iii for to travayle,
   That mekell beth of pryde.
This good sayle, y vndurstond,
The Erle of Northumberland,
Ros, clyfford, and Egremond—
   The trouthe is not to hyde.

79

Ther is a toppe the mast on hyght,
The shyp to defende in all hys ryght;
With his foomen when he schall fyght,
   They dare hym not a-byde.
The Erle of Shrovesbury the toppes name,
He kepeth the shype from harme and blame;
The Erle of Wylchyre, one of the same,
   That kepeth the shyp from drede.

Thys good shype hath ankers thre,
Of bether mettel ther may non be,
To strenthe the shyp be londe and se,
   When he woll stop hys tyde.
The furst anker, hole & sounde,
he is named the lord beamond;
Willys and Ryveres trouthe yn them found,
   In worship they hem gyde.

Now help, saynt George, oure lady knyght,
And be oure lode-sterre day & nyght,
To strengthe oure kynge and england ryght
   And fell oure fomenus pryde.
Now is oure shype dressed in hys kynde,
With hys taklynge be-for and be-hynde;
Whoso loue it not, god make hym blynde,
   In peynes to a-byde! [11]

The formal expectancies of such a poem are increasingly predictable as it goes along, and while perhaps the Wars of the Roses gave a special rhetorical point and seriousness to the names of the King's lieutenants, still as a metaphorical equation their procession here is always less and less novel. After a few stanzas we know more or less what to expect. A gradual anesthesia is avoided perhaps by the intricacy of the rhyme scheme and its own metaphorical effects

[11] "The Ship of State" (1458), collected in *Historical Poems of the XIVth and XVth Centuries*, ed. R. H. Robbins (New York, 1959), 191–193.

(e.g., in the third stanza "lyght," "ryght," and "bryght," are equated metaphorically; this is later replaced by equations of "hyght," "ryght," and "fyght"; and somewhat less consistently, of "knyght," "nyght," and "ryght"), but even the rhyme scheme has its repetitive aspects: the complex of words that are rhymed with "abyde" is a rhythmically monotonous sequence, however paradoxical and analytic it may be.

A poem like "The Ship of State" is entirely typical of the mode in its "purer" forms. Lest we accuse the example of being monotonous only because it is extensive and comprehensive, let me give a briefer case, to show that the lack of metaphorical surprise, the anesthesia, can operate under the most unlikely conditions. One would expect it not to characterize riddles and epigrams, but there also we find it. Take the simple modern example of Yeats's "Three Movements."

> Shakespearean fish swam the sea, far away from land;
> Romantic fish swam in nets, coming to the hand;
> What are all those fish that lie gasping on the strand? [12]

Here is the extreme of rigidity and simplicity, inasmuch as the poem, a riddle, depends on one image repeated three times, whereas another poem might have taken three different kinds of animal life and contrasted them under the one heading of living creatures. The "fish" are, from one point of view, agents, but they are easily enough considered the imagery of the poem. Here the curious animated metaphor of the first line gradually loses its strangeness, and we are finally left with an idea that fits in precisely with the ideas we already have, ideas the poem itself has given us. Surprise diminishes as the analogy is extended, because we see more and more clearly the

[12] Reprinted by permission, from W. B. Yeats, *Collected Poems*, copyright 1933 by The Macmillan Co., renewed 1961 by Bertha Georgie Yeats. Quoted in Tuve, *Elizabethan and Metaphysical Imagery*, 144: "This tripartite image would have been called *aenigma* by the slower-minded and *allegoria* by the quick. If anyone doubts that it 'beautifies the subject,' let him try to state Yeats' idea without it."

meaning of the hidden tenor. In most cases allegories proceed toward clarity, away from obscurity, even though they maintain a pose of enigma up to the very end. Take for example a political poem by Bertolt Brecht, "The Stone Fisherman."

> The big fisherman has appeared again. He sits in his rotted
> boat and fishes from the time when the first lamps flare up
> early in the morning until the last one is put out in the evening.
>
> The villagers sit on the gravel of the embankment and watch him,
> grinning. He fishes for herring but he pulls up nothing but stones.
>
> They all laugh. The men slap their sides, the women hold on to
> their bellies, the children leap high into the air with laughter.
>
> When the big fisherman raises his torn net high and finds the
> stones in it, he does not hide them but reaches far out with his
> strong brown arms, seizes the stone, holds it high and shows it
> to the unlucky ones.[13]

This parable of leadership in which the leader does not give his people what they need, but instead gives them "stones," does not cease to be enigmatic. It nevertheless *is* gradually less and less so for the reader who pursues the puzzle to the last line. Since the poet wants his reader to struggle over the hidden meaning, he is asking the reader to remove surprise, to lessen the unexpected, rather than the opposite.[14] With prose fiction this is no less true: Hawthorne's "The

---

[13] "Der Steinfischer," tr. H. R. Hays, in Bertolt Brecht, *Selected Poems* (New York, 1959), 144 (copyright 1947 by Bertolt Brecht and H. R. Hays; reprinted by permission of Harcourt, Brace & World, Inc.).

[14] Panofsky, writing of Dürer's allegorical engraving, *The Knight, Death and the Devil*, remarks on the high degree of system apparent in such work. "Based as it is on accumulated research and observation, Dürer's equestrian group bears all the earmarks of a scientific paradigm" (*Albrecht Dürer* [Princeton, 1948], 154). System tends to counteract the element of fantasy in such art, as it also counteracts the extravagant "spooks and phantoms" of modern "fantastic art." On this see Jurgis Baltrušaitis, *Anamorphoses ou perspectives curieuses* (Paris, 1955); *Aberrations: Quatre essais sur la légende des formes* (Paris, 1958); G. Hugnet, *Fantastic Art Dada Surrealism*, ed. A. H. Barr (New York,

Birthmark" leaves the reader with a gradually more sure sense that the birthmark is the insignia of life itself, by virtue of the imperfection it implies, and such in fact turns out to be the case when Aylmer finally succeeds in removing the birthmark from his wife's body. In "Rappaccini's Daughter" Hawthorne moves in two directions at once: while the action becomes increasingly restless and dramatic, the iconography settles into an increasingly sure interpretive pattern, so that by the close of the story we have a fixed idea of the particular contagion that is attached to Rappaccini's garden.[15] Older allegories much more obviously display the diminishing of metaphoric surprise.[16] Suppose that, like a major section of Hawes's *Passetyme of Pleasure*, the work is built on an educational program, whereby the parts of Grammar are studied, then the parts of Rhetoric, then the parts of Music and Mathematics, then of the Physical Sciences, including iconographic treatments of the five senses. This

----

1936). Cf. the discussion of images in Romanesque art in D. W. Robertson, Jr., *A Preface to Chaucer: Studies in Medieval Perspectives* (Princeton, 1962), 151–156. Robertson stresses the abstractive character of the monsters; they were partly magical, partly philosophical emblems.

[15] This garden is a *hortus conclusus*, which we recognize because, among other reasons, Hawthorne emphasizes the barriers between it and the city around it, a city compared to a desert—to reinforce the Eden parallel.

[16] On the *hortus conclusus*, see D. W. Robertson, Jr., "The Doctrine of Charity in Mediaeval Literary Gardens," *Speculum*, XXVI (1951), 24–49; and the account in Freeman, *English Emblem Books*, 173 ff., of Henry Hawkins' emblem book, *Parthenia Sacra* (1633), including a reproduction of the central image, the closed garden, a garden that includes the whole "cultivated" universe. Frye has discussed the mythic value of the *hortus* in *Anatomy*, 141–155 and 199–200. Johnson's *Rasselas* moves out of the garden, a movement discussed briefly by Krappe, *Genèse des mythes*, 61–62, where the story of Rasselas' journey is recounted in an Indian version some 2,000 years old. In English iconography one major Baroque text would be Browne's *Urne Buriall and the Garden of Cyrus*, ed. John Carter (Cambridge, 1958); in the quincunxial shapes of this garden, the circular shape is changed into a network shape, with reticulated diamond patterns comprising the whole, while the interest of the writer lies in articulating the static paradigm, rather than in the older questing action of a *Romance of the Rose*. On the garden in *The Romance of the Rose* see Robertson's *Preface to Chaucer*, 92–96.

poetry can only *fail* to achieve liveliness by virtue of its symmetrical, predetermined rhythmic order.[17] Once one has begun with one part of the formula, one is logically committed to all parts. In this general way allegory is unlike Aristotle's "metaphor."

The part-whole relationship. If this view is correct and there are difficulties with the equation of allegory and metaphor that outweigh its convenience, we may remedy the difficulty by a further look at the image as being governed by the whole figure; we might even assume that in some sense the whole determines the part. We need a term to suggest the symbiosis of part and whole. It may help to recall the classic distinction between *trope* and *figure*, the former a play on single words, the latter on whole groups of words, on sentences and even paragraphs.[18] Allegory must fall into the latter category. The best instance of truly *figured* speech would be an extended piece of ironical discourse, in which the complete discourse is pervaded by doubt, double meaning, and ironic detachment.

In the figurative form of irony the speaker disguises his entire meaning, the disguise being apparent rather than confessed. For in the trope the conflict is purely verbal, while in the figure the meaning, and sometimes the whole aspect of our case, conflicts with the language and the tone of voice adopted; nay, a man's whole life may be coloured with irony, as was the case with Socrates, who was called an ironist because he assumed the role of an ignorant man lost in wonder at the wisdom of others. Thus, as continued metaphor develops into allegory, so a sustained series of tropes (e.g., ironic tropes) develops into this figure.[19]

The picture of Socrates, so eloquent in the context of Quintilian's humanistic educational treatise, suggests a new approach to our problem.

[17] Of Hawes, Lewis writes: "It is at once his strength and his weakness that he writes under a kind of compulsion. Hence the prolixity and frequent *longeurs* of his narrative, but hence also the memorable pictures, whether homely or fantastic, which sometimes start up and render this dreariness almost 'a visionary dreariness'" (*Allegory of Love*, 280–281).

[18] On trope vs. figure: Tuve, *Elizabethan and Metaphysical Imagery*, 417; and Quintilian, *Institutes*, VIII, ii, secs. 44–47; IX, i, secs. 1–28.

[19] Quintilian, *Institutes*, IX, ii, secs. 44–47.

Teleologically controlled tropes. Perhaps instead of considering how the parts, the particular tropes of irony and double meaning, have the power to produce a total allegorical figure, we might ask whether the total figure, which in Socrates' case was a kind of symbolic life, does not give particular symbolic force to the part. The whole may determine the sense of the parts, and the parts be governed by the intention of the whole. This would yield a concept of a teleologically ordered speech. To say that "a man's whole life may be coloured with irony" is to imply that a whole life was "charted," in Kenneth Burke's term, as if under the control of a superior, final cause—the medieval poet's fourth level of symbolic control, the anagogic.

Two kinds of teleologically controlled tropes come to mind at once: metonymy and synecdoche.

Synecdoche is described by Quintilian as "letting us understand the plural from the singular, the whole from a part, a genus from the species, something following from something preceding; and *vice versa.*" [20] A synecdoche could then easily fit the logical criterion of an element of an allegory, since in itself it would always call to the reader's mind some larger organization of symbols to which system it bore an integral relationship.[21] If a man says, "My hand on it, then," we understand a larger engagement of the whole self, signified by the gesture of a handshake. Quintilian further equates synecdoche with *ellipsis*, which occurs "when something is assumed which has not actually been expressed." [22] Surely this is frequently the way allegory appears to us, which is clear from the examples given by Quintilian, for example,

Behold, the steers
Bring back the plough suspended from the yoke,

[20] *Ibid.*, VIII, vi, sec. 19.

[21] Thus Bentham in his *Handbook of Political Fallacies,* ed. with preface H. A. Larrabee (reprinted Baltimore, 1952), 174–178, relates what he calls "allegorical idols" to the structure of political authority. See Watson, *Shakespeare and the Renaissance Concept of Honor* (Princeton, 1960), "The Political Hierarchy," 82–90.

[22] Quintilian, *Institutes,* VIII, vi, sec. 21.

from which, as the rhetorician says, "we infer the approach of night." This inferential process, so much the essence of interpretive allegory, is a natural response to any fiction that is elliptical or enigmatic in any way.

It is but a short step from synecdoche to *metonymy*, which consists in the substitution of one name for another, and, as Cicero tells us, is called *hypallage* [exchange] by the rhetoricians. These devices are employed to indicate an invention by substituting the name of the inventor, or a possession by substituting the name of the possessor.[23]

Here, instead of a genus-species relationship (which Aristotle would have included under his first and second types of metaphor) we have primarily a cause-effect relationship, while once again the examples Quintilian gives are the purest allegory, of the kind we might label "personified abstraction" (employed in what rhetoricians would call a prosopopoeia).[24] For example: "Pale death with equal foot knocks at the poor man's door," and "There pale diseases dwell and sad old age." In either case there is a metaphoric interplay between tenor and vehicle, in terms of cause and effect, that is, in terms of a figurative action.

With these examples of metonymy we are back in the realm of agency, moving somewhat delicately away from the static type of true imagery (assuming that the perfect instance of an image is something fixed, like a geometric figure). Our earlier view was that all agents in allegory are becoming so fixed in sense that they begin to constitute images (that was indeed how they were introduced into the poem, for a personified abstraction is necessarily a sort of image).[25] While it may have been convenient to label these abstrac-

---

[23] *Ibid.*, sec. 23.

[24] Prosopopoeia (personification) is a figure, not a trope, since it is embodied usually in narrative or drama of some extent. See *ibid.*, IX, ii, secs. 30–33.

[25] The intermediate stage between an image and an agent is a *name*, i.e., a metonymy. To fix the agent into a name is to bring it from motion into rest. A poet like Crashaw, in whom metonymy abounds, plays on the sacred names, names of "divine ideas," in order to keep the *ecstasis* (a kind of movement of

tions "agents," it was recognized that they were not theoretically free enough and rich enough in "character" to be equated with the agents in a normal mimetic representation of action. The fact that with metonymies like those quoted by Quintilian we again have trouble distinguishing agent and image, only reinforces our view of the general allegorical transmutation of agency into imagery.

Taken together synecdoche and metonymy appear to contain the full range of allegorical part-whole relationships, the former allowing us to label *static* relations of classification (the *sail* is a qualitative subclass of the *ship*, in that it is a part thereof), while the latter allows us to label *dynamic* interactions between part and whole (the *sword* causes the *violent death*). Other more precise discriminations become possible. First, we can now be somewhat less abstract than we have been in our description of imagery. Second, we can settle on a generic term to include both synecdoches and metonymies.

The isolated image. The most striking sensuous quality of images in allegories is their "isolation" from each other. Allegorical painting and the emblematic poetry that takes after it display this very sharply. They present bits and pieces of allegorical "machinery," scales of justice, magic mirrors, crystal balls, signet rings, and the like. These devices are placed on the picture plane without any clear location in depth. Their relative sizes often violate perspective (they are often out of proportion), and at the same time they preserve their identities by being drawn with extremely sharp-etched outlines. This is not the result of a sheerly compositional criterion on the painter's part. "Isolation" of imagery follows from the need to maintain daemonic efficacy.

A peculiar characteristic of objects that are taken to have daemonic

---

the soul) from too much motion. See Ruth Wallerstein, *Richard Crashaw: A Study in Style and Poetic Development* (Madison, 1935), 85: "Crashaw, on the other hand, being of an ecstatic habit, chooses, like the makers of the lily symbol, to embody his idea in an object of sharp sensuous color and emotive power. This emotive power, or complex of suggestions, he uses as a sign, or metaphor, of his concept. Thereby he makes that single object the abstract *name* for the spiritual or intellectual concept he would express."

power (amulets, talismans, and the like) is that they are capable of existing solely as daemonic objects, almost as if the amulet were not related by nature to any other type of stone or gem. By cutting off the object in question from any function other than its daemonic, magical function, the user manages to address his particular talisman with total concentration.[26]

The type of allegorical imagery is then an isolated emblem. Three examples may suffice. The image may resemble, first, an astrological sign ("It is the stars, the stars above us, govern our conditions"), or, second, a banner carried in war or for some peaceable heraldic purpose, or, third, a signet ring that has authority, in that it possesses the power to gain immediate obedience from even a total stranger. Such devices are the allegorist's stock in trade. Each image tends toward a *kratophany*, the revelation of a hidden power.[27]

The talisman. Hawthorne's story "The Antique Ring" employs

[26] Attitudes toward statuary would be important here, since the statue can be conceived as a monument, isolating the image of the hero from the common, undifferentiated world of the nonhero. One can go further, to see which philosophical systems take their imagery from the fixed images of statuary (e.g., Parmenides) and which from the fluid images of music (e.g., Heraclitus). See Kroner, *Speculation in Pre-Christian Philosophy* (Philadelphia, 1956), 113.

[27] The term is used by Mircea Eliade, *Traité d'histoire des religions,* and elsewhere to mean "revelation of power." E.g., on the power residing in stones: "The hardness, the stiffness, the permanence of matter represents for the religious consciousness of primitive man a hierophany. Nothing could be more immediate or more autonomous in its force, nothing more noble and terrifying than the majestic boulder, the block of granite audaciously raised upright. Above all, stone *is.* It remains always itself and it subsists; and what is more important, it strikes. Even before he picks it up in order to strike with it, man himself runs into it. Not necessarily with his body, but in his sight at the very least. Thus he notes its hardness, its ruggedness, its power. The rock reveals to him something which transcends the precariousness of the human condition: a mode of absolute being" (*Traité,* 191). Worringer, *Abstraction and Empathy,* "Ornament," 51–77, shows how the semiabstract ornamental style using natural motifs (leaves, vines, etc.) is employed on account of its emotive, not its realistic (empathetic) significance. The ideal combination of stone and monument would be something like a pyramid, or sphinx, on which Mosheim has a valuable annotation in Cudworth's *Intellectual System,* I, 536, at which point Cudworth is discussing the origins of ancient Egyptian allegory.

the third of these devices.[28] Hawthorne departs from the legend that Elizabeth gave the Earl of Essex a signet ring which he was to return to her if he should ever fall into disgrace. The story recounts the deceit of the Countess of Shrewsbury, who promised to take the ring to the Queen and then deliberately kept it back from her, so that Essex was allowed to suffer death on the block. Hawthorne ascribes an increasingly powerful magic influence to the ring.

The diamond, that enriched it, glittered like a little star, but with a singular tinge of red. The gloomy prison-chamber in the Tower, with its deep and narrow windows piercing the walls of stone, was now all that the earl possessed of worldly prospect; so that there was the less wonder that he should look steadfastly into the gem, and moralize upon earth's deceitful splendor, as men in darkness and ruin seldom fail to do.

Again and again Hawthorne returns to the blood red color of the gem, an unlikely color in the ordinary scheme of things, since the gem is a diamond. (Starlike, it has a kind of astral influence.) The daemonic character of the device may be felt running throughout its history. While the Countess looks at Essex "with malignant satisfaction," an emotion that rises higher as she sees his state darkening, he reveals the belief that his whole destiny is tied to the power of the ring.

"This ring," he resumed, in another tone, "alone remains, of all my royal mistress's favor lavished upon her servant. My fortune once shone as brightly as the gem. And now, such a darkness has fallen around me, methinks it would be no marvel if its gleam—the sole light of my prison-

[28] "The Antique Ring" is from *Tales and Sketches*. Similar stories are "The Birthmark," "The Artist of the Beautiful," "Drowne's Wooden Image," "The Prophetic Pictures," "Chippings with a Chisel," "A Virtuoso's Collection." These stories betoken Hawthorne's interest in the work of art or artifice as an ikon possessing talismanic power. Even the birthmark is a talismanic image in that Giorgiana's husband, Aylmer, becomes an artist by virtue of trying to remove the mark, which is negatively an artifice, or rather, an artifice by negation. See the excellent Introduction by Newton Arvin to Hawthorne's *Short Stories* (New York, 1955).

house—were to be forthwith extinguished; inasmuch as my last earthly hope depends upon it."

"How say you, my lord?" asked the Countess of Shrewsbury. "The stone is bright; but there should be strange magic in it, if it can keep your hopes alive, at this sad hour. Alas! these iron bars and ramparts of the Tower are unlike to yield to such a spell."

The Countess is carefully presented here as a disbeliever in magic, so that when she betrays the Earl's trust and fails to deliver the ring to Elizabeth she suffers with double irony the burning influence of the ring—it was "found upon her breast," at her death, and there "it had imprinted a dark red circle, resembling the effect of the intensest heat."

Essex takes a double attitude toward the ring. He knows of course that it is a mere token and had an agreed-upon meaning for his Queen. But that matter-of-fact view does not occupy his thoughts. He senses the ring's occult value.

The condemned nobleman again bent over the ring, and proceeded:—

"It once had power in it,—this bright gem,—the magic that appertains to the talisman of a great queen's favor. She bade me, if hereafter I should fall into her disgrace,—how deep soever, and whatever might be the crime,—to convey this jewel to her sight, and it should plead for me. Doubtless, with her piercing judgment, she had even then detected the rashness of my nature, and foreboded some such deed as has now brought destruction upon my head. And knowing too, her own hereditary rigor, she designed, it may be, that the memory of gentler and kindlier hours should soften her heart in my behalf, when my need should be the greatest. I have doubted,—I have distrusted,—yet who can tell, even now, what happy influence this ring might have?"

Hawthorne pointedly draws attention to the circular form of the ring, so that we shall be aware of its concentrating, containing power.

But still Essex gazed at the ring with an absorbed attention, that proved how much hope his sanguine temperament had concentrated there, when there was none else for him in the wide world, save what lay in the compass of that hoop of gold.[29]

So natural is this concentration of interest and attention in the context of Hawthorne's fable, that we may forget how allegorical is the use of such "devices." Lest we assume Hawthorne is here solely interested in the occult, he moralizes the story with an almost ironic interpretation. The legend is inset in a discussion between two nineteenth-century Americans, Clara Pemberton and Edward Caryl. When at the close of Caryl's recitation, Miss Pemberton asks, "What thought did you embody in the ring?" he replies:

O Clara, this is too bad! . . . You know that I can never separate the idea from the symbol in which it manifests itself. However, we may suppose the Gem to be the human heart, and the Evil Spirit to be Falsehood, which, in one guise or another, is the fiend that causes all the sorrow and trouble in the world. I beseech you to let this suffice.

Hawthorne here might be understood as ironically defending the use of a Coleridgean "symbol," or a Hegelian "concrete universal,"

[29] The belief in the universe as *revealed* most perfectly in the form of the circle is apparent here. Presumably the earliest Western philosophic tradition of this sort is Parmenidean. "Parmenides held that there were bands crossing one another and encircling one another, formed of the rare and the dense element respectively, and that between these there were other mixed bands made up of light and darkness. That which surrounds them all was solid like a wall. That which is in the middle of all the bands is also solid, and surrounded in turn by a fiery band. The central circle of the mixed bands is the cause of movement and becoming to all the rest. He calls it 'the goddess who directs their course,' 'the Holder of Lots,' and 'Necessity'" (Aetios, quoted by Burnet, *Early Greek Philosophy*, 187). Burnet interprets Parmenides as follows: "The word *stephanai* (bands) can mean 'rims' or 'brims' or anything of that sort. . . . We seem, then, to be face to face with something like the 'wheels' of Anaximander" (187–188). The notion of the closed circle is of course central to the Ptolemaic cosmology, on which, in its Renaissance period of being attacked, see Nicolson, *The Breaking of the Circle: Studies in the Effect of the "New Science" upon Seventeenth-Century Poetry* (New York, 1960), espec. ch. i, "A Little World Cunningly Made"; also F. R. Johnson, *Astronomical Thought in Renaissance England* (Baltimore, 1937), ch. iv; Tuve, *Elizabethan and Metaphysical Imagery*, 420–421, no. M.

but the fact remains that his hero moralizes the image, and from our point of view it is an archetypal sort of image, the perfectly isolable, circumscribed, frozen gem.

The insignia. Our second example, the heraldic banner, represents isolation in another way. Banners, like signet rings, may serve practical purposes: in battle they provide rallying points, easily visible from a distance on account of their bright color and their height above the heads of both mounted and foot soldiers. But their significance seems early to have been enriched by the special value given to the iconographic designs embroidered upon them. They had the charismatic power of national flags in our own time.[30] We know of the standards of the Roman emperors and the banners (*vexilla*) of the legionnaires during the Empire. During the later middle ages banners were no less prominent a feature of massed political or military action. The anonymous Florentine chronicle that tells us about the revolt of the Ciompi in the thirteenth century puts emphasis on the use of banners for both tactical and charismatic purpose.

At seven P.M. on the said day the magistrates asked for all the flags of the guilds; and they wanted them in the Palace, solely because they did not want the *populo minuto* to be able to gather under its banner. So all the banners of the guilds were brought, because they knew of the plan that had been made, and thus it had been agreed that when they [i.e., the Ciompi] gave up their banner they would be cut to pieces and driven away. And all the bow strings of the bowmen would be cut. When the banner of the Angel was asked for, they did not want to give it, saying, "If this were foul play, to whom should we have recourse?" And they did not give it up.

When the Ciompi rebels were put down, there was a general search for the banners of all the recusant groups in the city.

All the banners of all the guilds and the "fat citizens" came into the square. All the magistrates, new and old, being in the palace advised

---

[30] The imagery of trees and forests produces a type of natural banner or flag; conversely the shrubbery of Eden is its heraldic ornamentation.

the leading magistrate that he should hang the flag of the *populo minuto* outside the window with the other flags; and he put it there. And there was great noise and shouting (in the square), "Throw it down, and throw those fools out."

Then the flag was hurled down. And it was torn apart and jumped on and thrown away. And then the two magistrates were told to go with God.

The magistrates after this execution of justice had all the churches searched for the banners and flags which bore the arms of the people and the Guelph party; and they were put in the palace; and [it was proclaimed] that no painter should paint any for any man, no matter of what class, no matter whether he was a citizen or a foreigner, on pain of death if he should be caught.[31]

This might be solely a matter of social action, in which the symbol "acts" very materially to bind men together into groups. The line is not easy to draw, however, between the use of banners in the revolt of the Ciompi and their use by a more refined chivalric group, knights in shining armor. Mario Praz has noted a sixteenth-century dialogue in which the banners are even more clearly emblematic than those of the Ciompi.

In our time, after the descent of King Charles the Eighth and Louis the Twelfth into Italy, whoever followed the military profession imitated the French Captains, and wished to adorn himself with elegant devices [*imprese*], which glittered on the knights, divided company by company, with different liveries, because they embroidered with silver-gilt their doublets, their cloaks, and on breast and back they wore the devices of their captains, so that the badges of the soldiers made a dainty and sumptuous pageant, and in the battles one could tell the boldness and bearing of each company.[32]

[31] "Cronaca prima d'anonimo," in *Il Tumulto dei Ciompi*, ed. Gino Scaramella ("Rerum Italicarum Scriptores," XVIII, iii; Bologna, 1934). I am indebted to Mr. Leo Raditsa for these passages, to which he drew my attention. See also, article "Flags," *Encyclopaedia Britannica*, 11th ed.

[32] Praz, *Studies in Seventeenth Century Imagery*, I, 48. Cf. Einhard, *The Life of Charlemagne*, ed. S. Painter (Ann Arbor, 1960), 51, on the different way the King would dress, depending on the occasion, daily or state: "He some-

The hieroglyphs of dress, embroidery of costume, emblems sewn into banners—they are beginning to look almost decadent, and at the same time more purely decorative and emblematic. The Renaissance is here returning to the language of a much earlier period. Langland, for example, had used the image of the banner in another scene of battle:

And then, before the trumpeters had time to blow, or the herald-of-arms to call out their names, these knights came clashing together in battle.

Hoary Old Age was in the vanguard, bearing before Death the banner that was his by right.[33]

When the allegorical author wishes to strike an immediate emblematic effect, he is likely to use something like "a banner with a strange device." The effect is often militant. Banners suggest one's national heritage or one's allegiance to a system of political or religious faith. This appears in Canto 8 of *The Lusiads*, where the legendary and actual history of the Portuguese is displayed in a series of banners on Vasco da Gama's flagship. Similarly, the festival production of Lindsay's *Ane Satyre of the Thrie Estaits*, as presented in Edinburgh,[34] makes great use of heraldic banners (which indeed we find in certain Brecht plays). The Estates enter briskly and soldierlike

---

times carried a jeweled sword, but only on great feastdays or at the reception of ambassadors from foreign nations." Note that "he despised foreign costumes, however handsome, and never allowed himself to be robed in them, except twice in Rome, when he donned the Roman tunic, Chlamys, and shoes. . . . On great feastdays he made use of embroidered clothes and shoes bedecked with precious stones, his cloak was fastened by a golden buckle, and he appeared crowned with a diadem of gold and gems, but on other days his dress varied little from the common dress of the people." Cf. Watson, *Shakespeare and the Renaissance Concept of Honor*, "Magnificence—the Accoutrements of Honor" (Princeton, 1960), 150–155.

[33] *Piers the Ploughman*, tr. J. F. Goodridge (Penguin ed., 1959), XX, 286.

[34] This is very much a festival production. *The Three Estates*, with its allegorical simplicity and stylization is well suited to such an occasion, rather like a *trionfo* in the Italian festivals of the Renaissance. Cf. Burckhardt, *Civilization of the Renaissance in Italy*, IV.

through the audience, carrying their banners to indicate their ranks. An iconography is latent in the spectacle.

Astral symbolism. The first instance of a typical allegorical image we gave was that of the stars. Astral symbolism, as for example it occurs in Marlowe's *Tamburlaine* or in Schiller's *Wallenstein*,[35] employs a clearly pinpointed symbol, the star. The actual physical isolation of the heavenly bodies from our own sphere is continually emphasized in such works, for whenever the poet draws attention to the influence of the stars (a daemonic influence in every case), he must at the same time remind us that this is action at a distance, that humans are under the control of distant bodies.[36] The remoteness of the stars is almost more important than their gemlike brilliance,[37] and the remoteness will be found throughout allegorical literature in the form of an almost Gnostic alienation of man from his Ulti-

[35] Schiller's *Wallenstein: A Historical Drama in Three Parts* exists in a translation by Coleridge, and more recently one by Charles E. Passage (New York, 1958). See especially the opening scene of the third play in the trilogy, *The Death of Wallenstein.*

[36] "The spatial concepts of the primitive are concrete orientations; they refer to localities which have an emotional colour; they may be familiar or alien, hostile or friendly. Beyond the scope of mere individual experience the community is aware of certain cosmic events which invest regions of space with a particular significance. Day and night give to east and west a correlation with life and death. Speculative thought may easily develop in connection with such regions as are outside direct experience, for instance, the heavens or the nether world. Mesopotamian astrology evolved a very extensive system of correlations between heavenly bodies and events in the sky and earthly localities. Thus mythopoeic thought may succeed no less than modern thought in establishing a co-ordinated spatial system; but the system is determined, not by objective measurements, but by an emotional recognition of values" (Frankfort, *Before Philosophy,* 30).

[37] "Bacchus to Ariadne," in Ovid's *Fasti,* tr. H. T. Riley (London, 1890), Bk. III, ll. 510 ff.: "He clasps her in his embrace, and, with kisses, dries away her tears, and he says, 'Together, let us seek the heights of heaven; united to me in wedlock, thou shalt take a united epithet. Henceforth, thy name altered shall be Libera. I will cause, too, that with thee there shall be a memorial of thy crown, which Vulcan gave to Venus, she to thee.' He keeps his word, and transforms its nine jewels into stars; by means of nine stars it still glitters in its golden radiance."

mate Cause. Man is "the stranger" on this earth, because his home, his astral resting place, remains so totally remote and cut off from him.[38] Astral imagery in this sense displays the highest degree of symbolic "isolation," for not only are the stars all separated from each other, like gems in a diadem, but they are even more distantly separated from man, who must adore and admire from a vast, alienating distance.[39]

The stars have a further virtue for the allegorist: they belong in constellations. They are known from the earliest times to move in a strictly ordered system of mutually dependent relations. The "fixed stars," stars whose relative motions do not vary, afford the perfect iconographic device.[40] System is nowhere more apparent to the

[38] On the "alien" in Gnostic theology, see Hans Jonas, *The Gnostic Religion*, 49-56. This is primarily a mystic notion, having nothing to do with political alienation. Cf., however, R. McL. Wilson, *The Gnostic Problem: A Study of the Relations between Hellenistic Judaism and the Gnostic Heresy* (London, 1958), ch. viii, "Diaspora, Syncretism and Gnosticism." The notion of man as the "alien," the "stranger" on earth, has profound effects on the kind of symbolism employed by Gnostic theology, on which see especially Jonas, Pt. I. In the political sphere the stranger is met with peculiar reactions, when, in the ancient world, he arrives at any new place. M. D. Legge, " 'To Speik of Science, Craft and Sapience' in Medieval Literature," *Literature and Science* (Oxford, 1955), 124, shows how this inhibition carries on up until the medieval period: "When you met a stranger in the Middle Ages you did not fence by talking about the weather. You carried on a rational conversation, and this you prefaced by firing a series of personal questions at him, designed to 'place' him by means of the categories. It was vital to discover whether you were talking to a man or a demon." This general subject, of the barriers to free travel and free international cooperation in the ancient world, has been treated by T. J. Haarhoff, in *The Stranger at the Gate* (Oxford, 1948). As the word "barbarian" suggests, this is a primarily cultural matter, involving, for example, language and dress, as well as the growth of political systems in the ancient world.

[39] Nicolson, *Voyages to the Moon*, 219: "I prefer to call the travels of my mariners 'cosmic voyages' since they lead not to outposts of civilization upon our maps, but *away from earth* to another world, usually in the moon or planets" (my italics).

[40] To the extent that emblematic objects are used in Neoplatonic magical theory (and in the poetry this theory influences), there is going to be a similar detachment of objects from background, with a resulting constellated order. One branch of Neoplatonic magic operates "through the occult qualities of

philosophic mind than in the systematic movements of the heavenly bodies. No wonder then that Henry Peacham used these very movements to describe the orderly character of allegory itself.

> The use of an Allegorie serveth most aptly to ingrave the lively images of things, and to present them under deepe shadowes to the contemplation of the mind, wherein wit and judgement take pleasure, and the remembrance receiveth a long lasting impression, and there as a Metaphore may be compared to a starre in respect of beautie, brightnesse and direction: so may an Allegorie be truly likened to a figure compounded of many stars, which of the Grecians is called *Astron,* and of the Latines *Sidus,* which we call a constellation, that is, a company or conjunction of many starres.[41]

Critics have long agreed with Peacham's analogy, in that it emphasizes the visual aspect of allegory. (I have already suggested there is a question about metaphor here.) This visual emphasis can be found in Aristotle, where "liveliness" sometimes has a strong sense of the "visually sharp image." Our word "image" itself has always troubled critics because it suggests that poetry must be essentially visual, and we have known this was nonsense, and therefore been embarrassed by our major term for poetic texture. But since I. A. Richards showed the fallacies of a naïve visual theory of imagery, by attacking its stronghold, the eighteenth-century literalism of Lord Kames, it has been easier to accept a *synaesthetic* notion of

---

things, that is, their forces or virtues other than elemental ones; these qualities are usually thought to be caused by the planets, to correspond to a certain planet's character, and they are used to induce or reinforce the required planetary influence."

"The main magical importance of occult qualities is in the resultant planetary grouping of objects, which can then be used by the other forces; one can, for example, make a picture, song or oration solarian by representing solarian objects (heliotrope, honey, cocks, etc.), or one could just sit and imagine them —in both cases one's imagination would become more solarian. These groups of objects may also comprise human beings, who can be used in the same way" (Walker, *Spiritual and Demonic Magic,* 79).

[41] *The Garden of Eloquence* (1593; facsimile ed. by W. G. Crane [Gainesville, Fla., 1954]), 25–26.

"image." [42] An image can be referred to any of the senses. In allegory, however, there does seem to be a penchant for the purely visual. This would be the one area in which Lord Kames's naïve visualism is exactly the right notion of imagery.

Diagrammatic isolation. A visualizing, isolating tendency is bound to appear wherever system is desired, since the perfect form of imagery for such purposes will be something like a geometric shape. [43]

[42] Richards, *Philosophy of Rhetoric*, ch. i. In the eighteenth century there was perhaps a more than usually strong delight in "verbal opsis," the imitation of visual realities by the effects of pure sound, as when alliteration makes us think of a visualized assault. Cf. an earlier example—Donne: "Spit in my face you Jewes, and pierce my side,/ Buffet, and scoffe, scourge, and crucifie me." "The most remarkable sustained mastery of verbal opsis in English, perhaps, is exhibited in *The Faerie Queene*, which we have to read with a special kind of attention, an ability to catch visualization through sound" (Frye, *Anatomy*, 259). On "representative metre" see Dr. Johnson's "Life of Pope," where Johnson conducts the original of Dr. Richards' experiment with the sound-sense relationships in Milton's "Nativity Ode." The whole of Johnson's account shows him at his best—acute, generous, humorous and categorical: "Beauties of this sort," he concludes, "are commonly fancied; and, when real, are technical and nugatory, not to be rejected, and not to be solicited." One of the clearest modern cases of "verbal opsis," where the "musical" quality predominates, is the poetry of E. E. Cummings, while Cummings' use of flower imagery is, as Blackmur showed, highly ornamental.

[43] "Spatial ideas are our clearest ideas, and it is very difficult not to clothe any idea which we wish to picture clearly in spatial forms" (Dean Inge, *Mysticism in Religion* [London, 1918], 81). "Spatial" need not always imply a very sensuous reality. Erich Auerbach has spoken of "the antagonism between sensory appearance and meaning, an antagonism which permeates the early, and indeed the whole, Christian view of reality. . . . The total content of the sacred writings was placed in an exegetic context which often removed the thing told very far from its sensory base, in that the reader or listener was forced to turn his attention away from the sensory occurrence and toward its meaning. This implied the danger that the visual element of the occurrences might succumb under the dense texture of meanings" (*Mimesis: The Representation of Reality in Western Literature*, tr. W. R. Trask [Anchor ed., New York, 1957], 48). It may be that an inhibition, a conflict of motives, produces the weird visual world of surrealist painting, where there is some sort of opposition to a natural visual world, and a preference for disturbed shapes. Surrealistic painting combines the "sensory base" and the "exegetic context." In the words of Stephan Körner, *Conceptual Thinking: A Logical Analysis* (Cam-

This Platonic source for allegorical imagery is certainly justified in terms of Plato's own practice; his tendency toward allegory is too well known to require commentary. It can perhaps be ascribed to a major need, in the Platonic system, for permanent images to convey the fixed ideas with which dialectic argument is going to operate. Quite apart from anything we say about Plato's metaphysical assumptions, to support the stress of vigorous dialectic argumentation, the "ideas" must be given a quasi-visual clarity of outline. The diagrammatic (Coleridge referred to *Prometheus Bound* as the "great paradigm," [44] *deigma* being a term in scriptural exegesis) and the geometric are both highly schematized means of thinking.[45] By such abstractive means the poet can isolate the forms of nature and human conduct and can subject them to analysis.[46] If reality is imaged in

bridge, 1955), 213: "In painting, aesthetic meaning is united with representation, and even with theoretical meaning. The latter enters, for instance, into surrealist paintings whose Freudian symbols tend to become discursive in the hands of those who paint according to theory." On the spatializing of time, see Ernst Cassirer, *The Philosophy of Symbolic Forms* (New Haven, 1955), III, 187. Ancient Egyptian art and the older North European art, as studied by Frankfort and Worringer, respectively, shows this spatializing of the temporal flux by means of ornamental forms.

[44] "On the Prometheus of Aeschylus," in *Essays and Lectures on Shakespeare and Some Other Old Poets and Dramatists* (Everyman ed.), 326–351. This lecture was read at the Royal Society of Literature, May 18, 1825.

[45] Dionysius of Halicarnassus takes *hyponoia* ("undermeaning") to be more or less synonymous with *schema* ("outline"). See Pépin, *Mythe et allégorie*, 87.

[46] This separating process accompanies any medieval *moralitas*, e.g., the *moralitas* of Henryson's "Orpheus and Eurydice," *Poems and Fables*, ed. H. H. Wood (Edinburgh and London, 1958):

> ffair phebus is the god of sapience;
> Caliope, his wyfe, is eloquence;
> Thir twa mareit gat orpheus belyfe,
> Quhilk callit is the pairte intelletyfe
> Off manis saule, and undirstanding fre,
> And seperat fra sensualitie.
> Euridices is our effectioun,
> Be fantasy oft movit up and doun;
> Quhile to ressone it castis the delyte,
> Quhyle to the flesche it settis the appetyte.

diagrammatic form, it necessarily presents objects in isolation from their normal surroundings, precisely what we found in the case of emblematic painting and poetry.

Surrealist isolation. Art history provides a conceptual framework in which to place this effect of "isolation." Surrealistic art is surreal precisely because its images are all "isolated" in the sense in which I have being using the term.[47] One can show a clear line of development from fantastic art of earlier periods, where thematic message is always prominent (Bosch, Brueghel, Dürer, Goya), through certain

------

> Arestius, this [hird] that cowth persew
> Euridices, is nocht bot gud vertew,
> That bissy is to keip our myndis clene. [425-437]

In the ordering of sermons this method produces "divisions" on a text. The method is to segregate the parts of a parable or "sentence" into processional steps.

[47] On the most primitive, early instances of a surreal art, see Waldemar Déonna, *Du Miracle grec au miracle chrétien: Classiques et primitivistes dans l'art* (Basel, 1956), II, 88. This early ceramic art is mainly concerned with the deformation of natural shapes, e.g., animal limbs, bird beaks, tree limbs. As a modern instance of isolation, the surrealist Paul Nougé thus describes the work of René Magritte: "The method itself consists in isolating the object by breaking off its ties with the rest of the world in a more or less brutal or in a more or less insidious manner. We may cut off a hand and place it on the table, or we may paint the image of a cut-off hand on the wall. We may isolate by using a frame or by using a knife, but even more by a deformation, or a modification, in the subject of an object—a woman without a head, a hand of glass. Or by a change of scale—a lipstick the height of a forest. Or by a change of scenery—the Louis-Philippe table on a field of ice, a statue in a ditch." This art might well be hermetic, and its constructional principle could be generalized to apply to whole social communities: "We all have our personal fetishes. The collective fetish is possible only in hermetic and highly unified communities. And this exactly describes the surrealist group at its inception. . . . Breton and his disciples invented a mythological kingdom in the heart of postwar Paris" (Germaine Brée, in *An Age of Fiction* [New Brunswick, 1957], 52).

Camus' short story, "Jonas, ou l'artiste au travail," in *L'Exil et le royaume* (Paris, 1957), tells of an artist's self-imposed exile, in the manner of a fairy tale. The artist goes up onto a scaffolding and will not come down again, while he works solely within his own imagination, but not in fact on the canvas. Jonas, of course, is the prophet swallowed by the whale—and the comic flavor of the apocryphal story lingers here.

sublime and picturesque painters of the eighteenth and nineteenth centuries, to the modern schools of Dada and surrealism in France. When this surreal imagery is rendered in poetry, the poet takes the same liberties with perspective; he makes his poem temporally discontinuous; he makes spatial relationships discontinuous.[48] A riddle, after all, is a verbalized, surrealistic collage, with a hidden meaning that draws the parts together "under the surface." Lautréamont's classic definition of *l'humour noir*, "the chance meeting of a sewing-machine and an umbrella on an operating table," fits the pattern of enigmatic allegory; like an Eisenstein montage it challenges us to interpretation by means of an elliptical form and fragmented imagery.[49] We need to remember that the marked isolation of objects within a painting by Dali or Ernst and a story by Kafka has an exact counterpart in the paintings of the Italian renaissance painters like Piero di Cosimo or Bellini,[50] and similarly in the precise counting of pieces

[48] Although it is advisable to distinguish mannerism from surrealism, the two tendencies have in common a cult of *deformation*. In brief, surrealism deforms by recombining the parts of bodies, mannerism by stretching and compressing the parts. In both there is a tendency to overemphasize the part, as if in a serious caricature. E.g., the effect in a poet like Crashaw, of whom Miss Wallerstein observes: "Then, secondly, Crashaw's Marinism is apparent in an insistence upon the physical detail of the subject, detail that is often trivial, with a resultant sensationalism. Finally, it is a schematic analysis of the emotions, using the dialectic of violent contrast, an analysis that gives the passions the same aridity as the concrete detail with which they are bound up" (*Richard Crashaw*, 108). Curtius has given a general summary of the problem of mannerism, in *European Literature*, 273–301. "A danger of the system is that, in mannerist epochs, the ornatus is piled on indiscriminately and meaninglessly" (274). This suggests a surreal imagery where perspective is absent and the "packing density" is excessively high.

[49] Cf. Curtius, *European Literature*, 97, on the *topos* of "The World Upside-down" (*similitudo impossibilium*). Examples would be Donne's "Go and Catch a Falling Star," which is a riddling poem, Edward Lear's nonsense poems, Lewis Carroll's nonsense poems and prose fables.

[50] Watkins, in *Shakespeare and Spenser*, has reminded us of the kinship between Spenser and a painter like Bellini or Piero di Cosimo. Cf. Mario Praz, *The Flaming Heart: Essays on Crashaw, Machiavelli, and Other Studies in the Relations between Italian and English Literature from Chaucer to T. S. Eliot* (New York, 1958), 12: "In a sense Spenser, compared with Ariosto,

of iconographic machinery in a poem like Lydgate's *Reson and Sensualitie*, Hawes's *Passetyme of Pleasure*, Phineas Fletcher's *The Purple Island*.

A comparison between what allegorical painting actualizes and what allegorical literature leaves to the imagination to "see" will show that the visual clarity of allegorical imagery is not normal; it does not coincide with what we experience in daily life.[51] It is much more like the hyperdefinite sight that a drug such as mescaline induces.[52] It is discontinuous, lavish of fragmentary detail—whether

marked a return to the ideals of the Middle Ages, just as Chaucer did in respect to Boccaccio in his *rifacimiento* of the *Filostrato*, and both in this respect and in his taste for pageants and allegories, he offers a striking resemblance to the Italian mannerist painters, with whom he has in common also a contrast between the vividness of painstakingly reproduced details and an unreal, arbitrarily constructed space." Robertson discusses the Romanesque treatment of unstructured, or nonstructuring, space in *A Preface to Chaucer*, 156–161; the later Gothic treatment, 176–188.

[51] Speaking of the *extremes* of allegory or realism, Auerbach notes a "half silly, half spectral distortion of ordinary average occurrences in human life," as in Apuleius, or Kafka, or the fourth-century historian, Ammianus Marcellinus, on whom see *Mimesis*, 43–66. See also, Paul Goodman, "The Real Dream," *Midstream*, V, no. 1, 86–88. When a painter wishes to draw attention to his creative act in reproducing the "real world," he frequently uses the device of *trompe-l'oeil*. See Robert M. Adams, *Strains of Discord: Studies in Literary Openness* (Ithaca, 1958), ch. iv, "*Trompe-l'Oeil* in Shakespeare and Keats." A perfect case, in painting, would be the composite mural of Peter Blume, *The Eternal City*, where there are not only *trompe* effects, but a combination of the sublime and picturesque landscape such that one can perceive, paradigmatically, their generic relationship to the allegorical. On this painting, see Kenneth Burke's note, *The Philosophy of Literary Form: Studies in Symbolic Action* (New York, 1957), 325–326.

By drawing attention to himself, or to an imagined spectator as in the Blume painting, the artist immediately starts a critical train of thought. One interprets the scene from the imagined spectator's point of view; the double view amounts to an allegorizing of an imitation. Mimetic art, Aristotle had seemed to say, need not introduce such double perspectives; even the author can stay out of his fiction, and in fact Aristotle counted his absence a beauty of Homeric composition. (The chorus had been a device of perspective, but we associate the choral speech with the need for dramatic commentary and dramatic irony, and these in turn with the allegorical impulse.)

[52] Tuve, *Elizabethan and Metaphysical Imagery*, 108, speaks of allegory's "sharp-etched detail as of vision or dream."

highly symmetrical, as in Dürer's design for a monumental gateway, or wildly random, as in a fantasy of Bosch or Goya. Whether the daemonic imagery is controlled or uncontrolled, its so-called "illustrative" character is more than merely "tacked on" to a moral discussion. Allegorical imagery must be illustrative, because its discontinuous nature does not allow a normal sense world to be created.[53] In the picture plane of the typical representational painting, objects, regardless of their importance in the scheme of things, will be compelled to obey the laws of perspective. Objects in the background will be drawn small, objects in the foreground will be drawn large. Such a picture plane will yield to the eye of the per-

[53] Epic simile would be an instance of effective, but isolated, decorative illustration of a more basic structure. Wallerstein noted this consequence of the rhetorical theory of Tesauro, in *Richard Crashaw*, 69: "The effect of the rhetoric or poetic guide was, then, to emphasize ingenuity in figure, gaudy decoration, and externality. The result was to develop the figure at the expense of the whole. In the large and leisurely movement of the epic poem, with its broad picture of life, the extended simile, which begins in a luminous description of the object figured and then moves on to complete its own beautiful scene before returning to the narrative, is an element of great organic beauty in that it helps to create that ample background scene and that sense of a whole world which are so necessary to the manifold life of the epic." In Homer epic simile is frequently used to give a microcosmic-macrocosmic contrast between the two worlds of war and peace. There is, always, some sense of interruption when epic simile is used, and this discontinuity seems essential to the use of the figure. A simile is always a partial digression and thus enters discursive sermons and essays quite pleasingly. Of the seventeenth-century divine, Jeremy Taylor, John Buchan observed, "When a simile occurs to him, his fancy elaborates it almost to the extent of allegory" (*A History of English Literature* [New York, 1923], 223). The same might be said of Robert Burton, e.g., in the simile of the hawk that begins the "Digression of Air": "As a long-winged Hawk, when he is first whistled off the fist, mounts aloft, and for his pleasure fetcheth many a circuit in the Air, still Soaring higher and higher, till he be come to his full pitch, and in the end, when the game is sprung, comes down amain, and stoops upon a sudden: so will I, having now come at last into these ample fields of Air, wherein I may freely expatiate and express myself for my recreation, a while rove, wander round about the world, mount aloft to those etherial orbs and celestial spheres, and so descend to my former elements again" (*The Anatomy of Melancholy*, ed. Floyd Dell and P. Jordan-Smith [New York, 1927; reprinted 1948], II, sec. 2, member 3, "Air Rectified. With a Digression of Air," 407).

ceiver what we know as "the real world." [54] (With some representational artists distortions in perspective occur, but usually in order to exaggerate what we might call "realistic errors" of perception.) An allegorical world gives us objects all lined up, as it were, on the frontal plane of a mosaic, each with its own "true," unchanging size

[54] On the related notion of constancy, see M. D. Vernon, *A Further Study of Visual Perception* (Cambridge, 1954), ch. i.

Note the important passage in Robertson, *A Preface to Chaucer*, 149–150: "Since the order of the whole in Romanesque art is always an artificial rather than a natural order, however, the parts viewed either from the point of view of later art, or from that of 'real life,' may seem to acquire a kind of autonomy. The 'individualizing' or 'isolating' tendency which Riegl observed in late antique art pervades Romanesque art as well, and this is true whether we are considering larger units or the representation of the human figure. If we compare a typical Romanesque church with a French Gothic cathedral, the aisles of the former seem to be separated from the main body of the nave as if they were almost distinct rooms, set off by the long 'aqueduct' structure of the main arches, and the transept and the choir are separate geometrical entities. From the outside the various parts have an 'additive' effect, as though one shaped bloc had been added to another. Again, when groups of figures appear in sculpture or in illumination, individuals are separated from one another by arcades, nimbuses, mandorlas, or, even in instances where no such mechanical separation occurs, they seem to act independently without reference to each other. In [an illumination from the 'Shaftesbury Psalter'] the Child seems suspended between the Virgin's outstretched knees, and His posture is simply an echo of the Virgin's posture except for a slight turn of the head toward the suppliant nun. He does not look at the nun, and the nun does not actually look toward Him. There is no effort to integrate the group as a whole in a coherent spatial continuum so that they might react naturally to one another. In effect, they remain, so far as space and time are concerned, essentially isolated. A disregard for a continuum of this kind is characteristic of the period, so that a single figure may appear in different guises in the same representation, or, as in late antique art, a series of actions by a single person may be either crowded into a single representation or portrayed by repeating his figure within the framework of a single scene. . . . The same kind of isolation requiring an intellectual act of integration on the part of the observer is common in Romanesque iconology. Thus Dr. Joan Evans [in *Cluniac Art in the Romanesque Period* (Cambridge, 1950), 23] calls attention to the 'symbolic integration' of the decorations in the apse of Cluny, where the various separate elements have no visual coherence, but a coherence that can be appreciated only with reference to the meanings which may be derived from them" (copyright Princeton University Press, 1962).

and shape. Allegory perhaps has a "reality" of its own, but it is certainly not of the sort that operates in our perceptions of the physical world. It has an idealizing consistency of thematic content, because, in spite of the visual absurdity of much allegorical imagery, the relations between ideas are under strong logical control.

Surrealist isolation of parts would certainly follow from the tendency of agents to become images, for that tendency appears whenever any agent is possessed by a daemon, itself finally becoming a daemon, and therefore hierarchically isolated as an intermediate creature somewhere on the ladder of perfection.[55] Religious painting demonstrates this isolation in showing descents of angels who visit mankind in completely discrete, discontinuous forms. Even more

[55] "In all acts of worship, even the most elaborate and intense, it is possible to claim—as was, in fact, maintained over and over again by defenders of images at all times—that the icons served merely as a symbol, a reminder, a representative of the deity or saint for whom the honor is intended. Wherever magic is involved this claim tends to become void. The common denominator of all beliefs and practices, which attribute magic properties to an image, is that the distinction between the image and the person represented is to some extent eliminated, at least temporarily. This tendency to break down the barrier between image and prototype is the most important feature of the cult of images in the period under review [the era after Justinian]" (Ernst Kitzinger, "The Cult of Images Before Iconoclasm," 100–101). By this breakdown Kitzinger means, for instance, that the image of the saint could act in the saint's place, to work a miracle—the image becomes truly the saint's persona. That such magic is not far from a pseudorational explanation, and therefore in this also resembles allegorical fictions which are as unreal as they are philosophical and rational, appears from the following account by Kitzinger: "The manner of the alleged intervention of the image is also worth noting. According to Euagrius the image was instrumental in kindling a fire which consumed an artificial hill built by the Persians as an assault tower. It brought about this effect through the intermediary of water which was sprinkled on the divine countenance before being applied to the fire. The seemingly paradoxical, and therefore all the more miraculous, phenomenon of fire being fanned by water is based on Procopius' account where it is given a perfectly rational explanation. But it also brings the Edessa story into line with a group of miracle stories in which the images—like saints and relics—exercise their beneficial effects through some intermediary substance" (104). "The story reveals not a new and more intense faith, but a new desire to make the object of that faith palpable." Palpable ideas—the material of allegories.

isolation is apparent when we turn to the diabolical imagery that accompanies the histories of saints or pictures of the Day of Judgment. So too the imagery of modern surrealism, metonymic and synecdochic in character, presents the *objet trouvé*, which has a direct antecedent in the emblematic devices of the earlier centuries. These latter devices are likewise "found objects," although they are organized into traditional iconographies which we recognize more readily than the chiefly Freudian iconography of surrealism. Take the following emblematic stanza from George Herbert's "Affliction."

> My thoughts are all a case of knives,
>> Wounding my heart
>> With scattered smart;
> As watering-pots give flowers their lives.
>> Nothing their fury can control,
>> While they do wound and prick my soul.

The fourth line is as discontinuous and lacking in "constancy" as Lautréamont's "chance meeting." Only the underlying ideas hold the stanza together, while in twentieth-century surrealist art it is mainly the new Freudian theory of unconscious motivation that holds the refracted imagery together. In both cases the total effect is the creation of barriers between images. Critics have differed over what to call these barriers. Some might say of Herbert's fourth line, that it exemplifies "wit," a *discordia concors*, or violent yoking together of opposites. Others would rather associate this wit with the *humour noir*, the absurd, of the surrealists.[56] But this wit and the

---

[56] It is tempting to contrast Dr. Johnson's attack on the absurdity of allegory with the modern Surrealist praise of absurdity, as if "absurd" meant the same thing in both cases. With historical settings taken into account, this might be a fair alignment, if we think only of the formal, visual absurdity of mixing planes of reality without regard to the organization of the physical space and time in which we live. A typical Johnsonian attack would be his criticism of Dryden's *The Hind and the Panther:* "The scheme of this work is injudicious and incommodious; for what can be more absurd than that one beast should counsel another to rest her faith upon a pope and council?" He then speaks of "the incongruity of the fiction," an incongruity that surrealism actually goes

demonstration of the absurd are no doubt very close to each other.

The price of a lack of mimetic naturalness is what the allegorist, like the Metaphysical poet, must pay in order to force his reader into an analytic frame of mind. Ellipsis in speech has just this effect, in much the same way that any fragmentary utterance (the rhetorician's *aposiopesis*) takes on the appearance of a coded message needing to be deciphered. We shall find that a strict order of elements is another aspect of the allegorical coding process, but for the moment it suffices to point out that by having a surrealistic surface texture allegory immediately elicits an interpretive response from the reader. The silences in allegory mean as much as the filled-in spaces, because by bridging the silent gaps between oddly unrelated images we reach the sunken understructure of thought (the biblical exegetes' "under-thought," *hyponoia*, the Russian schoolboy's "undertext").

One final effect of isolation needs to be observed. It makes a very precise delineation of the particular image not only possible, but actually highly desirable. The allegorist's abstract thematic intention does not prevent him from making a precise verbal delineation of objects; if anything he is encouraged to go too far toward precision. This excess is likely to occur in any tenaciously accurate documentary work, or whenever allegory is overtly ornamental, as in the aureate Scottish Chaucerians or in a poem like the fourteenth cen-

---

out of its way to produce. Few artistic movements could have shocked Dr. Johnson as deeply as would our modern Surrealism.

On the absurdity of time relations in allegorical art, recall Shaftesbury's *Second Characteristics*, ed. Benjamin Rand (Cambridge, 1914): having said that the allegorical painter, "when he has made choice of the determinate date or point of time according to which he would represent his history, is afterwards debarred the taking advantage from any other action than what is immediately present," Shaftesbury continues, "it may however be allowable, on some other occasions, to make use of certain enigmatical devices, to represent a future time: as when Hercules, yet a mere boy, is seen holding a small club, or wearing the skin of a young lion . . . and though history had never related of Hercules, that being yet very young, he killed a lion with his own hand; yet this representation of him would nevertheless be entirely conformable to poetic truth" (35–36).

tury *Pearl*.[57] The texture of allegory is "curiously inwrought," worked in ornamental detail. This is not realism; it is surrealism.

Kosmos: the allegorical image. The oldest term for ornamental diction, *"kosmos,"* appears in Aristotle's list of the eight types of words that constituted, as he saw it, poetical language. "Every word is either current, or foreign, or a metaphor, or an ornament [*kosmos*], or newly coined, or lengthened, or contracted, or altered." [58] It is this buried term,[59] familiar to us in somewhat disguised and certainly

[57] See E. V. Gordon's "Introduction" to his edition of *Pearl* (Oxford, 1953), pp. xi–xxix.

[58] *Poetics*, 1457b (I use the Greek plural form, *kosmoi*, for "ornaments").

[59] On ornament, see Quintilian, *Institutes*, VIII, ch. iii, sec. 61. For one of the earliest instances that allegory (*hyponoia*) and ornament are aspects of the same process, see Pépin, *Mythe et allégorie*, 85, on the fact that Euripides calls an ornamented shield "the symbol of the fate reserved for our city." For a general discussion of *kosmos* see Lane Cooper, *Aristotelian Papers* (Ithaca, 1939), "The Verbal 'Ornament' [*Kosmos*]," 101–128. Also, Henry Wells, *Poetic Imagery* (New York, 1924), ch. ii, "The Decorative Image"; A. Warren and R. Wellek, *Theory of Literature* (New York, 1949), 211, on the work of Wilhelm Worringer. Edward Bloom, in "The Allegorical Principle," *ELH*, XVIII, 164, takes the usual view of ornament as something tacked on, something "merely" decorative.

Harry Berger's signal service to the study of ornament has been his theory of "conspicuous irrelevance," for which see *The Allegorical Temper: Vision and Reality in Book II of Spenser's* Faery Queene (New Haven, 1957), chs. v, vi, vii. It is not an entirely new notion: Grierson, for example, found Spenser "at his best when most irrelevant" (*Cross Currents in English Literature of the Seventeenth Century* [London, 1929], 56).

Empson gave a full reading of an ornamental passage, Shakespeare's fable of the builder-bees in *Henry V*, I, ii, 320 ff., as an ambiguity of the third type. Notice the context in which Empson made this analysis: "There is a variety of the 'conflict' theory of poetry which says that a poet must always be concerned with some difference of opinion or habit between different parts of his community; different social classes, ways of life, or modes of thought; that he must be several sorts of men at once, and reconcile his tribe in his own person. It is especially to generalized ambiguity of the third type that this rather limited formula will apply" (*Seven Types*, 128).

Panofsky treats this ornamental art in his discussion of Dürer's "decorative phase." This phase found Dürer experimenting with daemonic forms. His Great Triumphal Car is as much a represented daemon as it is in any important sense decorative. But in fact, as many artists' sketches (notably Leonardo's)

debased form in its Latinate derivatives, *ornatus* and *decoratio*,[60] that I wish to revive and use, for it fills the requirements of an allegorical image: first, it must imply a systematic part-whole relationship; second, it should be capable of including both metonymy and synecdoche; third, it should be capable of including "personifications"; fourth, it should suggest the daemonic nature of the image; fifth, it should allow an emphasis on the visual modality, specifically on visual or symbolic "isolation," not to say surrealism; finally, it should be such that large-scale double meanings would emerge if it were combined with other such images.

Just how kosmos is the essential type of an allegorical image will appear as soon as the term is defined. It signifies (1) a universe, and (2) a symbol that implies a rank in a hierarchy. As the latter it will be attached to, or associated with, or even substituted for, any object which the writer wants to place in hierarchical position.[61] The classic

---

would show, the decorative and the daemonic are visual partners. This is quite apparent in the decor of the masque or in the combined use of the fantastic and the mechanical in certain Renaissance emblem books. Of the Platonic emblem writers Edgar Wind remarks: "Their books of heroic devices, so rich in moral marvels and myths, are interspersed with pictures of mechanical inventions, admirable machines which harness the secret forces of nature in order to release them for a dramatic effect. Placed next to the classical columns and sirens, diamonds and laurels, salamanders, porcupines and unicorns—symbols which continue to convey their heroic lesson in the language of fable—the new waterwheels, bellows, catapults, rockets, bombards, and barbacanes seem like brutally prosaic intruders, realistic contrivances in a setting of fantasy. But to the inventors themselves—Leonardo da Vinci among them—they exemplified the magical forces of nature, forces which man carries also in his own breast" (*Pagan Mysteries in the Renaissance* [London, 1958], 96). The very rich development of ornamental art in the nineteenth century suggests a similar concern with the daemonic, which reaches its height, perhaps, with *art nouveau*, and above all with the great master of that style, the Catalan architect Gaudi.

[60] The etymological connections of *decorum* and *decoration*, *polite*, *police*, and *expolitio*, *cosmic* and *cosmetic*, *costume* and *custom*, with all their minor variants (e.g., "ornamental gardening," "proper dress") all demonstrate the same fundamental duality.

[61] As Bentham put it, "Of this device, the object and effect is, that any unpleasant idea that in the mind of the hearer or reader might happen to stand associated with the idea of the person or the class, is disengaged from it: and

example of a kosmos is the jewelry worn by a lady to show her social status, or any other such sartorial emblems of position.[62]

As in English, the Greek term *kosmos* has a double meaning, since it denotes both a *large-scale order* (macrocosmos) and the small-scale *sign of that order* (microcosmos).[63] It could be used of any

---

in the stead of the more or less obnoxious individual or individuals, the object presented is a creature of the fancy, by the idea of which, as in poetry, the imagination is tickled—a phantom which, by means of the power with which the individual or class is clothed, is constituted an object of respect and veneration" (*Works*, IX, 76; quoted in C. K. Ogden, *Bentham's Theory of Fictions* [London, 1932]).

[62] St. Cyprian, "The Dress of Virgins," in *The Fathers of the Church*, XXXVI, tr. and ed. R. J. Deferrari (New York, 1958), ch. v, 35: "No one on seeing a virgin should doubt whether she is one. Let her innocence manifest itself equally in all things, and her dress not dishonor the sanctity of her body. Why does she go forth in public adorned, why with her hair dressed, as if she either had a husband or were seeking one?" This is important to the Church doctrinally, as well as ethically, for the worship of the Holy Virgin. See also Cyprian, "On the Unity of the Catholic Church," in *The Library of Christian Classics* (London, 1956), V, 128: "In the Gospel there is a proof of this mystery of unity, this inseparable bond of harmony, when the coat of the Lord Jesus Christ is not cut or rent at all. The garment is received whole and the coat taken into possession unspoilt and undivided by those who cast lots for Christ's garment, asking who should put on Christ. Holy Scripture says of this: 'But for the coat, because it was not sewn but woven from the top throughout, they said to each other, Let us not rend it, but cast lots for it, whose it shall be.' He showed a unity which came from the top, that is from heaven and the Father, a unity which could by no means be rent by one who received and possessed it. Its wholeness and unity remained solid and unbreakable for ever. He who rends and divides the Church cannot possess the garment of Christ. In contrast, when at Solomon's death his kingdom and people were being rent, the prophet Ahijah, meeting King Jeroboam in the field, rent his garment into twelve pieces." This figure recurs frequently throughout the Christian era as a sign of total, unbroken unity in the state or in any such community, and furthermore in the mind, when mind and state are being paralleled.

[63] Cf. Plutarch, *Moralia*, tr. W. W. Goodwin (Boston, 1878), Bk. II, ch. i, "Of the World," 132: "Pythagoras was the first philosopher that gave the name of kosmos to the world, from the order and beauty of it; for so that word signifies. Thales and his followers say that the world is one. Democritus, Epicurus, and their scholar Metrodorus affirm that there are infinite worlds in

decoration or ornament of dress, any embellishment, any costume particularly denoting status, any heraldic device that might accompany the donning of such a costume; [64] it could be used for a signet ring or good-luck charm if either were related to a hierarchic rank,

an infinite space, for that infinite vacuum in its whole extent contains them. Empedocles, that the circle which the sun makes in its motion circumscribes the world, and that circle is the utmost bound of the world. Seleucus, that the world knows no limits. Diogenes, that the universe is infinite, but this world is finite. The Stoics make a difference between that which is called the universe, and that which is called the whole world;—the universe is the infinite space considered with the vacuum, the vacuity being removed gives the right conception of the world; so that the universe and the world are not the same thing."

[64] The theatre, where as Frye observes "the rhythm of decorum" obtains, has always recognized the iconographic function of dress. Donatus, "On Comedy and Tragedy," in *European Theories of the Drama*, ed. Barrett Clark (New York, 1947), 45: "They always bring on Ulysses in Greek costume either because he finally pretended madness when he wanted to be ruler so that he should not be forced ignorantly to go to war, or because of this unusual wisdom under the cover of which he was of such great help to his comrades. For his nature was always that of a deceitful person. Some say that the inhabitants of Ithaca, like the Locrians, always wore *pallas*. The actors impersonating Achilles and Neoptolemos wear diadems though never royal scepters. The reason of this convention is held to be that they never entered the rites of conspiracy with the other Greek youths to carry on the war with Troy, nor were they ever under the command of Agamemnon. . . . The old men in comedies wear white costumes, because they are held to be the oldest sort. Young men wear a variety of colors. The slaves in comedy wear thick shawls, either as a mark of their former poverty, or in order that they may run the faster. Parasites wear twisted *pallas*. Those who are happy wear white robes; the unhappy wear soiled robes; the rich wear royal purple, paupers wear reddish-purple; the soldier carries a purple chlamys; a girl wears a foreign robe; a procurer, a robe of many colors; yellow, to designate greed, is given to the courtesan." What applies to costume also applies to drapery, e.g., the drapery (the "nets") in which Agamemnon is caught in Aeschylus' play.

On dress as an index to character and status, see Castiglione, *The Book of the Courtier*, tr. C. S. Singleton (New York, 1959), 121 ff. With a courtesy book like Della Casa's *Galateo: or, The Book of Manners* (ch. vii) it is apparent that decorum means very loosely, conformity to the customs of the land and particular place. See the new translation of *Galateo* by R. S. Pine-Coffin (Penguin ed., 1958), 33.

which would be the case, for example, if one belonged to a secret society known only by the possession of such a ring or amulet.[65] Used adverbially and adjectivally, the word *kosmos* and its derivatives implied propriety and decorum (κοσμιοτης) in dress and manner, since to be adorned according to one's true rank in society would be to conform to propriety. With this adjectival usage we begin to shift over to the other equally important meaning of *kosmos*, its implication of a universe, as when both the Greeks and ourselves speak of "the new cosmology," or of "the cosmos as an infinite universe," and so on.[66] This is the meaning that has survived, which suggests what appears to be valid on philological grounds, that the sense of universal large-scale order is the primary one. That elements of such an order must partake of its overall systematic nature is apparent from another meaning determined by lexicographers, namely, *law*, a meaning thus determined because the word *kosmos* was in special instances used for *a magistrate*, the lawgiver, the one who lays down the universal system under which the elements of society are ordered, under which all citizens find their places.[67] In this case, as in the commoner meaning, *ornament*, the part implies the whole and the whole the part, and neither part nor whole can do without

[65] A password may become the magical equivalent of the visual ikon. Cf. Ogden and Richards, *The Meaning of Meaning* (8th ed., New York, 1959), 27, 28.

[66] For a brief account of the philosophical and scientific background for cosmology, see Cassirer, *An Essay on Man*, 67 ff.; also, R. G. Collingwood, *The Idea of Nature*; Kroner, *Speculation*, "The Rise of Cosmology," 73–87; A. D. Ritchie, *Studies in the History and Methods of the Sciences* (Edinburgh, 1958), ch. x, "Cosmologies." For a recent modern scientific account of work being done in cosmology, see D. W. Sciama, *The Unity of the Universe* (New York, 1961); Fred Hoyle, *Astronomy* (New York, 1962). The field is currently enjoying a great surge of interest and activity. For the medieval background the most important work is perhaps Roques, *L'Univers Dionysien*. Notice that, since one synonym of *kosmos* is *taxis*, the major work of Ptolemy (100–170 A.D.) is entitled *Syntaxis;* the Ptolemaic system has the extremely important effect, for allegory, of establishing a system of *enclosures,* bands, rings, bracelets, wheels, or whatever one wishes to call the "spheres."

[67] See Frankfort, *Before Philosophy*, 137 ff., "The Cosmos as a State."

the other. Microcosmos and macrocosmos are complementary to each other.[68] This looks very like a synecdochic relationship, pure and simple—a matter of solely cognitive thought—but that it involves special emotive tensions will soon appear. Kosmos implies these tensions sometimes rather indirectly, sometimes quite openly, but in either case kosmos remains the most useful term for naming the elements of any symbolism, such as allegory, that establishes a hierarchy of more and less powerful agents and images.

Allegories are based on parallels between two levels of being that correspond to each other, the one supposed by the reader, the other literally presented in the fable. This is well known. A typical modern study of systems of correspondence would be E. M. W. Tillyard's handbook, *The Elizabethan World Picture*. This book might have been titled, *The Elizabethan Cosmos;* the sense of cosmos would here be double, as it should be, for in fact Tillyard deals with the elements of Elizabethan allegorical poetry and in general with Eliza-

---

[68] Plutarch, "On the Cessation of Oracles," in *Moralia*, tr. C. W. King (London, 1903), 74, discusses the prophetic practices of those who "pretend small things to be the signs of great ones," from which one understands something of the magical significance of the microcosmic-macrocosmic relationship. It is surprising to find these beliefs recurring in the mid-nineteenth century, in George MacDonald's *Phantastes* (1858), ed. Greville MacDonald (Everyman ed., 1916), ch. xii: "They who believe in the influences of the stars over the fates of men, are, in feeling at least, nearer the truth than they who regard the heavenly bodies as related to them merely by a common obedience to an external law. All that man sees has to do with man. Worlds cannot be without an intermundane relationship. The community of the centre of all creation suggests an interradiating connection and dependence of the parts. . . . No shining belt or gleaming moon, no red and green glory in a self-encircling twin-star, but has a relation with the hidden things of a man's soul, and, it may be, with the secret history of his body as well. They are portions of the living house wherein he abides." One thinks of the medieval theologian, Nicholas of Cusa, who said that "God is an intelligible sphere, whose center is everywhere and whose circumference is nowhere"; see Jorge Luis Borges, "The Fearful Sphere of Pascal," *Noonday 3* (New York, 1960). On the early development of systematic notions of the part/whole relationship in cosmology, see S. Samburskly, *Physics of the Stoics* (London, 1959), *passim*, but especially ch. iv, "The Whole and Its Parts"; Friedrich Solmsen, *Aristotle's System of the Physical World* (Ithaca, 1960).

bethan poetry to the extent that it is allegorical, at the same time
setting forth, typically by reference to lines like those of Shakespeare's Ulysses when he speaks of the Great Chain, the cosmic
hierarchy which is manipulated by poets to make parallel lines of
symbolism.[69] The ladder of the Great Chain can be treated horizontally, as Tillyard shows, and we then have the matrix for allegory,
since it follows that if there are ranks for all things there are also
specific things representative of each rank and thus a certain narrow
choice in the symbolization of each rank. Thus, for example, the play
Coriolanus is full of animal imagery because that imagery provides
a "level" corresponding to what is the main symbolic "level" of the
play, the fable of the body politic, told by Menenius Agrippa. But
that imagery in turn is based on two more levels, the levels implied
by the microcosmic and the macrocosmic "body." [70] The human

[69] On the roots of the idea of the Golden Chain, see Ludwig Edelstein, "The
Golden Chain of Homer," in *Studies in Intellectual History* (Baltimore, 1953),
48–67. Tylor, *Origins of Culture*, I, 117, and Mircea Eliade, *Images et symboles*
(Paris, 1952), "Le Dieu Lieur," suggest that, while the chain is a vestige of an
umbilicus which is both worshipped and resented, other concepts of bondage
also enter this governing image of hierarchical order. The classic text in English is Lovejoy, *The Great Chain of Being: A Study of the History of an Idea*
(Cambridge, Mass., 1953). Lovejoy's work is particularly important for the
study of allegory because it emphasizes the effect of "otherworldliness," a
variety of Puritan *ascesis*. See, finally, Leo Spitzer, *Classical and Christian
Ideas of World Harmony* (New York, 1944–1945).

[70] There is a tendency for the ornamental image of clothing external to the
body to merge with the body itself, and we find in fact an extensive use of the
body-image in allegorical and mythopoeic poetry. A perfect instance: the
kosmoi of clothing and jewelry (ring and bracelet and crown) in *Cymbeline*.
Perhaps the most extensive critical work on English poetry, centering on this
figure, is John F. Danby's *Poets on Fortune's Hill: Studies in Sidney, Shakespeare, Beaumont and Fletcher* (London, 1952), where the study of hierarchic
thought in the Renaissance leads directly to a study of the body-image. See,
e.g., Danby, 42, 50, 63, 85, 131 (concerning the image of the body as cosmos in
Antony and Cleopatra). See the brief entry in Curtius, *European Literature*,
136–138; Curtius observes: "The field is immense and unexplored. An entire
volume could be filled with examples from patristic literature alone." Note,
besides this entry on "corporal metaphors," the previous section on "alimentary
metaphors." I am indebted to Mr. Joseph Pequigney for the reminder that

organism becomes the system of hierarchy, with the head (reason and will) at the top, and other members of the body at lower levels, until we get to the "great toe of the assembly," a spokesman for the citizens. There can be as many such corresponding levels as there are orders within nature and within the spirit world.[71] A truly scientific

there is just such a metaphor in *Paradise Lost*, V, 414–431; Milton develops the figure into a kind of cosmic digestive system, analogous to the "fable of the belly" in Plutarch and Shakespeare. On Platonic use of the body-image, see Marignac, *Imagination et dialectique*, 71–98. During the middle ages this image provides the standard notion of the organization constituting the state. See Otto Gierke, *Political Theories of the Middle Age*, tr. F. W. Maitland (reprinted Boston, 1959), 24: "Like Mankind as a whole, so, not only the Universal Church and the Universal Empire, but also every Particular Church and every Particular State, and indeed every permanent human group is compared to a natural body (*corpus naturale et organicum*). It is thought of and spoken of as a Mystical Body. Contrasting it with a Body Natural, Engelbert of Volkersdorf (1250–1311) already uses the term 'Body Moral and Politic.'" As Gierke points out, it was possible to deduce various consequences about internal organization from this overall metaphor. For example, there is a kind of political health (wholeness) that results when "every part is perfectly fulfilling its own proper functions" (26). The standard modern treatment is Ernst Kantorowicz, *The King's Two Bodies* (Princeton, 1957).

The most interesting developments in this field are, however, not rhetorical, but psychoanalytic, where work has in fact been done to remedy the lack of knowledge observed by Curtius. Not only does Otto Rank deal with the mental significance of the body-image in his *Art and Artist: Creative Urge and Personality Development* (New York, 1932)—this still remains the classic work in the psychoanalysis of art, far more important, for example, than the work of Ernst Kris—but, from the purely clinical side, recent research has been collected and studied by Seymour Fisher and S. E. Cleveland in *Body Image and Personality* (New York, 1958). Much of what is found in the study of poetry, for example the idea of the "untorn garment," can be now given some fairly systematic interpretation in terms of the psychology of the body-image. Works like *The Song of Songs*, *Polyolbion*, and *The Seasons*, where nature, civil order, and human body are analogous, could presumably be reinterpreted in the light of psychoanalytic findings.

[71] The body can become a building, a fortress, "the castle of the body," or it can become a natural burgeoning, as in the analogy between body and garden; after the invention of automatic machinery other daemonic analogies become available. Any armoring of the body makes it into a kind of fortress, hard, rigid, and impregnable. The elaborate heraldic armor of the Renaissance, so-called "historical" armor, then decorates the human fortress with the signs of its

view of the universe would attempt to reduce the number of corresponding levels to zero, though in practice we find that physics, chemistry, and astronomy do use these metaphoric constructs as ways of guessing what might be answers to empirical questions.[72] At an early stage of any science we can expect allegory; conversely it could be shown that allegories are often the simulacra of scientific theory, the main difference being that our moral and mystical allegories are not subjected to empirical tests. Thus it is not surprising to find that the image of the body as a universal order, which we find in Shakespeare's *Coriolanus*, is an image that dominates early Greek scientific cosmology.[73]

In poetry also Greek literature provides perfect examples of the allegorical use of kosmos, in the clearest possible way. Homer's description of the shield of Achilles lays down the pattern for all later uses of the dress, the costuming, the armoring,[74] of the human body

---

strength. See, for example, the quite fair parody of these devices in Thomas Nashe, *The Unfortunate Traveller*, in *Works*, ed. R. B. McKerrow (Oxford, 1958), II, 271–278—the description of Surrey's tournament.

[72] On the area of "physical" exegesis see Pépin, *Mythe et allégorie*, 86: "It is more often a question of teaching in the area of physics, and Proclus, defining allegorical interpretation, declares that 'here physical phenomena are made the ultimate objects of hidden meanings in myths.'"

[73] See Collingwood, *The Idea of Nature*, 3–4. In the very detailed etymology of the term "*kosmos*," Boisacq notes a connection of the sense, "order; usage; beautiful conformation," with the Latin *corpus*, and thence with Indo-European roots in terms for "body; matrix." See Emile Boisacq, *Dictionnaire etymologique de la langue grècque* (Paris and Heidelberg, 1938), 500–501; also A. Juret, *Dictionnaire etymologique grec et latin* (Mâcon, 1942), 77. Maurice Charney, *Shakespeare's Roman Plays: The Function of Imagery in the Drama* (Cambridge, Mass., 1961) shows that *Coriolanus* employs an imagery of "isolation," which in turn is dependent on the notion of a broken cosmic whole, whether of state, city, family or person.

[74] Pépin (*Mythe et allégorie*, 153–154) discusses the interpretation of such imagery, in the hands of the Stoic Crates. The particular armor is that of Agamemnon (Book XI). In a poet like Spenser the armor of body has the further value imparted to it by the Pauline injunction to "put on the whole armor of God," but it still has, especially with major characters like Arthur and Redcrosse, a cosmic reference. The imagery of sewing and embroidery is probably akin to the imagery of armoring. Cf. Marignac, *Imagination et dialectique*, 99–102.

as an allegorical symbolism for a larger system of ideas and things. Throughout the *Iliad* the poet is careful to describe the adornment of both soldiers and citizens, whence we derive a sense of the order of battle and the order of a peaceful existence. Homer's ornamental, structuring use of simile—epic simile has always been considered an ornamental device par excellence—gives the reader a double point of view, by which the poem communicates an idea of two antithetical worlds, one at peace, the other at war. Simile and *kosmos* are continually in use for these "cosmic" purposes, and if the *Iliad* is predominantly a mimetic nonallegorical poem it *is* allegorical at precisely those moments of ornamental emphasis. Similarly in the *Odyssey*, Aristotle (*Poetics*, 1460a) finds the *locus classicus* of ornament when the hero lands beside the Cave of the Nymphs, on his return to his homeland, a passage which, if not so apt for allegorical reading as the story of Circe's Isle, is later the object of intense exegetical treatment in the hands of the Neoplatonist Porphyry.[75] Such a passage stands out with sharper focus for the very reason that ornamental simile does not occur often in the *Odyssey*.[76]

The emotive nature of ornament. While on the one hand the kosmos adorns and marks specific ranks, it has on the other hand more than a "merely" decorative or "merely" hierarchical function.[77] Nothing could be more likely to arouse intense emotional response

[75] Porphyrius, *Commentary on Odyssey XIII*, tr. Thomas Taylor (London, 1823). On Neoplatonist allegorizing, see André Chastel, *Marsile Ficin et l'Art* (Paris, 1954), 136–162. Chastel, like Edgar Wind, *Pagan Mysteries in the Renaissance*, emphasizes the role of magic in the Neoplatonic interpretation of image and experience.

[76] Virgil, more than Homer, was typically the "cosmic" poet. See Curtius, *European Literature*, 444. Since ornament is timeless, "something taken away from time," it is in that sense a Platonic Idea and partakes of the Divine. Curtius finds in Von Hofmannsthal the search of this "timeless European mythology."

[77] For a typical use of ornament as "mere ornament" (i.e., something superadded, extraneous, or the like) see Middleton Murry, *The Problem of Style* (London, 1960), 9–11. Tuve, *Elizabethan and Metaphysical Imagery*, 112–113, has attacked this view as applied to the Elizabethan use of the word "ornament." She gives Yeats's poem *Three Movements* as an example of ornamented style, in which it is quite clear there is nothing extraneous to the one central figure.

than the status symbol, since the person observing the wearer of
the kosmos may or may not belong to the same rank as the wearer,
in which case there will be feelings of solidarity, or a desire to
emulate, or a feeling of envy, any of which may be aroused by the
sight of the ornament. "The verb *kosmein* is explained as a process of
likening the object you wish to praise (and have accepted) to a
better object with a fine name." [78] Notice that there is nothing neutral
about the process: to adorn, in the rhetorical sense of *kosmein*,
means to elevate a lower rank to a higher one.[79] Dress and costume

[78] Lane Cooper, "The Verbal 'Ornament,'" 106. Cooper provides numerous
instances of ornamental diction which may appear to us merely hackneyed, but
which probably is hackneyed because it so powerfully suggests status, and is
overused for that reason.

[79] In the Early and Medieval Church the emotive character of ornamentation
led to serious disputes. Tertullian, "On Idolatry," 100: "Is it to honour a god,
you ask, that the lamps are put before doors and the laurels on posts? No indeed, they are not there to honour a god, but a man, who is honoured as a
god by such attentions. Or so it appears on the surface. What happens in secret
reaches the demons." E. G. Holt, *A Documentary History of Art* (Anchor
ed., New York, 1957), I, 19 ff., gives the materials of this dispute. St. Bernard
argues against church ornament: "Hence the church is adorned with gemmed
crowns of light—nay, with lustres like cart-wheels, girt all round with lamps,
but no less brilliant with the precious stones that stud them. Moreover we see
candelabra standing like trees of massive bronze, fashioned with marvellous
subtlety of art, and glistening no less brightly with gems than with the lights
they carry. What, think you, is the purpose of all this? The compunction of
penitents, or the admiration of the beholders? O vanity of vanities, yet no
more vain than insane! The church is resplendent in her walls, beggarly in her
poor; she clothes her stones in gold, and leaves her sons naked" (20). Bernard
especially singles out for attack the deformed, surrealist, grotesque images of
"unclean apes, those fierce lions, those monstrous centaurs, those half-men,
those striped tigers, those fighting knights, those hunters winding their horns.
Many bodies are there seen under one head, or again, many heads to one body,
etc., etc." Countering this kind of argument, the Abbot Suger writes: "We
applied to the perfection of so sacred an ornament not only these but also a
great and expensive supply of other gems and larger pearls" (28). The lavish
ornamentation of St. Denys is rationalized in part by being given allegorical
interpretation: "And because the diversity of the materials such as gold, gems
and pearls is not easily understood by the mute perception of sight without
a description, we have seen to it that this work, which is intelligible only to
the literate, which shines with the radiance of delightful allegories, be set down

can become instruments of social climbing, by this process, and in the social sphere if one spots a social climber, an Osric, or a Pamela, one can be sure the ascent is aided by a use of *kosmoi*, whether of speech, manner, or dress.[80] Ostentation of dress may be a matter of private vanity,[81] but as a "cosmic" device it raises the wearer to an equality with the best-dressed "man of distinction"; and, on the contrary, when a person of rank affects crude or poor dress, we are aware of a deception as to status, an "ironic" attempt to undercut actual social position.

Leveling and lowering is then a primary function of kosmos, no less than its elevating function. By likening an object we wish to dispraise to a worse object with a poor name, we achieve a downward movement.[82] It is most important to see that ornament can be bad as well as good, hateful as well as desirable, that the Chain of

---

in writing. Also we have affixed verses expounding the matter so that the allegories might be more clearly understood" (29).

[80] See Dorothy Van Ghent, *The English Novel* (New York, 1953), "On *Clarissa Harlowe*," and "Clarissa and Emma as Phèdre" in *Modern Literary Criticism*, ed. Irving Howe (Boston, 1958), where it is made clear that the imagery of clothing being torn is central to the main dramatic moments of the novels. Clothing similarly plays a major role in other eighteenth-century novels, e.g., in *Pamela* and in Francis Kirkman's "The Counterfeit Lady Unveiled," in *The Counterfeit Lady Unveiled and Other Criminal Fiction of Seventeenth Century England*, ed. Spiro Peterson (New York, 1961). Fine clothes are one device of the confidence man.

Note the equally standard cosmetic devices in Jonson's *Epicoene*. "Still to be neat, still to be dress'd" is cosmetic in imagery and meaning. Throughout Elizabethan and Jacobean drama the function of ornament is always a universalizing one. One essential aspect of the "world is a stage" commonplace is the cosmetic dressing up of the actors; the painted face needs to be "read," like an enigma. Thus, in Eliot's allusions to *Hamlet* we are prepared for the line "Prepare a face to meet the faces that you meet." We are told that through the surface we read the true interior design. Similarly with the rhetoric of the court in *Cymbeline*.

[81] Cf. *The Consolation of Philosophy*, 50: "Though Nero decked himself proudly with purple of Tyre and snow-white gems, none the less that man of rage and luxury lived ever hated of all."

[82] The figure *meiosis* lowers its object, rather than making it of higher esteem. See Tuve, *Elizabethan and Metaphysical Imagery*, 197, 203.

Being leads down as well as up, which was the very situation found in our study of the allegorical agent. The term "daemonic" was reserved for devils only by a late and naïve tradition; the more liberal view gave to daemons an intermediate position and maintained precisely the present view of the kosmoi, that like them the agents can be either above or below mankind. The effect of meeting an allegorical agent is to be raised (by an angel) or lowered (by a devil), but in no case to be unaffected with respect to the rank of the daemon.[83] The same influences are exerted by allegorical imagery, in a more obvious way.

The didactic function. Allegories are classically used for didactic and moral suasion. They may, during times of political revolution, present totally new theories of ethics, or during conservative eras, old theories which have been rendered otiose by time. Much is made by some critics of the fact that allegory usually presents a traditional "given," an accepted, proverbial moral world view, and gets it across by fresh illustrations. The argument is made that the suasive power of the Given saves such an art from being "merely illustrative," or rather, saves the added-on character of the imagery from becoming a deadly cloying influence over the internal body and vigor of an unadorned fable. But this seems to me too tame a view. In fact the old saws of religion and morality need far more than mere illustration to bring them to life. They need their own proper ornaments, the signs that go with them systematically, as the vestments of the priest go with the Mass, or the insignia of his uniform go with the military dictator or the five-star general. There is no separating individual rank from hierarchical system, and there is no avoiding the emotive nature of the particular symbols.

[83] For example, Young Goodman Brown, meeting the vision of the Devil in the woods; his course is at that point influenced by magic powers. Or Giovanni Guasconti, meeting Beatrice, in "Rappaccini's Daughter"; love in a simple way is not possible, given her daemonic nature. This is not to say that characters in mimetic literature do not affect each other, but, from the hero's point of view, there is always *choice* in a mimetically rendered situation. But in allegory the hero always accepts the terms of the daemon, even if it be a good daemon.

Rhetorical incitement to desire and action. Allegory belongs ultimately in the area of epideictic rhetoric, the rhetoric of praise and ceremony,[84] since it is most often used to praise and condemn certain lines of conduct or certain philosophical positions. Even when, as with the botanical poetry of Erasmus Darwin, it seeks to organize nature into a scientific hierarchic system, it still is praising the higher orders and dispraising the lower orders.[85] There is no choice about our feelings in these matters. We are, I think, unable to rank items without admitting implicit preferences. The rhetorician, on his side, must calculate the emotive effect of a language of kosmos when he seeks to sway a particular kind of reader. Thus,

we must take into account the nature of our particular audience when making a speech of praise; for, as Socrates used to say, it is not difficult to praise the Athenians to an Athenian audience. If the audience esteems a given quality, we must say that our hero has that quality, no matter whether we are addressing Scythians or philosophers. Everything, in fact, that is esteemed we are to represent as noble. After all, people regard the two things as much the same.[86]

Aristotle realistically points out, in effect, that regardless of their true merits men think well of themselves, and a shrewd encomiast will pretend a nobility, even when it is not there, in order to praise his client. The technique assumes first of all a widely accepted idea

[84] W. P. Ker, *Epic and Romance: Essays on Medieval Literature* (London, 1896; reprinted New York, 1957), 328 ff., has an account of the ceremonial tendency in medieval romance, which he connects with characteristic "descriptions of riches and splendours." In the case of monuments such a ceremonial aim is obvious enough: see, on this point, Paul Goodman's article, "Notes on a Remark of Seami," in *Kenyon Review*, XX (1958), 547–554; also C. S. Lewis, *A Preface to Paradise Lost* (London, 1960), ch. viii, 52–61, "Defence of This Style."

[85] Darwin has quite technical notes and commentary in *The Temple of Nature, or, The Origin of Society* (London, 1803), including additional essays on "spontaneous vitality of microscopic animals," "the faculties of the sensorium," "volcanic fires," "the mosquito," "reproduction," "hereditary diseases," "chemical theory of electricity and magnetism."

[86] Aristotle, *The Rhetoric* (*Works*, XI), ed. W. D. Ross, tr. W. R. Roberts (Oxford, 1924), 1376b.

of what *is* noble; it requires the symbolic use of stock attributes—imputed virtues—that are to account for the client's actions, which amounts to a sort of "character witnessing." "Praise is the expression in words of the eminence of a man's good qualities, and therefore we must display his actions as the product of such qualities." [87] To achieve this effect the orator brings out a stock of kosmoi. It is not enough to say what a man did; one has to say that he did it out of the highest motives, and certain typifying images need to be associated with these motives.

Now praise for real or imputed virtue has the effect of arousing people to action. "To praise a man is in one respect akin to urging a course of action. . . . Whenever you want to praise anyone, think what you would urge people to do; and when you want to urge the doing of anything, think what you would praise a man for having done." [88] A clear instance of this procedure occurs in Shakespeare's *Richard II*, Act II, scene 1, where old John of Gaunt, waiting for Richard to enter, says that he wishes to breathe his last "In wholesome counsel to his unstaid youth." Gaunt believes that "the tongues of dying men/ Enforce attention like deep harmony." His celebrated speech may be quoted here, because it is just such an attempt to "enforce attention," and it works by the rhetorical use of ornament —*kosmos* in the original sense—to hold up an ideal for a good king or citizen. The lines are often frankly proverbial, suggesting the wisdom of an older man. Ironically, the speech is not heard by the young king, who enters immediately after its conclusion; ironically also the speech runs from the height of the cosmic ladder to its bottom, from praise to dispraise.

> Methinks I am a prophet new inspired [Gaunt says]
> And thus expiring do foretell of him:
> His rash fierce blaze of riot cannot last,

[87] *Ibid.*

[88] *Rhetoric*, 1368a. The *Areopagitica* combines this epideictic manner with a prophetic intention, e.g., the section beginning "Next, it is a lively and cheerful presage of our happy success and victory."

For violent fires soon burn out themselves;
Small showers last long, but sudden storms are short;
He tires betimes that spurs too fast betimes;
With eager feeding food doth choke the feeder:
Light vanity, insatiate cormorant,
Consuming means, soon preys upon itself.

These platitudes are suddenly lifted by the inspired sequence of images:

This royal throne of kings, this scepter'd isle,
This earth of majesty, this seat of Mars,
This other Eden, demi-paradise;
This fortress built by Nature for herself
Against infection and the hand of war;
This happy breed of men, this little world,
This precious stone set in the silver sea,
Which serves it in the office of a wall,
Or as a moat defensive to a house,
Against the envy of less happier lands;
This blessed plot, this earth, this realm, this England,
This nurse, this teeming womb of royal kings,
Fear'd by their breed and famous by their birth,
Renowned for their deeds as far from home,
For Christian service and true chivalry,
As is the sepulcher in stubborn Jewry
Of the world's ransom, blessed Mary's Son;
This land of such dear souls, this dear, dear land,
Dear for her reputation through the world,
Is now leased out, I die pronouncing it,
Like to a tenement or pelting farm:
England, bound in with the triumphant sea,
Whose rocky shore beats back the envious siege
Of watery Neptune, is now bound in with shame,
With inky blots and rotten parchment bonds:
That England, that was wont to conquer others,
Hath made a shameful conquest of itself.

> Ah, would the scandal vanish with my life,
> How happy then were my ensuing death!

Each one of the praising anaphoras contains a conceptual, prophetic image of England's destiny, and as such the anaphoric listing is the framework of an undeveloped allegory. The symmetrical forms, as well as the cosmic content of the speech, are means by which it seeks to "enforce attention."

Here the moral and didactic suasion of allegory is couched in the language of praise and dispraise. Even so, Shakespeare makes the spectator somewhat ironical toward Gaunt. We can almost sympathize with the King's anger at being admonished by Gaunt, for when Richard does finally arrive, Gaunt does not spare his feelings. But there is a subtler rhetorical control being exerted here. We might question whether Shakespeare did not include the obviously sententious saws of Gaunt's first lines in the speech I have quoted for the sole purpose of undercutting any irony we might turn against the sudden afflatus of the praise. Such praise is vulnerable enough. It carries a little too much purpose, a little too intense an involvement in the noble destiny.

The commonest attack upon allegory is that it has the very effect which Aristotle's "praise" implies, namely "urging a course of action." Allegory is said to have too much "message," to lack the natural disinterest of art, to lack its organic autonomy.[89] Admittedly,

[89] Because of the change, over time, of ethical standards, the poet needs to consider the generality of *his* decorum, if not that of any given character he might portray. Thus Shelley says, in his *Defence of Poetry* (Oxford, 1932), 132–133: "A poet therefore would do ill to embody his own conceptions of right and wrong, which are usually those of his place and time, in his poetical creations, which participate in neither. By this assumption of the inferior office of interpreting the effect, in which perhaps after all he might acquit himself but imperfectly, he would resign a glory in a participation in the cause. There was little danger that Homer, or any of the eternal poets, should have so far misunderstood themselves as to have abdicated this throne of their widest dominion. Those in whom the poetic faculty, though great, is less intense, as Euripides, Lucan, Tasso, Spenser, have affected a moral aim, and the effect of their poetry is diminished in exact proportion to the degree in

the mode depends on kosmoi which in turn depend upon systems of status that are too strict to allow a free play of artistic imagination. When allegories force on their readers an ethical command whose artistic necessity is doubtful, they are presenting an ideal image of "what you would praise a man for having done." This image of the praiseworthy is extraneous to the high mimetic function which seems —especially if one is schooled by the *Poetics*—to be the central contribution of Western art.[90]

"Mere" ornament no longer exists, in this view. Rather ornament takes on the sense it clearly had in the middle ages and earlier. On the theoretical side a work like the *Celestial Hierarchy* of Pseudo-Dionysius the Areopagite,[91] forming the basis for Dante's imagery

---

which they compel us to advert to this purpose." On Spenser's diction and didactic purpose, see Ben Jonson's *Discoveries*, the section entitled "Praecipiendi modi."

Empson's *Some Versions of Pastoral* (New York, 1960), ch. v, "Bentley and Milton," is a study of ornament in the Aristotelian double sense. See especially 170–183, where Empson shows Bentley reacting to the "cosmic" implications of particular ornamental passages of *Paradise Lost*, and then altering them to remove these implications.

The fact that *any* passage of any work can be so treated need not denature the concept of "ornament," since some passages are clearly written with their cosmic implications high in the scale of intentional weight. If one were to take Richards' "communication tunnel" described in *Speculative Instruments*, ch. i, and apply it to the use of ornament, one would conclude that ornament puts most of its semantic and tonal weight on "influencing."

[90] Or, perhaps, acts which it is relevant neither to praise nor dispraise, acts which are not subject to the claims of "poetic justice," whether they be heroism or villainy.

[91] Pseudo-Dionysius the Areopagite, *De coelesti hierarchia*, in Migne, *Patrologia graeca*, III. A French translation exists by Maurice de Gandillac, *Oeuvres complètes du Pseudo-Denys, L'Aréopagite* (Paris, 1943); English translation, *On the Divine Names and Mystical Theology*, tr. C. E. Rolt (New York, 1940). Mazzeo, *Medieval Cultural Tradition*, 214, summarizes the cosmology of Pseudo-Dionysius as follows: "Dionysius expresses the concept of order primarily through the use of three terms: *taxis* or 'military' order; *kosmos*, the notion of the universe as good order, a term with aesthetic overtones; and *metron*, the concept of measure also applied to God as the measuring principle. These terms along with 'harmony' refer both to the idea of order and

as well as his symbolic world view, and on the practical side the poem of Dante contains the whole range of human achievement within the rhetoric of praise and dispraise.[92] But there are innumerable cases and kinds of ornamental art which need to be analyzed for their double meaning, their "cosmic" meaning:[93] Anglo-Saxon oral poetry, its imagery all "curiously inwrought";[94] the ornaments of

to a particular order." Roques, *L'Univers Dionysien*, gives the best general treatment of the subject.

Even in the middle ages there may be a cultivation of ornament for its own sake. But Edgar de Bruyne doubts this: "It is undeniable that the Middle Ages were given to the beauty of what we call 'glitter and gold,' but it would be absolutely wrong to say that they were limited to this primitive esthetic; it is necessary, as we shall do, to integrate this esthetic of brilliant beauty in a much more vast ensemble.

"First of all, even with the decorative arts art is admired chiefly for the themes which it realizes. A beautiful work of art is a subject which interests the spirit, represented with a perfect technical skill. The more universal the subject, the finer the work, so long as it be executed with the virtuosity of technique. This sense of the universal appears equally in the minor arts as well as in churches, in sermons, in poems" (*Etudes d'esthétique médiévale* [Bruges, 1946], II, 70—my translation).

[92] Auerbach, in *Mimesis*, the chapters on "Farinata and Cavalcanti" and "Frate Alberto," is concerned with the establishment of an intermediate style, neither high (sublime) nor low (naturalistic), under the democratizing influence of Christianity. A *Commedia* presumably requires such a style. A complaint, such as Alanus' *Complaint of Nature*, does not need it, since such a poem is couched consistently in the language of dispraise, and is indeed "naturalistic." See M. D. Chenu, *La Théologie au douzième siècle* (Paris, 1957). Also, Tuve, *Elizabethan and Metaphysical Imagery*, 225, on the Christian mixing of high and low styles. At this point decorum and ornament are on the level of a complete world view.

[93] The most available examples would be in the area of "popular art"—the art that adorns everyday, useful objects. For many illustrations of the frequently daemonic, consistently ornamental figuration of popular art, see Margaret Lambert and Enid Marx, *English Popular Art* (London, 1951). The subject is vast: ornament has an unlimited use in the visual arts. On medieval art, see Emile Mâle, *The Gothic Image* (reprinted New York, 1958), ch. i; Joan Evans, *Cluniac Art of the Romanesque Period*—these works, with others by Evans noted in the Bibliography, give some idea of the ornamental tradition.

[94] The effect is strongest when the Anglo-Saxon poetry involves either real

baroque poetry, as well as of baroque music and architecture; [95] the rococo façades of churches; the mazy twirls and hidden dells of picturesque art and landscape gardening; [96] the dress of duplicitous characters in eighteenth-century crime literature; [97] the dress of Carlyle's *Sartor Resartus;* [98] the stock devices and emblems of mod-

---

or spiritual wealth; e.g., *The Phoenix,* tr. C. W. Kennedy, *Early English Christian Poetry* (London, 1952), 238.

> Fair-breasted that fowl and comely of hue
> With varied colours; the head behind
> Is emerald burnished and blended with scarlet.
> The tail plumes are coloured some crimson, some brown,
> And cunningly speckled with shining spots.
> White of hue are the backs of the wings,
> The neck all green beneath and above.
> The strong neb gleams like glass or gem;
> Without and within the beak is fair.
> The eye is stark, most like to stone
> Or shining jewel skilfully wrought
> In a golden setting by cunning smiths.

The passage continues in this vein, and concludes with the iconographic significance of the rich plumage:

> Fair and goodly and marked with glory.
> Eternal the God who grants him that grace.

[95] Cf. Wallerstein, *Richard Crashaw,* 109, on the latent animism of Crashaw's "baroque" style; it is as if this style, and its equivalents in music and architecture, were recreating the vegetable world, a world of exuberant leafage. Cherubs appear to sprout; ornaments appear to be engrafted; with rococo this vegetable growth becomes a sort of jungle, as in the baroque churches of Central and South America.

[96] See below, the discussion of picturesque as daemonic ornament, Chapter 5.

[97] I have already referred to Kirkman's "The Counterfeit Lady Unveiled"; perhaps clothes are important in all fiction; it is certain, however, that here they play a dramatic role which has to do with status, and deception as to status. Notions of courtesy stress the value of sartorial emblems: see Castiglione, *The Book of the Courtier,* II, 121–123.

[98] *Sartor Resartus* may in fact be read as a treatise on *kosmos,* since it takes clothes for the basis of a symbolic vocabulary, and clothes in turn represent the cosmic totality of human body and of all systems analogous to the body. The Duke of Windsor's autobiography, *Windsor Revisited* (Cambridge, Mass.,

ern political fictions, such as the Russian propagandist works of the post-Revolutionary period [99]—all these and innumerable other instances of ornament could be shown to imply, within an emotively charged system of beliefs, a hierarchical system.

In this way the common, vague notion of rhetorical ornament comes to include all categorizing figures of speech [100]—but is that a useful generalization? Only if it is understood that allegorical imagery puts pressure on the reader to accept given hierarchies. The emotive pressure of the status symbol is more important than the fact that it can be referred to a categorical system.

Generalization of the term. The history of rhetoric shows a gradual generalization of the term *ornament*, until ornament includes all the figures of speech and all tropes, as, for example, in Puttenham, in the third book of *The Arte of English Poesie*.[101] Gradually decorum (*exornatio*) has come to include any device of style.[102] Can one

---

1960), totally preoccupied with clothes as symbol of status, illustrates the original cosmetic devices in modern dress.

[99] See Stravinsky's *Poetics of Music* (New York, 1956), ch. v, on the allegorization of Soviet music. The "literary" readings of music are felt by the "pure musician" to be a superadded encrustation of a "pure" original.

[100] In this generalized form, ornament is "properly" applied to any object or person or work, in order that it be adjusted to a prevailing norm. Ornament becomes the overall aim of the "courtesy book."

[101] George Puttenham, *The Arte of English Poesie* (1589 [Cambridge, 1936]).

[102] See Tuve, *Elizabethan and Metaphysical Imagery*, 141–142, on *expolitio*, one of the systems of *exornatio*. Also *ibid.*, 247: "Neither a modern nor a seventeenth-century image is to be judged indecorous by virtue of its being unconventional. I hope that I have shown that imagery can be entirely in line with orthodox pronouncements on decorum even though it be unconventional, homely, rough, difficult to understand. It can be decorous though it be used to abase rather than amplify a matter, though it be ironic, an understatement, vitriolic in its satirical force. It can be decorous when it surprisingly juxtaposes the grand and the colloquial, and whether it takes the shape of elaborate hyperbole, of brief witty analogy, or of dark and profound symbol. It has to meet but one criterion—that it suit with the true 'height' of the cause which the poet has in hand. This is precisely where the modern poet cannot entirely follow his predecessors. He can no longer range subjects in an order of elevation or importance." See also *ibid.*, 143, 234.

therefore isolate a particular device called *kosmos?* I would argue, yes, if one is willing to admit the gradual concurrent emergence of *prose* stylistics, or perhaps of what we could call scientifically neutral, unadorned prose, in opposition to the poetic techniques which are employed whenever one wants to sway an audience—sway them in any direction whatever. For poetry, by the time of the Renaissance, is the chief means of moral suasion available to mankind—and there is for this reason a *poetics* of the pulpit, where sermons were delivered in prose, and by the time of the Renaissance poetry has, in the most general way, accepted a cosmic function.[103] Poetry is the expression of man's "erected wit" in the sense that by poetry man can help his fellow to rise in the ranks of Christian society and in the company of spiritual beings. Poetry is more than mere verse, as distinguished from prose. It is also to be distinguished from the prosaic. We need further to recall that the rhetoricians of Elizabeth's day wrote for a courtly, or a court-aspiring audience, and their rhetoric sets its sights on the Court. The Court becomes the microcosmos for a celestial hierarchy, no less because England is a Protestant kingdom. It is possible to define "propriety" clearly enough, then, no matter how general a term it becomes, because we keep clearly in mind that propriety is always a matter of hierarchy. Propriety is not just what someone wants you to do; it is not even what the most powerful people want you to do, though that element of power enters in the background of all allegories. It is what they want you to do, *as a result of their representing the established order.* The authorities point out to us what our "place" is, or point out what should be our proper "calling" in life.

Cosmogonic ornamentation. Christianity provides a sanction for a "cosmic" poetry. The "calling of the tune"[104] was accepted by all

---

[103] See W. R. Mueller, *John Donne, Preacher* (Princeton, 1962); also Joan Webber's analysis of Donne's sermons, *Contrary Music* (Madison, 1962).

[104] The phrase gives the title to one of the longer articles in *The Philosophy of Literary Form.* The subject is a major one for Burke, as witness the emphasis in Parts II and III of *A Rhetoric of Motives.*

members of medieval society and most members of Renaissance society, for the good reason that Christian cosmogony, as well as cosmology, showed the rightness of their acquiescence. It is apparent that one can create a symbolic world, as well as interpret one into nature. Critics have often been disturbed that there are two seemingly contrary allegorical procedures, the interpretive and the creative, which would be exemplified on the one hand by Biblical exegesis and on the other by works like *The Divine Comedy* and *The Faerie Queene*. Obviously when a poet sets out to write allegory, like Dante or Spenser, he forces the reader into an extreme consciousness of differences in status. As far as imagery is concerned then, the art of allegory will be the manipulation of a texture of "ornaments" so as to engage the reader in an interpretive activity.

Christianity, however, makes this technique much easier than would be the case in a purely mechanistic universe, because Christianity sees the creation of the world as an establishment of a universal symbolic vocabulary.[105]

[105] "The whole world is a symbol" (Emile Mâle, *The Gothic Image*, 31). In the seventeenth century, when the meaning of Egyptian hieroglyphics became a much-bruited problem, there was a general adherence to this view that Nature constituted a universal vocabulary of symbols. Cf. Sir Thomas Browne, *Religio Medici*, 46; man's symbolizing skills allow him to live in "divided and distinguished worlds," which he bridges by seeing or interpreting their symbolic connections. See also Browne on the hieroglyphical painting of the Egyptians, in *Pseudodoxia Epidemica, Works* (London, 1928–1931), ed. G. Keynes, III, 137–138. Liselotte Dieckmann has shown how Sir Thomas Browne was in a way destroying the reality of old accepted fantasies. "No one will take the she-bear as a symbol of a 'man deformed, but later taking on normal shape' (Horapollo, II, 83) if the story of the she-bear is not true." That would certainly be so if art (and also the *Pseudodoxia*) were truly a science. But they are not. Fantasies are not so easily destroyed, and Browne creates as many new fantasies as he kills old ones. See Dieckmann, "Renaissance Hieroglyphics," *Comparative Literature*, IX (1957), no. 4, 308–321.

Professor Praz has found in this hieroglyphic world view, which at the same time Browne both fostered and criticized, a basis for the *concetti* of the baroque poets. "Seventeenth-century men saw instances of *argutezza* in every aspect of the universe. All the phenomena of the surrounding world, all the categories of learning, supplied them with suggestions for this mental idiosyn-

There was, first of all, *"in principio"* the first creation—*prima creatio* of the primordial matter; there was next, under the influence of the Divine Ideas, the information of this matter; which embellished the visible world—*"expolitio, exornatio,"* finally, there came the activity of the world, moving under the control of the universal soul, towards its end. To each of these steps there corresponds in fact one of the stages of "nature" which offers itself to the researches, the explications, the contemplations of the scholar.[106]

"Nature" here meant the whole visible cosmos, open to the poet's eye; it was an organized world, a world forever deprived of disorder. God's Providence banished chaos.

Before the ornamentation of the universe, God had created matter, this unformed chaos, which possessed in itself a rudiment of beauty but was still full of ugliness to the extent that it did not yet present discernible forms . . . Moses and Chalcidius agree in calling the stars the ornament of heaven and animals the ornament of earth: the *ornatus* of the world, that is, primary matter differentiated according to weight and number, circumscribed within certain contours, taking on shape and number, presenting determinate, beautiful forms.[107]

With the "imprint of divine ideas upon matter" [108] (a notion nowhere more prominent than in the work of the greatest allegorist of

---

crasy of theirs" (*The Flaming Heart*, 206). Cf. Lovejoy, "Nature as an Aesthetic Norm," in *Essays in the History of Ideas*, under Group C: "'Nature' in general, i.e., the cosmical order as a whole, or a half-personified power (*natura naturans*) manifested therein, as exemplar, of which the attributes or modes of working should characterize also human art." On "The Poem as Hieroglyph," see J. H. Summers, *George Herbert: His Religion and Art* (Cambridge, Mass., 1954), ch. vi.

[106] De Bruyne, *Etudes d'esthétique médiévale*, II, 257 (my translation).

[107] *Ibid.*, II, 257. The first banishment of chaos is described in the Book of Genesis, on which see the exegetical reading of Philo, in *Works*, tr. and ed. F. H. Colson and G. H. Whitaker (Loeb Classics ed., London, 1929), I. St. Basil speaks of the initial "ornament of the world" (*kosmou kosmon*), on which see Roques, *L'Univers dionysien*, 53.

[108] According to De Bruyne, William of Conches "is in agreement with all the other masters of Chartres in explaining the stage of the *exornatio* as the

imprint of divine ideas upon matter, by the intermediary of those forms which are their created images. Two ideas need to be kept in mind here, important as well for esthetics as for metaphysics. First, the 'ornamentation,' 'the differentiation' of Chaos or the agglomeration of matter into determinate shapes is made through a mixture of elements presided over by Harmony. (This gives rise to the *esthétique musicale* of Bernard Sylvestris and Alanus.) . . . The second more profound point: each 'form' enables the created being to be 'equal to itself,' stable, constant, a norm, the perfection of its own species to the extent that one can be equal to this form" (*Etudes*, II, 273).

For Christian theology the most important moment of the original *exornatio* is the endowing of material man with his soul. This is described allegorically in Hugh of St. Victor's *Soliloquy on the Earnest Money of the Soul*, tr. Kevin Herbert (Milwaukee, 1956), 24–25: "How exalted and glorious you have been made, my Soul! What does such attire signify but that He who clothed you has been preparing you as his spouse for his bridal chamber? He knew for what sweet task you were destined and what raiment was needed; therefore, he gave what was fitting. . . . Without He adorned you with the senses, within He enlightened you with wisdom, giving the one as an outer garment, the other as inner garb. His gifts of the senses are, as it were, precious and resplendent jewels for display, and the faculty of wisdom within is like the natural beauty of your countenance. Indeed, your attire far surpasses the beauty of any gems and your countenance is the most beautiful of all. Certainly such beauty is most befitting for one who would enter into the chamber of our Heavenly King." This cosmetic notion of the soul is ancillary to the idea that the Soul is the bride of Christ, which Hugh of St. Victor proceeds to develop at length in the following pages of the *Soliloquy*. He is mainly concerned with the danger of defiling the perfect, fitting raiment; he wants to show that the sacraments, the rite of baptism, for example, have a cosmetic function; they will return the soul to its prefallen state. "You are truly in ignorance, my Soul. You do not know how vile you have been in the past, how degraded, how ugly and filthy, unkempt, and dissipated. You were certainly loathsome and unclean. How can you therefore seek to go so quickly into that chamber of modesty and chasteness, unless by some care and zeal you first regain your former comeliness? This is the reason for the delay, this is why your Beloved has withdrawn from you and has neither embraced you nor given His sweet kisses to you. For truly the defiled ought not to touch the clean nor should a base person have sight of the beautiful. However, when you have been fittingly prepared and clothed, without embarrassment you will at last enter into and remain in the bridal chamber of your heavenly Spouse. Then your past disgrace will be no source of shame to you, for you will be free of all stain and reproach" (28). Hugh goes further with the allegory: "Let us consider next the kinds of ointments and cosmetics, the diet, and the vestments which are made ready in the regimen of the espoused. . . . In this room of preparation you will first find

the ancient world, Philo Judaeus),[109] the ornament of the world "comes forth"; there is an *ex*ornation of matter, which is primarily felt to be beautiful but which has hierarchic order for its basis. Thus the terms for beauty in this medieval scheme, *speciosum* and *formosam*, derive from the concepts of class and form.[110] To take but one

---

the font of baptism and the basin of regeneration in which you wash away the stain of past sins. Next the chrism and the oil, in the unction of which you are bathed by the Holy Spirit. Then anointed and imbued with the unction of gladness you come to the table and take there the nourishment of the body and blood of Christ. Filled and refreshed within by this you dispel the harmful emaciation of previous hungers and in a wondrous manner are rejuvenated with the recovery of your former strength and figure. Next you put on the garments of good works and by the fruit of almsgiving, with fasts and prayers, with holy vigils and other deeds of piety you become arrayed as though with finery of the most varied kinds. Finally the fragrance of the virtues comes forth and their sweet odors welling up dispel all the stench of past filth, so that somehow you seem to be wholly changed and transformed into someone else. You are become more joyful, more keen, more vigorous. The mirror that is Holy Scripture is also given to you so that you may see there your own visage and know that the arrangement of your garments does not have anything unfitting" (30–31). The whole Christian life-pattern is set forth here in cosmetic terms, even to the mirror (the *speculum*) in which the lady examines her adorned self. The metamorphosis of the soul, by which it becomes truly Christian, pure, and whole, is noticeably not only an organic-seeming change; it follows from the change of externals, or rather, externals are the allegorical imagery that stands for an inner reformation. We might speak of endocosmic and ectocosmic imagery, for the "inner garb" and the "outer garment." Cf. "fashion," meaning created form, or outer appearance.

[109] Cf. Wolfson, *Philo*, I, 120 and 295 ff., on Philonic interpretation of Genesis; also Daniélou, *Philon d'Alexandre*, 129 ff., on cosmological interpretation, and 168–172, on the cosmos in Philo's system. It is important to see the stress in Philo on the *ideal* character of the Divine Imprint: "In reality, the true Philonic allegory is that which we find in the *Allegory of the Laws* and which concerns not the cosmos and man who is in the cosmos, but the hidden mysteries of the hypercosmic world, as well as the spiritual journey of the soul which rises above the visible world and finally arrives at the world of God" (Daniélou, *Philon d'Alexandre*, 135). This is a sublime tendency, in the technical, eighteenth-century sense of the word.

[110] Thus Castiglione in *The Book of the Courtier*, IV, 337, considers all beauty under the aspect of a concept of universal order: "But to speak of the beauty we have in mind, namely, that only which is seen in the human person and especially in the face, and which prompts the ardent desire we call love, we

central example, the medieval allegory of virtue and vice prefers the beautiful form of the Tree as its embodiment, not only because of its suggestion of the light delicate leafy foliage, but even more because of the articulate exfoliation.

Thus the parable of the two trees is used during the twelfth century to the point of threadbareness, the reason being that the highly articulated structure of the growths of nature could lodge complicated systems of abstraction and their upward development could be interpreted step by step—or rather, branch by branch.[111]

will say that it is an effluence of the divine goodness, which (although it is shed, like the sun's light, upon all created things), when it finds a face well proportioned and composed of a certain radiant harmony of various colors set off by light and shadow and by measured distance and limited outline, infuses itself therein and shines forth most beautifully and adorns and illumines with grace and a wondrous splendor the object wherein it shines, like a sunbeam striking upon a beautiful vase of polished gold set with precious gems." And later: "Behold the constitution of this great fabric of the world, which was made by God for the health and conservation of every created thing." Speaking of the heavenly bodies, "These things have an influence upon one another through the coherence of an order so precisely constituted that, if they were in the least changed, they could not exist together and the world would fall into ruin; and they also have such beauty and grace that the mind of man cannot imagine anything more beautiful." Again and again Castiglione comes back to the idea that beauty is *formosam*, order and harmony above all.

[111] Adolf Katzellenbogen, *Allegories of the Virtues and Vices in Mediaeval Art* (London, 1939), 67. Quintilian, *Institutes*, VIII, iii, secs. 7–11, uses the imagery of the garden to suggest what should be the proper cultivation of an ornamental style. He prefers a garden with fruit-bearing trees in it, rather than merely decorative flowers and shrubs. The model symbolic tree is one with artificial limbs, as in the Bower of Bliss, or Cyrano de Bergerac's *States and Empires of the Sun*: "When Cyrano's traveller in inter-stellar space arrives on the surface of the sun, he finds himself lying under a remarkable tree of which the trunk is made of gold, the branches of silver, the leaves of emeralds and the fruit of rubies and other precious stones. On the top of the tree a nightingale is singing disconsolately. As he watches, two successive metamorphoses take place. First, one of the fruits, a pomegranate, of which the pulp is composed of rubies, changes spontaneously into a little man, as a result of what Cyrano calls an effervescence of seething, which he cannot for the moment distinguish clearly or analyze. Later the whole tree reveals itself to be a microcosm. It disintegrates into its component parts (all of which appear as little men), and these minute creatures dance around in the air (the traditional way of imagining the atoms is as motes dancing in the sunlight), and having

There is then a constant harmony of creative and interpretive vision as soon as one accepts the medieval theocentric cosmology of a Pseudo-Dionysius. Man, in his divinity, could imitate the creation of the world by his artistic efforts, and the scholar could regard himself as participating in the creation by an active aesthetic response to nature, taking it "cosmically" rather than hedonistically.[112] The modern question as to how we relate the interpretive and the creative activities could not arise before a break-up of the medieval world view. Modern empirical science, on the other hand, depends in part upon the disjunction of creative (imaginative and synthetic) and interpretive (empirical and analytic) mind, a major intellectual shift which might explain the modern distaste for allegory.

Sources of authority. There is, however, a bridge from the medieval concept of a creative gloss to the modern form of allegorical literature, for allegory is no less vigorous today than during the earlier centuries.[113] We find an old-world tradition still carried on

---

danced around in ever-narrowing orbits, they finally come together again to form a man of great beauty and perfect shape" (J. S. Spink, "Form and Structure," in *Literature and Science,* 145). Another common, probably much more primitive notion, is that the tree is identified with Woman, as in Paracelsus, *Selected Writings,* ed. J. Jacobi (New York, 1951), 100 ff.

The tree is finally the grandest of nature's "flowers," for which Biblical parables have only praise, as being "natural" ornament. Isidore of Seville (*Etymologies,* ed. W. M. Lindsay [Oxford, 1911], XIX, chs. xxx, xxxi; XI, ch. x) distinguishes between *natural* and *artificial* ornament, the former pertaining to the beauties of the human body or of nature, the latter to jewelry or clothes. This gives a terminology for modern advertizing, as well as for higher fictions. See De Bruyne, *Etudes d'esthétique medievale,* I, 79.

[112] This had been the crux of the quarrel between the Abbot Suger and his critics. He insisted that the wealth of his Abbey was "cosmic" and merely reflected the proper glory of God, while his critics read the display in simpler, more material terms. A St. Bernard would see only the deprivation of the poor which must follow upon such conspicuous expenditures. See note 79, above.

[113] Quintilian, *Institutes,* VIII, iii, secs. 63–64, seems to be describing procedures of style which we would call "naturalism"—a heightened awareness of physical detail. E.g., of a boxing scene he says, "Other details follow which give us such a picture of the two boxers confronting each other for the fight, that it could not have been clearer had we been actual spectators." Is this not a definition of naturalism?

through various kinds of literary documentary.[114] That medieval allegory is often encyclopedic is well known;[115] modern science fiction too provides a fantasy world of pseudoscientific documentation, allowing for a similar cosmic ornament. The vocabulary differs in detail, but in general the jargon of modern science fiction is manifestly ornamental; it is an encrustation upon simple romantic plots, the adornment of a daemonic fiction. On a more serious level of work we have the sociological treatise-novel, exemplified at its best by Zola or Dreiser, but imitated by lesser novelists of extreme left or right tendency, by an Upton Sinclair or an Ayn Rand. One notices in all such works a tendency to overdo the detail, to exaggerate the proofs of social depravity, and most of all to exaggerate the influence of social *system* on human existence. Such traits are essentially those of an ornamental art, taking ornament in our sense. Here, as with the older literature, there is always a governing authority at the top of the symbolic ladder, and the critic attempting to account for the dynamics of a documentary literature will look, as he would with *The Divine Comedy* or *The Pilgrim's Progress*, for that authoritarian power.

Nowhere is this authoritarian base more evident than during that period when rhetoricians most vigorously developed the concept of the "garment of style," which I take to be the common *generalized* form of the theory of *kosmos*.[116] During the Elizabethan period it

[114] See M. D. Chenu, *La Théologie au douzième siècle*, ch. i, "La Nature et l'homme"; also ch. vii, "La Mentalité symbolique." Also, Curtius, *European Literature*, ch. vi, "The Goddess Natura."

[115] "Encyclopedia" means during the middle ages, the circle drawn about the Seven Liberal Arts and their immediate extensions into scientific and religious knowledge. Curtius, *European Literature*, 302–347, has shown the importance of "The Book as Symbol" during this period; see especially 344, on the Cosmos as a book. The encyclopedic movement *around* all knowledge suggests the containment of the temporal flux by a process of historical commemoration and this in turn finds a primitive symbol in the *ouruboros*. For this in iconographic representation see Freeman, *English Emblem Books*, 96. Kroner, *Speculation*, 100, observes that one early pre-Socratic usage of *logos* makes it equivalent to "collection."

[116] See Tuve, *Elizabethan and Metaphysical Imagery*, ch. iv, "The Garment of Style."

is apparent that the Court, with its real political power on the one hand and its ideal, moral, and aesthetic sanctions on the other, could set the standard of "dress" that would be the pattern for rhetorical as well as actual costume.[117]

And as we see in these great Madames of honour, be they for personage or otherwise never so comely and bewtifull, yet if they want their courtly habillements or at leastwise such other apparrell as custome and civilities have ordained to cover their naked bodies, would be halfe ashamed or greatly out of countenance to be seen in that sort, and perchance to then thinke themselves more amiable in every mans eye, when they be in their richest attire, when they go in cloth suppose of silkes or tyssiues and costly embroderies, then when they go in cloth or in any other plaine and simple apparrell. Even so cannot our vulgar Poesie shew it selfe either gallant or gorgious, if any lymme be left naked and bare and not clad in his kindly clothes and coulours, such as may convey them somewhat out of sight, that is from the common course of ordinary speach and capacities of the vulgar judgment, and yet being artificially handled must needs yield it much more bewtie and commendation. This ornament we speak of is given to it by figures and figurative speaches, which be the flowers as it were and coulours that a Poet setteth upon his language by arte, as the embroderer doth his stone and perle, or passements of gold upon the stuffe of a Princely garment, or as th'excellent painter bestoweth the rich Orient coulours upon his table of pourtraite.[118]

Here courtly bearing and costume are the types of "good" ornament; presumably the plainer clothes of a merchant's wife would be models

[117] One of the best modern treatments is H. D. Duncan, *Language and Literature in Society* (Chicago, 1953), where the use of status symbols is fully discussed, stressing the effect of social pressures on symbolic behavior.

[118] Puttenham, *Arte of English Poesie*, III, ch. i. Later, ch. vi, Puttenham observes that the high style is vulnerable to attack because it tends toward over-inflation. In such a case it "cannot be better resembled than to these midsommer pageants in London, where to make the people wonder are set forth great and uglie Gyants marching as if they were alive, and armed at all points, but within they are stuffed full of browne paper and tow, which the shrewd boyes underpeering, do guilefully discover and turne to a great derision."

for a "middle" style; and of a peasant's or a lower-class citizen's wife, of the "lower" style.[119]

The Renaissance drama actually develops a type of dramatic literature which is based on the "cosmetic" use of ornament. The masques, designed and presented in the most lavish richness of decor, are intended to praise and reinforce the high standing of leaders of the state. They do this both visually and verbally. The words of the masque are allegorical and in effect explicate the costuming, the dancing, and the background scenery which give a dazzling aesthetic surface to this art form. There is always a strong suggestion of the daemonic in this spectacular imagery,[120] and the faery-tale atmosphere of the masques comes about naturally. One step further beyond the pastoral world, the fairy world of Oberon and Cynthia allows completely free play with ideal notions. It also allows a Ben Jonson to reinstate society according to a perfect plan. Nothing is impossible to the establishment of justice in this world.

In England, where the Italian Renaissance is felt after a suitable time lag, the next stage after the masque, if we are looking for a dramatic kosmos, is the emerging musical drama that rises, it might be argued, out of the repressive censorship of the Interregnum. Musical declamation, accompanied by dances and by the elaborate creation of a magical decor, allows for a drama that does not seem to be about the real world.[121] The musical drama, and another off-

[119] On Renaissance emblematic decoration of private homes, see Freeman, *English Emblem Books,* 50–51.

[120] See Frye, *Anatomy,* 290, on the relationship between the daemonic and the masque form. The costuming frequently indicates this kinship, by suggesting grotesque intermixtures of human, animal, bird, and vegetable forms.

[121] One of the remarkable facts of the history of opera is the continuing reliance on magical agencies, even in modern works like *The Rake's Progress* and *Porgy and Bess,* not to mention more recent operatic ventures into science fiction.

Manfred Bukofzer, "Allegory in Baroque Music," *Journal of the Warburg Institute,* III (1939–1940), nos. 1–2, 1–21, gives an initial statement of a theory of musical allegory and includes a list of baroque texts which themselves theorize about such music. Motions of sound can be ordered to make analogies with

shoot, the later heroic drama, do not offend censorship because their very material removes the play from a mimetic representation. Drama employs an official decorum under these repressive circumstances. It is possible that the drama revives under the courtly tutelage of Davenant, because he is able to draw on the imagery of royal power to establish an ornamental vocabulary.

The courtly standard, however, is but one principle according to which the cosmic hierarchy may be ordered.[122] Others are pos-

------

patterns of ideas: "The Analogies in Music may refer only to one voice, or to all the voices, to the rhythm, to the harmony alone, to the setting and instrumentation alone, or simply to the intensity of the sound" (9). Most important for the present theory of allegory is Bukofzer's view, a typical one, I believe, that the old notion of a bond between the musical modes and the human emotions has "cosmological, not musical reasons." Musical astrology is not confined to the ancient world, but also appears in China, Babylonia, India, and Java. By the baroque period these cosmo-musical associations have become conventional rules, "part of the general humanist equipment" (5). Music, like literature and the visual arts, therefore has its *topoi,* e.g., the musically descending scale that marks a descent into Hell, the ascending scale that marks a spiritual ascension. Schweitzer's allegorization of Bach seems more cogent than ever.

[122] Presumably the more fixed hierarchic systems elicit greater ambivalence in feelings about any given rung of the ladder. Eliade has shown how this is the case for the Indian, whose mythology of dependence upon the Divine is also a mythology of rebellion. See *Images et symboles,* 155: "We know how Indian thought is dominated by a hunger for deliverance and how its most characteristic terminology reduces itself to polar formulas like 'enchained-delivered,' 'bound-unbound,' 'attached-detached,' etc. The same formulas run through Greek philosophy: in Plato's cave, men are held back by chains which prevent them from moving and turning their heads (*Rep.* VIII, 514 et seq.). The soul, 'after its fall, was taken, was put in chains . . . ; it was, they say, in a tomb and in a cave, but in returning back towards thought, it frees itself from its bonds . . .' (Plotinus, *Enneads,* IV, 8, 4; cf. IV, 8, 1: 'The march towards intelligence is, for the soul, deliverance from bondage' " (my own translation).

In popular thinking the ambivalence of the imagery of knots and chains creates two opposed kinds of charms. "It is significant that knots and ribbons are used in the marriage ceremony, to protect the young couple, while it is indeed a knot which would prevent consummation of the marriage. But this ambivalence is one of those we observe in all magico-religious uses of knots and ties. The knots provoke the sickness and also they ward it off or cure the sick man; strings and knots work sorcery against a man and also protect him

sible, and we can expect kosmos to generalize along different lines
with each successive era. For the Greeks order was chiefly a matter
of public political honor, up until the growth of mystery cults; for
the Romans *pietas* in the domestic sense plays a greater part, and we
get a proliferation of ornaments peculiar to local petty gods, which
Cassirer called the Roman "bureaucratic gods"; the medieval conception in turn was more likely to involve a sort of spiritual honor,
Christian "grace" or feudal allegiance, since rank is related to the
order of divine forms presented in the phenomena of the created
universe and in the secular pattern of Christian Providence. Christian
eschatology might seem to our eyes a more rigid and fixed conception of hierarchy than the Greeks knew, yet to this very extent the
medieval period was more favorable to the creation of poetical allegories. What is decorous becomes gradually more clearly determined
and more readily known, in the main, until with the Renaissance
once again public affairs of a secular kind assume a central place in
the teaching of rhetoric.

Antiauthoritarian shifts in status. No simplification of those great
western waves of tradition need be given here, especially since, with
the emergence of the baroque in architecture, and subsequently in
music, with the emergence of similar baroque, metaphysical, Gongor-
ist poetic conceits as the organizing principles of poetry, we seem to
be witnessing a confusion of *kosmos.* It is as if degree were being
taken away, to be replaced experimentally by deliberate *discordia
concors.* This only appears to be confusion; more closely viewed, it
is seen to be irony, as in the common parodies of Petrarchan conceits.
Certain poems by Donne, or Shakespeare's sonnet, "My mistress' eyes
are nothing like the sun," make sport of the fragility of Petrarchan

---

from sorcery; they hinder childbirth and make it pass easily; they preserve new-
born children, and make them ill; they bring death and hold it far off" (Eliade,
Images et symboles, 147). Ilse Aichinger has recently employed the imagery of
knots in her story, "The Bound Man," in the collection, *The Bound Man and
Other Stories,* tr. E. Mosbacher (New York, 1956).

praise.[123] This irony is a process not of confusion, but of dispraise; it marks downward movement in the hierarchy—its kosmoi being no less "ornamental" for all that—or, as a medieval poet would have

---

[123] The Metaphysical poets share this defiance of convention and hierarchic idiom in poetry, on which see Tuve, *Elizabethan and Metaphysical Imagery*, 196.

At an earlier phase of history the lack of decorum had implied an openly political or social defiance of hierarchic order. No better instance of this semi-political "criterion of decorum" could be found than the prose interchapter following the "tragedy" of Richard III, in *The Mirror for Magistrates*. As elsewhere in *The Mirror* this interchapter serves a complex function—somewhat like the dialogues in the *Canterbury Tales*, it gets the discontinuous structure from one point to another, bidding leave to the story just told, bidding welcome to the one about to be told. The tragedy of Richard, Duke of Gloucester, seems to Baldwin and his interlocutors a poorly versified tale, and the grounds on which they object to the meter are carefully spelled out: "When I had read this [the tragedy], we had much talke about it. For it was thought not vehement ynough for so violent a man as kyng Richard had bene. The matter was wel ynough lyked of sum, but the meeter was mysliked almost of all. And when divers therefore would not allowe it, what (quoth one). You knowe not wherevpon you sticke: elles you would not so much mislike this because of the Vncertayne Meter. The cumlynes called by the Rhetoricians *decorum*, is specially to be observed in al thinges. Seyng than that kyng Rychard never kept measure in any of his doings, seing also he speaketh in Hel, whereas is no order; it were agaynst the decorum of his personage, to vse eyther good Meter or order. And therefore, if his oracion were far wurse, in my opinion it were more fyt for him. Mars and the Muses did never agree. Neyther is it to be suffred that their milde sacred Arte shoulde seeme to proceede from so cruell and prophane a mouth as his: seynge they them selves do vtterly abhorre it. And although we read of Nero, that he was excellent both in Musicke, and in versifieng, yet do not I remember that ever I saw any song or verse of his makying: Minerva iustlye providing, that no monument should remayne of any such vniust vsurpacion. And therefore let thys passe euen as it is, which the wryter I know both could and would amend in many places, save for kepying the *decorum*, which he purposely hath observed herein.

"In deede (quoth I) as you saye: It is not meete that so disorderly and vnnatural a man as Kyng Rychard was, shuld observe any metrical order in his talke: which notwithstanding in many places of his oracion is very wel kept: It shalle passe therefore even as it is, though to good for so yll a person. And to supplye that whych is lackinge in him, here I haue Shores wyfe, an eloquent wentch, whyche shall furnishe out both in meter and matter, that which could

perhaps said, it marks a *katagogy*, an opposition to the more familiar *anagogy*.

In the *Anatomy of Criticism* Frye has argued that Western literature shows a steady trend "downward" in that it has become increasingly more and more ironic in tone and point of view.[124] Its heroes, from once being gods, demigods, and superhumanly strong mortals, have become "less than men," until, as Frye points out, Thackeray calls *Vanity Fair* "a novel without a hero." Modern authors like Orwell and Kafka go even further and show heroes who are reduced to the status of vermin (though surely medieval allegory and the Aesopian tradition generally had shown man to be a species of animal).[125] Whether there are countermovements in this downward progress does not much matter, since kosmos in general is leaning toward the side of debasement, whereas it had once tended either in the opposite direction, upward, or had chosen a middle course and had represented a full hierarchy from top to bottom, just as Plato's ladder of love reaches to both highest and lowest forms of love. The modern movement begins with authors like Defoe, the first journalists, and proceeds to such masters as Zola and the American naturalist novelists. Ugliness of detail is no indication that ornament is any less involved, as Henry James observed of Zola,[126] the Zola who

---

not comlily be sayd in his person. Marke I praye you what she sayeth, and tell me howe you like it" (*The Mirror for Magistrates*, ed. L. B. Campbell [Cambridge, 1938; reprinted New York, 1960], 371-372).

[124] Page 34. Thus Bentham devotes his *Handbook of Political Fallacies* to the debunking of authority; his attitude is ironic.

[125] The recent publication of Giovanni Battista Gelli's *Circe*, ed. R. M. Adams (Ithaca, 1963), in the Tom Brown translation (1702), allows us to assess a major Renaissance recurrence of the metamorphic tradition.

[126] Henry James's comments on Zola are the most illuminating that I know on the nature of modern, naturalistic allegory: " 'Well, I on my side,' I remember Zola saying, 'am engaged in a book, a study of the *moeurs* of the people, for which I am making a collection of all the "bad words," the *gros mots*, of the language, those with which the vocabulary of the people, those with which their familar talk, bristles.' I was struck with the tone in which he made the announcement—without bravado and without apology, as an interesting idea

wrote "great romantic allegories," using government White Papers to provide information, his equivalent of the medieval *formosum involucrum*. Kafka's allegory, despite the desire of his admirers to call it by the more fashionable name of "myth," elaborates an imagery which we can call "ornamental" in both the strict and the loose sense of the term, even though at first we may not know exactly how to read the cosmic significance of his floating imagery. But that is the point: with Kafka kosmos becomes imbued with doubt and anxiety; hierarchy itself causes fear, hatred, tentative approach, tentative retreat. The sure sense of one's place in the sun has gone. The sure identification of the hero with governing political or cultural ideals has gone. Doubt inhibits action. Piety of any kind becomes difficult or impossible. "O for a household god to keep by me," Kafka cries out in his *Diary*. The horrid scales and joints of the metamorphosed

---

that had come to him and that he was working, really to arrive at character and particular truth, with all his conscience." This last phrase tells us James does not think Zola's method will work; a novelist does not write "with all his conscience."

Yet the documentary's beauty may affect us by a sort of statistical aesthetic; we are touched, not by forms, but by textures. "It was the fortune, it was in a manner the doom, of *Les Rougon-Macquart* to deal with things almost always in gregarious form, to be a picture of numbers, of classes, crowds, confusions, movements, industries—and this for a reason of which it will be interesting to attempt some account. The individual life is, if not wholly absent, reflected in coarse and common, in generalized terms; whereby we arrive precisely at the oddity just named, the circumstance, that, looking out somewhere, and often woefully athirst for the taste of fineness, we find it not in the fruits of our author's fancy, but in a different matter altogether. We get it in the very history of his efforts, the image itself of his lifelong process, comparatively so personal, so spiritual even, and, through all its patience and pain, of a quality so much more distinguished than the qualities he succeeds in attributing to his figures even when he most aims at distinction. There can be no question in these narrow limits of my taking the successive volumes one by one—all the more that our sense of the exhibition is as little as possible an impression of parts and books, of particular 'plots' and persons. It produces the effect of a mass of imagery in which shades are sacrificed, the effect of character and passion in the lump or by the ton. The fullest, the most characteristic episodes affect us like a sounding *chorus* or *procession* [my italics], as with a hubbub

Gregor Samsa are then no less ornaments than the invented trappings of Swift's Flying Island, or the forest images of *Comus*,[127] or the heraldic costuming of knights in *The Faerie Queene*. We need to remember this, since our ideas of what is "proper" may still be somewhat influenced by Victorian ideals and may be somewhat lacking in irony.

Expanding images of the universe. In conclusion it may be said that when empirical science assumes a dominant role in modern culture it becomes reasonable to think of the cosmos in everyday terms, or rather in physical and natural terms, and as a result there is a general loosening of the idea of ornament as the insignia of the universe. More and more phenomena have to be crowded into the universe

---

of voices and a multitudinous tread of feet. The setter of the mass into motion, he himself, in the crowd, figures best, with whatever queer idiosyncrasy, excrescences, and gaps, a being of a substance akin to our own. Taking him as we must, I repeat, for quite heroic, the interest of detail in him is the interest of his struggle at every point with his problem." From Henry James's article, "Emile Zola," in *The Future of the Novel*, ed. Leon Edel (New York, 1956), 169–170.

See also *ibid.*, 191, for Henry James's account of *L'Assommoir* (filmed as *Gervaise* by René Clément): "I have said enough of the mechanical in Zola; here in truth is, given the elements, almost insupportably the sense of life." James judged *L'Assommoir* "the most extraordinary record" of Zola's genius: "The tone of *L'Assommoir* is, for mere 'keeping up,' unsurpassable, a vast deep steady tide on which every object represented is triumphantly borne. It never shrinks nor flows thin, and nothing for an instant drops, dips or catches; the highwater mark of sincerity, of the genial, as I have called it, is unfailingly kept." Sincerity—that word heralds an art where the reader will be thinking more of the creator's frame of mind, than of his creations; it is an art unthinkable before the days of "originality." See also, A. Bronson Feldman, "Zola and the Riddle of Sadism," *American Imago*, XIII (1956).

[127] The forest frequently suggests charm, enchantment, and magical influence, as for example in "Young Goodman Brown," and in general in picturesque groves, on which see Lovejoy, "The Chinese Origin of a Romanticism," in *Essays*, 116 and 120, where the words "charm" and "enchant" have more than their usual debased evaluative meaning. See also Lovejoy, "The First Gothic Revival," *Essays*, 162, and for a modern instance, Thomas Mann's story, "A Man and His Dog," the section entitled, "The Hunting Ground."

that science keeps discovering, while the process of discovery is itself a sort of overall expansion. Kosmos has to expand with the expansion of knowledge itself.[128] At this point one may wonder whether the concept of kosmos still has boundaries.

Here lies the precise usefulness of the term, since our definition allows poetic ornament and its systematically ordered fictions to assume a wider and ever wider variety of colors as civilized existence grows ever more complex. We need only keep the original *hierarchic intention* in mind and to ask whether any given instance of imagery has this "cosmic" function, or whether it is not rather intended to *show* us something we had not thought of before (metaphor), or to arouse vague quasi-religious feelings (symbol), if we can make these rough distinctions.[129] It may be that the generalization of the term kosmos corresponds to a gradual secularization of life, where authoritarian hierarchies become multiple instead of unitary, where there is no longer any single all-pervasive religious orientation of existence. We shall expect more allegories to have ornaments in keeping with the anxiety and uncertainty of modern value judgments, and in fact this "ambivalent kosmos" becomes in an author like Kafka the dominant type of allegorical image. On the other hand there is a degree of optimism accompanying scientific exploration, especially in the fields

---

[128] It is thus an error to assume that all kosmoi will have to stand for conservative values; they may be the banners of revolution, as in Russian "socialist realism."

[129] The problem here is chiefly with the term "symbol." My own insistence on the function of awe, taboo, ambivalence, and my use of a Freudian model that shows allegory's kinship with religious ritual, might suggest a contradiction here. There is none, however. Religious ritual needs to be sharply distinguished from religious emotions in their more profound and "oceanic" character. The latter are presumably elicited by "symbol," if we grant the one condition that such emotions do not carry us into an otherworldly state. They carry us perhaps into an otherworldly attitude toward this world, but the interest aroused by "symbol" presumably should remain with this world. Otherwise Romantic theory becomes the mere perversion and watering-down of orthodox religious beliefs.

of medicine and of space travel, where the arrow of progress points always outward, however afraid we are of the consequences.[130] There is bound to be a continuing of science fiction, to the point where some of it becomes science without fiction, and at that moment writers will have to search out a strong new authoritarian language, that is, unless allegory falls more and more into the mold of documentary fiction. For naturalistic fables the range of the imagery would be nothing less than the range of natural phenomena itself, and at that point the loosening-up of the term *kosmos* would be complete.

[130] Cf. Robert Sheckley, *Untouched by Human Hands* (New York, 1960), and Albert Pohl and C. M. Kornbluth, *The Space Merchants* (New York, 1953), on the narrowing of the human horizon as the physical horizon expands. This theme gives a certain irony to the recent Soviet film, *The Letter That Was Never Sent*, a film dedicated to Soviet explorers and spacemen, a "pure" allegory made with consummate art. The film is furthermore an instance of the sublime and picturesque modalities of imagery; it concludes with an almost classic image of the "natural sublime," in which the hero is both defeated and glorified by Nature.

3

Symbolic Action:
Progress and Battle

IN the *Poetics* the analysis of tragic drama describes an "action" which, besides having a beginning, middle, and end, besides being presented to the audience in a probable way with reasonable expectations aroused and finally fulfilled, has also the property of eliciting surprise in the audience exactly as Aristotle had said metaphor would elicit surprise.[1] Here also something happens which does not fit in "with the ideas you already have." Basing the plot on a sequence of set expectancies about what the main characters will do and on the unexpected interruption of the drama by reversals and discoveries, Aristotle demands of his perfect tragic playwright that he take his audience by surprise, gaining attention and participation (*empatheia*) in this way, yet without using to excess the most surprising device of all—the supernatural event.[2] Such an event is described by Aristotle

[1] On "imitation of an action," see *Poetics,* 1450b.
[2] On reversal and discovery, see *Poetics,* 1452a, b. "But again, Tragedy is an imitation not only of a complete action, but of events inspiring fear or pity. Such an effect is best produced when the events come on us by surprise" (1452a). On the species of discovery (*anagnorisis*), *Poetics,* 1454b.

in the *Poetics:* the statue of a wicked man falls down on that very person as he happens to be walking underneath it, an accident clearly expressing arbitrary, divine intervention in the world of natural probability, "for incidents like that we think to be not without a meaning." And while Aristotle calls for a restrained use of the *deus ex machina*, he is even more skeptical when it comes to dramatic presentation of merely random events. His concept of probability allows no function for random chance in a good mimetic plot; accidents without any moral significance should be kept out of the perfect drama. In tragedy and, one supposes, in comedy Aristotle would disallow such events because they represent a totally arbitrary *ad hoc* imposition of outside authority and power on the natural scheme of things. The *Poetics* assumes, I think, that nature never suspends its own laws for such occasions. Even the gods should obey a kind of nature and act according to the probable, predictable course of their own higher destiny. The Aristotelian delight in nature is a delight in order, a distrust of fantasy, a canonizing of perception—the chief tool of inductive thought—and above all an unwillingness to toy with the irrational. Thus he is led to say that "those, however, who make use of the Spectacle to put before us that which is merely monstrous and not productive of fear, are wholly out of touch with Tragedy." [3] The mimetic poet must impose limits, derived from nature, on his choice of mimetic object.

Chapter 2 of the *Poetics* indeed stresses the diversity of nature precisely because Aristotle wants to insist on the control of object choice; yet he would not have it thought that mimetic drama is thereby fatally restricted. There is "God's plenty" in this natural range of things, people, and events imitated. We might argue that

[3] *Poetics,* 1453b. There is a close connection between ornamental speech, spectacle, and the "wonderful" or "marvelous" (*thaumastos*). In fact all such effects are effects of wonder, and conversely the supernatural is in some sense always an ornament to our familiar world of natural probability. Marvelous events, in turn, are those which appear to occur by chance, but which also are agencies of "poetic justice."

only by restricting and by rejecting supernatural materials wherever possible can mimesis remain mimetic.

At the same time, because it parallels the diversity of nature, mimetic art can display formal variety; at any given moment a good play will have various possible routes that it may follow (if it did not, there would be the special circumstance, an impasse, that requires the arrival of a *deus ex machina*), and this variety of outcome is mirrored in an endless variety of forms which mimetic plots can assume. This is not to say, however, that mimetic drama never deals with the supernatural, but rather that as an object of mimesis, for example the appearance of Heracles in Sophocles' *Philoctetes*, the supernatural comes into the play only after natural probabilities have been shown to reach an impasse.[4] Only when miracle itself is the sole means of concluding an action does a *deus ex machina* make sense for Aristotle. He would, for instance, applaud the use of the King in this role, in Molière's *Tartuffe*, because throughout the play Tartuffe has been equated with a devil and at the end has assumed the powers of a full-fledged Satan. Only a demigod, the Sun King, can overthrow such a power and restore the balance of nature. Under these circumstances nature calls out for help from the supernatural and we get, if not a "probable impossibility," at least a "necessary impossibility." Otherwise the mimetic dramatist has to prevent magic from entering the causal system of his plot. If it be his purpose to question the role of the supernatural, he can then introduce it as a psychological problem met by characters who are shown acting

[4] Paul Goodman, *Structure of Literature* (Chicago, 1954), 49–58, gives an analysis of the *deus ex machina* in the *Philoctetes*. The *deus* is necessary for the breaking of the impasse; "an impasse is an action so handled as to 'end' before the exhaustion of the possibilities. Gratuitous elements are the probability for action in an impasse." Notice here the careful distinction which Goodman preserves, between "possible" and "probable." "Gratuitous elements" are normally possible, but not probable; by appearing with the *deus* they emphasize the existence of a presiding God or Necessity who ultimately rules the action by fiat.

naturally within the world of the play. They regard the magical as a phenomenon which is anomalous for their own idea of nature. This is the case with any of those numerous instances in Greek drama, as well as in the Homeric epics, where the chorus or some other character tries to explain the relationship between human motivation, especially anger and lust, and the will of the gods. A more modern instance would be *Hamlet* (as opposed to *The Tempest* or *Cymbeline*), where the supernatural is treated partially as a case of perverted nature, in short, of insanity.

Mimetic drama then appears to question any case of a power that intervenes from above to control man's actions arbitrarily. It questions whatever will prevent human character from gradually modifying itself. It revels in change of character, therefore, and constantly shows, as Aristotle pointed out, that discoveries and reversals are not merely intellectual changes, "from ignorance to knowledge," but more important, are emotional changes "from love to hate, or hate to love." Above all, natural growth and natural decay seem to be the prime concern of the mimetic artist.

We begin with Aristotle's mimesis because in questioning the supernatural it questions the central devices of allegory and presents the strongest possible contrast with allegory. Allegory, it might seem, is equally at home with reversals and discoveries, with changes of character from love to hate and hate to love; but these are by no means probable natural changes; they are always imposed changes, like the metamorphosis of thieves in the "Inferno" or the quasi-medical changes of victims in Hawthorne's *Tales*. When an arbitrary conversion occurs at the end of an action, we must ask if that is not the moment when mimesis gives way to allegory. The *deus ex machina* is necessarily a magical device, whose anti-mimetic force may be suspected from the fact that it comes in to prevent an impasse, after the exhaustion of all *probable* routes of escape. Allegory is structured according to ritualistic necessity, as opposed to probability, and for that reason its basic forms differ from mimetic plots in being less diverse and more simple in contour.

No doubt we can imagine fables that appear to be as free in formal arrangement as any mimetic drama, but notice that such works will tend to fall into the category of satire, and satire, as we shall see, is on the borderline of the mode, since it directs allegory against allegory, irony against irony. The normal case is different, however. The following pages intend to show how allegory returns to ever simpler patterns of action. The mode is radically reductive and in that is at war with mimesis.

The two fundamental patterns. The tendency is for allegories to resolve themselves into either of two basic forms, and they do not merely arise out of the bare rudiments of these two forms; they keep returning to insist on them. The two may be labeled *battle* and *progress.* The former perhaps begins in Western literature with Hesiod's account of the gigantomachia,[5] the battle between titanic creatures for control of the world, but it comes into greater prominence when it is psychologized, with the *Psychomachia* of the early Christian poet Prudentius.[6] Progress begins with the allegorical interpretation of the *Odyssey,* the *Argonautica,* and especially the *Aeneid.*[7] What I wish to show in this chapter is that "symbolic action" can be formed into progresses and battles, and that fictions of this type necessarily have double meanings, and necessarily have daemonic agency and cosmic imagery.

Progress, real and ideal. The allegorical progress may first of all be understood in the narrow sense of a questing journey. There is usually a paradoxical suggestion that by leaving home the hero can return to another better "home": Christian leaves the City of Destruction, where his family home is, to reach the true home of all

---

[5] *Theogonia.* See the analysis of Hesiod, in F. M. Cornford, *The Unwritten Philosophy,* ed. W. K. C. Guthrie (Cambridge, 1950).

[6] Prudentius, *Works,* tr. and ed. H. J. Thomson (Loeb Classics ed., London, 1949), I, 274-343. Thomson translates *psychomachia* as "the fight for mansoul," which echoes Bunyan's imitation of Prudentius, *The Holy War.* On the *Psychomachia,* see Lewis, *Allegory of Love,* 66-73, and Katzellenbogen, *Allegories of the Virtues and Vices,* ch. 1.

[7] See Curtius, *European Literature,* 203-214, "Poetry and Philosophy."

believers, the Celestial City.[8] Sometimes, having made the journey, the hero comes back to his original home so much changed that he cannot any longer hold his former position: of this Gulliver would be a case; in his story there is a suggestion that his voyage has removed any chance he might have of returning to a resting place. Self-knowledge is apparently the goal, and with a disillusioned image of the self before him, Gulliver cannot tolerate his "home" or his family. Sometimes the journey leaves the traveler on the point of decision to return home, and then we know that another thematic function has been served, besides self-knowledge. Johnson's *Rasselas*, not unlike its model *Candide*, shows a group of travelers who are seeking to know their own desires, but who learn the vanity of their wishes only by experiencing the world outside the Happy Valley.[9] Though they must know themselves, they must also know what are the true conditions of human existence. When they have tested this harsh reality, they have also tested themselves: "Of these wishes that they had formed they well knew that none could be obtained." The progress of Imlac and his young friends has failed, and knowing their failure, they can only retrace their steps. This kind of failure, drawn enigmatically, is the "goal" of the hero of *The Journey to the East*,

[8] Bunyan's Proem to the Second Part of *The Pilgrim's Progress* makes specific reference to the Pilgrim Fathers' journey to a new home in America. This analogy had a powerful effect in justifying the Progress: "Tell them that they have left their house and home,/ Are turned Pilgrims: seek a world to come." A similar "argument" of the moral quest occurs in The Proem to Book II of *The Faerie Queene*, while the newly discovered islands to the west provide a symbolic location for *The Tempest*.

[9] *Rasselas*, ch. xlix. Two things are striking about this closing chapter of the novel: the fact that it ends with the "time of the inundation of the Nile," and the fact that Pekuah wishes, vainly, to retire to the convent of St. Anthony, while the princess wishes, vainly, to found "a college of learned women"—by which we understand the contrast between Nature's endless cycle and Man's endless drive to transcend Nature—on which see, Mircea Eliade, *The Myth of the Eternal Return*, tr. W. R. Trask (New York, 1954; reprinted as *Cosmos and History*, New York, 1959), *passim*; also Eliade, *The Sacred and the Profane*, tr. W. R. Trask (New York, 1961), 68–113.

an ironical modern progress by Hermann Hesse.[10] Such fables tell a story of actual journey, and we can easily trace the moment of arrival at the destination. It is easy to discern this typical, simple sort of allegorical progress. It is represented by voyages, land journeys, air journeys, some of which are realistically represented, others of which are the sheerest fantasy. But there is always a material description of travel from a home to some distant place, and then either a return, or a continuation of the voyage ad infinitum. Usually, as the story moves the hero farther from his home, the imagination of the author is fired by his freedom from the requirement of plausibility, and we often get quite visionary tales as a result.

The progress need not be plausible, as long as the momentum of symbolic invention is great.[11] It does not even need to involve a physical journey.[12] Travel is not the only way one can change places. The whole operation can be presented as a sort of introspective journey through the self; Kafka's "The Burrow," with its ruminations, would be a good instance. One can travel through a catalogue of objects recalled to mind without any physical displacement occurring. In that sense an encyclopedic poem which gives all the points

[10] The final image of *The Journey to the East,* tr. Hilda Rosner (New York, 1957): "Only slowly did it dawn upon me. Only slowly and gradually did I begin to suspect and then perceive what it was intended to represent. It represented a figure which was myself, and this likeness of myself was unpleasantly weak and half-real; it had blurred features and in its whole expression there was something unstable, weak, dying, or wishing to die, and looked rather like a piece of sculpture which could be called 'Transitoriness' or 'Decay,' or something similar." This monumental image merges and flows into that of a stronger person, the President Leo.

[11] The case with picaresque, where just so long as there is "one great end," as Fielding said of the *Odyssey,* the wandering sequence of events is no disadvantage. This "one great end" is usually the return home, frequently in the special sense that the hero is often a foundling and has to find out who he is in order to receive his inheritance. Note that in true picaresque the rogue is *compelled* always to keep moving; the sheriff drives him out of town.

[12] The basis of Joyce's *Ulysses,* where besides a mimetically rendered physical movement there is a predominant flow of mental events.

of doctrine in a given science is "traveling" through an intellectual countryside.[13] All that is required for this to be a progress is that it have a constant forward motion, that it be unremittingly directed toward a goal, that it attempt an undeviating movement in a given direction.

We began with a fine example of an ideal progress, "The Phoenix and the Turtle." The form of this poem is given by its subject, a funeral procession, a mass for the dead, where every stanza constitutes a slow paced ritual step toward the threnody that concludes the poem. Another form very close to this funerary, processional form is the common medieval sequence of the procession of the Seven Deadly Sins, and yet another is the Dance of Death. In the latter the progress is a sort of list, beginning with the King or the Pope, and moving downward in the hierarchic scale until the dance is joined by the humblest servants of God and King.[14] Nothing so well marks the ritual pattern of this dance as the identical framing of each person in the sequence when it is given visual illustration, as by Hans Holbein. Here, as with daemonic agency in general, movement and action are finally stilled.

The medieval "testament," [15] in which the narrator leaves all his worldly goods to survivors who are representative figures com-

[13] Cf. Spenser, *The Faerie Queene*, VI, proem, i.

[14] Auerbach, speaking of "the interplay between the epideictic style of knightly ceremony and a starkly creatural realism which does not shun but actually savors crass effects," shows how allegory and naturalism go hand in hand (a notion strongly reinforced by Huizinga's *Waning of the Middle Ages*): "What is common to the two elements and holds them together is certain factors in the sensory taste of the period: ponderousness and somberness, dragging tempo, strongly charged coloration. As a result its epideictic style has often a somewhat exaggerated sensory impressiveness; its realism often has a certain ponderousness of form and at the same time something directly creatural and fraught with tradition. Many realistic forms—the Dance of Death for example—have the character of processions and of parades" (Auerbach, *Mimesis*, 216–217).

[15] Villon's *Testament* is perhaps the most important example; Villon breaks the monotony of the catalogue by interpolating ballads into the body of the testament. See E. C. Perrow, "The Last Will and Testament as a Form of Litera-

parable to those of the Dance of Death, resembles the medieval "complaint," which chronicles a sequence of ways in which the world is thought to be falling to pieces.[16] In both genres the poet gives his reader a parade of the orders of society and nature. The poetry takes on the form natural to its subject, that is, it becomes something like a list, a tabulation, a catalogue of complaint or legacy. These genres are next door to the more ambitious encyclopedic allegories of the middle ages, which contain all known facts, or all facts known to the author, besides all moral and philosophical lore. In order to set forth the large quantity of material at hand the poet stratifies his poem. This is most strikingly done when the poem is cosmogonic, like Hesiod's *Theogony*, Du Bartas' *La Sepmaine*, or Erasmus Darwin's *The Temple of Nature*, which is subtitled *The Origin of Society*. In such works there is an order of stages of creation, whether the six days of Christian myth, or some other division of the total creative process. A poem that tells its story day by day is always looking to the last day, the seventh, and in this sense it comprises an ideal journey.[17] With cosmogony the term "progress" must have the most intellectualized meaning, since it is not the hero who moves (though the author's persona may do so, under the guise of discoverer who narrates the poem),[18] but the whole cosmos that moves toward completion.

When the poet is dissecting rather than creating his universe, when he is cosmological rather than cosmogonic, he may prefer the satirical form known as "anatomy," in which digression becomes the rule, so

---

ture," from *Transactions of the Wisconsin Academy of Sciences, Arts, and Letters*, XVII (Dec. 1913) Pt. I.

[16] Cf. Alanus de Insulis (Alain de Lille), *The Complaint of Nature*, tr. Douglas Moffat ("Yale Studies in English Literature," XXXVI) (New York, 1908). On this general subject see J. D. Peter, *Complaint and Satire in Early English Literature* (Oxford, 1956).

[17] The week of the Creation is central to the exegetical tradition, as described in Wolfson, *Philo*, I, 120.

[18] This is the case with Dante and Spenser, and with the visionary tradition even as late as Blake.

much so that digression itself takes on the character of a ritual.[19] Far from being a free and easy meander by the wayside, the digressions in *A Tale of a Tub* are the most ordered, forced aspect of that work. It is true that the aim of anatomy is to gain some apparent freedom from the customary rigors of allegorical action, and there is a way of reading Swift, or a comparable modern author like Eugene Zamiatin, so that by thinking less of form and more of satirical message we experience a certain freedom from rigidity. The wit displayed at individual moments shifts our gaze from the overall order in which the parts are held. Thus, with Zamiatin's *We* there are so many strange metaphysical jokes and ironies (and frights) crowding in upon the reader that he may not realize how the book is set up in an endless ritual of chapters each of which has three main cruxes.[20] Zamiatin himself signals the cruxes with little enigmatic epigraphs, three to a chapter, and they are there for the reader to decipher, as he begins each chapter. He may disregard the signals, but the exegete has a ritual available for inspection and participation.

The norm of allegorical action in this type remains a straight-line movement that is obsessive in its single-mindedness. Quests in either romance (e.g., for the Grail) or national epic (e.g., the *Aeneid*) come to mind at once. Our first chapter showed how this straight line produces or conveys a daemonic effect, since the daemonic agent

---

[19] On "anatomy" see Frye, 308–314.

[20] Eugene Zamiatin, *We*, tr. Gregory Zilboorg (New York, 1959). Each chapter begins with an epigraph as follows:

	The Limit of the Function
Chapt. 24	Easter
	To Cross Out Everything
	The Descent from Heaven
Chapt. 25	The Greatest Catastrophe in History
	The Known—is Ended
	In a Ring
Chapt. 35	A Carrot
	A Murder

can only progress in one direction, or if he digresses like the narrator of *A Tale of a Tub* or of Rabelais' *Gargantua and Pantagruel*, he does so in an obsessional manner.[21] The daemonic agent has no choice but to go and then stay bound on his quest, whether for learning and self-knowledge, or for holiness, or for simple power, or for some object he himself cannot define, which may be the case with Kafka's favorite hero, K. We should take the words "progress" and "quest" in the loosest way, because there is manifestly a wide difference between the hero Dante of *The Divine Comedy*, the hero Christian of *The Pilgrim's Progress*, and the hero Gulliver in *Gulliver's Travels*, yet all are engaged in progresses. Our difficulty is aggravated by the fact that whole groups of people may be involved in the movement. In Zola's sequence of novels about the family of the Rougon-Macquart, a complex destiny of a crowd of people of different generations is played out in almost predestined form.[22] Even though the way is strewn with documentary notes far exceeding in number those of medieval encyclopedic works, the same fatalistic pattern is there. Another veil thrown over the progress may be the degradation of the characters in much naturalist fiction; but this merely reverses the direction, and anagogy becomes katagogy. The hero is bound no less on a quest if he be searching for his own ruin.

Battle: the psychomachia and ideological warfare. The same need to be rather flexible in interpreting action appears with the second major paradigm, the battle form. Prudentius in the *Psychomachia* establishes the battle as an allegorical action, and he describes an actual conflict on a field of battle. But again our term is only a label for a somewhat variable allegorical sequence. Common among the gentler permutations of this imagery of conflict are the "debate" and

[21] Coleridge's remarks on the psychology of humours in Sterne, Rabelais' imitator, make this obsessional order quite apparent. Swift's "Digression on Madness" provides a satirical "theory" of digression itself.

[22] See Hemmings, *Emile Zola* (Oxford, 1953), ch. i, on the pseudoscientific theories of heredity on which Zola based the concept of an inherited infection which was to predestine the members of this family.

the "dialogue" (of Socrates and Euthyphro, of owl and nightingale, of self and soul),[23] where the war is verbal and more ironical and polite than Prudentius' physical struggle. Swift here also provides a typical example with his *Battle of the Books,* a typical minor work, with a delicate savor of the scholar's study. The tradition of the debate is, however, a major one. *Prometheus Bound,* the work Coleridge took to be the fountainhead of allegory, is written in the debate form. *Prometheus Bound* reduces battle to the static suffering of an agon.[24]

Actual violence marks the commonest type of allegorical battle in our times, science fiction's "war of the worlds." This war turns out always to be a conflict of ideas and ideals, but its figurative base is nonetheless a technological military one, and its form is necessarily back and forth in a typical military fashion. Often, however, the two forms of progress and battle are conjoined to produce works like Čapek's *War with the Newts,*[25] where there is as much of the encyclopedic as of the psychomachic, or Orwell's *1984,* where a struggle of minds leads the hero, Winston Smith, to a doomed end, through a spiritual trial. Orwell's *Animal Farm* combines a fable of technological progress with a war between good and evil agents. Koestler's *Darkness at Noon* turns the war of nerves, a brain-washing, into a ritual of questioning and rumination. Here again we have evidence to support Frye's view that in modern literature progress is inverted.

[23] Panofsky discusses the tradition of the "debate," in *Galileo as a Critic of the Fine Arts* (The Hague, 1954). Typical examples: the medieval "The Owl and the Nightingale," Lydgate's *Reson and Sensualitie,* Marvell's "Dialogue between the Soul and Body," and "A Dialogue between the Resolved Soul and Created Pleasure." See M. C. Waites, "Some Aspects of the Ancient Allegorical Debate," in *Studies in English and Comparative Literature* (Radcliffe College Monographs, No. 15; London and Boston, 1910).

[24] A minor medieval example would be the alliterative poem, "Death and Life," although here the *agon* is confined to a relatively small portion of the poem, the actual confrontation of Life and Death. On *agon,* see F. M. Cornford, *Origins of Attic Comedy* (New York, 1961), 27–46.

[25] Karel Čapek, *War with the Newts* (1936), tr. M. and R. Weatherall, (New York, 1959).

The katagogic, regressive character of modern allegories comes out not only in their imagery, which is increasingly low and disgusting and ironical, but in their very forms, where the hero moves gradually into a more restricted range of action, into an imprisoning hole or cave.

Contrasts between progress and battle. Since progress and battle so often merge, it will be well to have an abstract idea of their main difference. They are superficially not identical in shape. The progress is manifestly a ritual form, but the battle may not at first appear to be so. Progress, after all, involves a sequence of steps in one main direction, and, as with the steps we take when we walk in procession, while minor irregularities are the norm, an *overall* regularity is equally the norm and at last overrides the smaller irregularities. Ritual tends to exaggerate equality of step. Sometimes it can openly do this, when form and content coincide, as in poems like "The Phoenix and the Turtle." Sometimes the coincidence lies under the surface, which would be the case with more extended allegories. It then becomes ncessary to go beneath the large-scale order of these works, to see what, in detail, brings about the ritual effect.

The same precise analysis into detail should likewise be applied to the battle form, where the effect is not exactly one of ritual, but is rather an effect of symmetry and balance. If these are not ritualistic qualities, it is only because ritual seems to imply a continued unfolding, a moving sequence, whereas symmetry suggests stasis and conflict caught at a given moment in time. But conflicts can be symmetrically duplicated and repeated within a work. As one side takes a swipe, so the other side takes one. The back and forth of battle, when translated to a mental conflict or an ideological warfare, becomes the symmetrical presentation of first the argument on one side, then the argument on the other. The debaters of the debate are presented in an equality, so that each side gets its fair share of the action. In many poems of the kind single alternating stanzas are allotted to each side, as they argue back and forth. The symmetry of form here also may be employed for a mixed formal effect. *The*

Pilgrim's Progress, for example, has debates inset into the narrated progress, while *The Faerie Queene,* essentially a battle form, mingles pastoral progresses with the "fierce wars" and "faithful loves."

Debates ever recurring, battles repetitiously taking on the same form, reversals and discoveries always couched in the same heraldic diction, such are the materials with which a medieval romance might achieve ritual form. These effects can be modernized; in Kafka, for example, the quest often takes on legalistic form, which in turn becomes an attempt to "get through" to the authorities of a vast bureaucratic state. (Bureaucracy, be it noted, implies separation into isolated compartments.) In allegories of more clearly political import the ritual quest ironically becomes a process of brainwashing, as in Orwell, or in Arthur Koestler's *Darkness at Noon.* Whatever the content of the action, however, the reader is expected to follow along in a sort of procession. He follows along because the sequence of repeated elements is a kind of symbolic *dance,* to use Kenneth Burke's word, and it holds his attention in a certain way. Both semantics and syntactics are component aspects of this "symbolic action." The daemonic agents and cosmic images of allegory are semantic elements, signs which act and represent, while the rhythmic character of allegories is in a large sense a syntactic element. Syntax, the sequential ordering of the parts, can be looked at either grossly or precisely. Grossly examined, it yields an overall rhythmic pattern, the kind of pattern established in Spenser by the use of books, cantos, and stanzas. It also yields an overall pattern of actions going on *within* those imposed structural forms—the duels and marriages of *The Faerie Queene,* for example, or the successive revelations recounted by Dante in the *Commedia.* These are macroscopic symbolic rhythms. On a microscopic level we must look at the way sentences and paragraphs are formed, in short at what we normally mean by the term "syntax." On this level we shall equally find that the poet assumes a characteristic rhythm, a gait by which we identify him. The "garment of style" almost seems to be a cause of the allegorical rhythm, in that the formal elements of kosmos are like armor on a medieval knight; they dignify him but they also stiffen him, locking him into a strictly measured gait.

Microscopic effects of syntax. On the level of small-scale effects, what rhetorical characteristics of form and action can we see? This should be a matter of agent and image, as much as of overall story line and syntax. The agent is daemonic, the image a cosmic metonymy or synecdoche; the former can only follow his quest, the latter is an essentially arbitrary label attached to a desired virtue or hated vice. Metonymies are above all *names,* and are emphatically kept to serve the needs of labeling and fixing the magical value of whatever they are applied to. When one chronicles a set of names which label aspects of virtue or vice, one is making a catalogue, and this in turn constitutes a ritual. To the extent that metonymies are chosen arbitrarily, they will need to be contained by some sort of externally imposed order.[26] The same need characterizes synecdochic imagery,

[26] One of the most suggestive accounts of the fundamental grounds of metaphor, as contrasted with metonymy, is Roman Jakobson's "The Cardinal Dichotomy in Language," *Language: An Enquiry into Its Meaning and Function,* ed. R. N. Anshen (New York, 1957), ch. ix, 155–173. Jakobson bases his comments on the work done with aphasics by Kurt Goldstein; see Goldstein, *Aftereffects of Brain Injuries in War* (New York, 1942); also, "Abstract and Concrete Behavior: An Experimental Study with Special Tests," *Psychological Monographs,* LIII (1941), 1–31. Goldstein found a cardinal dichotomy in language capacities, which seems capable of generalizing to normal prose and poetic uses. "Every form of aphasic disturbance consists in some impairment, whether severe or not, either of the faculty for selection and substitution or of that for combination and contexture. The former affliction involves a deterioration of metalinguistic operations, while the latter damages the capacity for maintaining the hierarchy of linguistic units. The relation of similarity is suppressed in the former, the relation of contiguity in the latter type of aphasic. *Metaphor is alien to the similarity disorder, and metonymy to the contiguity disorder*" (Anshen, *Language,* 169–170).

This negative argument has a positive side. "The primacy of the metaphorical way in the literary schools of romanticism and symbolism has been generally acknowledged, but it is still insufficiently realized that it is the predominance of metonymy which underlies and actually predetermines the so-called 'realistic' trend, which belongs to an intermediate stage between the decline of romanticism and the rise of symbolism and is opposed to both. Following the path of contiguous relations, the realistic author metonymically digresses from

and here also it is most convenient for the poet to list the elements of the whole. One sees this clearly in Menenius Agrippa's "fable of the belly" in *Coriolanus*. Once the hierarchic system is announced, an economy arises from listing, rather than more freely displaying, the cosmic order therein. The effect, as far as imagery in particular is concerned, is obviously a kind of symbolic isolation, an islanding of each part-image into a ritual or symmetrical narration.

More important for the action is the particular syntax in which the action is expressed. We need a syntactic description of the effects we have already seen, steady propulsiveness and exact symmetry. The former effect would seem to have a syntactic parallel in what is called *parataxis*. This term implies a structuring of sentences such that they do not convey any distinctions of higher or lower order. "Order" here means intensity of interest, since what is more important usually gets the greater share of attention. In parataxis each predication stands alone: "They ran. He wept. They ran again." Or else predications are joined by conjunctions of equality: "He ran, and they wept, and he ran again"; or "He walked, but the people ran." This means that paratactic sentences do not attempt modification by relative clauses, subordinating conjunctions, phrases in apposition, and the like. When such subordinating devices are employed, we have what is called *hypotaxis*, of which the style of Henry James would be an extreme example.

These two terms need to be pulled away from their linguistic context and employed somewhat as Heinz Werner's *Comparative*

---

the plot of the atmosphere and from the characters to the settings in space and time. He is fond of synecdochic details. In the scene of Anna Karenina's suicide, artistic attention is focussed on the heroine's handbag; and in *War and Peace* the synecdoches 'hair on the upper lip' and 'naked shoulders' are used to stand for the female characters to whom these features belong" (*ibid.*, 175).

In older terms these features are the "emblems" for certain characters; as such they are physical leitmotivs, and to the extent that they stand alone, they become demonic agencies. They are the magical names and emblems of a poet like Stefan George, as well as of the naturalistic authors Jakobson speaks about. They, like the leitmotivs in Wagner and Richard Strauss, are clearly obsessional in their rather pedantic repetition.

Psychology of Mental Development employs "parataxis"; Werner takes the term to mean the piecemeal behavior of young children or primitive peoples. We do not want to imply childlike or primitive behavior, but we do want our terms to have a roughly psychological meaning. Logically parataxis and hypotaxis are clearly distinct, because subordination and superordination are logical concepts. But Biblical parataxis differs psychologically from the very same syntactic order as practiced by a person giving directions to a stranger, and Henry James's hypotaxis goes so far in the direction of involuted, defensive complexity that it almost ceases to be a modifying style and comes full circle into parataxis, like an incredibly complicated telegram—the effect Max Beerbohm achieves in his parody of James, "The Mote in the Middle Distance." Such an effect is felt for other than logical reasons, or, to put the matter another way, the emotive effects of the syntax are not the same as their logical effects. Both types of syntax may display ambiguity, suggesting that there is a rhythmic order even deeper in its organizing force than the syntactic order.[27]

[27] The syntactic conditions of rhythm need still to be studied in full. First, for example, parataxis will be differently produced by English than by Navaho, which is by nature a stertorous, asyndetonic language. Even in English there are varying effects with sentences that might seem, syntactically, to be all similarly paratactic. There are also many subtleties of *parole* that could only be studied phonographically, i.e., as paralanguage. "The word Parataxis may be used in two senses: it may mean simply a lack of grammatical subordination such as we find in the language of children and some primitive people, or, secondly, it may be a rhetorical device by which a subordinate relationship is idiomatically expressed by a coordinately juxtaposed sentence, as when we say 'Knock and it shall be opened' instead of 'If ye knock, it shall be opened'" (S. O. Andrew, *Syntax and Style in Old English* [Cambridge, 1940], ch. xi, 87). Andrew finds that most Old English poetry has an ambiguity of meaning which implies subordination, even though the style remains philologically paratactic; we feel there are subordinate clauses in *Beowulf*, even though few appear on the page. Perhaps the oral poet, when reciting, inflected his half-lines and kennings in such a way that the listener had a strong sense of higher and lower importance, from one to the next, as an actor will pronounce his "asides" in a special tone of voice. But this does not change the fact of language, that the style is paratactic in form, if not intent. See Auerbach, *Mimesis*, 170–177,

Auerbach observed in his *Mimesis* the almost antithetical ways parataxis can be used. He noted the vivid oral usage which conveys untrammeled passion.

It was the vernacular poets who first saw man as a living being and found the form in which parataxis possesses poetic power. Instead of a thin, monotonous trickle of juxtaposition, we now [in a poem like *The Song of Roland*] have the *laisse* form, with its abrupt advances and regressions and its abundance of energetic new beginnings, which is a new elevated style. If the life which this stylistic procedure can seize upon is narrowly restricted and without diversity, it is nevertheless a full life,

---

on *Inferno*, Canto X, lines 22–78. He finds that, despite a "rapid succession of scenes, there is no question of any parataxis in Dante's style." The whole of Auerbach's chapter, "Roland against Ganelon," and Spitzer's essay on Diderot's style, in *Linguistics and Literary History*, are classic studies of the problem. Spitzer discerns in Diderot's *La Religieuse*, "a mechanical repetition of two alternating rhythmical patterns." The *style coupé* is called "breathless, tense, cramped."

The paratactic effect (psychological lack of higher and lower degrees of interest or value, "withdrawal of affect") seems to result even when the syntax conditions would seem to be subordinative. In short, sometimes hypotaxis produces the sense of no hierarchy, sometimes even it may enhance a lack of syntactic pause, rush, accent, and rhythm. By an unmodulated sequence of relative clauses (Ionesco satirizes this in his play *The Bald Soprano*, in the Firechief's tale of the headache), the writer can seem to be frustrating the very purposes of hypotaxis, which theoretically might be defined as a modulation to fit the fusive, suddenly altering, suddenly accelerating and decelerating pace of human response to the environment. Such an author, par excellence, would be William Faulkner, whose hypotaxis has no effect of variety, but rather creates a monotonous ground swell. We have evidence that this was Faulkner's aim, judging from his way of reading his own prose aloud. He droned, if we may judge from phonographic recordings.

See Alarik Rynell, "Parataxis and Hypotaxis as a Criterion of Syntax and Style," in *Lunds Univ. Arsskrift*, N.F. Avd. 1., XLVIII (1952), no. 3. Also, Wyndham Lewis's attack on Gertrude Stein, in *Time and Western Man* (New York, 1928) 53–65. Obvious American authors would be Hemingway, Faulkner, Agee—and their opposite number, Henry James.

Cf. also W. Nelson Francis, *The Structure of American English* (New York, 1958), 292 ff., on syntactic structures; G. H. Vallins, *The Pattern of English* (Penguin ed., 1957), where structure is related to the behavior of the verb in English.

a life of human emotion, a powerful life, a great relief after the pale, intangible style of the late antique legend. The vernacular poets also knew how to exploit direct discourse in terms of tone and gesture.[28]

All we have to do, to derive a model of ritual syntax from Auerbach's description, is to emphasize that parataxis seized upon a life "narrowly restricted and without diversity," or else to say that the forward rush of the *laisse* form might become an unchecked, compulsive rush. Examples are not lacking. Take for example the following passage from the *Complaint of Nature*, which shows the same syntax in both the original and its prose translation:

Nature weeps. Character passes away. Chastity is wholly banished from its former high station, and become an orphan. The sex of active nature trembles shamefully at the way in which it declines into passive nature. Man is made woman. He blackens the honor of his sex. The craft of Venus makes him of double gender. He is both subject and predicate. He becomes likewise of two declensions. He pushes the laws of grammar too far.[29]

True, the fourth sentence of this passage contains a relative clause, which has a subordinating effect and gives variety. The passage is therefore not totally unmixed. Furthermore, the very meaning of given words will sometimes introduce an element of subordination, though the syntax fails to do so, and this may help to vary the paratactic style. On the other hand the predominating effect is a listing and labeling of all the items in the complaint. The form is exactly what it would be in an ironical "testament," where the poet leaves to the world all the errors he is complaining of.

Oral, formulaic poetry employs the device of the kenning in a way that suggests a purely practical reason for the style of the *Complaint of Nature*. The kenning of Old English poetry, for example,

---

[28] Page 103. Auerbach deals extensively with syntactic effects, as befits a scholar in the linguistic tradition. See also, for example, *Mimesis*, 155 and 185. Robertson has a related treatment of the *Chanson de Roland* in his *Preface to Chaucer*, 163–171.

[29] *Complaint*, tr. Moffat, 3.

had been combined "in paratactic single file," because it was easy
to improvise in that manner. But poets like Alain de Lille, or William
Blake, or Walt Whitman do not write oral poetry, although they are
all preeminently paratactic authors. The following lines from Blake
were not meant to be recited by a bard in a mead hall.

> The citizens of New York close their books and lock their chests;
> The mariners of Boston drop their anchors and unlade;
> The scribe of Pennsylvania casts his pen upon the earth;
> The builder of Virginia throws his hammer down in fear.[30]

This passage and the one that follows it in Blake's *America*, like his
prophetic poetry in general, are paratactic. It is perhaps not necessary to quote Whitman at this point, since the passage from Blake so
obviously suggests Whitman. (Whitman, like Blake and Christopher
Smart, is a master of metonymy, outdone in this respect only by the
archmetonymist, Gertrude Stein.)

That this style can be more flowing and rhythmic appears from
much of the poetry of Shelley. One wonders, even so, just how long
the poet can effectively keep parataxis going. Consider what would
happen if Shelley had written several pages in the following stanzaic
form.

> The world's great age begins anew,
>   The golden years return,
> The earth doth like a snake renew
>   Her winter weeds outworn:
> Heaven smiles, and faiths and empires gleam,
> Like wrecks of a dissolving dream.
>
> A brighter Hellas rears its mountains
>   From waves serener far;
> A new Peneus rolls his fountains
>   Against the morning star.
> Where fairer Tempes bloom, there sleep
> Young Cyclads on a sunnier deep.

[30] *Complete Writings*, ed. Geoffrey Keynes (London, 1958), 201.

A loftier Argo cleaves the main,
    Fraught with a later prize;
Another Orpheus sings again,
    And loves, and weeps, and dies.
A new Ulysses leaves once more
Calypso for his native shore.

If this style of verse leans sometimes toward a freedom of line, hypotaxis can in its excess lean toward a "monotonous trickle of juxtaposition," which amounts to another kind of ritual. Coleridge complained of Dr. Johnson's balanced periods that they were merely verbal, by which he implied they were false antitheses, artificially constructed by Johnson out of nonexistent conflicts.[31] Fair or not, the accusation can theoretically be made against any overly symmetrical, or euphuistic, balanced periodic sentence. Such sentences are bound to be hypotactic, and in this one case at least we have no guarantee that the nominal opposite of parataxis produces an effect any less ritualized than parataxis itself. It would seem that the hypotactic abuse of symmetrical periods corresponds to the hyper-symmetrical forms we have found basic to one type of allegorical action. Johnsonian antithesis sets up a kind of miniature battle between conflicting elements of his thought; he is allegorical in this way as well as in his Latinate etymologizing, which he learns from

[31] Lecture XIV, "On Style," in *Misc. Crit.*, 220: "Johnson's style has pleased many from the very fault of being perpetually translateable; he creates an impression of cleverness by never saying anything in a common way. The best specimen of this manner is in Junius, because his antithesis is less merely verbal than Johnson's. Gibbon's manner is the worst of all; it has every fault of which this peculiar style is capable. Tacitus is an example of it in Latin; in coming from Cicero you feel the *falsetto* immediately." Note how Coleridge has just previous to these comments related the periodic style to the cultural development of a wider reading public, which suggests that status symbols are involved here. "The essence of this style consisted in a mock antithesis, that is, an opposition of mere sounds, in a rage for personification, the abstract made animate, far-fetched metaphors, strange phrases, metrical scraps, in every thing, in short, but genuine prose." This sounds rather like a description of a rage for allegory, on the syntactic and stylistic level.

Sir Thomas Browne, in whom the hieroglyphical tradition kept very much alive during the seventeenth century.

Symmetry of balanced elements, whether syntactic (in prose) or prosodic (in verse) are strongly served by the device of anaphora, a figure dubbed by Thomas Wilson, "the marcher." [32] The Anglo-Saxon allegory of the *Phoenix* provides a good instance from oral poetry; a very large percentage of the following lines and half lines will be seen to begin with either of two words, "No" and "or," and the effect is certainly what we should expect from a poem employing "the marcher."

> Naught hostile lodges in all that land,
> No pain or weeping or sign of sorrow,
> No age or anguish or narrow death;
> No ending of life or coming of evil,
> No feud of vengeance or fret of care;
> No lack of wealth or pressure of want,
> No winter storm or change of weather
> Fierce under heaven, or bitter frost
> With wintry icicles smites any man there.
> No hail or hoar-frost descends to earth,
> No windy cloud; no water falls
> Driven by storm. But running streams
> And welling waters wondrously spring
> Overflowing the earth from fountains fair.[33]

In the Bible comparable instances are the Beatitudes and the book of Ecclesiastes, with its roll of "times." In the latter at least it is easy to see the archetypal roll call of abstractions from the universal calendar.

To every thing there is a season, and a time to every purpose under the heaven:

---

[32] Puttenham, *Arte of English Poesie*, 208, calls anaphora the "figure of report," suggesting the catalogue, the inventory, the list. His example is from Raleigh, with whom the figure was a favorite device, along with detached illustrative simile.

[33] "The Phoenix," *Early English Christian Poetry*, 232.

A time to be born, and a time to die; a time to plant, and a time to
pluck up that which is planted;

A time to kill, and a time to heal; a time to break down, and a time
to build up;

A time to weep, and a time to laugh; a time to mourn, and a time to
dance;

A time to cast away stones, and a time to gather stones together; a
time to embrace, and a time to refrain from embracing;

A time to get, and a time to lose; a time to keep, and a time to cast
away;

A time to rend, and a time to sew; a time to keep silence, and a time
to speak;

A time to love, and a time to hate; a time of war, and a time of peace.[34]

This appears to be plain exposition, but if it is so, then it is rendered
more symbolic, and less simply expository, by its syntax; that is, the
rhythm here works rather against the expression of fact, and instead
creates a sort of incantatory sermon, personifying the "times," as
they lead on the procession, much as they would in a medieval allegorical tapestry, or as in Spenser. A high degree of syntactic symmetry here reinforces the rhythmic pulse which uses a calculated
monotony to produce a hypnotic effect.

The same archetypal rhythm is more apparent in lesser works, like
the familiar medieval procession of the Seven Deadly Sins. I would
maintain that ritualized rhythm is enough by itself to render exposition symbolic, as in the following instance from Gascoigne's *The
Steele Glas* (1576), where the anaphoras (here, the "figure of report") are underscored by the original punctuation.

> But now (aye me) the glasing christal glass
> Doth make us think, that realms and towns are rich
> Where favor sways, the sentence of the law,
> Where all is fish, that cometh to the net,
> Where mighty power, doth over rule the right,
> Where injuries, do foster secret grudge,

[34] Cf. Auerbach, *Mimesis*, 95–96, on the sublime style of Genesis.

Where bloudy sword, makes every booty prize,
Where banquetting, is counted comely cost,
Where officers grow rich by princes' pens,
Where purchase comes, by cozyn and deceit,
And no man dreads, but he that cannot shift,
Nor none serve God, but only tongue-tied men.
Again I see, within my glass of Steel,
The four estates, to serve each country soil,
The King, the Knight, the Peasant, and the Priest.
The King should care for all the subjects still,
The Knight should fight, for to defend the same,
The Peasant he, should labor for their ease,
The Priests should pray, for them and for themselves.[35]

This is the language of a Christian poet, aiming his address at a people who must believe in the hierarchy of the state, for whom all human action is but the doubtful simulacrum of a more permanent otherworldly state. In this instance of the lesser poet like George Gascoigne, where the overall prosodic and punctuational effects are simpler and easier to discern, we can well apply the words of Carlo Levi's *Of Fear and Freedom*, a modern study of authoritarian symbolism and behavior.

When the sense of the world is placed outside the world, when every action and every thought are a sacrifice to a deity, language foregoes its autonomous creative value and assumes a symbolic significance. Every part of the language, every single sentence, every word in the sentence, becomes a divine symbol; and every symbol, every word has an absolute value, identical with every other, because all of them equally contain and postulate a god. Every symbol becomes valuable, and dwells in isolation. Syntax dissolves; the single elements of a sentence acquire an equal importance, and equally suggestive powers.[36]

---

[35] *The Steele Glas*, in *English Reprints, George Gascoigne, Esquire*, ed. Edward Arber (London, 1869). Toward the end of the poem Gascoigne runs for 43 lines using anaphora, with a few minor interruptions in the form of lines starting with "and" and "but."

[36] Levi, *Of Fear and Freedom*, tr. Adolphe Gourevitch (New York, 1950),

This automatism, the loss of autonomy, this lack of syntactic freedom, this lack of response to an external world here and now, can come about under a kind of general religious pressure which a writer would feel only in the most diffuse way, perhaps not consciously at all. At any rate Levi's description of parataxis seems right in the context of allegorical literature, where we see it borne out even beyond the historical period he describes.

The primitive expression, that of the world which arose directly from the fall of the Empire and of the Latin language, was an expression, as we have seen, imbued with religiosity. Its syntax, therefore, is paratactic: every word, every image is closed in itself, complete, without ties, and equal in its value to every other one. The images, all equally symbolic, stand side by side, without correlation or opposition: discourse is a *mosaic*. The stress falls upon every word; all of them are on the same plane: there cannot be perspective. Furthermore, as there is no syntactic relationship, every single word must contain in itself the entire concept: inflections are abundant and complicated (dual number, third future tense, etc.).

Here we have, in brief, the description of an allegorical style such as I have already insisted on: the emblematic, isolated, mosaic imagery; the paratactic order; the ritual that accompanies religious observance; the lack of that perspective which would create a mimetic world; the microcosmic character of the imagery, where "every single word must contain in itself the entire concept."

A paradox emerges from these suggestions about rhythm: however hard it may be to isolate the rhythmic qualities of a symbolic

---

67 (copyright 1950 by Farrar, Straus & Co.; quoted by permission). Levi identifies parataxis (or, the effect of parataxis) with mosaic, lack of perspective, monotonous rhythm, symmetry forms, abolition of "tonality and composition" (see 72). See also Heinz Werner, *Comparative Psychology of Mental Development* (Chicago, 1948), on paratactic behavior in general. Christine Brooke-Rose, *A Grammar of Metaphor* (London, 1958), 64, 203, shows why, grammatically, a sustained allegory is likely to be monotonous, inasmuch as it requires an addition together of a group of "genitive metaphors" (synecdoches mainly) which must necessarily, in their referent, be tautological.

mode, we can record a more or less ritualized movement of ideas and events, and this movement oddly conflicts with the purported aim of most allegories, the hierarchical structuring of ideas and attitudes. Paratactic and hypotactic forces are at war with each other in the ritual. The authoritarian iconography should find its image in a varied hypotactic style, but, as I have noted, allegory subverts the hypotactic style (e.g., Euphuism) until it can become a pseudo syntax covering up an inherent lack of feeling. The term "parataxis" seems to stand, as I have used it, for a style by which feeling is either withdrawn from a danger situation (the psychoanalyst's "withdrawal of affect") or else so strictly channeled that it no longer shows the variability of normal instincts and drives. A galley slave's behavior will be paratactic, no matter what bank of oars he sits at.

The concept of a ritualistic rhythm has been defined in very general terms. In practice literary works all show minor variations that defy precise definition. It appears therefore that the concept of "actions," by which we mean the form taken by the story (Greek: *mythos*), has a usefulness other than for pointing to peculiar characteristics of particular works. The concept is useful because we need to think of allegory itself in very large terms; we need to understand the mode less in terms of the special subject matter of any given work and more in terms of the rhythm of the given work.

Rhythmic encoding. Finally the author communicates an allegorical intent, not by the content, but by the rhythm. How is this so? Very simply, we can understand the process in terms of an encoding technique. If one wanted to establish a code using a series of unfamiliar signals, let us say bell sounds of different pitches instead of dots and dashes, one would have to repeat certain key combinations in a sort of ritual. The listener who picked up the repeated sounds would at first see no message in them, but gradually would perceive the repetitive pattern, an imposed "code," and would try deciphering what he heard. Allegories are codes in this sense. Their enigmatic surfaces are known not to be random and accidental, by virtue of their periodic repetitions. For example, each of the four voyages in *Gulliver's Travels* begins with a permutation on the idea of ship-wreck. With the first there is little to the shipwreck besides sheer accident—man against nature. But as each successive shipwreck oc-curs, it becomes apparent that Gulliver is being landed on the strange islands and territories in a peculiar way; to be shipwrecked for him is always to experience a violent exclusion from safety, from social comfort and friendship. With each successive appearance of the figure there is an increased degree of human malevolence toward Gulliver. This malevolence in itself might also be an accident, like the storm of the first voyage, but the fact that the shipwreck recurs in variants of that first catastrophe indicates an underlying concept. The allegory expresses an idea of inevitable isolation, by this device of the wreck, and it is clearly iconographic to the reader because it has the status of a repeated unit of code.

The establishment of a code need not take long. Kafka achieves it almost at once, in his short story, "The Hunter Gracchus." In the opening paragraph his studiously paratactic rhythm sets off a number of compartmented elements, all of which are seen simultaneously, in a timeless cross section whose static order is prima facie emblematic, like the order in a De Chirico painting.

Two boys were sitting on the harbor wall playing with dice. A man was reading a newspaper on the steps of the monument, resting in the shadow of a hero who was flourishing his sword on high. A girl was filling her bucket at the fountain. A fruit-seller was lying beside his scales, staring out to sea. Through the vacant window and door openings of a cafe one could see two men quite at the back drinking their wine. The proprietor was sitting at a table in front and dozing. A bark was silently making for the little harbor, as if borne by invisible means over the water. A man in a blue blouse climbed ashore and drew the rope through a ring. Behind the boatman two other men in dark coats with silver buttons carried a bier, on which, beneath a great flower-patterned tasseled silk cloth, a man was apparently lying.[37]

[37] Tr. W. and E. Muir, in *Parables* (Schocken ed., New York, 1947), 91. Re-printed by permission of Schocken Books Inc. from *Parables and Paradoxes* by Franz Kafka; copyright 1936, 1937, by Heinr. Mercer Sohn, Prague; copyright 1946, 1947, 1948, 1953, 1954, 1958, by Schocken Books Inc.

This predominantly paratactic enigma is furthered in the second paragraph, where Kafka employs anaphoric repetition.

Nobody on the quay troubled about the newcomers; even when they lowered the bier to wait for the boatman, who was still occupied with his rope, nobody went nearer, nobody asked them a question, nobody accorded them an inquisitive glance.

I am not suggesting that a whole story must be encoded in this manner, but that such techniques cue the reader to think in terms of riddles. The technique is formal; the content is not especially enigmatic in itself.

The unfinished allegorical progression. Another paradigm for the action of allegories would be the mathematical concept of a progression. If a mathematician sees the numbers, 1, 3, 6, 11, 20, he would recognize that the "meaning" of this progression can be recast into the algebraic language of the formula: X plus 2^x, with certain restrictions on X.[38] What would be a random sequence to an inexperienced person appears to the mathematician a meaningful sequence. Notice that the progression can go on ad infinitum. This parallels the situation in almost all allegories. They have no inherent "organic" limit of magnitude. Many are unfinished like *The Castle* and *The Trial* of Kafka. The physically unfinished state of some of these works, despite certain obvious biographical limitations that appear when we study the amount of time the author had to finish his work (as in the case of Guillaume de Lorris and *The Romance of the Rose*, or Edmund Spenser, who died before he could finish *The Faerie Queene*, for "want of bread," if we can believe Ben Jonson), and the fragmented forms characteristic of others (e.g., *A Tale of a Tub*) need to be understood in dynamic terms. There is more than

---

[38] Scott Buchanan, in his *Symbolic Distance in Relation to Analogy and Fiction* (London, 1932), developed the analogy between metaphoric constructs and algebraic matrices which might be fully worked out (allegory) or only partially worked out (metaphor and symbol).

external biographic evidence to show how works come to be left unfinished.[39]

There is always a strong tendency for any ritual to remain essentially unfinished, in the sense that all rituals, whether religious or otherwise, show a tendency to increase in length and elaboration over time. The church ritual known as the liturgy tends to elaborate itself indefinitely until we get a fundamentalist "reformation," because each past order of worship is felt to have lost some of its original efficacy. As each ritual is elaborated, given new ornaments, given new stages and subdivisions, it necessarily increases in length. Two results are possible, and both can be found in allegorical literature. First, the poet can arbitrarily refuse to elaborate, and then we have a strong sense of "closure," as when he cuts off a procession of allegorical devices with what is called in medieval literature a "summation scheme." [40] The "Threnos" of "The Phoenix and the Turtle" is a classic example of the summation scheme closing the end of a potentially endless sequence of steps. The arbitrary closing of a

[39] Aristotle, on poetic magnitude, *Poetics*, 1449b, 1451a, 1452b, 1455b, 1459b and 1462b. See also R. M. Adams, *Strains of Discord, passim;* and on Kafka's unfinished forms, Heinz Politzer, *Franz Kafka: Parable and Paradox* (Ithaca, 1962).

[40] Curtius, *European Literature*, 289. The summation scheme is an optic device, since it makes the reader look back over the visually presented appearance of the poem. In this respect it is not unlike the repeated use of a typographical figure, e.g., Herbert's *Easter Wings*, on which see J. H. Summers, *George Herbert*, ch. vi, especially 143-145. In this connection see also Curtius, 284. Curtius appears to define "mannerism," of which these particular figures are meek relatives, as an obsessive deformation of natural usage. A style much given to "summation schemes" would soon begin to pall on the reader, like any obsessive act. This dullness is felt, for example, in the Theophrastian "Character." On a similarly "optic" device, cf. Sir Thomas Browne, *Works*, V, "Of Ropalic or Gradual Verses." Says Browne: "I must needs confess, I have no affection for it; as being utterly averse from all affectation in Poetry, which either restrains the phancy, or filters the invention to any strict disposure of words." Cf. also Victor Erlich, *Russian Formalism*, in the series *Slavistische Drukken en Herdrukken* (The Hague, 1955), 190 ff., on "rhythmico-syntactical parallelism."

romance by means of a marriage or a death is another instance, less obvious only because it seems a more material and less formal device. Perhaps poems like *The Divine Comedy* and *The Faerie Queene* show this arbitrary closure more strongly than most allegories, because not only do they exhibit it along the way, by what I would call a "segregation of parts" (e.g., the stanza forms of both poems), but they both are intended to close with a final homecoming in an ideal world.[41] *The Faerie Queene* was literally going to end where it began, at a marriage ceremony. As I interpret its final canto, *The Divine Comedy* suggests metaphorically that Dante the traveler could now serenely return to his earthly round of daily action. The poem ends on a note of triumphant peace.

> but already my desire and will
> were turning like a wheel moved evenly
>
> by the Love which turns the sun and the other stars.

It follows from the arbitrary nature of allegorical action itself, that it will go on as long as a daemonic agent is present, since, unlike the Dante who is gradually transformed, a daemon never tires or changes his nature. If he does change his nature, that happens only by his meeting a superior force, inevitably another daemon, and then the change is no less arbitrary than would be the continuation of a single-tracked action.[42] Critics have observed that when in a medieval

[41] For Blake the true epic is a cyclic vision of life, as described in Frye, *Fearful Symmetry*, 109–111. The archetypal round of the "eternal return" is the narrative, temporal equivalent of the encyclopedic enclosure of a total body of knowledge. This is not a matter of historical allegory, but of an historicizing allegory, on which see Cohen and Nagel, *An Introduction to Logic and Scientific Method* (New York, 1934), 359–360. I have omitted any serious consideration of historical allegory in the present work, because it is a large, and to some extent a secondary, area of allegorical technique. It is worth noting that no proper treatment of the historical allegory of Book V of *The Faerie Queene* is available at present.

[42] H. Frankfort, in *Ancient Egyptian Religion* (New York, 1948), ch. v, "Change and Permanence in Literature and Art," 141, discusses the hypostatizing imagery of a people otherwise living in terror of the flux—the net

chivalric romance or in a composite form like *The Faerie Queene*
the hero achieves a victory over a hostile agent, he is not brought
thereby into a state of repose; he is acclaimed, and then rewarded
by another task. This is the conventional way of expressing a tendency toward infinite extension. It is logically quite natural for the
extension to be infinite, since by definition there is no such thing as
the whole of any analogy; all analogies are incomplete, and incom-
pletable, and allegory simply records this analogical relation in a
dramatic or narrative form.[43] The interest of allegory perhaps re-

---

effect, in stylistic terms, was paratactic ritualized series of images, both in visual
art and poetry. Such an order appears in the early Christian allegory of Prudentius, *The Psychomachia*, where the poet underlines an episodic form by
allowing each scene to be just like that on either side of it. Later the ritual
appears in such popular works as Brant's *Narrenschiff*, or *Ship of Fools*—a
dance of death, by implication.

The processional character of the Dance of Death (see Auerbach, *Mimesis*,
217) has a living analogue in the processions of the Masques of the Seasons, or
of the Rivers in Spenser. Frye, *Anatomy*, 289, describes "spectacle" as processional and fragmentary in form. At the heart of the masque is a "triumph."

[43] T. E. Hulme, author of *Speculations*, argued a special case for analogy in
what he considered the highest kind of "imagist" poetry: "But where the whole
of the analogy is every bit of it necessary for accurate description . . . if it is
sincere, in the accurate sense, when the whole of the analogy is necessary to
get out the exact curve of the feeling or thing you want to express—there you
seem to me to have the highest verse." This might be called "the doctrine of
imagism." Hulme wanted a poetry in which cosmic systems (analogies as
wholes) completely and perfectly corresponded to each other. I. A. Richards
reacted strongly against Hulme perhaps because the latter was in fact arguing
for a sort of allegorical poetry. Thus to stress analogy was to stress a rigid
semantic counterpoint, an academic fugue instead of a free contrapuntal development. Richards attacked Hulme in *The Philosophy of Rhetoric*, 133–134:
"For one thing, there is no whole to any analogy, we use as much of it as we
need; and, if we tactlessly take any analogy too far we break it down." This
statement reiterates the standard caution on the use of allegory; Macaulay says
as much, criticizing Bunyan. Richards continued: "There are no such limits to
the relations of tenor and vehicle as this [Hulme's] account puts. The result
of the doctrine may be seen in those anxious, over-careful attempts to *copy*
perceptions and feelings *in words*, to 'hand over sensations bodily,' of which
modern prose at its most distinguished too often consists. Words are not a
medium in which to copy life. Their true work is to restore life itself to order."
In this last criticism Richards is recalling the fallacy of "representative metre,"

sides in the special sort of causal connection between scenes and between the different allegorical characters it establishes. After all, even a systematic literature needs an other than logical interest.

The "visual" nature of allegorical actions. If one studied ritual in kinesthetic terms, one would perhaps find that there is a characteristic physical response to its measured tread; one might find that the reader of highly ritualized prose exposition simply goes to sleep, becomes anesthetized by the monotony; or, one might find an ever heightened, if somehow hypnotic, involvement in the ritual—the effect of listening to a bolero or a fandango. But if one thinks of ritual in conceptual terms, which indeed allegory requires, one finds, I expect, a more coolly rational sort of response in the reader. The ritual imposes such order on movement that it in effect communicates a sense of plan, of metric design, of formula. And this sense in turn is a quasi-visual one of diagram, which one of allegory's favorite forms will demonstrate most readily. The masque and its cousin, the allegorical pageant, exemplify this "charting" effect of ritual, and from this example to others of a less obvious kind in allegorical narratives there is not a very great distance.

More strikingly than in narrative poetry or prose fiction, in the dramatic form of the masque the action is ritualized. The masque consists most simply of a procession, introducing sequences of vir-

---

and his attack could be broadened to include a fallacy of representative music, i.e., program music. We need to recognize the almost universal fascination this kind of art has had for the greatest composers. Henry Purcell, for one, uses allegorical devices continually; his trills indicate shivering, in the Spirit of Frost's aria, in *King Arthur;* musical shakes are emblematic of the word "shake," in *Dido and Aeneas.* But this is a baroque tradition, fully established in such a composer as Bach. The more interesting cases come later, since contrapuntal music is inherently iconographic, whereas homophonic music seems less so. (See above, Chapter 2, n. 121; also the works of Manfred Bukofzer cited in the Bibliography.) It is apparent that so-called "pure" music finds a fair compromise with the desire for iconography in the accompaniments to lieder and operatic arias and in ballet. With Wagner this tendency toward the iconographic completely overwhelms mimetic drama; what is left is an endless series of sublime and picturesque "effects." Consider his own design for the opera house at Bayreuth, with its orchestral "abyss."

tues or vices or figures of topical interest. This procession can allow a certain amount of formalized dramatic interplay between the dramatis personae, and irrelevant songs and dances may interrupt it, but since its aim is finally to do honor to the chief spectators of the masque, it is finally limited by a rather strict decorum. When variety enters the action of the masque, it properly does so in the form of a *polar* opposition to the primary movement, that is, in the antimasque. If such devices remind us of the complex antiphonal choruses of Greek drama, we should not be too quick to assume that the masque becomes thereby mimetic. The antiphonal chorus is almost liturgical in Greek drama and constitutes one of the clearest ties binding that drama to a religious origin. The variety within the masque is therefore like that of a complex liturgical procession; it remains fundamentally ritualistic, despite the appearance of color and contrast in costume, dance, and song. So clear, in fact, are the demarcations of parts in the masque that this minor genre is able to isolate ideal conceptions. The masque is an analogical metaphor physically extended in time and space before an audience, and its diagrammatic effect comes chiefly from its rigidity of presentation, from its segregation of parts.

Much the same sort of diagrammatic effect comes across in any merely literary allegory, as a product of the sort of ritualized action pattern that I have been describing. In his *Philosophy of Literature* Kenneth Burke has spoken of the "charting" and "mapping" functions of literature, but the notion is a very old one, as the terminology of biblical exegesis indicates. There we find allegorical language referred to by such terms as *"paradeigma," "figura," "typos," "schema,"* all of which have strong visual connotations. It will perhaps be argued that all figurative language shares this visual quality with allegory, and the term "image" will be adduced to show the general truth of this argument. True enough, and we need here only maintain that in allegory the visual characteristics of all figurative language are reduced to a sort of diagrammatic form or impression (e.g., *"emblema," "impresa"*). In allegory the "extension" of the metaphor, that is, the narrative of the action, produces something at the same time deader than the lively effects of metaphor and clearer than those effects. When allegory is called "pure," the adjective implies that it lacks ambiguity in the same way that a diagram essentially lacks it. For the suggestiveness and intensity of ambiguous metaphorical language allegory substitutes a sort of figurative geometry. It enables the poet, as Francis Bacon observed, to "measure countries in the mind." Bacon's phrase may suggest that allegory is always going to be an affair of the mind, not of the heart (which many a modern critic has tried to maintain), but this view, as we shall see, takes account of only one side of the problem. Allegory may also be taken as emotive utterance and in this light shows an internal structure of such force that we do not long remain cold analysts of the geometric paradigm. The popular appeal of many parabolic works, especially of those romances that are so modestly allegorical—the western, the detective story, the melodrama—lies in a countermovement; for the causal connections of scenes and characters—the reasons why they go together as they do, the way the characters influence and affect each other, and so on— these are not simply logical; they are not merely reasonable; they are to a high degree magical relationships which have only superficially the form of ordered arguments.

4

Allegorical Causation: Magic and Ritual Forms

EVERY story, however brief, every drama, however condensed, every lyric, however elliptical, must be united by some causal interconnection of events. Aristotle says in the *Poetics* that it is desirable for mimetic drama to depict only such events as might "probably" follow each other in causal sequence, which applies an empiricist's criterion to the judgment of the coherence of drama and epic. In more modern fiction we often speak of the "plausibility" of the action, by which we also understand a reference of the fiction to an external standard of publicly shared experience. Such criteria will often do to indicate why a particular audience finds a particular play or novel "timely" and "relevant" to the problems of living. What Frye has called the "criterion of plausibility" further implies certain techniques of representation and in general implies that fiction seems always more real, more true to life, if it assumes the guise of factual reporting. It will often be useful to speak of this guise, when the artist sets out to be a naturalistic author, in the manner of Defoe. However, literature may present sequences of events, absurd or chance happenings, which do not meet the Aristotelian criterion of probability, although certain devices of verisimilitude make them plausible. This is preeminently the case with naturalistic allegories.

In allegorical actions generally events do not even have to be plausibly connected. Reversals and discoveries arbitrarily imposed on the action, the *deus ex machina* introduced to rid the action of an impasse—these do not imitate Nature, though they may imitate ideas and theories. Even so, however, allegorical actions do hold together on their own principles of unity. We shall find that these principles require a suspension of disbelief in magic and magical causation. When plots and subplots are combined in certain ways, the effect of interplay between them is a causal one, and when major characters "generate" subcharacters, fractions of themselves, these fractions have peculiar causal interrelations. The dramatis personae in allegorical fictions will not have to interact plausibly, or according to probability, as long as they interact with a certain logical necessity. This necessity in turn appears, as a result of the rhythms of allegory, to take on a magical force. The agents of allegory can help, hurt, change, and otherwise affect each other "as if by magic." The purpose of this chapter is to spell out this mode of interaction.

Doubling: a magical causation. Empson's thesis in *Some Versions of Pastoral*, his major treatment of allegory, was that double plots are bound to suggest a magical relationship between the two levels on which these plots are told. In a play like *Troilus and Cressida* the major plot is mirrored by a secondary one, and the mutual mirroring is felt to have a magical force, as if one plot brought the other into existence, since the other was its double. Each plot recreates the logic, the coherence, the persuasive force of the other, and the result is that we get something like a miraculous reduplication of two worlds that "belong together." As Empson said of *Troilus and Cressida*,

the two parts make a mutual comparison that illuminates both parties ("love and war are alike") and their large-scale indefinite juxtaposition seems to encourage primitive ways of thought ("Cressida will bring Troy bad luck because she is bad"). This power of suggestion is the strength of the double plot; once you take the two parts to correspond any character may take on *mana* because he seems to cause what he corresponds to or be the Logos of what he symbolizes.[1]

Here "Logos" implies a highly charged system of symbolic parallels, presumably imaged in the kosmoi that contain whole universes in small details of ornament. The war story of *Troilus and Cressida* begins to have power over the love story, and love thence becomes a kind of war—a conceit well known from the literature of courtly love, but here distinguished by its being the result of a parallelism of form, the doubling of the plots.

What seems strange at first is the odd object toward which Empson directed his studies—the pastoral—and strange also that he should so loosely define pastoral that it includes chiefly the literature he calls "proletarian." The latter might better be termed the literature of class struggle. But Empson chose his object of study for good reason, since the poetry in question, where there are magical double plots, is a poetry whose main aim is to codify social, political, or spiritual hierarchies along the lines of class distinctions. Pastoral is always a literature of status differences. If it employs kosmoi, it will be allegorical. All the works studied in *Some Versions of Pastoral* are given exegetical readings (thus the word "versions") and are interpreted as instances of ambivalent feeling, the feeling one experiences in situations of acute social tension. Magically caused behavior is appropriate to this pastoral world, because in order to shift from one rung of the social ladder to another, one needs magical aid. When a story presents the rich and the great hobnobbing with the poor, it suggests they impart to the poor a degree of power,

---

[1] William Empson, *Some Versions of Pastoral*, "Double Plots," 32. See Empson, *Seven Types of Ambiguity*, 140, where Empson discusses allegory. He later remarks: "But this form of ambiguity, though it was prominent in early Elizabethan writings, was soon felt as a triviality and abandoned by the dramatic writers. For if you are thinking about several situations at once you are detached from all of them, and are not observing any with an immediate attention."

while the poor return the gift by conferring purity on the rich. The interplay that allows this exchange is imaged in the plot structure, which is always showing us how the two groups seem to change places, the courtiers becoming shepherds, the shepherds becoming courtiers.[2]

This theory, that double plots are related to each other so as to produce a magical interaction, ties in with the argument that the plots of allegories are either going to be symmetry plots or ritual plots, diagrammatic allegorical battles or programmatic allegorical quests. For Empson was describing the central tradition of English allegory, namely pastoral. Thus, for example, Yeats understood Spenser's *Faerie Queene:* he took it to be a poem about the struggles of the rising middle classes.[3] There is no need, however, to confine the role of double plots to pastorals. Symmetrical plot structures abound throughout literature wherever struggles of any radical kind occur. Any struggle between antithetical positions will arouse the kind of formalized doubling that Empson was interested in. Thus, in Thomas Mann's "The Blood of the Walsungs"[4] the theme of the Jewish versus the Aryan "races" is carried by a symmetrical opposition of the actual story Mann tells about the brother and sister, Siegmund and Sieglinde, and the story of their namesakes told in Wagner's opera. The parallel is exact down to the finest detail, and when the brother and sister go to the opera they witness the precise action which they themselves are about to engage in. They commit the very incest they have just witnessed, and Mann describes the effect of the witnessed scene as a magical causation over which they have no control.

[2] In his film, *A Nous la Liberté,* René Clair worked out an exact, symmetrical correspondence between the regimented lines of convicts in prison and similar lines of workers in a factory which finally, at the film's climax, becomes fully automated. Clair created a counterpoint of ideas by means of a corresponding counterpoint in the visual world.

[3] *Edmund Spenser,* a selection of poems, edited, with an introduction, by Yeats (Edinburgh, 1906). See also Yeats's letter to Lady Gregory, Dec. 4, 1902.

[4] This story is readily available in the paperback selection *Death in Venice and Seven Other Stories* (New York, 1958).

ALLEGORICAL CAUSATION

When the allegorical author divides his major character into two antithetical aspects, he is bound to create doubled stories, one for each half. This is what happens in the Jekyll and Hyde stories which abound in German romantic prose literature. Ralph Tymms has shown in detail how Hoffmann and others developed the idea of the *doppelgänger* with such psychological precision that the allegorical character of their writing is not apparent.[5] The fact, is, however, that the antitheses on which the German Romantic double is based are always antitheses of good and evil. They do not escape from their dualistic moral heritage. They allow for the simultaneous unfolding of more than one plot of similar form, and this has an inevitable allegorical effect. Psychological overtones plausibly overlay this iconographic intention. Psychology is such a good cloak that Tymms prefers to distinguish the psychological use of the double as separate from the allegorical use. The distinction remains valid if one narrows the sense of "allegorical" to include only the most conventional moralizing. Nevertheless, the sharply dualistic psychology of the romantics lends itself immediately to an exegetical reading.

Many seemingly nonpolitical works can be seen to portray class struggles under a surface of sentimental love interest, and these also need to be included. Such would be the typical modern allegories of Communist Russia, where a love story can only occur at the price of an iconographic attachment of all moments of that story to some higher thematic message about the current state of Soviet progress.[6] The manifest popularity of *Don Quixote* in Russia may have some-

[5] Ralph Tymms, *Doubles in Literary Psychology* (Cambridge, 1949). Tymms contrasts the psychological with the allegorical use of the double, the former involving a reality of mental life, namely the existence of hallucinations. The allegorical double is, by contrast, "trivial." This notion is an illuminating one, since it enables the critic to establish a basis for aesthetic valuation of Romantic literature. From my own point of view both the trivial and the truly "psychological" uses of the double are allegorical, and I feel sure that, given my own definition of allegory, Tymms would agree with this view.

[6] A Soviet love story, as reported by Ernest Simmons, led up to a scene between the two lovers, in which, on being asked by her lover what she most dearly desired, at the very moment, the heroine replied, "To meet Comrade Stalin face to face."

thing to do with its social message, its attack on a declining way of life.[7] A class conflict is the main burden of the double plot involving Sancho's turn as Governor. Throughout such stories there is a strong suggestion that servants are, or could be, rulers, if only they were given a chance, and the typical Spanish servant—a Sancho, a Figaro, or a Leporello in the Don Juan story—keeps challenging his master and sometimes even becomes the main character in the narrative. Similarly, the complex actions of the Italian *opera buffa*, which, for example, convey ideas of revolution and social upheaval by means of their double plots involving servants, can be included among the types employing magical parallelism. It is also clear that all the earlier mythological operas known as *opera seria* are allegorical in essence, and opera in general has remained a kind of highly ingratiating allegorical art. The word "operatic" has even been used to denote the more abstract, iconographic plotting that characterizes the political films of Eisenstein, suggesting that these too may be called pastorals in Empson's sense. With opera and film we can reach an extreme of grandeur and brilliance in spectacular presentation.

At the opposite extreme of magnitude we get short enigmatic poems, or epigrammatic fables, where there is no plot in the ordinary sense of the term. We therefore need to add a qualification to what we have said about double plots: when lyrics or other shorter fictional forms use parallel or symmetrical structures, the reader may not have a strong feeling of a plot being doubled, but may experience the lyric equivalent of that sort of doubling—the effect of a sestina, where six key terms are put through six parallel treatments in a group of six stanzas, turns out to be much the same as a narrative effect. The doubling works with imagery instead of action, but otherwise presumably produces magical relations between the terms thus displayed in parallel. Beyond this, the six key terms, each of which is a kosmos, require an interpretive rehearsal in the reader's

[7] See the Marxist reading of *Don Quixote* in *Cervantes across the Centuries*, ed. Angel Flores and M. J. Benardete (New York, 1947).

mind. This rehearsal is not left up to the reader's choice; it is forced upon him by the *envoi*, which takes up all six terms in one final microcosmic set of parallel statements. The *envoi* is more than a merely formal device; it has the effect of a *moralitas* at the end of a fable by Aesop.

Magic, accident, and miracle. To go further with the Empsonian concept of magical causation, we need to reconsider Aristotle's position on what holds stories together if they are presented mimetically in an organic plot where there is always a reasonable probability that something will or will not happen at any given moment. The mimetic poet avoids manifest impossibilities, unless he can somehow dupe us into thinking they might actually occur.[8] He avoids the use of the *deus ex machina* whenever possible, because the audience is never in doubt as to the arbitrary quality of daemonic intervention. (Thus many religious conceptions cannot be represented.) But in allegory plots are either ritualized or symmetrical, and for these we need another principle of combination of parts, something other than Aristotle's "probability." It will have to be a type of magical causation, for the following reason. Whenever fictional events come about arbitrarily through the workings of chance ("accidents") or are brought about by the supernatural intervention of a superior external force ("miracles"), this accident and this intervention have the same origin, in the eyes of religion and poetic tradition. The ancients assumed something that still holds good today for literature, though not for science, namely that so-called accidents always are the work of daemons. Even today when we say, "It happened by accident," we can sometimes mean that this chance occurrence has an occult cause. Normally, of course, we try not to ascribe occult causes. In Roman and medieval times, however, the goddess Fortuna gave a name and a cult to this belief in the magical causation under-

---

[8] Aristotle observes that it is better to have probable impossibilities than improbable possibilities. This criterion of plausibility remains central to the aesthetic of all Western art that pretends in any sense to be "mimetic." It can, however, by excessively rigid application become a cause of an allegorical, naturalistic art.

lying chance occurrences. Her iconographic use is nowhere more vigorous than in allegorical literature, and when "fortune" is identified with "fate" (the Virgilian *fatum*) the link between chance and external control becomes explicit.

For *battle* and *progress* two aspects of magical causation are relevant, and though they interpenetrate on most occasions, the one seems to apply chiefly to battle, the other to progress. *Homeopathic* magic, or as I shall call it, *imitative magic* is the basis of causality in allegories where symmetry predominates. *Contagious magic*, which may also be termed *metonymic magic*, is the basis for ritualized forms.[9] Once again, it must be remembered that the two classes do merge with each other in many cases.

Imitative magic. As described in *The Golden Bough*, imitative magic tries to bring real events which the magician wants to control into parallel with symbolic events. The latter are under his direct control. Thus, if he wants it to rain, he performs a rite that imitates the rain, perhaps pouring water out of a jug, or urinating on the ground. Or, if he wants to assist a woman in childbirth, he imitates the labor pains in a dance (the couvade) which is as exactly as possible parallel to the course of labor and delivery. By ending the dance

[9] The basic distinction, a somewhat academic one to be sure, is Frazer's in *The Golden Bough* (abr. ed., New York, 1951), ch. iii.

On the general function of magic, a classic text, though now superseded in details, is Bronislaw Malinowski, *Magic, Science and Religion* (Boston, 1948). Malinowski calls magic "the specific art for specific ends," an immediate difference from religion. "Magic is surrounded by strict conditions: exact remembrance of a spell, unimpeachable performance of a rite, unswerving adhesion to the taboos and observances which shackle the magician. If any one of these is neglected, failure of magic follows" (65). See the whole of sec. V, "The Art of Magic and the Power of Faith"—many parts of which are, to my mind, necessary to the understanding of the difference between allegory and myth. Malinowski makes a sharp distinction between magic and religion, which centers on the view that magic is a type of pseudo science. See also, Durkheim, *Elementary Forms of Religious Life,* chs. i, iii, vii, viii, and ix. For the Keio University *Studies in the Humanities and Social Relations,* I (Tokyo, 1956) Professor T. Izutsu has written a preliminary study of great interest, *Language and Magic: Studies in the Magical Function of Speech.*

properly, his magic parallel will enforce the happy issue of the woman's labor. In such dances it is absolutely necessary not to violate the imagined symmetry between symbol and fact, the slightest error of performance requiring the magician to start the whole process over again. The supposed causal efficacy of the parallel resides in its strict pursuance of all details. Here of course symmetry and ritual work together.

When the basic form of a work is the battle, the action takes on an oscillating motion. Prudentius' *Psychomachia* introduces first the Virtue, then the Vice, which is designated to attack the Virtue. The battle then takes on a seesaw rhythm.

Next to step forth ready to engage on the grassy field is the maiden Chastity, shining in beauteous armour. On her falls Lust the Sodomite, girt with the fire-brands of her country, and thrusts into her face a torch of pinewood blazing murkily with pitch and burning sulphur, attacking her modest eyes with the flames and seeking to cover them with the foul smoke. But the maiden undismayed smites with a stone the inflamed fiend's hand and the cursed whore's burning weapon, striking the brand away from her holy face. Then with a sword-thrust she pierces the disarmed harlot's throat, and she spews out hot fumes with clots of foul blood, and the unclean breath defiles the air near by.[10]

And another such entrance and duel:

Lo, mild Long-Suffering was standing with staid countenance, unmoved amid the battle and its confused uproar, with fixed gaze watching the wounds inflicted as the stiff javelins pierced the vital parts while she waited inactive. On her from a distance swelling Wrath, showing her teeth with rage and foaming at the mouth, darts her eyes, all shot with blood and gall, and challenges her with weapon and with speech for taking no part in the fight.[11]

Variety appears in the details, but the form of battle is almost stichomythic. That each side has its day is natural enough. But allegories tend to stress the equality of the two opposing forces, and

[10] Prudentius, *Psychomachia*, in *Works*, 283. [11] *Ibid.*, 287.

the implication is that by paralleling virtue and vice the poet is showing the latter to be magically overcome by its equal antithesis. The direct confrontation of the two is from the philosopher's point of view a dialectical process, but from the psychologist's point of view it is a primitive device invoking the occult belief that things which look alike must be somehow magically related to each other. Only a naïve person thinks he can directly defeat evil. A less primitive view assumes rather that evil is "the absence of good," according to Augustine's formula; Augustine would tend to say that by making a frontal attack on evil, as the Manichaeans do, one only creates new evil. But the allegorist assumes that, when virtue imitates vice at the moment of attack, it can, by that very isomorphic imitation, destroy its opposite. Perhaps to avoid a strict Manichaeism, major allegorists may allow a degree of confusion to exist at the very moment when Virtue attacks Vice. This happens in *The Faerie Queene*, where, as Empson points out in his *Seven Types of Ambiguity*, one cannot tell who "he" is when Spenser describes two combatants, using the third singular pronoun.

Types of doubling. Symmetries within plots may be of different kinds. They may be the seesaw of battle. They may be double plots involving two levels of society, each mirroring the other, as in Empson's examples. They may be repetitions of sections of a ritual, as when in anatomizing the Seven Deadly Sins each sin is presented in identical iconographic form, like a face card. Symmetries may occur in the sectioned details of description in the *blason*,[12] where each part of the human body is given its particular praise. They may involve large-scale effects, as in the triplicate structure of *The Divine Comedy*, or the isomorphism of Books I and II of *The Faerie*

[12] As in the poetry of the Arabian Nights, or Indian love poetry. The main instance in the Hebraic-Christian tradition is the "Song of Songs." The type is common, but it has interesting variants, as in "To His Coy Mistress" (an undressing poem), and "A Rapture," of Carew. The Marvell, like Donne's elegy, "To His Mistris Going to Bed," identifies the body and its adornments with the cosmos, the world.

Queene, or the balanced structure of court masques, where dance and counterdance present two levels of being which elicit an interpretive response from the audience. In all these cases we need to observe that the dialectical organization of thesis, antithesis, and synthesis does not serve a properly philosophical function. It serves a magical function.

This use of symmetrical parallels must also be distinguished from metaphor. In figurative language, as I understand it, an exact, total, unswerving correspondence between tenor and vehicle would destroy "liveliness." From being an intuitive perception, metaphor so controlled would become a mechanical illustration. From being based on sense experience, metaphor would lose its perceptual function to an overpowering logic. Instead true metaphor employs correspondences that cannot be carried out analogically to any great length. With both the allegorical extensions of correspondences and the imitative magic employed to induce a desired effect, the exactness of the parallel must be rigorously maintained. Whether we like it or not, the most strictly allegorical parts of Spenser are those where he traces the meaning of the two "symbols of the center," the House of Holiness and the House of Temperance in Books I and II, in which, once he has started the figure going, he keeps it going from turret to dungeon, omitting no major term of the correspondence between castle and conceptual system. Furthermore, imitative magic must be distinguished from a metaphorical process of expression in that metaphor does not seek the power over reality which is sought in the magical symmetry.[13] The magician is trying to control nature.

---

[13] See Suzanne Langer, *Philosophy in a New Key* (Mentor Books; New York, 1942), 141–148. Langer differentiates between myth and fairy tale, a distinction following from the distinction between mythology and demonology, fairy tale being based on the latter. The fairy tale is, as Plato said, a story told by nurses to frighten children into obedience; its appeal to the superego is immediate and lasting. It is the poetry of "poetic justice." Thus, *Mario and the Magician,* owing to the beautiful insistence on the attitude and presence of the children in the story, becomes a travestied fairy tale, and further, a critique of such

The mimetic poet using metaphor is only trying to understand nature; his art attempts to bring about catharsis of spent emotion. By means of his "message," on the other hand, the allegorical poet is furthermore trying to control his audience. He seeks to sway them by magic devices to accept intellectual or moral or spiritual attitudes. Having assumed that the audience participates in whatever is represented, the poet represents reality in the form of doubled plots or doubled characters.

Ultimately the imitative magic of allegory is based on the correspondence between microcosmos and macrocosmos, since it is necessary to have systems of images and agents that can be placed in a symmetrical relationship to each other. The allegorist takes over a large-scale parallel between clothes and human body, for then he can construct a story in which he tells on the one hand a history of a villain, and on the other the history of his costume. "If you cannot catch a thief, the next best thing you can do is to get hold of a garment which he may have shed in his flight, for if you beat it soundly, the thief will fall sick." [14] The overcoat is the very life-image of Gogol's Akaky Akakyevitch. Or you can tell the story of a petty bureaucrat on the one hand, while you tell the story of his nose, on the other, as Gogol did in "The Nose," if you wish to extend the notion of ornament from clothes to body. Somewhat like the play *Coriolanus* Jonson's *Sejanus* uses the microcosmic device of the body-image, by showing that the hero constantly fears physical dismemberment (while the state is in danger of political dismemberment), and this is the death that at last finds him.

Moving farther afield from the image of the body, the allegorist can construct a double plot in which animals act on one level what human beings are acting out on another level. A popular novel like

stories. It recalls the irony of the postwar German film, *Aren't We Wonderful?* where the same emphasis on the attitudes of children toward totalitarian power is brought to bear on the problem of power itself; this film recalls Clément's *Forbidden Games*, one of the great films of our time.

[14] Frazer, *The Golden Bough*, abr. ed., 44.

The Strange One runs two parallel stories at once, one telling of miscegenation between a white boy and an Indian girl, the other describing the mismating of two different species of geese.[15] Animal fables are built on this kind of parallel, except that they do not make it explicit. They, like *The Strange One*, depend on some idea of the Great Chain of Being, which allows a cross relation between different creatures that are at equal levels of dignity, differing only in that they belong to different species. Sometimes the line between man and animal is deliberately confused by the author. In *The Magic Flute* the bird-man Papageno and his bride Papagena belong initially to the animal world, but they look forward to a conversion, which finally occurs and allows them to enter the Great Chain at a higher stage of development.[16] Much of the literary interest in metamorphosis comes from the idea of liberation or imprisonment that it conveys; it continually turns humans into their bestial equivalents somewhere on the scale of the Great Chain, or frees them to live as humans, with free will.

The Great Chain disposes objects that not only have fixed places but furthermore elicit wonder and admiration. Aristotle points out that to achieve a marvelous, magical effect in a mimetic drama you must introduce ornamental language. The implication would be that the language of cosmic correspondence is an inherently magical language. This may indeed be so. There is reason to suppose it is so,

[15] Fred Bodsworth, *The Strange One* (New York, 1959). This same doubling of animal and human life-pattern appears in one of Tolstoy's major short stories, "Kholstomer." This story is, considering only the horse, not a fable. The story is *sui generis* in that it conveys a sense of the thought of the animal, or of a true, as opposed to fanciful, continuity between animal and human worlds. It accepts the Pythagorean notion of deep kinship throughout all Nature.

[16] The student of literature may find a special interest in this opera, because it has been translated by W. H. Auden and Chester Kallman and performed in this translation. The libretti of Mozart's Italian operas, by Da Ponte, are of considerable literary importance. These correspond in quality to the libretti produced for Verdi by Arrigo Boito, e.g., *Otello* and *Falstaff*, or those of Von Hofmannsthal for Richard Strauss.

judging from the way such symbolic vocabularies develop in the hands of the magus—Paracelsus, in the "doctrine of signatures," exemplifies the thinker whose cosmic language is intended to have magical, medicinal properties.[17] But there is a more important cause of the magic, namely, the doubling arrangement itself. Empson's

[17] Paracelsus (1493-1541) developed a concept of *mana*, to the extent that he believed man's imagination holds the power of symbolic causation: "If he [the magus] thinks of fire, he is on fire; if he thinks of war, he will cause war. All depends only upon man's imagination to be *Sun*, i.e., that he imagines wholly that which he wills." The magician or alchemist in this way has control over certain soul-forces which inhere in actual physical objects—he further may control the transfer of souls from one object to another, and to each stage of this metempsychosis are assigned specific alchemical symbols.

The alchemists' use of homeopathic magic, i.e., symmetry magic, appears in Paracelsus' "doctrine of signatures," on which see Jolande Jacobi's glossary to *Paracelsus: Selected Writings*, 333: "*Signature*: External characteristics corresponding to inner qualities, which serve as signs, by which everything internal and invisible can be discovered. The idea of the 'signature' underlies the Paracelsian doctrine that the similar can be cured by the similar; the higher a creature in the order of creation, the more difficult it is to discover its inwardness, the less unambiguously, thinks Paracelsus, does its inner nature manifest itself in its outward form. Most hidden of all is the essential core in man, whereas in plants, for example, it is often expressed in their form and colour." Cf. the allusion to this doctrine in T. S. Eliot, *The Dry Salvages*, line 191.

Paracelsus further connects this doctrine of signatures with a theory of astral, or sidereal, control. Thus, Jacobi, "Glossary," 330: "*Planet*: . . . The planets are also in man, they are his 'anatomy.' In keeping with his theory of the organic unity of the microcosm and macrocosm, Paracelsus believed that there was an inner, invisible connexion between the cosmic situation of each period (this includes the positions of the planets) and the course of human history—for instance, the outbreak of wars, the emergence of new arts, inventions, etc."

See further, Kurt Seligmann, *The Mirror of Magic* (New York, 1948), 318-322. On the spirit's power to move, on *pneuma* as vital, all-pervading force, see three articles in *Spirit and Nature* (papers from the "Eranos Yearbooks," Bollingen Series XXX; New York, 1954), by W. Willi, "The History of the Spirit in Antiquity"; by M. Pulver, "The Experience of the Pneuma in Philo"; and by M. Rahner, "Earth Spirit and Divine Spirit in Patristic Theology." See also the selection from *Paracelsus*, secs. v, and ii, "Man and His Body." For Renaissance and baroque developments see D. P. Walker, *Spiritual and Demonic Magic from Ficino to Campanella*; F. H. Wagman, *Magic and Natural Science in German Baroque Literature: A Study in the Prose Forms of the later 17th Century* (New York, 1942).

argument applies. In poetry any two systems of images put in parallel, and kept parallel, will appear to be magically joined—as readers of poetry we assume a primitive attitude and ask how two levels could fail to be united by occult affinity, if they are thus drawn together by formal correspondence. Beyond this, in attempting to explain the action of the parallel plots, we adduce the double meaning which is the chief defining attribute of allegory.

In conclusion we can say that when a main character of an allegory generates more than one double for himself, when he is fractionated into a number of other partial characters, this portrayal greatly increases the amount of plot symmetry. Each partial aspect that has been generated out of the main character is now available to the author for its development parallel to every other partial aspect. From being a person with a vague mixture of good and bad in his character, Sir Guyon is divided into partials of himself, and against each evil he has to fight the identical war. Spenser's favorite way of getting the doubling effect, however, is to play on man's illusion that he has a well-defined, unified ego. Spenser creates true doubles like Archimago and Duessa, who then assume particular aspects to fit each realm of virtue in which Redcrosse may be deceived. With the Fair and the False Florimell he extends the idea of deceptive appearance to cover the realm of aesthetics. In all these cases he is able, by the generation of subcharacters, to introduce symmetrical double plots. And once again, the creation of a double plot line enforces an allegorical interpretation, since, in effect, we always want to know which is the genuine and which the false representation.

Contagious magic: a consequence of ritual form. Form is an even more important determining factor when we consider the other major substructure of allegory, the ritual. Here we have a causal mechanism which anthropologists call "contagious magic." [18] This

[18] See Frazer, *The Golden Bough*, abr. ed., 32, and especially 41, on the imagined relation between the wound and the wounding agent, through the medium of the blood. Frazer himself found the two types of magic always merging and coexisting with each other. The line between them is primarily one of convenience rather than strict theory.

concept implies that instead of imitating precisely whatever is to be controlled, the magician takes some item of dress, some possession, even some leaving of the body such as a fingernail pairing or a lock of hair, and by casting a spell over this object he controls the destiny of the person with whom it was previously associated. Here the bond is contiguity, not similarity. Whatever "goes with" the object of the spell will suffice to bring that object under magic control. Here the man's clothes are used, not because they are like him, but because they belong to him; Gogol's use of the overcoat partakes therefore of both types of magic, as does the classic instance of such magic, Defoe's use of the footprint in *Robinson Crusoe*.[19] The tendency of writing that employs this sort of magic is toward an increasing use of metonymy, a phenomenon which has been ascribed by Roman Jakobson to the naturalist fiction of the nineteenth century, a fiction whose progenitors include Daniel Defoe.

Traditional allegory has a number of correlates in the field of contagious magic. The magic of wounds appears in the *psychomachia;* the magic of clothes and ornament appears in the *blason*[20]

---

[19] Coleridge recognized the connection between Defoe's work and what he called "Asiatic supernatural beings." The religious doubts of Robinson Crusoe are to some extent the result of his "confounding of God with Nature, and an incapacity of finding unity in the manifold and infinity in the individual"— cf. Coleridge, *Misc. Crit.*, 191–194, 292–300, for an important commentary on Defoe.

[20] For example, Henryson's "The Thre Deid Pollis" (*Poems and Fables*, ed. H. H. Wood [Edinburgh and London, 1958]), stanza 4, where the *blason* is ironic:

> O Ladeis quhyt, in claithis corruscant,
> poleist with perle, and mony pretius stane;
> With palpis quhyt, and hals [so] elegant,
> Sirculit with gold, & sapheris mony ane;
> Your finyearis small, quhyt as quhailis bane,
> arrayit with ringis, and mony rubeis reid:
> as we ly thus, so sall ye ly ilk ane,
> with peilit pollis, and holit thus your heid.

Normally the *blason* forms the basis of a genre of love poetry, as for example in *The Arabian Nights*, where its praise of the beloved becomes entirely con-

and in the festive allegorical procession; the magic of names is too widespread to be ascribed to any one kind of writing, but it predominates whenever the poet is trying to list virtues, vices, friends, or foes, as he would typically be doing in a moral fable. Swift's celebrated list of social parasites, ending with the dancing masters, would be an instance of a curse cast over whole groups of men, by the sheer invocation of their names.

What is the mechanism involved in these symbolic acts? For the first, as Freud noted, the sorting process of metaphor is replaced by the nonclassifying principle of contiguity. Metaphor, which puts things into classes by suggesting their essential qualities, is replaced by metonymy, which merely gives them new labels.

If a Melanesian gets possession of the bow by which he has been wounded he will carefully keep it in a cool place in order thus to keep down the inflammation of the wound. But if the bow has remained in the possession of the enemy, it will certainly be kept close to a fire in order that the wound may burn and become thoroughly inflamed.[21]

The weapon has *mana*, spiritual power, not because it is like the wound, but because it has caused the wound. What we see clearly as a primitive confusion about causality, the primitive would regard as a sophistication. By burning the man's coat, he could equally hurt him, and, if he knew the man's name only, he could take that name as an almost physical substitute for the real man and, by casting a spell over it, could hurt his enemy through an occult action at a distance. To the extent that primitive man, and the allegorist who resembles him, make the metonymy into a symbolically "solid" sub-

---

ventional. For an odd twist to the *blason* description, see Fletcher's "The Purple Island," *Poems*, ed. Alexander Grosart (London, 1869), IV, canto vii, stanzas 35–39, where, in keeping with character, the appearance of Hypocrisy is described almost entirely in terms of similes, so that we shall feel this is what he *seemed* to be.

[21] Frazer, *The Golden Bough*, abr. ed., ch. iii, quoted by Freud in *Totem and Taboo*. The James Strachey translation of *Totem and Taboo* is now available in Freud, *Works* (Standard ed., London, 1955), XIII.

stitute for the personal human agent, both are turning that sign into a daemonic agent. It may not be easy to determine how "real" the personification that results will seem to the reader of an allegory, but it is possible that the allegorical agents thus produced will be as "real" and powerful as were the Roman gods to the ancient Romans. When they made gods and goddesses out of Luck, Force, Success in Love, Success in War, and the like, they were employing these metonymic terms in the same way a primitive employs the metonymic objects of his cult. Coleridge, in discussing allegory, points out that we can never be sure just how individual a soul was being ascribed to personifications like the Roman Gods.

Of a people [i.e., the Romans] who raised altars to fever, to sport, to fright, etc., it is impossible to determine how far they meant a personal power or a personification of a power. This only is certain, that the introduction of these agents could not have the same unmixed effect as the same agents used allegorically produce on our minds, but something nearly resembling the effect produced by the introduction of characteristic saints in the Roman Catholic poets, or of Moloch, Belial and Mammon in the Second Book of *Paradise Lost,* compared with his Sin and Despair.[22]

This observation suggests that the criterion of realism is wasted on the theory of allegory. There is no important difference between a very real, human, semiabstraction (Moloch, Belial, or the like) and a very unreal, nonhuman abstraction (a Gluttony, a Fever, or the like), since as long as they take part in total forms that are ritualized or symmetrically ordered, the ritual *form of the whole* will determine the final effect of each agent. The apparent surface realism of an allegorical agent will recede in importance, as soon as he is felt to take part in a magical plot, as soon as his causal relations to others in that plot are seen to be magically based. This is an important point because there has often been confusion as to the function of the naturalist detail of so much allegory. In the terms I have been out-

[22] Coleridge, *Misc. Crit.,* 30.

living, this detail now appears not to have a journalistic function; it is more than mere record of observed facts. It serves instead the purposes of magical containment, since the more the allegorist can circumscribe the attributes, metonymic and synecdochic, of his personae, the better he can shape their fictional destiny. Naturalist detail is "cosmic," universalizing, not accidental as it would be in straight journalism.

Contagion in contagious magic. Nowhere is this policy of containment better exemplified than in the main tradition of Christian allegory, the treatment of morals as a war between virtue and vice. This *psychomachia* is rendered most frequently as the struggle between two warring armies of moral germs, the good and evil viruses. In a primitive view the contiguous elements of such a magic form are felt to be related as the viruses of a disease are related to the healthy members of the body. The Christian depiction of Sin has its parallels in Greek thought, where a similar tradition holds that moral perversion is an inherited, uncontrolled, unwilled sickness. The curse on the House of Atreus, which along with the means of Agamemnon's murder is often symbolized by a "net," is also, quite typically, likened by Aeschylus to a contagious pollution of the blood.

Contagion is the primary symbol of Christian allegory since that allegory is chiefly concerned with sin and redemption.[23] Prudentius'

[23] Origen, in the *Contra Celsum,* tr. Henry Chadwick (Cambridge, 1953), displays fully the connection between allegory and the fear of contagion. See IV, ch. xlviii. The ascetic rituals of the Gnostic religion are symbolic purifications; these rites purge the impure. See Hans Jonas, *The Gnostic Religion,* 144, 231–233, 270–281. I have already referred to the attack by Tertullian on icons, which is based on the belief in their contamination. Augustine's attack on stage plays, in the *City of God,* tr. G. E. McCracken (Loeb Classics ed., Cambridge, Mass., 1957), follows the same line.

On the relation of the fear of impurity to allegorical demonism, see E. R. Dodds, *The Greeks and the Irrational,* chs. ii, v, and viii especially. See Dodds also on the story of Leontius, 213. Dodds's book is one of the major texts for the study of the origins of allegorical literature.

A monograph needs to be written on the relation of ideas about contagious sickness and the characteristic modes of symbolic expression during eras prior to modern hygiene and sterilization. Owsei Temkin, in "An Historical Analysis

Hamartigenia likens the most sinful man (who happens to be a Manichaean) to a tainted murderer.

---

of the Concept of Infection," *Studies in Intellectual History* (Baltimore, 1953), points out that the Latin word *infectio* means a dyeing, a staining or coloring. ("What is Guilt? A stain upon the soul," says Hawthorne in one of his tales.) "The root meaning of this word (*inficere*) is to put or dip into something, especially a poison; or to stain something in the sense that it becomes tainted, spoiled, or corrupted. Indeed, the English word 'to stain' can still be used in the double sense of dyeing as well as polluting. Let us remember, then, that an infection is basically a pollution. And the same is true of the term 'contagion' which indicates a pollution, especially by direct contact. Peculiarly enough, the Greek verb *miaino* presents a counterpart to the Latin *inficere*. Here too the mere staining can be included together with physical or moral defiling. And the corresponding noun '*miasma*' originally meant any pollution or polluting agent. . . . This brief linguistic excursion will suffice to bring out a basic element in the concept of infection: impurity." One thinks of the miasmic fog in *Bleak House*. Temkin finds that although there was even in early times, before the birth of Christ, some understanding of the physical causes of leprosy, such a disease would mainly be treated as a magically caused and a magically curable sickness. "The guiding thought was that of a ritualistic religious taboo." Later, the so-called Hippocratic writings attempt a natural explanation of epilepsy, the "Sacred Disease." "Speculating on the significance of air, another Hippocratic author reasons that pestilences or epidemic fevers must be due to the air that all men inhale at the same time. 'So whenever the air has been tainted with such pollutions (*miasmasin*) as are hostile to the human race, then men fall sick. . . .' Keeping within the old terminology of miasma, a secularization has been achieved. The plague is no longer considered a punishment for religious or moral defilement; instead it has become the result of a defilement of the air, due to some mysterious agents suspended in it" (128). Here we must observe that in naturalistic allegories, like those of the Americans Sinclair, Norris, or Dreiser, or of Zola, the secularization has also occurred, but it makes for no less magic in the final analysis, since there are still those "mysterious agents suspended" in the air. The concept of air itself is not entirely free, at any time, of symbolic overtones, connecting it with the breath or the soul (the *pneuma*). Further, Temkin notes that "medicine from Antiquity to the Renaissance is replete with references to planets and conjunctions that breed pestilences and new diseases. The name for 'influenza' is derived from the influence of the stars" (128). See Henry Sigerist, *A History of Medicine* (New York, 1951), I, 267–296, and 395, n. 14. A readily available work is Johannes Nohl, *The Black Death,* tr. C. H. Clarke (New York, 1960). Nohl's chapters on diagnosis of the bubonic plague and on the Church's relation to medical practice will readily show that there was, throughout the Middle Ages,

He is a bloody Cain, one that hates unity, a cultivator of the world, who comes to sacrifice all befouled; his offering is unclean and savours of the earth, the earth of the mortal body, corrupt flesh lumped together of thick water and dust, whose nature it is to bloom richly with wickedness, pouring out prolific crops of sin in guilty men, and with the foulness of the flesh to kill the life of the soul. The flesh aims its weapons at its sister the spirit, and the spirit is swung about in a drunken brain, from which it contracts strong frenzies, being intoxicated with the maddening poison of the body. It splits the everlasting God into two Gods, daring to divide the Godhead indivisible, and is slain and perishes in denying the one God, while Cain triumphs in the death of his brother's soul.[24]

This sickness of the soul is also likened by Prudentius to a "madness." Sin came naturally to be identified with plague, since the plague was a reality in Europe well on into the eighteenth century. Thus Langland in *The Vision of Piers Plowman* is portraying a physical reality as well as a metaphysical belief when he chronicles the revenge of Conscience, who invokes the plague homeopathically to teach the sinners their true nature.

Then Nature heard Conscience, and coming out of the planets, he sent forth his foragers—fevers and fluxes, coughs and seizures, cramps, toothaches, catarrhs, and cataracts, scabby skin, diseases, boils, tumours,

---

a predisposition to explain contagious diseases by spiritualist, demonological systems running parallel to the true theory of physical contagion. Medieval diagnosis, a kind of pseudo science, would perhaps encourage any habit of mind that assumed symbolic causes. In this area of medicine and sickness we have a belief in "symbolic causation," as much as in the areas of alchemy and astrology. Even the word "health," suggesting wholeness, suggests the basic allegorical trope of the *whole body*, the untorn garment, the complete paradise, the *hortus conclusus*. The *hortus* is closed so that it may prevent disease from entering by contagion.

Daniel Defoe, the first great naturalistic writer of allegories, was also author of the *trompe-l'oeil Journal of the Plague Year*, a story of allegory's central fable, on which Camus drew for his epigraph to the allegory of *La Peste*.

[24] Prudentius, *Hamartigenia*, tr. H. J. Thomson (Loeb Classics ed.), Preface, lines 48-63.

feverish agues, fits of madness, and countless other foul complaints. And these foragers of Nature so pierced and preyed on the population, that a thousand at least had soon lost their lives. Then on all sides could be heard cries of "Mercy! Woe! for Nature comes, with dreadful Death, to destroy us all!" And the Lord who lived for lust shouted for his knight, Comfort, to come and bear his banner. "To arms! to arms!" cried this Lord. "Every man for himself."

And then, before the trumpeters had time to blow, or the herald-at-arms to call out their names, these knights came clashing together in battle.

Hoary Old Age was in the vanguard, bearing before Death the banner that was his by right. Nature followed with a host of cruel diseases, slaughtering thousands with foul contagion, and sweeping all before him with his plagues and poxes. Then Death came dashing after, crushing to powder both kings and knights, emperors and pontiffs. He left none standing, priest or layman, but so squarely that they never stirred again. And many a lovely lady, and the mistress of many a knight, sank down and swooned beneath Death's cruel blow.[25]

Here *psychomachia* and plague are combined in one terrible image whose physical reality gives all the greater force to the figurative, visionary, daemonic intention of that image. Plague here is both the cause and the effect of sin, both a human failing and a divine retribution.

The corollary of the idea that man the sinner is sickened by a pollution is the idea that the Christian who enjoys God's grace is "clean." Having shown the pollution of Belshazzar's wealth, and his death, the anonymous poet concludes the fourteenth-century alliterative poem, "Cleanness":

> Thus in a threefold tale I now have told
> How that uncleanness doth offend the sight
> Of our Dear Lord, who dwells in Heaven's height,
> Both work in Him to wrath, stirs up His ire;

[25] *Piers the Ploughman*, tr. J. F. Goodridge (Penguin ed., 1959), XX, 285–286. Cf. *Paradise Lost*, X, 532–545, where the bad angels fall, "Catcht by Contagion, like in punishment,/As in their crime."

Cleanness His comfort is, and His desire;
Who shine in seemliness shall see His face—
That we this vesture wear God send us grace,
To serve aye in His sight, in sweet solace.[26]

This poem introduces the theme of pollution by emphasizing its opposite, a spiritual hygiene.

At other times, as in the *Map of Man* translated by Joshua Sylvester, the disease is the product of the breath (*miasma*) of Satan, and this also was a standard medieval view with respect to the Black Plague itself, namely, that it was an effluence of evil spirits floating through the air.

I sing not, but (in sighes abrupt)
Sob out the State of Man, corrupt
   By th' Old Serpent's banefull breath:
Whose strong Contagion still extends
To every creature that descends
   From the old Little World of Death.[27]

At no time is the Christian believer ever allowed to forget that Sin and Death coexist in a symbiotic relationship. At times there is a breath of hope for the believer, as when he is told that by learning from the Scriptures, he will correct his fatal ignorance, which is itself the worst of diseases.

   Of soule the chiefest staine,
Contagion first, and chiefest yll, that, through the flesh doth raine,
Is Ignorance of truth and good, from whence out springeth than,
False judgment as the greatest plague, that happens unto man.

[26] Translated by Jessie Weston, in *Romance, Vision and Satire* (Boston, 1912), 169–170. The bejewelled verse of the anonymous *Pearl* depends likewise on the belief in contagion and the counteraction of it. The Pearl is a perfect, i.e., clean, talisman, and thus can stand for the virgin of the poem. Cf. Milton's *Comus*, lines 451–474.

[27] From Henry Smith, *Micro-cosmo-graphia: The Little-Worlds Description, or, The Map of Man*, tr. Joshua Sylvester (Grosart ed., privately printed, 1880), II, 97.

Whereof two Monsters are begot, folly, and wickednesse.
From these two, every yll proceedes, that man can here expresse.

This text—from Palingenius' *The Zodiacke of Life*,[28] in Googe's
Elizabethan translation—at least allows some hope for the student of
good. But other older views perhaps are the truly persistent ones,
according to which no easy education would allow for an escape
from contagion. Bloomfield has chronicled the views of the
fourteenth-century *Pricke of Conscience*, where the poet (perhaps
Richard Rolle)

records, on the basis of making the punishment fit the crime, the following maladies which various sinners must suffer: a quotidian fever will
wrack the proud, the covetous will have dropsy, the slothfull will suffer
"potage" and gout in their limbs. Ulcers, whitlows, and impostumes will
attack the limbs of the envious.[29]

This homeopathic medicine of the soul is based on the belief that the
idea of a particular sin has a peculiar magic efficacy to force a certain conformation of character onto the sinner, while an opposite
homeopathic dose of the same idea will correct the disease, driving it
out. This Dantesque notion seems very naturally to lend itself, as a
source of allegorical detail, to the rendering of a large-scale cosmic
poetic world. There is no unified concept of infection, empirically
related to a technique of mental hygiene, for example; there is only
an endless sequence of spiritual risks to be run, any one of which may
lead the Christian into sickness, that is, into a state of sin. In all cases,
however, as we have come to expect, there is a prototypic science of
psychosomatic medicine envisioned here. While, for example, it is
easy to see the system of symbolic contagion being exploited by
Camus in *La Peste*, it is less easy to see it in Kafka's political allegories such as *The Trial*. But the imagery of contagion, and the
miasmic form of clouding, infecting details, is not far to seek, and is

[28] Palingenius, *The Zodiacke of Life*, tr. Barnabe Googe, ed. with an introduction by Rosemond Tuve (New York, 1947), 163.
[29] M. W. Bloomfield, *The Seven Deadly Sins* (East Lansing, 1952), 205.

nowhere more central than in *The Castle*, where a kind of cloud permeates the surveyor's world and keeps him from ever "seeing" his goal.

Contagion as a generalized magical influence. It is necessary to allow this generalized description of contagious magic, because we do find major allegories which seem to avoid the content of sin, disease, miasma, plague. Of course, what matters more than a quasi-medical content is the form taken by that content, and in this case it is clear that contagious magic implies a ritual form.[30] Since the metonymic items of a curse or blessing are multiple, as purveyed by the medicine man who employs contagious magic, they require to be sequentially ordered into some sort of list, as in the following almost perfect example from Egyptian poetry:

THE CURSING LITANY

Mayest thou never exist, may thy *ka* never exist, may thy body never exist.

May thy limbs never exist.	Mayest thou never exist.
May thy bones never exist.	Mayest thou never exist.
May thy words of power never exist.	Mayest thou never exist.
Mayest thou never exist.	Mayest thou never exist.
May thy form never exist.	Mayest thou never exist.

[30] One can trace the origins of this form to very early doctrines of taboo, and thence to the Greek mystery religions. See Louis Moulinier, *Le Pur et l'impur dans la pensée des Grecs d'Homère à Aristote* (Paris, 1952), especially ch. ii, "Les Rites."

W. K. C. Guthrie, *In the Beginning* (Ithaca, 1959), discusses the connection between belief in a taboo on food and the Pythagorean doctrine of metempsychosis. One accepted the taboo on meat because one feared one might be eating the flesh of one of one's ancestors. Ovid concludes his *Metamorphoses* with the account (Bk. XV) of Pythagoras, and we can perhaps understand the key position Ovid gives to Pythagoras in the light of his supposed doctrine of metempsychosis. Transfer of the soul seems prerequisite to the idea that one body can plastically or organically change into another. Both conceptions depend in turn on an idea that purity is to be sought by avoiding contact, not by living in contact and thus strengthening oneself with one's own spiritual antitoxins.

May thy attributes never exist.	Mayest thou never exist.
May that which springs from thee never exist.	Mayest thou never exist.
May thy hair never exist.	Mayest thou never exist.
May thy possessions never exist.	Mayest thou never exist.
May thy emissions never exist.	Mayest thou never exist.
May the material of thy body never exist.	Mayest thou never exist.
May thy place never exist.	Mayest thou never exist.
May thy tomb never exist.	Mayest thou never exist.
May thy cavern never exist.	Mayest thou never exist.
May thy funeral chamber never exist.	Mayest thou never exist.
May thy paths never exist.	Mayest thou never exist.
May thy seasons never exist.	Mayest thou never exist.
May thy words never exist.	Mayest thou never exist.
May thy enterings in never exist.	Mayest thou never exist.
May thy journeyings never exist.	Mayest thou never exist.
May thy advancings never exist.	Mayest thou never exist.
May thy comings never exist.	Mayest thou never exist.
May thy sitting down never exist.	Mayest thou never exist.
May thy increase never exist.	Mayest thou never exist.
May thy body never exist.	Mayest thou never exist.
May thy prosperity never exist.	Mayest thou never exist.
Thou art smitten, O enemy.	Thou shalt die, thou shalt die.

Thou shalt perish, thou shalt perish, thou shalt perish.[31]

This comminatory rite is extreme, and the serial order of contagious contacts between agents in allegorical poems is usually made less rigid.[32] In Spenser the dramatis personae affect each other—that is,

[31] *Egyptian Religious Poetry*, ed. Margaret Murray (London, 1949), 64–65 (quoted by permission of John Murray Ltd.). This "cursing litany" is "an incantation against the serpent Apophis, the enemy of the Sun-God. The ritual symbolically causes the enemy's death, as the last lines show.

[32] Robert C. Elliott has traced the originating impulses of satire back to the primitive curse. This view is of course exactly parallel to several of my own; Elliott's *The Power of Satire: Magic, Ritual, Art* (Princeton, 1960) is a parallel analysis of a major branch of allegory which I have dealt with only incidentally. See also E. D. Leyburn, *Satiric Allegory: Mirror of Man* (New Haven, 1956), especially ch. i, "Definitions."

they bring about a plot through this specific type of causal inter-relation—by meeting in random orders, so it would seem, and in no very rigid sequence. (The same apparently random sequence characterizes picaresque romances.) Only in allegorical processions and tapestries and "chronicles" does a poet like Spenser allow the natural form of contagious magic to dominate the fiction.[33] Normally the ritualized sequence is less prominent, and it is only on a long view that the poem appears ritualistic. That it finally does appear so is because, like Aeneas, Spenser's heroes can never come to rest after a victory; no pause in the action ever is fully realized, and one senses in such a poetry an anxiety to get on to the next challenge, a strong suggestion that the poem is sickened throughout by its own acceptance of the idea of spiritual contagion.

Although the principle of magical contagion, by which characters in allegories interact, infecting each other with various virtues or vices, need not involve direct reference to magical practices or to magicians like Merlin or Simon Magus or Mann's Cipolla, this is

---

[33] Spenser, like many poets of his time, was influenced by Neoplatonic thought, on the one hand, and by the liturgical offices of the Church, on the other. It may be important for Spenser and his contemporaries that Neoplatonic magic, as in Ficino's *De Vita Coelitus Comparanda*, revives "a theory of astrological influence, ultimately stoic in origin, which postulates a cosmic spirit (*spiritus mundi*) flowing through the whole of the sensible universe, and thus providing a channel of influence between the heavenly bodies and the sublunar world" (Walker, *Spiritual and Demonic Magic*, 12). Walker shows that the iconography of the sacred Mass informs the Ficinian type of magic. Ficino's magic "has many sources. Perhaps the most important, though Ficino does not avow it, and may not even have been conscious of it, is the mass, with its music, words of consecration, incense, lights, wine and the supreme magical effect—transubstantiation. This, I would suggest, is a fundamental influence on all medieval and Renaissance magic, and a fundamental reason for the Church's condemnation of all magical practices. The Church has her own magic; there is no room for any other. The effort to make a sharp distinction between Christian rites and any kind of secular magic is apparent in many sixteenth-century discussions of such subjects. As one would expect, it is rare for anyone overtly to accept the connexion between magic and the eucharist" (*ibid.*, 36). On the origins of the theory of occult properties or immanent forces, see E. R. Dodds, *The Greeks and the Irrational*, 246–247.

often the case, or at least the author presents a figure somewhat like a magus, a wiseman of some sort—a "mad scientist" in science fiction, a "Hercule Poirot" in detective fiction, a wise country doctor in romantic "westerns," a sage in all cases. And the greatest allegories, whether intentional like *The Faerie Queene* or *Jerusalem Conquered* (the rewritten *Jerusalem Delivered*) or unintentional, like the *Odyssey* and *The Aeneid*, are governed by that sort of rigid destiny which can only operate through magical ordinances such as those of the oracle or of an all-powerful deity. It is not possible to think of such works in solely cognitive, rational terms. They are dynamic in nature. Their symbolic structure is a cause of sharp or pervading emotions in their readers, and for good reason. While the order of a ritual is always capable of acting on the cognitive level as a species of code, so that the reader tries to decode its allegorical meaning, on the emotive level such codes are highly charged by their very form. They occur, we shall see, in response to certain governing concerns that are thrust upon their authors. Allegory concerns itself with highly charged thematic contents that must be subsumed under the heading, taboo.

Contagion: the cure, symbolic isolation. In conclusion we can offer a reason for the emphasis on symmetry and ritual. Let us assume for the moment that the attitude toward sin characteristic of Christian allegory is the predominant one in allegory generally, that it is as true of *The Dunciad* as of the *The Divine Comedy*, as true of Kafka's *Castle* as of Milton's *Comus*, as true of *Brave New World* as of "Rappaccini's Daughter." Let us assume further that "sin" here is a general term for any contagious error, and that political depravity would be subsumed under it, if the work were a political allegory, that scientific error would be subsumed under it, and so on through all the varieties of allegorical literature. A chiefly formal critique has emerged, in that we have been talking about things like symbolic isolation, symmetry, and ritual. It is immediately apparent that the belief in contagion carries with it a belief about the measures that may be taken to avert the spread of disease. We are now speaking in terms of figurative language, but the effect is identical to what would occur if a genuine disease were the object of our fear. The classic response to contagion is to isolate those who have caught the disease. This was true in ancient times with the lepers; it was true during the middle ages with the bubonic plague (it appears from Thucydides that the Athenians had not thus handled the plague in 430 B.C.). Quarantines are still used today. The same procedure of isolation is followed with those who are in any way suspected of being unclean, who have become unclean by violating a taboo, and the strongest prohibitions are laid down by primitive societies to keep the unclean person from coming into any contact with others who are not thus violated. This cult of isolation which is laid down in the case of a violated taboo parallels the actual medical need to quarantine those suspected of carrying a contagious disease.[34] The two procedures are drawn even closer together in earlier times, when actual plagues are usually understood, as Langland understood them, to be divine retributions or products of otherwise otherworldly causes. Plagues follow, it was thought, upon the violation of tabooed objects or people or places.

In the storyteller's world there is of course only an imaginary

---

[34] The clearest instance of this is Camus's *La Peste*. But the same quarantining and isolation of the central characters from the "free" world occurs in Mann's *Death in Venice*, where Aschenbach finds the city being abandoned by the tourists, at the very moment when he is about to embrace its illness. In "Rappaccini's Daughter" we have, as Honig has observed, the story of a contaminata, and the same isolating process separates the garden from the world (the city). The notion of a corrupted Eden is, of course, infinitely varied in literature. Stories like *Robinson Crusoe*, Conrad's *Victory*, Aldous Huxley's *Island*, Golding's *Pincher Martin* (London, 1956), take the most extreme image of isolation possible, the island, and they tend to treat it as a substitute for Eden. E.g., *Victory*, III, ch. vi: "The civilization of the tropics could have had nothing to do with it. It was more like those myths, current in Polynesia, of amazing strangers, who arrive at an island, gods or demons, bringing good and evil to the innocence of the inhabitants—gifts of unknown things, words never heard before." On this isolating image, see Wallace Fowlie, "Mallarmé's Island Voyage," *Modern Philology*, XLVII (1950), no. 3, 178 ff., and Walter de la Mare's commentary, *Desert Islands and Robinson Crusoe* (London, 1930).

contagion and only an imaginary isolation. But the fact remains that a very large number of allegories are topographically based on the idea that the hero must be kept away from any contact with evil, otherwise he will pick up the evil illness. There are, for example, sacred places which are free of contagion—the House of Holiness and the House of Temperance in Spenser are examples.[35] These uncontaminated places can be of several kinds, their main claim to sacred value residing in their supposed centrality to a given universe. Mircea Eliade summarizes the main types as follows:

1. The Sacred Mountain—where heaven and earth meet—is situated at the center of the world.
2. Every temple or palace—and, by extension, every sacred city or royal residence—is a Sacred Mountain, thus becoming a Center.
3. Being an *axis mundi*, the sacred city or temple is regarded as the meeting point of heaven, earth, and hell.[36]

[35] On the temple, see Yrjö Hirn, *The Sacred Shrine* (London, 1958); W. R. Lethaby, *Architecture, Nature and Magic* (London, 1956); M.-M. Davy, *Essai sur la symbolique romane: XII siècle* (Paris, 1955); Otto Rank, *Art and Artist: Creative Urge and Personality Development,* ch. v, "Microcosm and Macrocosm"; ch. vi, "House-building and Architecture." The temple is central to medieval esthetics, both in architecture and in the symbolism deriving from architecture. "Beauty is found in four temples, that is, in the four forms where the spirit resides. These are: the human body, the mystical body of the Church, the soul in which God is reflected, and Christ, the incarnate Word." Here De Bruyne notes that the Cistercian theorist Thomas of Citeaux asks wherein consists the beauty of each of these four bodies. What are its effects? What does the Scripture say of it? What is its moral value? What are its ornaments? The main answer with regard to the human body is that its beauty is perishable, suspect, and vain, and stands always in contrast to the imperishable beauty of the Soul, of God, and of His Son (see De Bruyne, *Etudes,* III, 53). The "temple of the body" is carried over into later allegorical poetry as a cosmic imagery, informing, for example, a poem like Marvell's *Upon Appleton House;* the Spenserian temples and castles use the figure quite explicitly. In allegorical painting the castle can become elaborated to the point of resembling a city, as with Dante's City of Dis.

[36] On the "symbol of the center," see Eliade, *Cosmos and History,* "The Symbolism of the center," 12–17; also Eliade, *Sacred and Profane,* 73–76. The most important instances in classic literature are perhaps the placements of the oracles (their locus is called the "navel of the earth") and the placements

Yeats's Mount Meru is one of the examples Eliade gives. One thinks of Arlo Hill in the *Mutabilitie Cantos*. The summit of such a sacred, cosmic mountain is furthermore "not only the highest point of the earth; it is also the earth's navel, the point at which the Creation began." Thus it happens that any such center, like any sacred temples of Virgil's *Aeneid* or the "houses" and "castles" of *The Faerie Queene*, "is preeminently the zone of the sacred, the zone of absolute reality. Similarly, all the other symbols of absolute reality (trees of life and immortality, Fountain of Youth, etc.) are also situated at the center." [37] We therefore can expect the giant manifestation of the

---

of temples and seats of government, e.g., the Comitium in Rome. Plutarch, describing the mythic foundation of Rome in his life of Romulus, cites this perfect case of the center: "Romulus, having buried his brother Remus, together with his two foster-fathers, on the Mount Remonia, set to building his city; and sent for men out of Tuscany, who directed him by sacred usages and written rules in all the ceremonies to be observed, as in a religious rite. First, they dug a round trench about that which is now the Comitium, or Court of Assembly, and into it solemnly threw the first-fruits of all things either good by custom or necessary by nature; lastly, every man taking a small piece of earth of the country whence he came, they all threw in promiscuously together. This trench they call, as they do the heavens, Mundus; making which their centre, they described the city in a circle round it. Then the founder fitted to a plough a brazen ploughshare, and, yoking together a bull and a cow, drove himself a deep line or furrow round the bounds; while the business of those that followed after was to see that whatever earth was thrown up should be turned all inwards towards the city; and not to let any clod lie outside. With this line they described the wall; and where they designed to make a gate, there they took out the share, carried the plough over, and left a space; for which reason they consider the whole wall as holy, except where the gates are; for had they adjudged them also sacred, they could not, without offence to religion, have given free ingress and egress for the necessaries of human life, some of which are in themselves unclean.

"As for the day they began to build the city, it is universally agreed to have been the twenty-first of April, and that day the Romans annually keep holy, calling it their country's birthday. At first, they say, they sacrificed no living creature on this day, thinking it fit to preserve the feast of their country's birthday pure and without stain of blood" (*Lives*, "Dryden" tr. [Modern Library ed.], 31). Jacob Burckhardt describes the identical ritual, which took place at the founding of Constantinople (*The Age of Constantine the Great*, tr. Moses Hadas [New York, 1949], 346–349).

[37] Eliade, *Cosmos and History*, 18.

cosmic center to be reducible to a small form, a kosmos, "this jewel set in the silver sea." (Such an instance would be White Pond, in Thoreau's *Walden*.) [38] It is important for the focusing function these symbols have in romances and allegories, that, as Eliade remarks:

The road leading to the center is a "difficult road" (*durohana*), and this is verified at every level of reality: difficult convolutions of a temple (as at Borobudur); pilgrimage to sacred places (Mecca, Hardwar, Jerusa-

---

[38] See, throughout, the chapter entitled "Ponds." Note the description of White Pond in mythological/theological terms: "We have one other pond just like this, White Pond, in Nine Acre Corner, about two and a half miles westerly; but though I am acquainted with most of the ponds within a dozen miles of this centre, I do not know a third of this pure and well-like character. Successive nations perchance have drank at, admired, and fathomed it, and passed away, and still its water is green and pellucid as ever. Not an intermitting spring! Perhaps on that spring morning when Adam and Eve were driven out of Eden Walden Pond was already in existence, and even then breaking up in a gentle spring rain accompanied with mist and a southerly wind, and covered with myriads of ducks and geese, which had not heard of the fall, when still such pure lakes sufficed them. Even then it had commenced to rise and fall, and had clarified its waters and colored them of the hue they now wear, and obtained a patent of Heaven to be the only Walden Pond in the world and distiller of celestial dews. Who knows in how many unremembered nations' literatures this has been the Castalian Fountain? or what nymphs presided over it in the Golden Age? It is a gem of the first water which Concord wears in her coronet."

And further: "White Pond and Walden are great crystals on the surface of the earth, Lakes of Light. If they were permanently congealed, and small enough to be clutched, they would, perchance, be carried off by slaves, like precious stones, to adorn the heads of emperors; but being liquid, and ample, and secured to us and our successors forever, we disregard them, and run after the diamond of Kohinoor. They are too pure to have a market value; they contain no muck. How much more beautiful than our lives, how much more transparent than our characters, are they! We never learned meanness of them. How much fairer than the pool before the farmer's door, in which his ducks swim! Hither the clean wild ducks come. Nature has no human inhabitant who appreciates her. The birds with their plumage and their notes are in harmony with the flowers, but what youth or maiden conspires with the wild luxuriant beauty of Nature? She flourishes most alone, far from the towns where they reside. Talk of heaven! ye disgrace earth."

lem); danger-ridden voyages of the heroic expeditions in search of the Golden Fleece, the Golden Apples, the Herb of Life; wanderings in labyrinths; difficulties of the seeker for the road to the self, to the "center" of his being, and so on. The road is arduous, fraught with perils, because it is, in fact, a rite of passage from the profane to the sacred, from the ephemeral and illusory to reality and eternity, from death to life, from man to the divinity. Attaining the center is equivalent to a consecration, an initiation; yesterday's profane and illusory existence gives place to a new, to a life that is real, enduring, and effective.[39]

Camoens, in *The Lusiads* (Canto 9), has Venus devise this kind of sacred place, the Island of Love. Some doubts have been cast on the poet's allegorical interpretation of the Island and its delights. Some have suggested that only the pressure of official religious censorship would make the allegory necessary. That may be so. We are certainly familiar with such Aesopism. But it is easier to assume that when Camoens calls the erotic delights "symbols of the honors, delightful in themselves, that can make life sublime," he is thinking in almost mythic terms, or at least, apocalyptic terms. The Island is a true *locus amoenus*, and as such it cannot help symbolizing the highest reward, which is not pleasure, as Camoens takes care to point out, but rather fertility and, even more truly apocalyptic, immortality. For he says that Fame, which makes heroes immortal, has smiled on the heroes of Vasco da Gama's hard expedition to the Orient.

The examples from Eliade and from *The Lusiads* indicate that the cosmic center is a place free of contamination, and one might therefore say, a safe place. Classical history constantly reminds us this was the case, for the "right of sanctuary" demonstrated this magical property of temples and sacred places; the fugitive was theoretically untouchable if he stood on sacred ground. Such a positive value cannot always be ascribed to the symbol of the center. Literature and, unfortunately, history have presented the opposite kind of sacred place, and we commonly call it "hell." Prisons are such places, in fact or in imaginative "prison literature." Prometheus' rock was such a

---

[39] Eliade, *Cosmos and History*, 18.

place. The bottomless pit of Christian mythology is such a place. The islands in Golding's *Lord of the Flies* and *Pincher Martin,* especially the latter, are such hells. All these cases make us aware that the contagion may be walled in, instead of walled out, an irony of which many allegorists are acutely aware.[40] Spenser, for example, is fascinated by caves, and they are usually prisons—the Cave of Despair, the Cave of Mammon, the Cave of Proteus—where the hero or heroine is reduced to a state of the most acute ambivalence. Anxiety is not the mark of a Happy Valley. It is the mark of a terrible alienation from the comic world of love, marriage, dance, and merriment.

Allegory is thus not committed either to a good or an evil place of isolation; it can designate either an interior or an exterior plague, depending upon the author's confidence about the world he inhabits.

Microcosmic reduction of the symbolic center. Isolation operating in the mental and spiritual spheres can show yet another method. The allegorist can develop a sort of mental space, in which by concentrating the thought of the hero on a given object that hero seems to be placed *in* a symbolic center. Besides being places, the sacred, isolated *loci* can take the form of consecrated talismanic objects, or consecrated moments of time. Our notion of allegorical ornament requires such a reduction of the universal genus to the universal species, of

[40] With a sense of historic irony Thucydides provides an archetype of such places; at the end of Bk. 7, he describes the Syracusan prisoner-of-war camp—after the Athenian defeat in Sicily (413 B.C.): "Those who were in the stone quarries were treated badly by the Syracusans at first. There were many of them, and they were crowded together in a narrow pit, where, since there was no roof over their heads, they suffered first from the heat of the sun and the closeness of the air; and then, in contrast, came on the cold autumnal nights, and the change in temperature brought disease among them. Lack of space made it necessary for them to do everything on the same spot; and besides there were the bodies all heaped together on top of one another of those who had died from their wounds or from the change of temperature or other such causes, so that the smell was unsupportable. At the same time they suffered from hunger and from thirst. During eight months the daily allowance for each man was half a pint of water and a pint of corn. In fact they suffered everything which one could imagine might be suffered by men imprisoned in such a place" (*The Peloponnesian War,* 488).

kosmos in its macrocosmic sense to kosmos in its microcosmic sense. We find precisely this. Kosmos becomes the "sacred detail." Despite its small-scale magnitude it can substitute for any much greater and more obvious symbol of the center.

Homer's *Iliad* (Book XVIII) preserves for us the most remarkable of all such substitutions, the shield of Achilles, forged by Hephaistos.

> He made the earth upon it, and the sky, and the sea's water,
> and the tireless sun, and the moon waxing into her fullness,
> and on it all the constellations that festoon the heavens. . . .
> On it he wrought in all their beauty two cities of mortal
> men. And there were marriages in one, and festivals.
> They were leading the brides along the city from their maiden chambers
> under the flaring of torches, and the loud bride song was arising.
> The young men followed the circles of the dance, and among them
> the flutes and lyres kept up their clamour as in the meantime
> the women standing each at the door of her court admired them.
> The people were assembled in the market place, where a quarrel
> had arisen, and two men were disputing over the blood price
> for a man who had been killed. One man promised full restitution
> in a public statement, but the other refused and would accept nothing.
> Both then made for an arbitrator, to have a decision;
> and people were speaking up on either side, to help both men. . . .
> But around the other city were lying two forces of armed men
> shining in their war gear. For one side counsel was divided
> whether to storm and sack, or share between both sides the property
> and all the possessions the lovely citadel held hard within it.
> But the city's people were not giving way, and armed for an ambush.
> Their beloved wives and their little children stood on the rampart
> to hold it, and with them the men with age upon them, but meanwhile
> the others went out. And Ares led them, and Pallas Athene.
> These were gold, both, and golden raiment upon them, and they were
> beautiful and huge in their armour, being divinities,
> and conspicuous from afar, but the people around them were smaller. . . .

He made upon it a soft field, the pride of the tilled land,
wide and triple-ploughed, with many ploughmen upon it
who wheeled their teams at the turn and drove them in either
    direction.
And as these making their turn would reach the end-strip of the
    field,
a man would come up to them at this point and hand them a flagon
of honey-sweet wine, and they would turn again to the furrows
in their haste to come again to the end-strip of the deep field.
The earth darkened behind them and looked like earth that has
    been ploughed
though it was gold. Such was the wonder of the shield's forging.[41]

And Homer extends his cosmic image some sixty lines more, further
elaborating the total view of a society at peace, ruled, ordered, governed as if by music. This image gives Achilles' shield a magical
power; it is a *kratophany;* it is "the work of immortals." The glory
of such an object is its totality of comprehension; symbolically the
shield contains all that the Trojan War is being fought for, and it is
fitting that the final image is a timeless one, since Homer's world
view demands an "eternal return," the repetition of an archetypal
Golden Age. This shield differs markedly from the Virgilian shield,
forged for Aeneas by Vulcan, likewise a total cosmic image, a symbol
of the symbol of the center, but differing completely in time
scheme. Aeneas' shield shows a prophetic glimpse of the future, of
the actual Italy in which Virgil lived; it shows us Catiline, Cato,
Augustus Caesar, Agrippa, Antony—and while these historical persons are accompanied by mythological beings, the combination
produces no loss of historicity; indeed it produces an increase of
historical intensity, since Rome's future is felt to have compelling
necessity because it could be foreseen in the prophetic vision. The
shield *is* history.

[41] I have used Richmond Lattimore's translation of Homer's *The Iliad* (University of Chicago Press, 6th impression, 1957), lines 474–607, with a number
of lines omitted for the sake of brevity. The whole of the passage describing
the shield is relevant.

> All this Aeneas
> Sees on his mother's gift, the shield of Vulcan,
> And, without understanding, is proud and happy
> As he lifts to his shoulder all that fortune,
> The fame and glory of his children's children.[42]

It was this compression of history and all its glittering fortunes, its chance windfalls and deliberate, long-thought designs, that Hawthorne had imposed upon the signet ring of the Earl of Essex. The power of such a talisman is finally magical, as were the shields of Achilles and Aeneas, and in each case the reader is drawn into an iconographic frame of mind. That such is the tendency of these talismanic, cosmic devices appears very clearly from the Hesiodic imitation (or analogue) of Achilles' shield, namely the so-called Shield of Heracles, where the realism of Homer's description is replaced by a more obviously iconographic style. We find the poet using freely personified abstractions.

Upon the shield Pursuit and Flight were wrought, and Tumult, and Panic, and Slaughter. Strife also, and Uproar were hurrying about, and deadly Fate was there holding one man newly wounded, and another unwounded: and one, who was dead, she was dragging by the feet through the tumult. She had on her shoulders a garment red with the blood of men, and terribly she glared and gnashed her teeth.

And there were heads of snakes unspeakably frightful, twelve of them; and they used to frighten the tribes of men on earth whosoever made war against the son of Zeus; for they would clash their teeth when

---

[42] Virgil, *The Aeneid*, tr. Rolfe Humphries (New York, 1951), 232 (copyright 1951 by Charles Scribner's Sons; quoted by permission). This follows identification of Aeneas with Hercules, the killer of the bandit-figure Cacus. Hercules is the archetype not only of superhuman strength but also of civilization, of culture, of law, of stoic virtue, and later—by a natural medieval extrapolation—of Christian virtue and historical Christianizing progress. On this point, see Marcel Simon, *Hercule et le Christianisme, passim;* also, Jean Seznec, *The Survival of the Pagan Gods,* 25–26. The figure of Hercules as agent of Christian progress becomes central in Bk. V of *The Faerie Queene* and provides the symbolism of the center for that book; Hercules and Osiris are identified by Spenser in his mythos of Justice.

Amphitryon's son was fighting; and brightly shone these wonderful works. And it was as though there were spots upon the frightful snakes: and their backs were dark blue and their jaws were black.[43]

Here we have not only the rationalistic figures of Pursuit, Flight, Tumult, Panic and Slaughter, but also the more primitive conceptions of terror embodied in the snakes. Their daemonic power resembles that of the Medusa's locks.

It is perhaps only because we perceive a common effect of symbolic isolation that we liken these shields to the tiny circlet of Essex' ring. But that is enough. The ring becomes a whole universe of memory within the dreamer's mind.

But still Essex gazed at the ring with an absorbed attention, that proved how much hope his sanguine temperament had concentrated here, when there was none else for him in the wide world, save what lay in the compass of that hoop of gold. The spark of brightness within the diamond, which gleamed like an intenser than earthly fire, was the memorial of his dazzling career. It had not paled with the waning sunshine of his mistress's favor; on the contrary, in spite of its remarkable tinge of dusky red, he fancied that it never shone so brightly. The glow of festal torches,—the blaze of perfumed lamps,—bonfires that had been kindled for him, when he was the darling of the people,—the splendor of the royal court, where he had been the peculiar star,—all seemed to have collected their moral or material glory into the gem, and to burn with a radiance caught from the future, as well as gathered from the past. That radiance might break forth again. Bursting from the diamond, into which it was now narrowed, it might beam first upon the gloomy walls of the Tower,—then wider, wider, wider,—till all England, and the seas around her cliffs, should be gladdened with the light. It was such an ecstasy as often ensues after long depression, and has been supposed to precede the circumstances of darkest fate that may befall mortal man. The Earl pressed the ring to his heart as if it were indeed a talisman,

[43] This analogue to Homer appears in "Hesiod's Shield," *The Shield of Achilles*, attributed to Hesiod. I have used the translation of Hugh G. Evelyn-White, *The Homeric Hymns and Homerica* (Loeb Classics ed., London, 1929), 231.

the habitation of a spirit, as the queen had playfully assured him,—but a spirit of happier influences than her legend spake of.[44]

"The compass of that hoop of gold"—the Pearl in the alliterative poem of that name—the sword Excalibur—the multifoliate rose of *The Divine Comedy:* such images contain the cosmos of those works where they appear. They contain the universe and at the same time they have magical power, for good or evil, or as more usually is the case, for both good and evil commixed. As such images exist in literal isolation, so heroes and heroines may exist in isolation. The overriding cause of this must surely be something like the dominant fear of spiritual contagion we have been examining. The curious fact is that the best instances of kosmoi are all objects toward which a degree of ambivalence is felt; they are both good and bad at once. It is to this problem that we inevitably turn when we examine the thematic intention of allegory.

[44] From "The Antique Ring," which appeared originally in *Tales and Sketches;* now readily available in Hawthorne's *Short Stories.* Hawthorne is fond of the focusing effect by which a single, perhaps even minute, artifact becomes the iconographic nucleus of a curse or blessing.

5

Thematic Effects: Ambivalence, the Sublime, and the Picturesque

WHENEVER a literary work is dominated by its theme, it is likely to be called an allegory, on the grounds that thematic content is not usually so free of logical control that it could be there by accident.[1] The contrary assumption that mimetic art resists thematic excess follows from the way Aristotle defined mimesis, namely as an "imitation of an action," since "action" (*praxis*) in Aristotle's sense can and does exist without any extra help from secondary rationalizations, that secondary level which he called "thought" (*dianoia*). Such is not at all the case with allegory, where the secondary meaning arises immediately from the primary surface of literal narration or drama, and constitutes the *raison d'être* of the primary surface. Allegorical stories exist, as it were, to put secondary meanings into orbit around them;

---

[1] Frye, *Anatomy*, 90: "We have actual allegory when a poet explicitly indicates the relationship of his images to examples and precepts, and so tries to indicate how a commentary on him should proceed."

the primary meaning is then valued for its satellites. Much of the time the secondary meanings are obscured, actually withheld from view, in the same way that contrapuntal music cannot be heard in all its melodic lines at once, but rather one line after the other emerges from an ever-changing background. This is Frye's view of allegory, a view deriving from medieval statements about polysemous meaning. That allegory is dualistic or pluralistic in this sense needs very little comment today. Most of the adverse criticism, and some of the serious attempts at justification of allegory, have concerned themselves with this characteristic splitting which is the essence of the mode. Frye goes further than most critics when he observes that any critical practice which invokes several disciplines—e.g., history, psychology, semantics, rhetoric—is by definition reading literature polysemously, that is, allegorically.[2]

[2] I omit "character" from my comments, because in the Aristotelian scheme it is less crucial to the definition of mimesis than "action" (Auerbach, *Dante*, 1-10). But in prose fiction "character" assumes primary importance, and in fact whenever the distinction must be drawn between the *romance* forms and either (a) high mimetic drama and epic or (b) the novel, we invoke a conception of "character" as a point of difference. My own view that allegory is daemonic, in agency, would suggest a reason for the prevalent identification of romance and allegory, since a *daimon* is a member of the second level of Frye's five levels of heroes (halfway between a god and a man) and secondly daemonic action is fated and simplified according to the patterns of romantic quest. But Frye is able to distinguish romance and novel for much the same reasons: "The essential difference between novel and romance lies in the conception of characterization. The romancer does not attempt to create 'real people' so much as stylized figures which expand into psychological archetypes. It is in the romance that we find Jung's libido, anima, and shadow reflected in the hero, heroine, and villain respectively. That is why the romance so often radiates a glow of subjective intensity that the novel lacks, and why a suggestion of allegory is constantly creeping in around its fringes. Certain elements of character are released in the romance which make it naturally a more revolutionary form than the novel" (*Anatomy*, 304-305). This seems too modest a claim for allegory; it does more than creep in around the edges of romance; it is the very lifeblood of the type, since, without archetypal simplifications of character, romance would have no other *raison d'être*, but as it is, romance is the natural, popular medium for allegorical expression—for allegory in the best sense of the word, if we can give it a value.

Theological dualism. What concerns me in this chapter is another sort of dualism associated with allegory. This is not the dualism of double meanings, but dualism in its theological sense,[3] where it implies the radical opposition of two independent, mutually irreducible, mutually antagonistic substances: in short, the opposition of Absolute Good and Absolute Evil, such as one finds in a variety of Manichaean doctrines. It is found in all allegories that the thematic opposition of absolutes (Good and Evil, Ignorance and Enlightenment, Doubt and Certainty, or the like) is expressed by an ordering of imagery and agents which is equally dualistic.

Assuming that either *L'Allegro* or *Il Penseroso* were lost, we could from the one remaining poem make a good guess at what the other was about, and perhaps even tell in some detail just what the form of the lost poem would be. On what is the symmetry of the two poems based? May not both refer, though in antithetical terms, to a single, comprehensive tradition, the belief that the powers of darkness are forever at war with the powers of light? This ultimately Zoroastrian dogma carries with it a host of subdivisions of the light/dark duality.

It is ethical and dualistic in that the struggle between good and evil is projected into cosmology and symbolized by a warfare between light and darkness which is conceived on the one hand naturalistically and manifesting itself in a deification of shining heavenly bodies, veneration of fire, fear of defilement, and purificatory rites, and, on the other hand, mythologically as the vying for supremacy between Ormazd and Ahriman and their hosts of angels and demons. Man must choose between light and darkness, truth and falsehood, moral right and wrong, and thus gain either eternal bliss or agony.[4]

Allegories are of course not all traceable to a Near Eastern origin in some form of Zoroastrian or Manichaean heresy or cult, but still

[3] See, for example, the entry under "dualism" in the *Dictionary of Philosophy*, ed. Dagobert Runes (New York, 1942). In terms of Christian theology the question of dualist attacks on the orthodox position is of such scope that it can only be alluded to here. Frequently the issues center around some variant of Manichaean belief, which is the heresy of heresies.

[4] The entry under "Zoroastrianism" in Runes, *Dictionary of Philosophy*.

222

a marked dualism of some such kind does appear throughout the literature of Christianity and the postromantic period.[5]

The same sharpening of opposition, the same denial of a natural moral continuum, the same withdrawal of moral and ethical and spiritual problems into two polar opposites, affects agency. On the highest level of power God is set off eternally against Satan, Christ against Antichrist, the Virgin against the Whore of Babylon. These dualities parallel the duality of Ormazd and Ahriman, and, in Greek mythology, the duality of Zeus and Prometheus, and so easy is it to find such polar opposites in all religions that we may suspect we have, in allegory, the language of religion. This mode allows an expression of the means by which religions are elaborated into intellectualized doctrines more complex than their origins in primitive belief. The poet cannot often create direct images of deity, but he can mirror duality on the plane of the Gods, by showing us the deeds of knights and ladies. Here also dualism is the natural order of things. Redcrosse is warring to the death against Archimago, Una against Duessa, Calidore against the Blatant Beast. True, the powers of darkness are often pluralized, and then there is a "decomposition" of both villain and hero, and it is found that Redcrosse, for example, generates several subcharacters who are archetypally evil. He fights an Archimago of several guises, while he himself has several helpers, all of whom are equally generated by the hero.

There is probably no need to dwell at length on this primary trait of allegorical literature. It has often been noticed.[6] Allegorical dual-

[5] Since Manichaeism is the easiest of heresies to remember, and includes a variety of sects, it gets too much attention, and probably not enough close scrutiny. Dualistic thought is natural enough in any case, given the nature of the human mind, so it need not be ascribed to a Manichaean origin.

[6] See the passage already alluded to, in Coleridge, *Misc. Crit.*, 191-194, on the Near Eastern polytheism which results from an inadequate dualistic philosophy of good and evil. From a dual conception to a plural one is but a short step, as Catholic orthodoxy recognizes. Cf. Coleridge, on Apuleius (30-31): "The most beautiful allegory ever composed, the Tale of Cupid and Psyche, tho' composed by a heathen, was subsequent to the general spread of Christianity, and written by one of those philosophers who attempted to Christianize

ism in this sense is the natural result of the cosmic function of allegory, inasmuch as cosmologies of times earlier than our own depended on a "chain of being," in which, if one descended just a step lower than the lowest stage one could imagine, one reached a sort of absolute zero, Lucifer upturned in the pit of Hell, while his counterpart, Jehovah, stood at an absolute height of divine power and good.

The crux of the critical problem in the study of allegory is the way we interpret this dualism. If we simply accept the war between absolutes as the ground plan of all allegories, we are being naïve in one important respect. True, the war is always going on. But we should not assume the polar opposites are really separated by any distance. This above all is a case where the expression "extremes meet" is not a metaphor. It is a psychological fact, as we shall see.

Emotive ambivalence. In a word, allegorical literature always displays toward its polar antagonisms a certain ambivalence.[7] This much-used term does *not* mean "mixed feelings," unless we are willing to amend the phrase to "a mixture of diametrically opposed feelings." It is a term very easy to abuse. It can be used, however, if the discussion bears some relationship to psychology or comparative religion. There ambivalence is related frequently to the concept of taboo, and by means of this latter concept we can account for much that happens and much that does not happen in allegory. As I suggested when discussing the role of contagious magic, moral fables

---

a sort of Oriental and Egyptian Platonism enough to set it up against Christianity; but the first allegory completely modern in its form is the *Psychomachia* or *Battle of the Soul* by Prudentius, a Christian poet of the fifth century —facts that fully explain both the origin and nature of narrative allegory, *as a substitute for the mythological imagery of polytheism,* and differing from it only in the more obvious and intentional distinction of the sense from the symbol, and the known unreality of the latter—as to be a kind of intermediate step between actual persons and mere personifications" (my italics). This syncretic function of the mode seems to necessitate a degree of polytheism; that, in short, is what syncretism in this case means—the combination of pagan deities with the Christian monotheist system. Coleridge fully accepts the daemonic origins of allegory.

[7] See below, Chapter 6, 298–302.

are quite overtly concerned with taboos. Moral fables assert, symbolically, that some objects are sacred and some are sinful, and the
true believer should avoid the one and embrace the other. This seems
at first to be plain dualism of values. The idea of what is holy seems
so clear and self-evident. But when we seek the true meaning of
"sacred" in religious usage we meet a paradox, for it turns out that
"sacred" means both good and evil, both meeting at one time.

Freud is quite orthodox in his description of taboo, in his classic
text, *Totem and Taboo* (1918).

For us the meaning of taboo branches off into two opposite directions.
On the one hand it means to us, sacred, consecrated; but on the other
hand it means, uncanny, dangerous, forbidden, and unclean. The opposite for taboo is designated in Polynesian by the word *noa* and signifies
something ordinary and generally accessible. Thus something like the
concept of reserve inheres in taboo; taboo expresses itself essentially in
prohibitions and restrictions. Our combination of "holy dread" would
often express the meaning of taboo.[8]

The prohibitions that are discovered by the hero of the ethical fable
are not so much rational laws of a conditional sort; they are absolute
imperatives. The heart of moralizing actions becomes temptation,
which asserts the desirability of evil (a paradox inherent in the very
idea of absolute moral standards). When a man suffers from the
sudden onrush of a tabooed desire or idea, and when he cannot run
from this creature of his imagination, "the immediate consequence is

---

[8] Freud, *Totem and Taboo,* in *Basic Writings,* III, on "Animism, Magic and
the Omnipotence of Thought." Freud summarized his contribution to the
theory of taboo as follows: "The correspondence between taboo customs and
the symptoms of compulsion neurosis are most clearly manifested: 1. In the
lack of motivation of the commandments, 2. in their enforcement through an
inner need, 3. in their capacity for displacement and in the danger of contagion
from what is prohibited, 4. and in the causation of ceremonial actions or commandments which emanate from the forbidden" (*ibid.,* 829). And finally: "The
basis of taboo is a forbidden action, for which there exists a strong inclination
in the unconscious" (832). See also Franz Steiner, *Taboo* (London, 1956), and
J. C. Flugel, *Man, Morals, and Society* (New York, 1961), ch. x, "Taboo and
Its Equivalents."

certain to be a partial paralysis of the will and an incapacity for coming to a decision upon any of those actions for which love ought to provide the motive power." [9] This paralysis is nowhere more evident than in Plato's account of an ambivalent emotion, focused on the "taboo of the dead," the primitive prohibition against viewing the dead.

The story is, that Leontius, the son of Aglaion, coming up one day from the Piraeus, under the north wall on the outside, observed some dead bodies lying on the ground at the place of execution. He felt a desire to see them, and also a dread and abhorrence of them; for a time he struggled and covered his eyes, but at length the desire got the better of him; and forcing them open, he ran up to the dead bodies, saying, "Look, ye wretches, take your fill of this fair sight." [10]

At the moment when the paralytic state breaks, a splitting of consciousness occurs, and Leontius as it were separates the actions of his eyes from those of his true self; he displaces the guilt of the act onto them, and to do so he employs a central figure of allegory, personification.[11]

To illustrate this ambivalence in its most acute form, Freud quoted the *Symposium*, where Alcibiades says this of Socrates: "Many a time have I wished he were dead, and yet I know that I should be much more sorry than glad if he were to die: so that I am at my wits' end." As Freud remarked, "poets tell us that in the more tempestuous stages of love the two opposed feelings may subsist side by side for a

---

[9] Freud, *Totem and Taboo*, 821. Aristotle in the *Nicomachean Ethics*, III, ch. ii, gives a series of things which "choice" is *not*. Among them, "Still less is it anger; for acts due to anger are thought to be less than any others objects of choice." Aristotle may here be referring to the Platonic gloss on the story of Leontius, where Plato says that "sometimes anger goes to war with desire," creating a situation of acute moral conflict in the place of reasoned, balanced choice. On the Shakespearian handling of ambivalence—Watson, *Shakespeare and the Renaissance Concept of Honor*, chs. viii, ix.

[10] *Republic*, 439–440.

[11] Freud, *Totem and Taboo*, 857: "The projective creations of primitive man resemble the personifications through which the poet projects his warring impulses out of himself, as separated individuals."

while as though in rivalry with each other." [12] This "chronic coexistence of love and hatred, both directed toward the same person,"
becomes something more subtle when it is transferred to the sphere
of doubt and certainty. Along with the emotions that are ambivalent,
when this coexistence is in full force, there are likely to be intellectual
equivalents in the form of extreme doubt as to the good and/or evil
of the loved object. Franz Kafka's allegories are just as concerned
with doubt, which is intellectual, as they are with emotive ambivalence; or rather, with him the ambivalence of feeling becomes intellectual as well. The Christian allegory that deals with the hero's
search for holiness, which is a state of mind as well as of being, displays not only the tortures of the lover of God, but equally the tortures of self-knowledge. The hero is never, until final redemption
saves him, sure of himself; appearances may be deceptive, and he
therefore is most concerned to defeat the Duessas, the Archimagos,
the Guiles of this world. In Christian allegory deception is as much
a trait of the fallen world as is its sinful impurity.

Doubt, the intellectual concomitant of "ambivalence," is a central
fact of our secular love poetry, where the rhetoric defined by
courtly love always centers on some equation such as, Love is a
Warfare, or, the Desired Object is the Unattainable Object. Denis de
Rougemont may go too far in his treatise on erotic ambivalence,
L'Amour et L'Occident,[13] but that courtly love employs an ambivalent rhetoric (whatever its inner meaning) seems indubitable. If I
have stressed the theological origins of taboo (in the sense of *sacer*),[14]

---

[12] Freud, "Notes on a Case of Obsessional Neurosis" (1909), in *Collected
Papers*, III, tr. A. and J. Strachey, ed. Joan Riviere (London, 1950), 374.

[13] See Denis de Rougemont, *Love in the Western World*, tr. Montgomery
Belgion (Anchor ed., New York, 1957), 162–170, on the metaphorics of
ambivalent feeling. Cf. Maurice Valency, *In Praise of Love: An Introduction to
the Love-Poetry of the Renaissance* (New York, 1961)—a work with a more
literary purpose than De Rougemont's book; it treats the practices of troubadour poetry, whereas De Rougemont is concerned with a theme, the "love-
death," and with this undercurrent in the metaphorics of Western love poetry.

[14] On the concept of the holy (*sacer*) see Rudolf Otto, *The Idea of the
Holy*.

it is only to preserve a balance with our modern psychological concept of the emotive ambivalence which is always felt toward the loved object. For romantic allegory, such as De Rougemont treated, this latter emphasis seems to be correct, since romance in its normal meaning implies a relationship between the sexes. It was natural for a learned scholar to refer to *The Faerie Queene* as a poem "about the war between the sexes."

The poetry of ambivalence is a poetry of acute mental conflict, so disturbing that a philosopher might ask whether there is any virtue in the creation of such a literature. Even if the great polarities of moral speculation and mythic cosmology need to be reduced by a dialectical process to dramatic antitheses, the question still remains, as Plato's *Republic* posed it, whether the resulting conflict is good for men to witness, since they are bound to share in whatever they witness.

Philosophic ambivalence. The grandest and most challenging instance of an ambivalent mythos must surely be the first in Western literature, the *Prometheus Bound* of Aeschylus. This drama is intended to give the allegorical justification for the rule of law, but it has made a hero of the rebel Prometheus. It is intended further to justify belief in an all-powerful god, Zeus the perfect being, the One. (The cruelty of Zeus provides the emotional justification for Prometheus' rebellious conduct.) Coleridge has characterized the play for us: "The Prometheus is a *philosophema*, ταυτηγορικὸν,—the tree of knowledge of good and evil,—and allegory, a προπαίδευμα, though the noblest and the most pregnant of its kind." [15]

The major subject of the play is "the generation of the *nous*, or pure reason in man," and Coleridge interprets the various aspects of the Promethean fire to show the various excellences of this pure reason. In opposition to *nous* is the godlike law (*nomos*), and it is this opposition on which the drama rests, as an action.

Now according to the Greek philosopheme or *mythus*, in these, or in this identity (i.e., God, the One) there arose a war, schism, or division,

---

[15] "On the Prometheus of Aeschylus," in *Essays and Lectures*, 334.

that is, a polarization into *thesis* and *antithesis*. In consequence of this schism in the *to theion*, the thesis becomes *nomos*, or law, and the *antithesis* becomes *idea*.[16]

Coleridge takes us out of what he calls "the holy jungle of transcendental metaphysics" by showing that Zeus in the play is "the impersonated representation or symbol of the *nomos*," while Prometheus "in like manner is the impersonated representative of Idea, or of the same power as Jove, but contemplated as independent and not immersed in the product,—as law *minus* the productive energy." [17] While Zeus is active, involved totally in his action, ordering and creating at once, Prometheus is passive, suffering, and understanding. In him Mind is "bound to a rock, the immovable firmness of which is indissolubly connected with its barrenness, its nonproductivity. Were it productive it would be *Nomos;* but it is *Nous*, because it is not *Nomos*." [18] The conflict of Mind and Law is presented by Coleridge in metaphysical terms, yet it has a dramatic validity which he also stresses in his detailed commentary on the play. We conclude that if Prometheus were not to be liberated, as he in fact was in the third (now lost) play of the Aeschylean trilogy, we should have been faced with an intolerable conflict between ultimate opposites. But Alcides Liberator was to rescue Prometheus from his barren rock—precisely what occurs in Shelley's *Prometheus Unbound*.

Irony: the extreme degree of ambivalence. Classical rhetoric would make irony a subcategory of allegory, and yet the relationship of the two terms is not very clear. Perhaps the instance of *Prometheus Bound* will clarify this relationship, since, if no liberation of the hero occurred, the play would end on a note of grand irony, the hero remaining intellectually free, but physically imprisoned; at the same time nothing could be more evident than the allegorical modality in which Aeschylus and Shelley have rendered their image of the conflict between Zeus and Prometheus.

Irony we often equate with paradox, that is, with seemingly self-

[16] *Ibid.*, 338.   [17] *Ibid.*, 342–343.   [18] *Ibid.*, 345.

contradictory utterances where tenets normally in polar contradiction to each other are collapsed together into one single ambivalent statement. In irony and paradox extremes meet, while the tension of ambivalence increases proportionately. Because irony seems to collapse the multileveled segregations of allegory (e.g., a fourfold schema would collapse), it has been called "antiallegorical." [19] This seems to me an unfortunate usage, since irony still involves an otherness of meaning, however tenuous and shifty may be our means of decoding that other (*allos*) meaning. Rather, I think we might call ironies "collapsed allegories," or perhaps, "condensed allegories." They show no diminishing, only a confusion, of the semantic and syntactic processes of double or multiple-leveled polysemy. Where they do differ from an allegorical norm might instead be in the degree of emotive tension they manifest; anxiety increases in European literary works as they approach what Frye calls their "ironic" phase. One suspects that our modern ironists, our Kafkas, are managing to control both anxiety and fear, as perhaps the original ironist, the man in Theophrastus' character sketch, "The Ironical Man," controlled his much simpler fear and anxiety. But before judging this an inadequacy of modern literature let us reconsider the condition of Prometheus.

There are, says Kafka, four legends concerning Prometheus:

According to the first, he was clamped to a rock in the Caucasus for betraying the secrets of the gods to men, and the gods sent eagles to feed on his liver, which was perpetually renewed.

According to the second, Prometheus, goaded by the pain of the tearing beaks, pressed himself deeper and deeper into the rock until he became one with it.

According to the third, his treachery was forgotten in the course of thousands of years, the gods forgotten, the eagles, he himself forgotten.

According to the fourth, every one grew weary of the meaningless affair. The gods grew weary, the eagles grew weary, the wound closed wearily.

There remained the inexplicable mass of rock.—The legend tried to

[19] Frye, *Anatomy*, 91–92.

explain the inexplicable. As it came out of a substratum of truth it had in turn to end in the inexplicable.[20]

I have deliberately chosen this parable by Kafka because, recalling Coleridge, it indicates both the Aeschylean attitude and the further possibility of other even more ironic attitudes toward Prometheus. The original play is ironic enough: its conflict of *nous* and *nomos* leads to a moment of stasis, and Aeschylus' play, as we have it, implies the impasse which Shelley, following classical practice, resolved by the introduction of a *deus ex machina*. In consequence of the ambivalent claims of two kinds of power (in the absence of disinterested virtue), the action of *Prometheus Bound* is an agon and requires an overriding divine intervention if the impasse is to be broken. The normal human response to this play may be, "It is intolerable; we must break the impasse." But that is not the only possibility, and Kafka has suggested that our reaction follows from our misconstruing the true center of the action, which is not Prometheus, but the rock. This rock center is totally unlike a man center; unfeeling, unmoving, unthinking, unchanging, the rock is meaningless, purposeless, timeless, and totally beyond the fragile confines of human history and human progress; in short, the affair is naturally forgotten. One response to the parable will be: is there no hope if one denies the possibility of liberating Prometheus? Kafka has given his answer: Yes, there is a sort of dull, inhuman hope. Typically, Kafka's notion of the victim is that he is wearied by an impossible fight against an inexplicable enemy. The battle is infinitely sad.

Yet the possibility of another exit from the Promethean impasse was already suggested in classical antiquity, by Plato's Socratic dialogues, and these I take to be dramatic and philosophic proofs that we need not rely on a *deus ex machina*, if we can only "stay with it" in the ironic situation.

If irony is defined as the perception and oblique statement of the

---

[20] "Prometheus," in *Parables* (New York, 1947)—this parable translated by Willa and Edwin Muir. Reprinted by permission of Schocken Books Inc. from *Parables and Paradoxes* by Franz Kafka; copyright 1936, 1937, by Heinr. Mercer Sohn, Prague; copyright 1946, 1947, 1948, 1953, 1954, 1958, by Schocken Books Inc.

discrepancy between appearance and reality, we find it continually animating the method of Socrates; his irony is philosophic, like that of the psychoanalyst who gently raises the ironies of one's mental life to the surface of consciousness, where they can be lived with effectively. Thus the Socratic dialogues end on a note of uncertainty, or in a haze, or in the ambiguity created by multiple framing procedures. It would be an error to assume that Socrates was the Socrates of classical parody; he does not, as in Xenophon's *Symposium*, try always to make men feel inferior. True, Socratic questions will cut a man down to size if he is pretentious. But their tone is not hostile. They are intended to produce a state of equality—equality in our ignorance—so that if we finally want to feel wise, we must accept our folly. (If allegory is essentially epideictic in mode of address, irony is the converse: "praise by blame.") Whatever he argues politically and socially, the Platonic Socrates embraces a method which argues the intellectual equality of men, since his brightest man, the philosopher, is he who knows how little he knows. He, like Christ, has greatest power by abnegating the use of force. The ironic method allows us to live with the discrepancy between appearances and truth, since we are able to analyze our situation dialectically, thereby freeing ourselves of misconception. The ironies remain; the conflicts of *nous* and *nomos* are not resolved in this world; but they do not remain unobserved, and perhaps even, in little everyday situations, they can now be dealt with.

The ironic mode of the Platonic dialogues appears to follow from Plato's epistemology. With him things are an allegorical imitation of ideas, or, in another formulation, appearances are the allegorical equivalence of a higher reality. Thus it happens that a double movement characterizes the Platonic account of Socrates' thought. On the one hand there is the irony we have found in the demonstration of an equality in ignorance; on the other hand there is the often noted use of myth, which is here properly not mythos as eventful story, but mythos as paradigmatic story.[21] The Platonic distrust of

[21] Vladimir Jankélevitch, *L'Ironie ou la bonne conscience* (Paris, 1950), especially ch. ii, "La Pseudologie ironique, ou la feinte," 32–115.

sense experience has a positive consequence, for while he would say that such experience is merely a model of the truth (he calls it a "shadow"), Plato is yet left with the idea of a model. Models have their uses, and Platonic philosophizing, for one thing, could not exist without them. Removed as we are from the sun, we are yet aware of its heat and light, and of our own existence we know at least the bare outlines.

Mythos in Plato has a transcendental function. It is the philosopher's attempt to approach an epiphany. But it has also the lower function of sharpening our awareness of unmysterious aspects of reality, by allowing a sort of "withdrawal and return." The mythic core of certain Platonic dialogues, e.g., the *Symposium* and the *Phaedrus*, can thus be understood, I believe, as affecting us in two ways: like poetry it does indeed transport us to an ideal world and thereby denies the truth of our sense experience, but it also renews faith in the ideal grounds of belief, action, and thought and then lets us return more confidently to mundane problems. Mythos furthermore reminds us that the true assertion is always a question, the true statement always an enigma. Such a use of myth is capable of allegorical extension, as in the epistemological debate following Plato's parable of the cave (*Republic*, VII). These myths are archetypal and thus do not absolutely require to be explicated; but they do suggest paradigms and mathematical formulas. In their enigmatic imagery and statement we see the archetypal form which allegory takes. It is thus important to note that they are the consequence of an ironic world view. A Platonic belief in the value of myth, though at first sight it seems transcendentalism, follows from a belief in the rightness of "staying with it"—thus the Socrates of the *Apology*, the *Phaedo*, and the *Crito* stays to live and die in Athens, and at last finds himself writing verses.

"Difficult ornament" and the transition to modern allegory. The ambivalence that is expressed on the highest level of thought in *Prometheus Bound* and in the Socratic dialogues has been expressed in lesser degrees of intensity and significance by a host of writers since Aeschylus and Plato. If we wish to examine the transition from

medieval and Renaissance allegory to that of modern times, we must ask a fundamental question about this ambivalence: What is its expressive counterpart in the rhetorical theory of ornament? Since from the psychological point of view ambivalence appears at all stages in the history of allegory, the cultural growth of tradition and of idea needs to be shown working out a varying posture toward ambivalence, as each age succeeds the preceding age. When we ask what kind of ornament is intensely and perfectly allegorical—since all ornament to a degree provides an occasion for exegesis—we are trying to penetrate the sometimes adventitious variations of style and fashion that make each era think itself unique. Every period of history will have its own favorite vocabularies and its own special rhetorics. What then is the abiding tendency of an ambivalent polysemous literature, once one has discounted these particular aims? Medieval theory gives us a clue. It termed the kosmos of Scripture "difficult ornament." [22] "Difficulty" implies here a calculated obscurity which elicits an interpretive response in the reader. The very obscurity is a source of pleasure, especially to the extent that the

[22] Edgar de Bruyne, *Etudes d'esthétique médiévale*, II, 36 ff. Also Edmond Faral, *Les Arts poétiques du XII et du XIII siècle* (Paris, 1924), II, ch. iii, 89–91. De Bruyne summarizes medieval theory as follows: there are three levels of style—(1) *Genus amplum, grande, vel sublime;* (2) *Genus mediocre sive moderatum sive medium;* (3) *Genus vel subtile.* "The sublime ornaments are then rather like characteristics of the emphatic style, 'where one expresses one's thoughts by neologisms and archaisms, difficult or far-fetched metaphors, words that are grander than their subject-matter.' (Cornificius, IV, ii, 16) The grandiose approaches the emphatic, but does not quite fall into it. The medieval theoreticians are very much attached to these rules of literary theory; they pick them up and give them an original meaning. They translate *gravitas* by *difficultas:* as a result, the grand style—*oratio gravis*—for them is characterized by the *difficultas ornata*" (De Bruyne, *Etudes d'esthétique médiévale*, I, 53 (my translation).

Boccaccio, too, in his *Life of Dante*, says: "It is obvious that anything that is gained with fatigue seems sweeter than what is acquired without effort." This is a standard justification for the difficulty of allegory. The old attitude should be compared with adverse views of Eliot's and other modern poets' "obscurity." See Bk. XIV, sec. 12 of Boccaccio, *Genealogy of the Gods,* tr. by C. G. Osgood, as *Boccaccio on Poetry* (Princeton, 1930).

actual process of deciphering the exegetical content of a passage would be painfully arduous and uncertain.[23] Obscurity stirs curiosity; the reader wants to tear the veil aside. "The more they seem obscure through their use of figurative expressions," says Augustine, "the more they give pleasure when they have been made clear." [24]

[23] The obscurity of Scripture is ascribed to the clouding of man's insight, as a consequence of the Fall. Thus Milton says, "The end then of Learning is to repair the ruines of our first Parents by regaining to know God aright, and out of the knowledge to love him, to imitate him, to be like him, which being united to the heavenly grace of faith makes up the highest perfection" (*Tractate of Education* [1644], quoted by G. W. O'Brien in *Renaissance Poetics and the Problem of Power* [Chicago, 1956], 47).

[24] Training made up, to some extent, for the "difficulty." Cf. the mandate of Charlemagne (*ca.* 794) to Baugulf, abbot of Fulda, instructing the abbot in the need for monastic education: "Wherefore we exhort you not only not to neglect the study of letters but even with the most humble God-approved earnestness to vie in learning, so that you may prevail more easily and rightly in penetrating the mysteries of sacred literature. But, inasmuch as in the sacred pages are found embedded figures and tropes and other like forms of speech, no one can doubt that every one in reading those the more quickly understands (what he reads) in a spiritual sense the more fully he has before been instructed in the discipline of literature" (quoted by Laistner, in *Thought and Letters in Western Europe: A.D. 500 to 900* [Ithaca, 1957], 197). See also Laistner, 198–200, on Alcuin's method of riddling, which bears an ironic resemblance to the question and answer passages of Rabelais and Joyce. Alcuin, in a "Dispute" (*disputatio*), says to his pupil, "Since thou art a youth of good abilities and natural gifts, I will put before thee some other wonders (*i.e.* riddles). Try if thou canst guess them of thyself."

Bernard Huppé provides other instances from St. Augustine: "No one has any doubt that some things are understood more readily through figures of speech; and that when something is searched for with difficulty it is, as a result, more delightfully discovered" (*De Doctrina*, 2, 7–8). Huppé points out that "what he [Augustine] attacks is not meaningful obscurity, but meaningless rhetorical display. The rhetoric of the Second Sophistic may have dismayed him not because it taught obscurity, but because it treated obscurity as an end in itself" (*Doctrine and Poetry* [Albany, 1959], 11). Note the parallel with the "mere ornament" view.

In the Renaissance period the *Polyolbion* (1613) of Drayton failed of public acclaim, it seems to me, because it demanded an exegetical labor that was already out of fashion, and was not easily apprehensible in the new form Drayton's topographical poem gave it. He anticipated the revival of Longinus by appealing to the same criterion of mental effort to be found in the treatise

Committed to attack scholastic pedantry, the modern critic may accuse Augustine of opening the door to mere hairsplitting, a secondary, superficially clever activity of mind. Francis Bacon, speaking for the Renaissance, suggested this unhappy picture of the schoolmen when in his essay, "Of Studies," he remarked, "they are *cymini sectores*." Yet such a critique flies in the face of the manifest requirements of Scripture, which, however much exegetes may have exaggerated, does possess a frequently enigmatic surface. Augustine is pointing to a cosmic uncertainty embodied in much of Scripture, in response to which he can only advocate an interpretive frame of mind, which for him becomes the occasion for an *ascesis*. The mixture of pain and pleasure, an intellectual tension accompanying the hard work of exegetical labor, is nothing less than the cognitive aspect of the ambivalence which inheres in the contemplation of any sacred object. Whatever is *sacer* must cause the shiver of mingled delight and awe that constitutes our sense of "difficulty."

The twentieth-century reader may find this equation of "difficulty" and ambivalence more readily understandable if he remembers his own experience in reading Donne or Herbert. Donne's obscurity is not, as Dr. Johnson seems to have implied, merely clever, nor has all been said when Johnson observes that "to write on their plan it was at least necessary to read and think," for the immediate excitement of Donne's poetry involves a mingling of feeling and thought.

On the Sublime. Several times in his "Preface: To the General Reader" he attacked the "dull and slothful ignorance," the "stupidity and dullness" of his contemporaries, and demanded that the reader exert himself to discover the hidden and learned antiquarian sense of his poem. "If, as I say, thou hadst rather (because it asks thy labour) remain where thou wert, than strain thyself to walk forth with the Muses, the fault proceeds from thy idleness, not from any want in my industry." I think it could be shown that *Polyolbion* is, with *The Faerie Queene* and *Paradise Lost*, one of the most comprehensive and powerful of English sublime poems, though failure to understand its allegorical use of the body image has kept it from any general public favor.

A modern conception of "difficult beauty" is noted in A. Warren and R. Wellek, *Theory of Literature*, 233–234, where the authors discuss Bosanquet's *Three Lectures on Aesthetic* (London, 1915).

There is furthermore every technical reason for maintaining that Donne's extended figures are allegories in little; they conform to the standard notion of an extended metaphor. Herbert's poetry has recently been treated under the properly seventeenth-century rubric, hieroglyphical poetry,[25] while its subject matter—notably in poems like "The Collar"—is ambivalence itself, just as its purpose is the definition of the holy, and its form, the "steps to the temple," is a clear case of ritual. Herbert even tries to define the virtues of "difficult ornament" in his two "Jordan" poems, while in "The Forerunners" he studies the nature of figurative language in general.

No doubt a history of allegory would make much of these and other Metaphysical poets, since their works display the transitional conflicts and doubts attendant upon that breakdown in accepted ideas which Marjorie Nicolson has called "the breaking of the circle." Such an aim is beyond the scope of the present general remarks, and instead I wish to leap forward in time, to the eighteenth century—perhaps missing thereby the crucial period of transition—when the breakdown of the medieval and Renaissance world view is more advanced. We find what amounts to a loss of confidence in the old sources of authority and in the old matrices of poetic language. Numbers of scholars have shown the stresses imposed upon writers as a result of this breakdown, and here I can only suggest one or two of its probable consequences.

By the mid-eighteenth century the old belief in a cosmic hierarchy

---

[25] John Hughes, *An Essay on Allegorical Poetry* (London, 1715), used this terminology—his definition of allegory seems influenced by the tradition of Scriptural exegesis. "An Allegory is a Fable or Story, in which, under imaginary Persons or Things, is shadow'd some real Action or instructive Moral; or, as I think it is somewhere very shortly defin'd by Plutarch, it is that in which one thing is related, or another thing is understood. It is a kind of Poetical Picture, or Hieroglyphick, which *by its apt Resemblance conveys Instruction to the Mind by an Analogy to the Senses; and so amuses the Fancy whilst it informs the Understanding.* Every Allegory has therefore two senses, the Literal and the Mystical; the literal sense is like a Dream or Vision, of which the mystical sense is the true Meaning or Interpretation." (The italicized words anticipate Coleridge.)

of spiritual and temporal powers had undergone a softening, if not by any means a total alteration. The cosmic matrix for imagery such as Spenser, Shakespeare or even Milton could draw on no longer carried conviction with the poet who must equally reckon with the rising waves of scientific skepticism and with the progressive widening of middle-class materialist values.[26] Christian revelation now needed to be shored up by "natural religion," and when we actually find eighteenth-century attempts to revive the understanding of inspired revelation, as in Bishop Hurd's twelve sermons, *An Introduction to the Study of the Prophecies*,[27] we are looking at the avowed revival of an apparently moribund art. Here, as with his comments on romance and Gothic literature, Hurd is something of an antiquarian; he seeks a rhetoric which his contemporaries no longer immediately recognize. The twelve sermons have special importance as a symptom of the times. When a critic has to preach a sermon on "the style and method of the Apocalypse," we may suppose he is filling a gap in rhetorical theory left by the gradual erosion of scriptural authority. Prophecy and apocalypse no longer elicit the correct response. Bishop Hurd, for all his genius, remains a minor figure in the world of ideas. But it is not as if the gap could not be filled by other means. The history of changing taste during the Age of Reason shows how unnecessary it was for critics and poets and theologians to revive scriptural inspiration and its literary products.

[26] "Materialism" in the scientific sense of mechanistic causal theories has an immediate effect on allegorical vocabularies. We get a new iconography of the daemonic when, in the mid-eighteenth century, a natural philosopher like Lamettrie conceives of "l'homme machine" and "l'homme plante." The more or less concurrent development of Mesmer's theory of animal magnetism provides amusing as well as serious daemonic allegory, e.g., Mozart's *Così fan tutte* and his early opera, *Bastien und Bastienne* (K. 50). Hypnosis gives the daemonic hero a special power.

[27] *An Introduction to the Study of the Prophecies Concerning the Christian Church; and, in Particular, Concerning the Church of Papal Rome: In Twelve Sermons, Preached in Lincoln's-Inn-Chapel, at the Lecture of The Right Reverend William Warburton, Lord Bishop of Gloucester* (2d ed., London, 1772).

The "grandeur of generality" had other sources, chiefly in a reinterpreted Nature, which could replace the old notion of an unchanging cosmic hierarchy, and then secondly, and perhaps more important, in a reinterpreted Mind. For the eighteenth century sees the appearances of nature become, increasingly, phenomena in their own right. Nature is seen to surround physically, and this environment becomes an object of empirical study. At the same time psychology turns thought in upon itself and begins to develop a gradually more and more psychologized "human nature." Revealed religion with its emphasis on the *sacer* gives way to varieties of natural religion. There is no need to chronicle the changes here. What counts for the present inquiry is to ask: Where can the poet find analogical matrices in this new world view? If the sacred has suffered a loss of centrality, despite the continuance of Sunday sermons on Christian topics, then in some way the reinterpreted Nature and Mind may provide a replacement for the sacred, as long, at least, as major allegory is to be expected.

Lovejoy, in *The Great Chain of Being*, showed in detail that the necessary notion of cosmic hierarchy did not die during the eighteenth century, but rather underwent a gradual change under pressure from the ideological forces of natural religion, of cosmic optimism, of biological science, until the great chain of being is "temporalized," that is, until it is no longer a static hierarchy of eternally fixed ranks, but is now an evolving hierarchy of beings who are slowly and proportionately becoming more perfect.[28] Thus Bonnet argues:

The same gradation which we observe today between the different orders of organized beings will doubtless be found also in the future state of our globe; but it will follow proportions which will be determined by the degree of perfectibility of each species.[29]

Toward this world view the allegorical author must inevitably turn, since he requires some kind of hierarchical matrix, some abiding cosmic structure, on which to base his fictions. At first one might

[28] *The Great Chain of Being: A Study of the History of an Idea*, chs. iv–x.
[29] *Ibid.*, 286. The quotation is from Bonnet's *Palingénésie*, I, 174.

suspect that if visionary allegory died, it died in the eighteenth-century periodical essay, where it was used to display the ironies of polite society.[30] Dr. Johnson, who attacks the mode sometimes, is at other times himself a practitioner. (Opinions differ as to the success of his *Rasselas*.) Perhaps influenced by William Law, he marks a strange return to an earlier homiletic tradition.[31] But that is not the only possible route for the mode to follow. The temporalized chain of being opens up a whole new world, in which the old allegorical "progress" will take on even grander scope than it had when individual perfection was its goal. Now whole societies, whole technologies, whole cultural ideals are seen developing in a progressivist vision. We can look ahead to the novel of social reform and political struggle.

Perhaps even earlier, in the seventeenth century, allegory noticeably had begun to shift its ground, coming alive again in a profoundly new notion of man's place in the cosmic order of things. One example —Johnson on Milton—may serve metaphorically to recall the mentality of the period of transition away from the Renaissance. Johnson is discussing the style of *Paradise Lost*. As always with Milton, Johnson here also may have mixed feelings. He has been praising the expansionist character of Milton's imagery.

He [Milton] expands the adventitious image beyond the dimensions which the occasion required. Thus, comparing the shield of Satan to the orb of the moon he crowds the imagination with the discovery of the telescope, and all the wonders which the telescope discovers.[32]

This crowding of the imagination can only occur after the scientific revolution in which a Galileo gets men to look again, to stand off again, away from Nature, not in awe of Nature, but in direct confrontation and perception of it. How strange then that this directness of sight should once more be the occasion of those same feelings that

[30] See E. C. Heinle, "The Eighteenth Century Allegorical Essay" (Ph.D. dissertation, Columbia University, 1957).

[31] See W. J. Bate, *The Achievement of Samuel Johnson* (New York, 1955), 134 and 162.

[32] "Life of Milton," in Johnson, *Works*, II, 43.

characterize man's attitude toward the holy. The awe generated here is not unlike that generated by a Biblical text in the eyes of Augustine, and in the similar situation we are not surprised to find a similar sense of conflict. Milton's sublime crowding of the imagination is a deeply unsatisfied mental state.[33] It has value for Johnson for that very reason: the "wonders which the telescope discovers" feed not merely man's desire for practical knowledge, they also feed the "hunger of the imagination." This hunger is always occasion in Johnson for a powerful ambivalence, as W. J. Bate has so eloquently shown in his book, *The Achievement of Samuel Johnson*.

The telescope has then discovered two new centers of wonder.

[33] Thus Johnson (*ibid.*, 42) describes Milton's sublime poem: "He had considered creation in its whole extent, and his descriptions are therefore learned. He had accustomed his imagination to unrestrained indulgence, and his conceptions therefore were extensive. The characteristic quality of his poem is sublimity; . . . his natural port is gigantic loftiness. . . . The appearances of nature, and the occurrences of life, did not satiate his appetite of greatness. To paint things as they are, requires a minute attention, and employs the memory rather than the fancy. Milton's delight was to sport in the wide regions of possibility; reality was a scene too narrow for his mind. He sent his faculties out upon discovery, into worlds where only imagination can travel, and delighted to form new modes of existence, and furnish sentiments and action to superior beings, to trace the counsels of hell, or accompany the choirs of heaven."

The resulting style "never fails to fill the imagination," but lacks "the freshness, raciness, and energy of immediate observation." Johnson stresses allusion in Milton: "the spectacles of books" are a means of sublimity, since at every point the reader is led from one scene to an allusive second scene, to a third, and so on. Johnson's Milton has, we might say, a "transumptive" style. Thomas Wilson, in *The Arte of Rhetorique:* "Transumption is, when by degrees wee goe to that, which is to be shewed. As thus: Such a one lieth in a dark Dungeon: now in speaking of darknesse, we understand closenesse, by closenesse, we gather blacknesse, and by blacknesse, we judged deepenesse." As Quintilian describes it, transumption is a minor device, "a change from one trope to another," in which commonly the poet goes from one word to another that sounds like it, to yet another, thus developing a chain of auditory associations getting the poem from one image to another more remote image. "But metalepsis (transumption) is a trope to claim as an acquaintance, not to use: the commonest example is *cano* equals *canto, canto* equals *dico;* therefore *cano* equals *dico* (*canto* being the metalepsis)" (Quintilian, *Institutes*, VIII, vi, 37-39). Milton uses a less tricky method, his allusion (itself usually considered a figure) being "transumptive."

First and most obviously it unties the knotted braids of the constellations and lets us see nature with some clarity. But secondly it gives our minds, as perceiving organs, a new control over, or at least involvement with, the nature perceived. While the physical bounds of the universe expand, the imaginative boundaries of mind also expand.[34] In this double process we have, I think, the grounds for a new allegory, even before the idea of progress gains much impetus in the thoughts of poets and philosophers. We have by no means destroyed authority. We have not destroyed the possibility of accidental events "we think to be not without meaning," in short, marvellous events. We have not destroyed hierarchy. We have not made feelings of awe impossible. All these ideal activities are preserved, but in a new framework. The scientist (and now the poet becomes a sort of scientist) will be the conquistador of that new cosmos. Throughout the period following the foundation of the Royal Society, science presents new technical obstacles to the poet;[35] yet greater than these is the grandeur science imparts to whatever it influences.

The new poetry begins perhaps with Milton, but in him there is

[34] "The 'natural sublime,' that obsessive form of romantic sensibility, was the symbolic projection of the new model (the new 'infinite universe') just as the romantic imagination was, in a sense, of the new model of the mind" (Ernest Tuveson, *The Imagination as a Means of Grace: Locke and the Aesthetics of Romanticism* [Berkeley, 1960], 2)—see also ch. iii, "The Rationale of the 'Natural Sublime.'" Tuveson quotes Henry More's "*Democritus Platonissans*":

> "Wherefore with leave—the infinite I'll sing
> Of Time, of Space: or without leave; I'm brent
> And all my spirits move with pleasant trembeling,
> With eagre rage, my heart for joy doth spring."

Notice then that "the new philosophy and the mystique of space demanded a new epistemology. . . . The conception of God must be purely spiritual and rational, and must be 'uncontaminated' by the imagination, that is, by the physical sensations," *ibid.*, 63.

[35] See Basil Willey, *The Seventeenth Century Background*, ch. x, "The Heroic Poem in a Scientific Age," 219–262. Ch. iv, "On Scriptural Interpretation," chiefly on Sir Thomas Browne, is also relevant.

still much of the old world view, notably in his model of the universe. More problematic is the case of preromantic poetry, in which critics have stressed the emergence of a new subjectivism. This subjectivism constitutes a deliberate bias toward the narrator as hero, which we see already forming in *Paradise Lost*. The romantic hero is a perceiver, a dreamer, more importantly a responder and observer, a participator. His eye may be fixed to the eyepiece of the telescope, whereby the orb of the moon becomes a whole new world, comparable to the shield of Satan—and then we remember, to the shield of Achilles and to the shield of Aeneas. The hero learns at the same time an unaccustomed lability before his natural environment, from which he seeks to frame new cosmic systems.

Criticism almost immediately makes a theory which conforms to this new aesthetic experience, and this theory involves two hitherto unstressed concepts. Besides defining beauty, the aestheticians of the eighteenth century adduce the two rubrics of the sublime and the picturesque. These terms name the direction taken by allegory after "the breaking of the circle." The process of breakup had shown no catastrophic, clearly discernible moments at which we could say, "Now the springs of allegorical poetry will have to be renewed." Yet the gradual shifting of emphasis in both poetry and criticism to a concern with scientific prowess, with sensibility and subjectivism, with infinite human perfectibility, constitutes the changed condition under which a poetry of theme and idea will survive.

Most historians and theorists of the sublime in recent years have, I believe, gone even too far in emphasizing the subjectivism of the so-called "sublime emotions." Psychologically oriented, these critics have been reluctant to grant that a passage like Johnson's description of the Miltonic sublime, in which science is the new power and authority, involves not merely the new perceiver—Galileo, the hero of the Renaissance—it even more crucially involves an idealist philosophy. Samuel Monk, whose work *The Sublime* gives a rich historical account, allows primary importance to the "subjectivism of Kant," toward which, he argues, the theory of the sublime gradually moves.[36] From a certain point of view that is unquestionable. But Kant would very likely have said, "By 'subjectivism' I suppose you mean 'idealism'?" The tendency of the theory of the sublime is to reinforce a new concept of authoritarian control, so that if one thinks of the sublime as a totally or even predominantly subjective experience, one runs a risk of confusing personal attitudes with philosophical ideas, subjectivism with idealism. Ideas are a dialectically apprehensible source of authority. Yet as a result of emphasizing the growing stress on the poet's self-involvement with Nature, certain modern critics overrate the private character of romantic and pre-romantic experience. The idealist intentions of romantic poetry get lost to sight, as do the visionary Platonistic origins of that poetry (although lip service is surely paid to Plato's ghost). Most historians and critics of the transition to the romantic period are rightly interested in the development of psychology, but they do not go far enough; they end with their demonstration that a psychological movement occurs. That is but part of the story. Beyond the new mentalistic orientation, as presented in a work like Abrams' *The Mirror and the Lamp*,[37] there is a far more profound movement, the mythopoeic, which in some cases achieves true myth, in most cases achieves allegory. The new psychology becomes the basis of a new iconography. In effect, that iconographic development seems to be a main concern of *The Mirror and the Lamp*.

Primary among the emotive characteristics of the sublime and its little brother the picturesque is the same sort of ambivalence we have already noted. Monk mentions this in his paraphrase of Kant, with which he opens his study of the sublime, but then seems to forget it,

---

[36] Samuel Monk, *The Sublime: A Study of Critical Theories in XVIII-Century England* (Ann Arbor, 1960).

[37] Chs. iv, vi, vii, viii. See ch. x, sec. 3, "The Poem as Heterocosm," 278, on the "poem of the marvelous," by which a critic like Bodmer understood (and here I quote Abrams' summary) "a second creation, and therefore not a replica nor even a reasonable facsimile of this world, but its own world, *sui generis*, subject only to its own laws, whose existence (it is suggested) is an end in itself."

in spite of the fact that ambivalence occupies a central position in Kant's and every other formulation. Similarly we need to give a fresh estimate of the nature of enthusiasm, which is not simple excitement bordering on hysteria. If Kant and Schiller and before them Burke had been concerned with sensationalist raptures over Nature's grandeur, they would have indeed been describing a subjectivism. But they were concerned with an "enthusiastic" experience based on an oceanic involvement of the Self with the universe. We need to be aware that enthusiasm in the eighteenth century is a religious notion, the term suggesting certain consequences of ritual behavior.[38]

Reexamined as a type of idealist thought, not as subjectivism, the sublime appears to provide a cosmology for the poet. It provides particularly for the requirement of a "difficult ornament" and in that respect does not break the tradition of an ambivalent literature.

Allegory and the sublime. In Kantian terms the Miltonic "crowding" of the imagination is "an absolute overstraining of the faculties." [39] Any poetry that does this will exercise the intellect and

[38] Ronald Knox, *Enthusiasm: A Chapter in the History of Religion with Special Reference to the XVIIth and XVIIIth Centuries* (Oxford, 1950).

[39] I am indebted to Paul Goodman's remarks on the sublime, in his *Structure of Literature.* Goodman has put his finger on the main problem to be considered with respect to the psychology of the sublime: Kant's "absolute overstraining of the faculties." And he has made the link between this overstrain and the overstrain caused by enigmatic or riddling allegories. I have merely tried to develop some further aspects of this observation. "Consider the Delphic Oracle, where the same words have a double set of meanings. In such ambiguity we are directed outside the work for clarification—for instance, we think of the well known cunning of the Tripod. But it is just by dwelling on the unity of what is presented, with its embarrassment of riches, that we are forced to feel and think beyond what is presented" (*Structure*, 253). Often this effect of embarrassment occurs quite trivially, as Goodman points out, in works of a *trompe-l'oeil* character (and we might add, in surrealist works) or in works of "the uncanny," that is, demonic works, where the intent is more serious. See Freud's article "The Uncanny" (1919) in *Collected Papers*, IV.

Note that Lord Kames invokes the Kantian idea of "overextension of the faculties," but with him it forms the basis of a criticism. He dislikes the extension of an allegory—"a metaphor drawn out to any length, instead of illustrating or enlivening the principal subject, becomes disagreeable by *overstraining the mind*" (my italics). Lord Kames is censuring allegory for the

rouse the mind from ennui. We noted earlier that one effect of the epideictic force of allegory is that the mode incites action, and precisely that effect seems to have been the original aim of Longinus' treatise *On the Sublime*. It furthermore characterizes the aims of aestheticians who rework the Longinian theory. To begin with Longinus, that his treatise displayed anger and concern over a period of cultural stagnation and further aimed at a cultural rejuvenation appears from the tenor of the whole treatise, but most from the concluding chapter of *On the Sublime*, where Longinus states that his main hope was to counteract the decadence of his age.[40]

I maintained that among the banes of the natures which our age produces must be reckoned that halfheartedness in which the life of all of us with few exceptions is passed, for we do not labour or exert ourselves except for the sake of praise or pleasure, never for those solid benefits which are a worthy object of our own efforts and the respect of others.[41]

We are, in short, as he says, "slaves of pleasure," and we need to be roused from our dullness. (At once the concept of the sublime comes into focus as an eighteenth-century concern.) The sublime aims at "the eagerness of mutual rivalry and the emulous pursuit of the foremost place" (XLIV, 2). This arousal had been a main aim of Pope's

---

very reason earlier centuries had praised it, namely its "difficult" ornament. What would Spenser have thought had he read, "However agreeable long allegories may at first be by their novelty, they never afford any lasting pleasure: witness the *Fairy-Queen*, which with great power of expression, variety of images, and melody of versification, is scarce ever read a second time." He would have objected to an unbalanced praise of secondary virtues, and asked: What of the general plan of the poem? Admittedly, this is attacking Lord Kames at one of his weakest points, for it is just after these quoted passages that he launches into the erroneous visual theory of metaphor which Richards exposed in his *Philosophy of Rhetoric*, depending somewhat on Campbell's *Philosophy of Rhetoric* (London, 1776).

[40] Charles P. Segal has fully documented this view in his article, "ΎΨΟΣ and the Problem of Cultural Decline in the *De Sublimitate*," *Harvard Studies in Classical Philology*, LXIV (1959), 121–146. Segal stresses the cosmic implications of *hypsos*.

[41] Longinus, *On the Sublime*, tr. W. Rhys Roberts (Cambridge, 1907), ch. xliv.

two *Epistles* on the proper use of riches, while his *Dunciad* appears at once to be a classic in what we should call the burlesque sublime.[42] Graver poems like the sublime odes of Collins and Gray, and later of Shelley, have the direct and serious function of destroying the slavery of pleasure. The much-vaunted "animation" of personified abstractions in eighteenth-century verse begins in this light to mean something quite allegorical.[43] It is not, as critics have sometimes implied, a matter of visual vividness; but these are devices with considerable *ideational* vividness. The sublime poem does not in fact suggest the world of nature or of metaphor;[44] it suggests ideal Shelleyan worlds—the enthusiasm for the ideal.

[42] See Reuben A. Brower, *Alexander Pope: The Poetry of Allusion* (Oxford, 1959), ch. vii, "Essays on Wit and Nature," sec. 2, "The Scale of Wonder," 206-239. Wonder is the emotion proper to cosmic speculations.

[43] C. F. Chapin, *Personification in Eighteenth-Century English Poetry*, 45, 50, discusses the "vehement feelings" associated with the use of this device.

[44] See A. O. Lovejoy, *Essays in the History of Ideas*, v, " 'Nature' as Aesthetic Norm," 69-78. Also, Lovejoy's *Great Chain of Being*, chs. vi-x, *passim*.

It may seem odd that while many of the sublime effects were sought in natural scenery, wild cataracts, the Alps, the stormy ocean, etc., I would maintain authorization was sought outside the *cult* of Nature. But there is no contradiction here, as long as authority implies a sanction of a higher kind, something higher than a mere source of physical imagery. The authority of any major artistic mode must be metaphysical or religious, and I think the metaphysics and religion behind the sublime were a new ideal *conception* of nature, not nature itself in its raw physical state (such as would provide the documentation of a "naturalistic" fiction). Lovejoy showed how many different conceptions of the norm of Nature there could be—some would authorize allegory, some mimesis, some even mythological writing. "Nature" became a "verbal jack-of-all-trades"—and had always been "the chief and most pregnant word in the terminology of all the normative provinces of thought in the West." "And the multiplicity of its meanings has made it easy, and common, to slip more or less insensibly from one connotation to another, and thus in the end to pass from one ethical or aesthetic standard to its very antithesis, while nominally professing the same principles" (*Essays in the History of Ideas*, 69). Thus, the norm (though not the *cult*) of Nature could authorize an allegory based on the depiction of average types (the Soviet sort of allegory, the statistical kind), or it could authorize a true mimesis of natural human passions seen in the full range of their action, or it could authorize a strict allegory of essences, Platonic Ideas, "imperfectly realized in empirical reality." My general point is that all these various "Natural" norms are to be distinguished from truly Scriptural

247

Enumerating those five main qualities of literature that conduce to sublime effects, the treatise *On the Sublime* began with two that by themselves define a nonmimetic, nonmythical mode. In the summary Monk gives we perceive that the sublime is a special sort of poetry of ideas.

The first and most excellent of these [qualities] is a boldness and grandeur in the *Thoughts*. . . . The second is call'd the *Pathetic*, or the power of raising the passions to a violent and even enthusiastic degree; and these two being genuine constituents of the *Sublime*, are the gifts of nature, whereas the other sorts depend in some measure upon art.[45]

Neither Aristotelian mimesis nor any sort of mythmaking of a primitive sort (as opposed to the sophisticated creations of a Blake or a Shelley) could be thus described, since mimesis gives first place to imitation of actions, not primarily the thoughts generated about those actions, while myths give first place to an even more radical

---

norms. They are a different kind of notion, though notions even so, and not simple renderings of an objective, empirical, "external nature." If we seek the particular authorization of the sublime in the aesthetic norm of "Nature," as Lovejoy outlined its varieties, we would find that authorization in his Type C, "*Nature in general, i.e., the cosmical order as a whole, or a half-personified power (natura naturans) manifested therein, as exemplar, of which the attributes or modes of working should characterize also human art,*" and only in certain subdivisions of this norm, namely No. 7, "uniformity," No. 10, "regularity: nature as geometrizing," No. 11, "irregularity, wildness," No. 12, "fullness, abundance and variety of content, insatiable fecundity—and as consequence of these, as sometimes conceived, juxtaposition of sharply contrasting features." These are all possible features of the sublime and sometimes—for example, the last one—necessary to it (or to its ironical half-brother, the picturesque). We can say therefore that the sublime is the child of but one variant of the norm of Nature; or, putting the matter conversely, here is a sublime variant in the norm of Nature—one of its variants is the sublime. For some reason allegory was not openly identified with this variant in Romantic theory, and therefore the Romantics could not easily find authorization for allegory. They did not perceive, it would seem, that anything sublime is inherently allegorical. For an account of Lovejoy's No. 12, see his *Great Chain of Being*, ch. x, "Romanticism and the Principle of Plenitude."

[45] Monk, *The Sublime*, 13.

mimesis, in which action completely crowds out what Aristotle calls "thought." Instead we have an ideological art whose passion has a strangely highpowered, exaggerated, artificial drive. This exaggeration appears in the cult of "original genius," as well as in the cult of enthusiasm, while both trends show a latter-day revival of traditional beliefs in daemonic possession.[46] The daemonic has been rendered polite. Monk himself has quoted a passage from Edward Young that well illustrates this new daemonology and shows the conversion of awe from the religious to the aesthetic sphere. "Learning we thank, Genius we revere; That gives us pleasure, This gives us rapture; That informs, This inspires; and is itself inspired; for Genius is from Heaven; Learning from Man." [47]

The almost mystical daemonic overtones of this mode, in which genius is the ability to make the sublime response, seems to have been largely overlooked by commentators, perhaps because such an influential work as Burke's *Philosophical Inquiry into the Origin of Our Ideas of the Sublime and Beautiful* has always seemed a primarily psychological treatise on sense experience, with main emphasis on the so-called "causes" of the sublime emotions. Even Burke's account, however, includes major references to completely ideal stimuli.[48] Objects in nature are Burke's main "cause," but the sublime reaction to those objects immediately takes on an idealized, intellectualized cast. The causes are always types of excessive sensory stimulation, an overloading of the *mind* that somehow often leads to naïve reflections on man's higher destiny.

Burke found that excessively grand scenes, endless sequences of

[46] Johnson seems to resist this view of inspired natural genius, though himself very much concerned with the attempt to define genius in his own antiromantic terms. Thus, in "The Life of Cowley" he speaks of genius as large general powers accidentally determined to some particular end. He is likely to stress traditional skills, at the same time asking always for "novelty" (following Aristotle).

[47] Monk, *The Sublime*, 102.

[48] Edmund Burke, *A Philosophical Inquiry into the Origins of the Sublime and the Beautiful* (World's Classics ed., London, 1906–1907), II, sec. ix, 125.

visual or auditory stimuli, such as colonnades or bell-ringing sounds, could affect the mind by a kind of stunning arousal. He was interested in physical textures that could produce "the artificial infinite." [49] In all cases the mind must be struck by the labor involved in the creation of the sublime object.

Another source of greatness is *Difficulty*. When any work seems to have required immense force and labour to effect it, the idea is grand. Stonehenge, neither for disposition nor ornament, has anything admirable; but those huge, rude masses of stone, set on end and piled on each other, turn the mind on the immense force necessary for such a work.[50]

Above all, any objects that can convey the idea of infinitude will be sublime, and it is striking that Burke mentions specifically those works which remain unfinished, as producing the peculiar pleasure of the sublime. It is a pleasure of anticipation, in which the mind is aroused and "the imagination is entertained with the promise of something more, and does not acquiesce in the present object of the

[49] *Inquiry*, II, sec. ix, 125: "It is in this kind of artificial infinity, I believe, we ought to look for the cause why a rotund has such a noble effect. For, in a rotund, whether it be a building or a plantation, you can nowhere fix a boundary; turn which way you will, the same object still seems to continue, and the imagination has no rest." Man can artificially reproduce these natural divisions and series. Kafka's fable, "The Great Wall of China," shows the construction of "a secure foundation for a new Tower of Babel," a sort of religious Pentagon—a bureaucratic foundation for a reaching an Absolute. Imperial China suggests sets of beliefs, sets of languages, sets of warring interests, sets of ambivalent feelings—"so vast is our land that no fable could do justice to its vastness, the heavens can scarcely span it—and Pekin is only a dot in it, and the imperial palace less than a dot." This frustrating vastness Kafka means to be ironically taken, since the Imperial Palace is also equal in this nightmare to the Empire itself, which in turn is equal to the heavens. Kafka shows this by his fable within a fable. The wall is archetypal in compulsive symbolizing, since it is the means of enclosing the symbolic "center," the *hortus conclusus*, or any other encapsulating area.

[50] *Inquiry*, II, sec. xii, 127. Poe, on reading Hawthorne: "The deepest allegory, as allegory, is a very, very imperfectly satisfied sense of the writer's ingenuity in overcoming a difficulty we should have preferred his not having attempted to overcome."

sense." [51] Schiller argued the same point from a philosophic position: "We must of necessity go beyond the physical order, and seek the principle of conduct in quite another world," for which purpose sublime poetry exists.[52] The enigmatic forms of allegory are actually being invoked by Schiller, since he is demanding a poetry of ideas, as opposed to sense experience.

For the sublime, in the strict sense of the word, cannot be contained in any sensuous form, but rather concerns ideas of reason, which, although

[51] *Inquiry*, II, sec. xi, 127. The overextension of the mind is by no means a concept developed only in the eighteenth century. It has old religious origins. The Alexandrian exegete Origen speaks of "an extension of thought in pondering and considering the beauty and the grace of all the things that have been created in the Word" (*The Song of Songs: Commentary and Homilies*, tr. and annotated R. P. Lawson [Westminster, Md., 1957], 29; see also 40). Before him Philo Judaeus had had the same thought, employing an astronomical image to convey the range of that extension, viz., his commentary "On the Creation," in *Works* of Philo (tr. and ed. F. H. Colson and G. H. Whitaker [Loeb Classics ed., London, 1929], I, 55). This is one of the great paeans to the sublimity of the human intellect: "The human mind evidently occupies a position in men precisely answering to that which the great Ruler occupies in all the world. It is invisible while itself seeing all things, and while comprehending the substances of others, it is as to its own substance unperceived; and while it opens by arts and sciences roads branching in many directions, all of them great highways, it comes through land and sea investigating what either element contains. Again, when on soaring wing it has contemplated the atmosphere and all its phases, it is borne yet higher to the ether and the circuit of planets and fixed stars, in accordance with the laws of perfect music, following that love of wisdom which guides its steps. And so, carrying its gaze beyond the confines of all substance discernible by sense, it comes to a point at which it reaches out after the intelligible world, and on descrying in that world sights of surpassing loveliness, even the patterns and the originals of the things of sense which it saw here, it is seized by a sober intoxication, like those filled with Corybantic frenzy, and is inspired, possessed by a longing far other than theirs and a nobler desire. Wafted by this to the topmost arch of the things perceptive to mind, it seems to be on its way to the Great King Himself; but, amid its longing to see Him, pure and untempered rays of concentrated light stream forth like a torrent, so that by its gleams the eye of the understanding is dazzled."

[52] Blake seems to be thinking like Schiller, when in his famous statement he says, "Allegory addressed to the Intellectual Powers, while it is altogether hidden from the Corporeal Understanding, is my Definition of the Most Sublime Poetry" (*Complete Writings*, II, 246).

no adequate representation of them is possible, may be excited and called into the mind by that very inadequacy itself which does admit of sensuous presentation.[53]

One must, as allegorists know, "have stored in one's mind a rich store of ideas," if one is to affect and be affected by the conceptions of an ideal poetry.[54] The simple image of the wild ocean, the massive mountain, the yawning chasm is not enough; one must come to such an imagery with a desire to see its paradigmatic meanings.

Allegory and the picturesque. The theory of the picturesque develops collateral to that of the sublime. Picturesque art has perhaps existed for millennia, but as a cult it takes its departure from the

[53] Friedrich Schiller, *Essays Aesthetical and Philosophical* (London, 1882), 134. The essay "The Sublime" is chiefly concerned with man's "moral education"—"an *aesthetic* tendency which seems to have been placed there expressly: a faculty awakens of itself in the presence of certain sensuous objects, and which, after our feelings are purified, can be cultivated to such a point as to become a powerful ideal development. This aptitude, I grant, is *idealistic* in its principle and in its essence." We might call it the "faculty of being moved by the sublime," or of "being moved to think in a sublime manner." It is a mode of being free intellectually. Its archetypal play would be something like Beethoven's opera *Fidelio*.

[54] See Kant, *The Critique of Aesthetic Judgment*, tr. and ed. J. C. Meredith (Oxford, 1911), "Analytic of the Sublime," 97. Kant argues that the stars brought near by telescopes are not sublime; only the *idea* of the infinitely-distant-brought-close can be sublime: "*That is sublime in comparison with which all else is small.* Here we see that . . . nothing can be given in nature, no matter how great we may judge it to be, which, regarded in some other relation, may not be degraded to the level of the infinitely little, and nothing so small which in comparison with some still smaller standard may not for our imagination be enlarged to the greatness of a world. Telescopes have put within our reach an abundance of material to go upon in making the first observation, and microscopes the same in making the second. Nothing, therefore, which can be an object of the senses is to be termed sublime when treated on this footing. But precisely because there is a striving in our imagination towards progress ad infinitum, while reason demands absolute totality, as a real idea, that same inability on the part of our faculty for the estimation of the faculty of things of the world of sense to attain to this idea, is the awakening of a feeling of a supersensible faculty within us." This imagined telescopy is what Johnson praised in Milton.

seventeenth- and eighteenth-century fads of landscape "improvement," the cultivation of "special effects" in gardening, and by extension the cultivation of these effects in the visual, literary, and even
musical arts. Picturesque might best be defined as inverse, or microscopic, sublimity: where the sublime aims at great size and grandeur,
the picturesque aims at littleness and a sort of modesty; where the
sublime is austere, the picturesque is intricate; where the sublime
produces "terror," or rather, awed anxiety, the picturesque produces
an almost excessive feeling of comfort; with all the other aspects of
the one there will be found inversions in the other.

Uvedale Price, the leading theorist of the picturesque and the
writer on whom the following argument is based, would seem to
agree generally with Burke's understanding of the nature of the picturesque, though Burke has less to say on the subject. Burke remarks
that "the last extreme of littleness is in some measure sublime" (II,
sec. vii). Price shows how the picturesque duplicates the sublime not
only in its peculiar exaggeration of certain aspects of magnitude, as
Burke's remark suggests, but how furthermore it has the same stimulating function we have noticed—the same ideological function, the
same strong ambivalence. Price's picturesque employs an essentially
"difficult" ornament, however mild the "difficulty" may seem.

The source of difficulty is no longer what it had been during the
middle ages and Renaissance. It had been the esoteric, arcane, veiled
nature of figurative speech. Now the "difficulty" is shifted to a more
purely sensuous function. The picturesque challenges the spectator,
but not at first sight by figurative meanings. It challenges by a direct
attack on the senses, such that, while picturesque art is pleasing, it is
likely to mix pleasant scenes with troubling, disturbing scenes of a
morbid nature. This pleasurable pain is the main concern of Uvedale
Price's treatise *On the Picturesque*,[55] in which the author considers

---

[55] I have used the text, Price, *On the Picturesque*, edited, with interpolated
commentary, by Sir Thomas Dick Lauder (London, 1842). The work first
appeared as *An Essay on the Picturesque, as Compared with the Sublime and
the Beautiful* (London, 1794).

actual landscaping, not artistic renditions following these outdoor creations.

According to Price's view the picturesque landscape plays with surrealistic deformities in nature, what Price would call the "pleasing deformity of a clump." [56] Such landscaping plays with the idea of textural surface itself, and when painters imitate landscape, their art becomes nothing but surface, seeking to agitate the senses of the beholder. This agitation is more than surprise. It is friction, attack, inflammation of the senses. Thus it happens that Price uses the metaphors of warfare—deploying his clumps and copses like dragoons and light-armed bowmen—to convey the intention of the picturesque landscape.[57] Admittedly Price complains that others before him, the "levelling" improvers, have used their trees and shrubs like "bodies of men drilled for the purposes of formal parade," and he rejects this rigid form of landscape improvement, but on the other hand, he is only substituting a much more subtle kind of ornament, a subtler kind of warfare on the senses, where sudden ambushes take the place

[56] Price, *On the Picturesque*, ch. ix, 182, on pleasing deformity: "Clumps, like compact bodies of soldiers, resist attacks from all quarters. Examine them in every point—walk round and round them—no opening, no vacancy, no stragglers! but, in true military character, *ils font face partout*. I remember hearing, that when Mr. Brown was High-Sheriff, some facetious person, observing his attendants straggling, called out to him, 'Clump your javelin men.'" Price then makes a very remarkable extension of his military metaphor; he continues the discourse with the "belt." "The next leading feature to the clump in this circular system, and one which, in romantic situations, rivals it in the power of creating deformity, is the belt. Its sphere, however, is more contracted. Clumps, placed like beacons on the summits of hills, alarm the picturesque traveller many miles off, and warn him of his approach to the enemy; —the belt lies more in ambuscade; and the wretch who falls into it, and is obliged to walk the whole round in company with the improver, will allow that a snake with its tail in its mouth, is comparatively but a faint emblem of eternity" (183). This allusion to the *ouruboros*, playful as it is, still indicates the symbolic intent of such improvements of landscape, the tenor of the *paysage moralisé*.

[57] Recall that a major synonym for *kosmos* is *taxis*, the term for "military order."

of frontal attacks. Indeed, his treatise *On the Picturesque* is a remarkable study of the techniques of sheerly sensuous agitation.

One principal charm of smoothness, whether in a literal or a metaphoric sense, is, that it conveys the idea of repose; roughness, on the contrary, conveys that of irritation, but at the same time of animation, spirit and variety.[58]

Speaking of buildings and architectural columns, Price says:

If the whole, or a considerable part of them, were to be covered with sharp projecting ornaments, the eye would be harassed and distracted, and there would be a want of repose; on the other hand, if the whole were smooth and even, there would be a want of spirit and animation. But how different is the scenery in forests! Whoever has been among them and has attentively observed the character of those parts, where wild tangled thickets open into glades,—half seen across the stems of old stag-headed oaks and twisted beeches—has remarked the irregular tracks of wheels, and the footpaths of men and animals, how they seem to be seeking, and forcing their way, in every direction—must have felt how differently the stimulus of curiosity is excited in such scenes, and how much likewise the varied effects of light and shadow are promoted, by the variety and intricacy of the objects.[59]

The use of the word "stimulus" indicates the interest Price is taking in the problem of boredom and its cure; he is at the same time something of an animist, a polite daemonologist, with his "old stag-headed oaks." Seen from the perspective of the past fifty years, picturesque art loses for us its stimulating effect, strangely enough because it sought stimulation too directly, and also on too superficial a basis. Yet the social purpose of the picturesque is never cloaked by its practitioners, painters like Cole or Allston in this country, nor by a theoretician like Price. We may wonder if this cult, and the corresponding cult of the sublime, are not an answer to a growing ennui on the part of the leisured classes. With the picturesque, art begins to deal in "effects" rather than organic forms.

[58] Price, *On the Picturesque*, 111.   [59] *Ibid.*, 114–115.

Discords in music, which are analogous to sharp and angular objects of sight, are introduced by the most judicious composers, in their accompaniments to the sweetest and most flowing melodies, in order to relieve the ear from that languor and weariness, which long continued smoothness always brings on. But, on the other hand, should a composer from too great a fondness of discords and extraneous modulations, neglect the flow and smoothness of melody, or should he smother a sweet and simple air beneath a load even of the richest harmony, he would resemble an architect who, from a false notion of the picturesque, should destroy all repose and continuity in his designs, by the number of breaks and projections, or should try to improve some elegant and simple building, by loading it with a profusion of ornaments.[60]

Price's warning against abuse of picturesque effects is a warning against the tendency to indulge in ornament for its own sake.[61] Sheer sensuous excitement may become an artistic aim. "Effects"

[60] *Ibid.*, 108.

[61] "Almost all ornaments are rough, and most of them sharp, which is a mode of roughness; and, considered analogically, the most contrary to beauty of any mode. But as the ornaments are rough, so the ground is generally smooth; which shows, that though smoothness be the most essential quality of beauty, without which it can scarcely exist—yet that roughness, in its different modes and degrees, is the ornament, the fringe of beauty, that which gives it life and spirit, and preserves it from baldness and insipidity" (*ibid.*, 107). This passage emphasizes the stimulus-quality of ornament, and therein differentiates it from the beautiful. But it also points out the ideal function of ornament, a function "analogically considered," and opposed to the beautiful here also, in that Price's ornament is intended to animate, enliven, excite human response and perhaps therefore to have a moral purpose, a general stimulation of the mind such that it may be ready for higher purposes. The cult of sheer sensation here may seem anti-intellectual and amoral; so in a way it is. But it is the creation of new idols, new gods and shrines—picturesque ones hidden away in grottoes, at the ends of vistas. Frye, discussing the cult of beauty in art (related to the cult of the picturesque, in eighteenth-century theory), remarks on "the importance, after accepting the validity of (the archetypal) view of literature, of rejecting the external goals of morality, beauty and truth. *The fact that they are external makes them ultimately idolatrous, and so demonic*" (*Anatomy*, 115, my italics). The picturesque stimulus is likewise demonic. Baltrušaitis concentrates on this matter in his *Aberrations*, ch. iii and iv. See Geoffrey Scott, *The Architecture of Humanism* (Anchor ed.), 70—78, on picturesque as "a demand on our attention."

begin to need an aesthetic of their own. They are regarded as sufficiently meaningful in their function of arousing attention, which is understandable only if attention itself has languished.

Many people seem to have a sort of callus over their organs of sight, as others over those of hearing; and as the callous hearers feel nothing in music but kettle-drums and trombones [our hi-fi sets?], so the callous seers can only be moved by strong oppositions of black and white, or by fiery reds. I am therefore so far from laughing at Mr. Locke's blind man for likening scarlet to the sound of a trumpet, that I think he had a great reason to pride himself on the discovery.[62]

This passage makes the typically Pricean suggestion that modern listeners are jaded and need an excessive stimulation if they are to be roused at all into wonder. But can this excess have the desired effect? The middle-class notion of the picturesque no doubt plays gently with wonders—perhaps "lovely" seaside scenes, with old row-boats dotted about on the beach, are enough to stir the vacationing city dweller.[63] The almost perverse cultivation of surprise is based on a "bold contrast," but because picturesque objects are smaller and less tied to ideas and cosmic notions than are sublime objects [64]—

[62] Price, *On the Picturesque*, 129.

[63] Surrealist painting shows a marked kinship with the picturesque and sublime. Max Ernst employs picturesque "jungles"; De Chirico employs sublime colonnades and vistas almost as if he were visualizing the requirements set forth in Burke's *Inquiry*. See James Thrall Soby, *Giorgio de Chirico* (New York, 1955), 120: some of Chirico's later "composed landscapes" use inset landscape paintings standing on easels, and these are picturesque in a deliberate way. Ernst, in his satire on middle-class picturesque, makes collages of Empire engravings, in which he mixes the boudoir scene with its lace curtains, damasked and antimacassared *chaises longues,* and shadowy nooks and corners, so that we have something like an indoor equivalent of the old "improvement" of the landscape. See also Marcel Jean, *The History of Surrealist Painting,* tr. S. W. Taylor (New York, 1960).

[64] See Price, *On the Picturesque*, ch. iv, 96 ff., on the distinction between the picturesque and sublime, which is for Price mainly a matter of size, uniformity, and solemnity, in all of which the sublime exceeds the picturesque.

Both sublime and picturesque scenes share the power of eliciting ambivalent fascination, but they may perhaps finally be distinguished in two major char-

they are closer to human scale—we should ask what we learn about allegory if it is in fact at times picturesque.

The effect of such excessively irritant detail is to anesthetize. We may say that the picturesque work does not have "proper magni-

___

acteristics, (1) the magnitude of the elements in each, the immense versus the minute, and (2) in consequence of the picturesque's reduction of sublime grandeur to minute textural intricacy, the more approachable, more charming, more comfortable effect of picturesque scenes. The standard notion that "picturesque" means "picture-like" or "depictable" (as, for example, Jean Hagstrum discusses fully in *The Sister Arts: The Tradition of Literary Pictorialism and English Poetry from Dryden to Gray* [Chicago, 1958]) is, I think, almost meaningless unless, as Hagstrum suggests, there is a connection made between the "picture-like" and the diagrammatic or the emblematic. To picture in a picturesque manner meant to paint ideas into landscapes, to impose themes on nature, or, looking at the matter in reverse, to extract from certain particular natural scenes certain equally particular ideas or, more obscurely, to evoke particular feelings. Both sublime and picturesque scenes can be depicted, but the latter seem to be the result of moving into a more accessible, more genteel sublimity, a weak sublimity. Instances of this could be found in the arts, but a rather more striking case would be one from real life. I have chosen the account in James Boaden's *Memoirs of Mrs. Inchbald* (London, 1833), II, 131–134, where the burning of a number of London theatres is described. Boaden remarks that "Mrs. Inchbald was at all times fond of sublime objects, and had missed the sight of Covent-Garden theatre in flames; but her situation at the top of No. 163 in the Strand, by the side of the New Church, giving both a direct and reflected view of the horrors attending the destruction of Holland's Drury-Lane theatre, we are happy to lay her descriptive letter on the subject before our readers:—

To Mrs. Phillips.

'Sunday, Feb. 26, 1809

'I saw nothing of the conflagration of Covent-Garden theatre, but was a miserable spectator of all the horrors of Drury-Lane. I went to bed at ten, was waked at a quarter before twelve, and went into the front room opposite to mine, while the flames were surrounding the Apollo at the top of the play-house, and driven by the wind towards the New Church, which appeared every moment to be in danger.

'I love sublime and terrific sights, but this was so terrible I ran from it; and in my own room was astonished by a prospect more beautiful, more brilliantly and calmly celestial, than ever met my eye. No appearance of fire from my window except the light of its beams; and this was so powerful, that the river, the houses on its banks, the Surrey hills beyond, every boat upon the water,

tude," in Aristotle's sense.[65] It presents only a texture, though theo-reticians of the picturesque would have pointed to their vistas and "artificial waters" as breaking the texture. These breaks, however, serve only to heighten the general effect of textural congestion. Here ornament has fallen away from any structure beneath, a fact clearly illustrated in the textbooks on the picturesque, where a single land-scape is given two alternate and arbitrary "plantations," the one neo-classic, the other picturesque, showing that the underform is not felt to demand one single ornamentation which alone is organically "right" for it. The picturesque clothing of this landscape is preferred because it brings with it a sensuous excitation which the mind accepts as good in itself.[66] Clothing, of the landscape as of the body, here

---

every spire of a church, Somerset House and its terrace on this side,—all looked like one enchanted spot, such as a poet paints, in colours more bright than nature ever displayed in this foggy island.'" From this letter we might con-clude that the picturesque is a beautification of the terrible. Certainly, by re-moving herself from the direct sight of the fire, Mrs. Inchbald was enabled to see it "such as a poet paints," without extreme terror, and yet with a residue of terror and a mingled "celestial" delight consequent upon that terror. Mrs. Inchbald is saying in effect that there is a degree of sublimity in which the ambivalence is too great to be supported, but the picturesque diminishes this tension to an aceptable level.

[65] "The picturesque has no connection with dimension of any kind, and is as often found in the smallest as in the largest objects" (Price, *On the Pictur-esque*, 96). Price means that this mode is defined by a textural quality more than by any factor of outline.

[66] Notice the cosmetic metaphors of clothing in the following passage from Sir William Chambers' *Dissertation on Oriental Gardening*, quoted by Love-joy, in "The Chinese Origin of a Romanticism," *Essays*, 127: "We admire Nature as much as you do; but being of a more phlegmatick disposition, our affections are somewhat better regulated: we consider how she may be em-ployed, upon every occasion, to the most advantage; and do not always intro-duce her in the same garb; but show her in a variety of forms; sometimes naked, as you attempt to do; sometimes disguised; sometimes decorated, or assisted by art; scrupulously avoiding, in our most common dispositions, all resemblance to the common face of the country, with which the Garden is immediately surrounded; being convinced, that a removal from one field to another, of the same appearance, can never afford any particular pleasure, nor ever excite powerful sensations of any kind."

again implies a cosmology in the larger sense. The artificial landscape is treated by its theoreticians just as if it were a woman's body, to be dressed in the picturesque or sublime ("Roman") manner.[67]

> Let sweet concealment's magic art
> Your mazy bounds invest;
> And while the sight unveils a part,
> Let fancy paint the rest.[68]

This stanza suggests most vividly the curious veiling which seems to be at the heart of cults like that of the sublime and the picturesque.[69] The picturesque scene is meant to titillate, not excite naturally by a promise of movement and climactic pleasure. This stanza was used

[67] On the relation between ornament and the body, see Kenneth Clark, *The Nude: A Study in Ideal Form* (Anchor ed., New York, 1959), 369–370. "Decoration exists to please the eye; its images should not seriously engage the mind or strike deep into the imagination, but should be accepted without question, like an ancient code of behavior. In consequence, it must make free use of clichés, of figures that, whatever their origins, have already been reduced to a satisfactory hieroglyphic."

[68] Shenstone's verses are quoted by Chapin, *Personification*, 56. Price says the same of the picturesque: "Many persons, who take little concern in the intricacy of oaks, beeches, and thorns, may feel the effects of partial concealment in more interesting objects, and may have experienced how differently the passions are moved by an open licentious display of beauties, and by the unguarded disorder which sometimes escapes the care of modesty, and which coquetry successfully imitates" (*Of the Picturesque*, 70). But the whole art of the picturesque is so obviously to veil that it may not need remarking. It employs a range of devices by which this veiling becomes a stimulus to *curiosity*, though not to liveliness. "Curiosity" here means an almost prurient fascination with whatever is hidden, and it relates, on the pathological end of the scale, to neurotic fetishism, which would be its extreme or parodistic form. Price sums up the experience of the picturesque thus: "The effect of the picturesque is curiosity" (98).

[69] One cannot help thinking of the old notion that allegory itself is a "veil" interposed between the exegete and the true vision of God's Word. For example, St. Augustine, echoing Origen, in *The City of God* (Bk. XVII. 20): "But now the Song of Songs is a certain spiritual pleasure of holy minds, in the marriage of that King and Queen-city, that is, Christ and the Church. But this pleasure is wrapped up in allegorical veils, that the Bridegroom may be more ardently desired, and more joyfully unveiled, and may appear."

to illustrate a certain picturesque decorative tendency; I am reading nothing into it that a nonpsychoanalytic critic, a conservative critic, C. F. Chapin, has not already read into it. The verses also remind us that the "fanciful" creatures of the picturesque, like other creatures of the fancy, are conceived as separate from the structure they are adorning. Unlike the figures of imagination, which cling and interweave, these remain volatile, like airy spirits, like the daemons from which in fact they come down to us. Chapin shows in his *Personification in Eighteenth-Century English Poetry* how the figures of the fancy become the details of picturesque art, and how they are related to the "machines" of the older allegory, through such poetry as Pope's *Rape of the Lock*, where part of the satirical mock-epic background is the creation of a secondary fairy world, parallel to a third analogical world, of the ombre game.[70]

Pope writes that his grotto at Twickenham wants "nothing to complete it but a good statue with an inscription." Such a statue would serve as a symbol of the grotto as a whole; it would act to personify "the aquatic idea of the whole place." Joseph Warton compares the kind of pleasure which such landscape statuary imparts to the pleasure one receives from the insertion by the poet of "oblique" moral reflections in passages of scenic description.[71]

If here the allegorical nature of "machines" and thence of picturesque landscape is not a fully conscious allegory, but remains rather on the spiritualist plane, it dates back historically to the consciously allegorical use of machines in Renaissance masques and Restoration heroic drama.

Grotesquerie: ambivalent picturesque. When the cultivation of such spiritualism becomes morbid, or introspective, we get something like Flaubert's *Temptation of St. Anthony*, behind which lies a long tradition of pictorial grotesquerie. As Henry James put it:

Tremendously pictorial M. Flaubert has certainly succeeded in being, and we stand amazed at his indefatigable ingenuity. He has accumulated

[70] Chapin, *Personification*, 54 ff.   [71] *Ibid.*, 56.

a mass of curious learning; he has interfused it with a mass of still more curious conjecture; and he has resolved the whole into a series of pictures which, considering the want of models and precedents, may be said to be very handsomely executed. . . . But for the most part M. Flaubert's picturesque is a strangely artificial and cold-blooded picturesque—abounding in the grotesque and the repulsive, the abnormal and the barely conceivable but seeming to have attained to it all by infinite labor, ingenuity, and research—never by one of the fine intuitions of a joyous and generous invention.[72]

Henry James was asking for another sort of picturesque, a light-hearted one. But though he criticized Flaubert for "labor, ingenuity, and research," such are the very marks of medieval allegory, from which Flaubert's picturesque descends. Such must almost necessarily be the character of an encyclopedic allegory.

Flaubert's grotesquerie belongs to the Gothic tradition.[73] A similar symbolism appears in the cult of the exotic detail known as *chinoiserie*.[74] This branch of picturesque displays as well as any we could choose the ideal function of the mode, as well as its marked emotive ambivalence. We notice immediately that here, as with picturesque in general, there is a strong desire to confront the spectator with dead, dying, or decaying objects.[75] These objects, which would normally be repulsive, are here made into objects of desire. William Chambers' *A Dissertation on Oriental Gardening* (1772) provides a vivid description of this grotesquerie.

The plantations of their autumnal scenes consist of many sorts of oak, beech, and other deciduous trees . . . placing amongst them decayed trees, pollards, and dead stumps, of picturesque forms, overspread with

[72] Henry James, "Flaubert's *Temptation of St. Anthony*," in *Literary Reviews and Essays*, ed. Albert Mordell (New York, 1957), 149–150.

[73] His St. Anthony is akin to "Monk" Lewis' Ambrosio, in *The Monk*.

[74] The following discussion is based on Lovejoy's essay, "The Chinese Origin of a Romanticism," in *Essays*, 99–135.

[75] See Price, *Of the Picturesque*, ch. ix. Price calls for a good deal of carefully disposed "rubbish." This is a traditional emblem of the passing of Empire; on which imagery, see O. W. Larkin, *Art and Life in America* (New York, 1949), ch. xvi, "Westward the Course of Landscape."

moss and ivy. The buildings with which these scenes are decorated are generally such as indicate decay, being intended as mementos to the passenger. Some are hermitages and almshouses, where the faithful old servants of the family spend the remains of life in peace, amidst the tombs of their predecessors, who lie buried around them: others are ruins of castles, palaces, temples, and deserted religious houses; or half-buried triumphal arches and mausoleums, with mutilated inscriptions, that once commemorated the heroes of ancient times: or they are sepulchres of their ancestors, catacombs and cemeteries of their favourite domestic animals; or whatever else may serve to indicate the debility, the disappointments, and the dissolution of humanity: which, by cooperating with the dreary aspect of autumnal nature, and the inclement temperature of the air, fill the mind with melancholy, and incline it to serious reflections.[76]

This orgy of gloom is but the prelude to some truly wild self-indulgence in Gothic excess. The picturesque scene is gradually made more and more savage, as the traveler is invited to pass by tombs, "pale images of ancient kings and heroes, reclining on beds of state; their heads are crowned with garlands of stars, and in their hands are tables of moral sentences"—past precipices and waterfalls that threaten to engulf him, past deep gullies "filled with Colossal figures of dragons, infernal furies, and other horrid forms, which hold, in their monstrous talons, mysterious cabbalistic sentences, inscribed on tables of brass," past violent explosions of fire, places where he hears nothing but yells of torment, the roaring of bulls, and howls of ferocious animals and the croaking of ravenous birds. Now, what is strange about this mad landscape is not only that it is intended to incline the mind to "serious reflection" (thus the large number of "sentences" inscribed on various kinds of tablets), but further that it is not at all unpleasant to the traveler. Just around the bend he is to be met by a delightful change of scene.

His road lies through lofty woods, where serpents and lizards of many beautiful sorts crawl upon the ground, and where innumerable apes, cats and parrots, clamber upon the trees to imitate him as he passes; or

[76] Chambers' *Dissertation* (2d ed.), 37-38, quoted by Lovejoy, *Essays,* 130.

through flowery thickets, where he is delighted with the singing of birds, the harmony of flutes, and all kinds of soft instrumental music: sometimes, in this romantic excursion, the passenger finds himself in spacious recesses, surrounded with arbors of jessamine, vine and roses; or in splendid pavilions, richly painted and illumined by the sun: here beautiful Tartarean damsels, in loose transparent robes, that flutter in the scented air, present him with rich wines or invigorating infusions of Ginseng and amber, in goblets of agate; mangostans, ananas, and fruits of Quangsi, in baskets of golden filigree; they crown him with garlands of flowers and invite him to taste the sweets of retirement, on Persian carpets, and beds of camusathskin down.[77]

One cannot resist the feeling that here Chambers' explanatory *Dissertation* has shifted to irony. The luxurious implications of the final scene show, however, an odd contrast in the way in which normally threatening creatures, the serpents and lizards, have been made into creatures of delight. Here also the ambivalence of attitude is strong, since even the dangers of the place are met with pleasure. Finally, however, this exotic landscape is one where, as Chambers' traveler proceeds, delight is experienced in an open confrontation of terrifying objects, and although Chambers was describing solely what he could imagine as the perfect *chinoiserie*, he still conveys the essence of an attitude. In the description that follows we see how far "difficult ornament" has come from its earlier value as "cosmic" figuration; it now includes the most exotic and frightening images— "difficult" will now mean "threatening," instead of "obscure" or "arcane." In this change is mirrored the general change of allegorical procedures as they strike the beginnings of the preromantic era. Gone is the iconography of the Holy Scripture, though this is an apocalypse. The period of naturalism is not so far distant.[78]

---

[77] *Ibid.*, 42–44, quoted Lovejoy, *Essays*, 131.

[78] I say this advisedly. Lovejoy interprets the *chinoiserie* of Chambers as "anti-naturalism." See *Essays*, 126 ff. "Chambers represents the Chinese artists as justifying their methods expressly on the ground that all improvements are deviations from the natural." This is true enough, as far as it goes. But the irony of this anti-naturalism is that it fosters a kind of detailed, surrealistic

The trees are ill formed, forced out of their natural directions, and seemingly torn to pieces by the violence of tempests: some are thrown down and intercept the course of the torrents; others look as if blasted and shattered by the power of lightening: the buildings are in ruins; or half consumed by fire, or swept away by the fury of the waters: nothing remains entire but a few miserable huts dispersed in the mountains; which serve at once to indicate the existence and wretchedness of the inhabitants. Bats, owls, vultures, and every bird of prey flitter in the groves; wolves, tigers and jackalls howl in the forest; half-famished animals wander upon the plains; gibbets, crosses, wheels and the whole apparatus of torture, are seen from the roads; and in the most dismal recesses of the woods, where the ways are rugged and overgrown with poisonous weeds, and where every object bears the marks of depopulation, are temples dedicated to the king of vengeance, deep caverns in the rocks, and descents to gloomy subterraneous habitations, overgrown with brushwood and brambles; near which are inscribed, on pillars of stone, pathetic descriptions of tragical events, and many horrid acts of cruelty, perpetrated there by outlaws and robbers of former times: and to add both to the horror and sublimity of these scenes, they sometimes conceal in cavities, on the summits of the highest mountains, founderies, lime-kilns, and glass works; which send forth large volumes of flame, and continued clouds of thick smoke, that give to these mountains the appearance of volcanoes.[79]

It is quite true, as Lovejoy observes, that Mason wrote a satirical epistle to Sir William Chambers, based chiefly on this passage of the *Dissertation*.[80] On the other hand, it is exactly the final scene Chambers described which Hawthorne used, in all seriousness, in his *Ethan Brand*. And Shelley was to employ scenery not unlike that of the picturesque and sublime horrors here described. Chambers him-

---

cultivation of detail, which in turn develops into the excessive documentary of the Naturalist writers. Lovejoy presumably means "naturalism," then, in the simple sense of "conforming to a natural norm." In fact, a later work like *La Faute de l'Abbé Mouret*, of Zola, is pure picturesque landscape gardening (to produce a new Eden, called "Paradou") and is daemonic in much the same manner as Chambers' imaginary scenes.

[79] *Ibid.*, 44–45, quoted Lovejoy, *Essays*, 132.   [80] Lovejoy, *Essays*, 132.

ALLEGORY

self is understood by Lovejoy to be "seeking to introduce a kind of aesthetic 'Romanticism,' " which in literature produces the Gothic novel.[81] This trend was in turn finally going to yield to the symbolist movement, and therefore to a movement which we normally distinguish from the writing of allegory.[82] Yet in the last analysis

[81] See the introduction by William Axton to Maturin's Gothic novel, *Melmoth the Wanderer* (1820; reprinted Lincoln, 1961): Axton argues that the Gothic novel is essentially a revolutionary fiction. One thinks of Shelley's early, unfinished romance, *The Assassins*.

Cf. the review in *Time Magazine*, LXXVIII, no. 1 (July 7, 1961), of Russell Kirk's Gothic novel, *Old House of Fear*. The reviewer makes a standard error. Having quoted Kirk's own assertion that his book is "in blushing line of direct descent from *The Castle of Otranto*," the reviewer proceeds: "He is wrong. Historian Kirk (*The Conservative Mind*) has expertly stuffed his book with all the claptrappings of the Gothic romance, but what he has actually achieved is a political morality tale." Then the review, as if unaware that it is defining Gothic romance, describes *Old House of Fear* in entirely daemonic terms; the two subheads of the article are "Demon Ideology" and "Political Exorcist," both of which recall that ideologies are always daemonic when pushed to a fanatic limit. The novel was classic allegory, right down to its use of an "island of Carnglass," in the Outer Islands of the Hebrides, "the microcosmos of modern existence."

[82] The surrealists and the Dada movement share this desire to stimulate a torpid middle class. Axton quotes De Sade to the effect that "it was necessary to bring hell to the rescue," and much the same diabolism characterizes these two modern movements. The parallel process in the picturesque channeling of ideas can be easily seen in modern surrealism, where the artist looks about for the *"merveilleux du quotidien."* "The surrealist anti-novel is a direct transcription, not of the irrelevant routines, but of the surprising and unexpected shocks of life" (Brée, in *An Age of Fiction*, 137).

See also, on this point, Anna Balakian, *Surrealism: The Road to the Absolute* (New York, 1959). Balakian quotes Breton's requirements for the surrealist image (123 ff.): (1) It embodies contradictions. (2) One of the terms of the image is hidden. (3) "The image starts out sensationally, then abruptly closes the angle of its compass"—i.e., it embodies a deception, a sudden, shocking frustration of whatever we had expected. (4) "The image possesses the character of a hallucination." (5) "The image lends to the abstract the mask of the concrete." (6) "The image implies the relation of some elementary physical property"—what better proof that we are dealing with a decapitated allegory, whose aim is indeed, as Tzara and Breton insisted, an automatic search for a new absolute, a new dogma.

"It seemed to us that the world was losing itself in vain, that literature and

266

Chambers' peculiar brand of "Gothic" Romanticism has an iconography. Its peculiar material was the exotic and frightening, but especially the sublime variants of romantic scenes. Its aim was finally a moral one, in that it sought to give the mind new stimuli to reflection; it was full of "sentences." In this way it was a thematically charged art.

The essential psychic kinship of the sublime and picturesque with the main tradition of allegory lies in their moralizing tendency and in their emotive ambivalence. Schiller insists on this ambivalence:

The feeling of the sublime is a mixed feeling. It is at once a painful state, which in its paroxysm is manifested by a kind of shudder, and a joyous state, that may rise to rapture, and which, without being properly a pleasure, is greatly preferred to every kind of pleasure by delicate souls. This union of two contrary sensations in one and the same feeling proves, in a peremptory manner, our moral independence. For as it is impossible that the same object should be with us in two opposite relations, so it follows that it is we *ourselves* who sustain two different relations with the object. It follows that these two opposed natures should be united in us, which, on the idea of this object, are brought into play in two perfectly opposed ways.[83]

This perfect description of ambivalence, related as it is to the cultural determinants bringing about such states of mind, required a terminology which we possess, but which Schiller lacked; thus Kant argued that "since the mind is not simply attracted by the [sub-

---

art had become institutions which, on the periphery of life, in place of serving man, had made themselves the instruments of an outmoded society. They served war and, while expressing good sentiments, they covered with their prestige an atrocious inequality, a sentimental misery of injustice and vulgarity. . . . Dada took the offensive and attacked the world system in its totality, in its fundamentals, for this system embodied human stupidity, that stupidity which ends in man destroying man, along with all material and spiritual goods" (T. Tzara, *Le Surréalisme et l'après-guerre* [Paris, 1947], 19). This catastrophic view leads to one of the great figures, the total destruction of life on earth, after which new life is believed to spring up: the myth of the phoenix, the myth of the millennium.

[83] Schiller, "The Sublime," in *Essays Aesthetical and Philosophical,* 133.

267

lime] object, but is also alternately repelled thereby, the delight in the sublime does not so much involve positive pleasure as admiration or respect, i.e., merits the name of a negative pleasure." [84] By this means the imagery of the sublime "transports and ravishes the mind beyond the narrow circle of the real, beyond this narrow and oppressive prison of physical life." [85]

Spenser's epic: the sublime poem. After Milton's *Paradise Lost* [86]

[84] Kant, "Analytic of the Sublime," in *Critique of Aesthetic Judgment*, 91.

[85] Schiller, "The Sublime," 110.

[86] See Coleridge's *Misc. Crit.*, Lecture X, on Milton's sublimity, which reflects "an under consciousness of a sinful nature, a fleeting away of external things, the mind or subject greater than the object."

Hazlitt, "On Chaucer and Spenser": "With all this Spenser neither makes us laugh nor weep. . . . But he has been unjustly charged with a want of passion and of strength. He has both in an immense degree. He has not indeed the pathos of immediate action or suffering, which is more properly the dramatic; but he has all the pathos of sentiment and romance—all that belongs to distant objects of terror, and uncertain imaginary distress. His strength, in like manner, is not strength of will or action, of bone and muscle, nor is it coarse and palpable—but it assumes a character of vastness and sublimity seen through the same visionary medium, and blended with the appalling associations of preternatural agency. We need only turn, in proof of this, to the Cave of Despair, or the Cave of Mammon, or the account of the change of Malbecco in Jealousy" (*Hazlitt on English Literature*, ed. Jacob Zeitlin [Oxford, 1913], 30).

There is a problem here, however. The sublime appears to have suggested *vagueness*, the *impalpable*, to early commentators, and hence we have to admit that its signification was not a clear one. Anton Ehrenzweig, in *Psychoanalysis of Artistic Vision and Hearing* (London, 1953), 54, quotes Warton's commentary on the Miltonic description of Satan: "His stature reached the sky, and on his crest sate Horror plum'd"—"We have," says Warton, "no precise or determinate conception of what Milton means. And we detract from the sublimity of the passage in endeavouring to explain it, and to give it a distinct signification. Here is a nameless terrible grace, resulting from a mixture of ideas, and a confusion of imagery." Another commentator, Dr. Newton, had given the standard reading: "Extravagant! . . . Horror is personified and made the plume of his helmet."

Similarly, the description of Spenser's Dissemblance in the following quotation is surrealistic, and hard for the critic of an earlier time to explain. Of the line, "And her bright browes were deckt with borrowed haire," describing Dissemblance in *The Faerie Queene*, III, xii, 14, Coleridge says: "Here, as too often in this great poem, that which is and may be known, but cannot *appear*

the favorite eighteenth-century example of a sublime poem would be *The Faerie Queene*. This work is extraordinarily spacious and grand in design; it is enigmatic; it challenges all our powers of imagination and speculation; it "proves, in a peremptory manner, our moral independence"; it further is marked by ambivalence of attitude toward moral dichotomies. We can approach the assessment of this ambivalence by asking to what extent Spenser achieves that stimulating, exciting surface texture which characterizes the sublime or the picturesque. To what extent does Spenser entertain the "painful state" Schiller speaks of? Does *The Faerie Queene* ever elicit "two contrary sensations in one and the same feeling?"

Spenserian ambivalence. Spenserian ambivalence is not simple. We find it throughout the poem: Book I, the ambivalence resulting from the sense of sin, the archetypal Christian *taboo;* Book II, the ambivalence of appetite and will [87] (Guyon, some readers have felt, is not "temperate" in Aristotle's sense); Book III, the ambivalence of the fear of sexual impurity; Book IV, a continuation of Book III, centering, officially, on the conflict of loyalties, or conflicting friendships; Book V, the ambivalence which Coleridge spoke of in his explication of *Prometheus Bound,* between idea and law (Artegall displaces the repressive cruelty onto Talus, like a G.H.Q., as Davis says); [88] Book VI, perhaps the least openly ambivalent of the six (though even here, as Frye points out, the final vision of Serena is a depiction of *sparagmos,* the ripping apart of the goddess).[89] The "Mutability Cantos" are broadly philosophical and religious, and contain in essence the problems of the various other Books.

---

from the given point of view, is confounded with the visible. It is no longer a mask-figure, but the character of a Dissembler" (*Misc. Crit.,* 39).

[87] The interpretation of Bk. II as a fable patterned on the story of Achilles' wrath accords fully with the concept of a prevailing Spenserian ambivalence, since such a wrath springs from frustration, more than outright challenge. Achilles is the arch-brooder, the resentful one, suggesting a degree of reserve in his emotional make-up. On this view, see A. C. Hamilton, *The Structure of Allegory in The Faerie Queene* (Oxford, 1961), 116-123.

[88] B. E. C. Davis, *Edmund Spenser,* 125.   [89] Frye, *Anatomy,* 148.

Some critics would define Spenserian ambivalence more narrowly. Watkins spoke of "the excessive carnage" in *The Faerie Queene*, which suggests ambivalence in its sadomasochistic phase.[90] Hazlitt said that Spenser "luxuriates equally in scenes of Eastern magnificence; or in the still solitude of the hermit's cell—in the extremes of sensuality or refinement"; [91] and Grierson noted:

It is not only Guyon but the reader whose moral alertness is lulled by stanzas such as these, and their tone is that which predominates in one's memory of *The Faerie Queene* [referring to II, xii, 74–75]. . . . The moralist must convince us that the sacrifice is required in the interest of what is a higher and more enduring good, that the sensuous yields place to the spiritual. It is this Spenser fails to do imaginatively, whatever doctrine one may extract intellectually from the allegory.[92]

These quotations suggest the ambivalence of sensual indulgence and puritan asceticism. Another critic, B. E. C. Davis, reminds us that "the Legend of Justice is manifestly not at unity with itself," [93] and his analysis of the problem suggests the doctrinal ambivalence of Law versus Freedom, the old one of *nomos* and *eros*, which Bishop Nygren treated at length in its religious aspect,[94] which Plato had dealt with in broadly political terms.

Most critics seem to think that Spenser resolves the inner conflicts of his poem by abandoning his own puritanism (not a doctrinaire Calvinism) at just the right moment, and for its allegorical rigors substituting a freer mythopoeia, or else a Platonic ideal of balance. For example, H. S. V. Jones has argued in favor of Book V that Artegall creates a character of Lord Grey "answering to the Roman type of the judge merciful in temper but stern in the execu-

---

[90] W. B. C. Watkins, *Shakespeare and Spenser* (Princeton, 1950).

[91] Hazlitt, *Lectures on the English Poets*, "On Chaucer and Spenser," in *Complete Works*, ed. A. R. Waller and A. Glover (London, 1902), V, 35.

[92] Grierson, *Cross Currents in English Literature*, 54.

[93] Davis, *Edmund Spenser*, 124.

[94] Anders Nygren, *Agape and Eros*, tr. A. G. Hebert and P. S. Wilson (London, 1933), *passim*. M. C. D'Arcy, *The Mind and Heart of Love* (New York, 1947), ch. ii, discussed Nygren's views, with those of De Rougemont.

tion of justice." [95] This *politique spiritualiste* is seen as opposed to a Machiavellian *politique materialiste*.[96] Without trying to assess this view, we can assume that it contains a seed of doubt, that perhaps the two *politiques* are self-destructively intermingled in Spenser's Book V.

Another version of Spenserian ambivalence was seen by J. W. Saunders, who argued in his article "The Façade of Morality" [97] that Spenser was writing out of a new moral decorum, the rising dualistic ethic of the "new" middle classes—of the Peter Wentworths, who made "merit" the measure of hierarchical status, of the London shopkeepers who made shopkeeping success their sign of godliness. Saunders preceded his discussion of Spenser with a general survey of the sociological problem, under the heading "Ambivalence in Tudor Poetry." Such a title must not mislead us; it does not refer to the acute personal ambivalence from which I believe the *writer* writes, but rather to the large cultural force which makes *writers*, in the plural, write in a largely didactic or propagandistic way. It is thus unfortunate that Saunders, using an argument Yeats himself came to, stumbled on the word "schizophrenia." There is nothing schizophrenic about the compulsive behavior resulting from ambivalence, at least as we know it in its public artistic form. The poet may isolate groups from each other, may isolate himself from society by his own introspection, but that does not make him

[95] Jones, "Spenser's Defence of Lord Grey," *University of Illinois Studies in Language and Literature* (Urbana, 1919), V, 151–219.

[96] On this general subject, see the collection of essays, *Christianismo e ragion di stato: L'Umanesimo e il demoniaco nell'arte*, ed. Enrico Castelli (Rome, 1953). To a very considerable extent the idea of the daemonic in statecraft becomes prominent with the appearance of Machiavelli. See, for example, Daniélou, "Le Démoniaque et la raison d'état," in *ibid.*, 27–34; also Gerhart Ritter, *The Corrupting Influence of Power*, tr. F. W. Pick (London, 1952), from *Die Dämonie der Macht*.

[97] Saunders, "The Façade of Morality," in *That Souereign Light: Essays in Honor of Edmund Spenser 1552–1952*, ed. W. R. Mueller and D. C. Allen (Baltimore, 1952). See also, for effects of ideology on imagery, J. B. Fletcher, "Some Observations on the Changing Style of *The Faerie Queene*," *Studies in Philology*, XXX (1934).

"schizophrenic"; the latter is a condition whose symptoms are of no special use, and, if beautiful, are disturbingly beautiful. Schizophrenia is, after all, an extreme pathological state. It denotes the advanced cases of split-mindedness. Yet the fact remains that Spenser was deeply concerned with the classification of social groups, and he would be likely to take this problem in the light of his own orientation, a middle-class one. He could not attack his Queen; he could and did attack her counselors. For the artist, after the medieval period, patronage and the pursuit of patronage become matters that may entail the most violent conflicts of allegiance.

Social ambivalence is not always easy to show in Spenser, however, because his poem is a largely idealized defense of the Establishment. More readily apparent are the deeper kinds of psychological conflict we have already seen. These might be subsumed under the heading of taboo, since a tabooed person or object is defined as one that elicits emotions in diametric conflict. Of the three kinds of taboo which Freud treated in *Totem and Taboo*—of enemies, of rulers, of the dead—all can be illustrated by Spenser's poem. Most marked of all is the taboo of the ruler: Gloriana is the unapproachable yet infinitely desirable object of courtly desire. She is at once the avenging Britomart, the melting Amoret, the chaste, athletic Belphoebe, the transparently beautiful Florimell, the just Mercilla, the truthful Una—and she is others whom we have not met, who were to be heroines of later books. Always we must remember that Spenser did not finish his poem. That is a main fact to be considered in Spenserian criticism from the formal side. The taboo on Gloriana holds the poem together, even unfinished, like a retreating glow of light around the deity, lambent in the distance, deadly when we approach it. While the taboo keeps the courtier from his actual Queen, and the reader from the final vision of the fictive Queen, it ineluctably draws both courtier and reader into her embrace.

These speculations suggest there is much ambivalence in the Spenserian epic. We need not quarrel over its name. When a critic denies its presence, he thereby undercuts the high seriousness of the poem. Thus, while Douglas Bush perhaps still speaks for a number of critics in his *Mythology and the Renaissance Tradition in English Poetry*, he there gives a disturbingly bland account of Spenser's characteristic manner:

Indeed he was not of a nature to be conscious, as Tasso was, of disturbing conflicts. He remains, among other things, the wistful panegyrist of an imagined chivalry, the bold satirist of ugly actuality, cosmic philosopher and pastoral dreamer, didactic moralist and voluptuous pagan, puritan preacher and Catholic worshipper, eager lover and mystical Neo-Platonist.[98]

In the light of the theory of ambivalence, however, this account appears inconsistent; Bush's own list of attributes presents a Spenser full of conflict, while all the violence in Spenser contradicts the denial of a similarity (in this respect) between Spenser and Tasso. How can a man write much about endless fighting, tyranny, and deceit, and not "be conscious . . . of disturbing conflict"? Bush does a disservice to Spenser by sentimentalizing him—Spenser is hardly "wistful." It would have been fairer to attempt to explain the striking lack of dramatic excitement in *The Faerie Queene*. The excitement of reading Spenser, is so to speak ours, not Spenser's. We bring it to the work; the work does not, like a mimetic work, present us with a series of events capable in their autonomy of exciting our attention and sympathy. On our first encounter the figures are miniature, like the knights Proust imagined on his bed, jousting in the playful light of a magic lantern. But as we read our way *into* Spenser, his figures grow large with another size, of dull reverberations, by alluding to other cultures, other religions, other philosophies than our own.

Forms of infinite magnitude and detail. When a poem like *The Faerie Queene* has a core of profound ambivalence, when it is built upon clusters of "antithetical primal words," the tendency to

---

[98] Bush, *Mythology and the Renaissance Tradition in English Poetry* (Minneapolis and London, 1932), 88.

achieve sublime magnitude overall and picturesque precision in detail can hardly be unexpected. Themes (*dianoia* and *hyponoia*) have important effects on the magnitude and texture of poems. On the one hand the sublime work is defined as having, or suggesting, infinitely large outlines, while on the other the picturesque work has, or suggests, infinitely small refinements of detail within the whole outline. *Paradise Lost*, of which Dr. Johnson remarked that "no man ever wished it longer," demonstrates both tendencies—in precisely the proportion to which the poem has allegorical meanings. Spenser's epic likewise is so far sublime that its completion would have been an inconceivable achievement, while its picturesque texture has been a source of endless critical commentary and wonder.

On a "romantic," a "Gothic," or a "medieval" view these excesses have high value. Bishop Hurd could well praise the movement of a poem toward episodic "Gothic" complications. But a more classic view, defined by Aristotle in the *Poetics*, would reject the development of the sublime outline and the picturesque texture in allegorical works. Aristotle admires dramas that share the organic, organismic unity of living, moderate-sized creatures—man appears to be his standard of scale. Leviathan and the insect—neither will do for the model of a mimetic hero. They have no dramatic relation to a natural human scale. On this basis Aristotle can justify his preference for plays over epic poems; the latter run the risk, which Homer alone avoids, of becoming "thin and waterish." Besides the risk of a diffused effect, perhaps worse than it, is the danger that if a work is too long or puzzlingly minute in detail, it will not be quite perceptible either to the sensual eye or to the mind's eye. Neither memory nor imagination will be able to retain an image of "a creature, say, one thousand miles long." Aristotle questions the value of such a difficult, indirect perception, and we can suppose he would similarly question "difficult ornament." This is a matter of taste perhaps, and it may be that, had Aristotle turned his attention more fully on *Prometheus* than on *Oedipus*, he would have found a *raison d'être* for the sublime. As it is, we must await the later terms, sublime and picturesque, to name the thematic uses of distortion in natural magnitude.

It might be possible to invent new terms, or to modify the term "mannerism" or the term "baroque," in such a way as to provide a terminology. For present purposes, however, the eighteenth-century labels will serve, especially since I am not concerned to fill out the differences between different historical periods. I would not insist on the labels sublime and picturesque being referred solely to eighteenth-century art history, though that should bear out their appropriateness in the present theory. Freely employed, they point adequately to devices of both later and earlier periods.

Both the sublime and the picturesque can assume new guises, which happens, for example, in commercial art and in surrealism. A Dali, an Ernst, a De Chirico, a Peter Blume, and many others provide evidence of this in the visual arts. Literature is more complex, and we must search to find the symbolic sublime and picturesque. Consider, however, the vast indefinite pseudo articulation of the surveyor's ignorance in *The Castle* and of the prisoner in *The Trial*. The machine in Kafka's story "In the Penal Colony" [99] recalls the horrors of Gothic and of science fiction, but it also recalls the devices of the landscape in Chambers' *Dissertation*—it is an instrument of hell. The desire for decay and decrepitude described by

[99] "In the Penal Colony" is available in the collection *The Penal Colony: Stories and Short Pieces*, tr. Willa and Edwin Muir (New York, 1961), 191–230; also in *Selected Short Stories of Franz Kafka*, tr. Willa and Edwin Muir, with an introduction by Philip Rahv (New York, 1952). Speaking of the role of H. G. Wells in the pioneer stages of modern science fiction, Kingsley Amis remarks: "The time machine itself, the Martians and their strange irresistible weapons in *The War of the Worlds*, the monsters in the first half of *The Food of the Gods*, the other world coterminous with ours in "The Flowering of the Strange Orchid," all these have had an innumerable progeny. What is noticeable about them is that they are used to arouse wonder, terror, and excitement, rather than for any allegorical or satirical end" (*New Maps of Hell*, 32–33). This sort of distinction results, I believe, from an excessively narrow notion of allegory; as a sublime modality it perfectly conforms to the wondrous, terrifying, exciting literature Amis has described. A machine is of course inherently wonderful, if regarded at all in human perspective.

Uvedale Price reappears in Kafka's story "A Hunger Artist," [100] while his parables have the most obvious connection with oracular, sublime language. "The Hunter Gracchus," [101] for example, begins with the typical iconographic "coding" process which results from paratactic form, and it continues through an enigma until Kafka is able to end on a note of infinite openness.

"Extraordinary," said the Burgomaster, "extraordinary.—and now do you think of staying here in Riva with us?"

"I think not," said the hunter with a smile, and, to excuse himself he laid his hand on the Burgomaster's knee. "I am here, more than that I do not know, further than that I cannot go. My ship has no rudder, and it is driven by the wind that blows in the undermost regions of death."

Whatever the genre, this literature takes on "open forms," tending always to develop so many involutions of imagery and theme, or so much scope overall, that it finally produces either actually or psychologically unfinished works. It is a question, then, solely from the point of view of magnitude, whether allegorical works can be organically unified. Zoologists hold that for every physically functioning unit of a body there is an optimum range of size—and conversely certain gross and minute sizes impose limits upon physical function. In much this way there are functional disabilities inherent in the picturesque texture and, perhaps more so, in the sublime outline. Yet this may finally not be a disadvantage. Openness of purpose, strained by an opposite encapsulating tendency, may be the true virtue of the mode.

Now in the aesthetic estimate of such an immeasureable whole, the sublime does not so much lie in the greatness of the number, as in the fact

---

[100] *The Penal Colony*, 243–256. Note that the artist is transformed into a panther, a medieval emblem of Christ, for which see *The Bestiary*. Heinz Politzer, *Franz Kafka: Parable and Paradox*, 307, notes the conclusion of Meno Spann that the beast is a leopard.

[101] In *Selected Short Stories of Franz Kafka*, 129–147. The story of the Great Wall is also archetypal for allegory—the building is endless, the means are compartmentalized and bureaucratic, the tone is doubtful and anxiety-ridden and, finally, bored and anaesthetic.

that in our onward advance we always arrive at proportionately greater units. The systematic division of the cosmos conduces to this result. For it represents all that is great in nature as in turn becoming little; or, to be more exact, it represents our imagination in all its boundlessness, and with it nature, as sinking into insignificance before the ideas of reason, once their adequate presentation is attempted.[102]

For Kant there is no problem in finding a "true," "natural," sublime somewhere in the real world; he needs no Alps, no actual Grand Canyons, no actual Saharas, because the *idea* of these wastes and grandeurs will be enough to elicit an intermediate, but higher, sublimity, which is on its way to becoming the true sublime, i.e., power completely ideal in conception. As Kant puts it, and here he echoes both Plato and the Alexandrian exegete Philo Judaeus, the sublime in nature makes the mind "sensible of the appropriate sublimity of the sphere of its own being, even above nature." So, if nature is not quite grand enough, not quite uncanny or enigmatic enough to present, in a poem, an image of the sublime, that matters little, as long as the reader is enabled by the inadequate actual poetry to reach an ecstasy of intuition. In these terms we can assess the aim of Shelley, both in the Longinian *Defence of Poetry* and in his major poems, including the *Prometheus Unbound*, to revive a desire to emulate the ideal agent. In this ultimate sense there is an emotive function for allegory. Shelley wanted his readers to struggle with the grand and confused scenes of his odes, with the obscure metaphysics of his *Prometheus*, for which purpose he elaborated a highly ornamental style. If the style was and still remains difficult, that puts it in the main tradition of prophetic literature. We may conclude this chapter by observing that, when "difficult ornament" is most "difficult," it is usually because the poetry is prophetic, like the prophetic books of the Bible or Blake's prophetic poem *The Four Zoas*. The poet can always justify his obscurity, no matter how deep, because he claims to be presenting an inspired message. This is not mere allegorical cleverness. It is the attitude of the prophet who in turn

[102] Kant, *Critique of Aesthetic Judgment*, 105.

is reading the mind of some higher Being. Whether we can believe in this view is a matter of private metaphysics. But it was certainly Shelley's view, when he claimed for the great poets that they are "legislators." He seems to have meant that they give mankind the laws of thought, if not of expedient practicality. Allegory thus would reach its highest plane in a symbolism that conveys the action of the mind.

6

Psychoanalytic Analogues:

Obsession and Compulsion

OVER half a century has passed since Freud laid the groundwork
for a psychoanalytic theory of symbolism in his *Interpretation of
Dreams*,[1] and in the meantime his methods and his orientation toward the dynamic character of symbolic behavior have radically
altered our ideas about language,[2] whether in everyday life or in
specialized uses such as religion or literature. There is no need to

---

[1] Sigmund Freud, *The Interpretation of Dreams*, tr. James Strachey (2d
print., New York, 1956). This supplants the old Brill edition (Modern Library
ed.). On allegorical interpretation of dreams see 96–100, and 524 on Silberer's
notion of "anagogic interpretation."

[2] On the notion of a "dynamic" psychology, see Freud, *Interpretation*, chs.
vi and vii; "Formulations regarding the Two Principles in Mental Functioning,"
Collected Papers, IV; also the article "Repression" in the same volume. A review article by Sandor Rado, "Psychodynamics as a Basic Science," is in his
Psychoanalysis of Behavior: Collected Papers (New York, 1956). The most
illuminating collection of essays in this field is, I believe, David Rapaport's
Organization and Pathology of Thought (New York, 1951). Rapaport includes
two selections of papers on "Symbolism" and "Fantasy-thinking."

justify a tempered employment of Freudian concepts, despite the technical objections that have been raised against them by psychologists and philosophers. For whereas Freud and his successors may have failed to construct an adequate behavioral theory that can be experimentally tested, and may have failed to meet epistemological criticism from philosophy, they have not failed in their description of symbolic action. The naïve assumption would be to see in psychoanalysis a reductive sort of methodology; rather it is almost too willing to see in the dream, in the neuroses, and in the "psychopathology of everyday life" a wide range of cultural contents.[3] There is no strait-jacketing in this methodology; if anything, its fault is an opposite tendency to overcomplicate the processes by which feeling is expressed symbolically. Of the particular syndrome which I wish to emphasize, Freud said: "The wildest psychiatric fantasy could not have invented such an illness, so different, so striking, and so individual is the symptomatology." [4] He was willing to admit that in spite of the techniques of interpretation he advocated, many dreams would finally resist full interpretation, would remain too enigmatic to be understood analytically, while on the other side it might happen that an overly ingenious interpreter would read too much into a dream. Freud, and the shrewdest of his successors, were well aware of the complications of symbolic behavior. We need have no fear, either, that he was unaware of the conventional tricks and skills of literary artists; his awe of these skills knew no bounds, and was equaled only by his own skill in the art of exposition.[5]

Applications of psychoanalysis. Psychoanalytic concepts need

[3] Freud, *The Psychopathology of Everyday Life* (1901) (Standard ed., London, 1953–1962), VI, or in *Basic Writings of Sigmund Freud.*

[4] Quoted by Wilhelm Stekel, *Compulsion and Doubt,* tr. Emil A. Gutheil (New York, 1949), Introduction, I.

[5] See Ernest Jones, *The Life and Work of Sigmund Freud* (New York, 1957), III, ch. xv, "Art," ch. xvi, "Literature." Also, Ludwig Marcuse, "Freuds Aesthetik," PMLA, LXXII (June 1957), 446–463. Relevant essays by Freud have been collected in *On Creativity and the Unconscious,* ed. Benjamin Nelson (New York, 1958).

therefore no general justification. But there is a difficulty about their use which is specific to literary criticism. They have been far too much used in a genetic way, that is, as a way of ascertaining why a given author wrote as he did, or why a given character in a fiction acts as he does. These two kinds of genetic criticism need a word of comment.

The first is a psychobiographical approach to literary history. To explain the literary behavior of a given author, the critic plays the part of a diagnostician relating literary symptoms to biographically known causes, which will usually be traumatic events of the author's childhood and adolescence. The critic may read Franz Kafka's "Letter to my Father," and from this and other such personal documents he constructs an etiology of Kafka's writing behavior. Or, by an analysis of Swift's letters and his *Journal to Stella*, the critic accounts for the obsessional scatology that pervades Swift's fictional works. Or, by a similar analysis of Ezra Pound's letters, he attempts to determine where the line of sanity is to be drawn in the *Cantos*. Freud's essays on artists are mainly of this sort, and in "The Relation of the Poet and Day-dreaming" (1908) he argued that by technical devices the poet is able to make his fantasies and daydreams public,[6] to make them pleasing for an audience to share in, to make them into adequate substitutes for real satisfactions—chiefly sexual—that would otherwise be lacking in the artist's life. Such arguments are bound to be concerned in large part with the poet's life and character and environment—a concern which we as critics may wish to reserve for the literary historian, on the ground that psychobiography is strictly speaking a nonformal, nonaesthetic concern.

The second familiar genetic criticism stemming from Freudian theory is very like the first, but is focused on the fictional worlds thus created. Ernest Jones's study of the motivations in *Hamlet* uses the theory of the Oedipus complex to account for the seeming contradictions in Hamlet's behavior.[7] Henry Murray has similarly

[6] *Collected Papers*, IV, 182–192.
[7] Ernest Jones, *Hamlet and Oedipus* (Anchor ed., New York, 1955).

treated Melville's *Pierre*.[8] Freud again sets the pattern for this in his essay on Dostoyevski,[9] and in essays on "The Theme of the Three Caskets," [10] on "Those Wrecked by Success," [11] which dealt with the revelation of character in *The Merchant of Venice* and *Macbeth*. In this as in the other case the critic attempts to find out the sources, the origins, the causes of behavior; he is only secondarily concerned with literary form, although character analysis may well move over into analysis of reversals and discoveries, and thence of dramatic form.

If, however, we are to find adequate formal criteria in psychoanalysis, we shall need especially to examine the neuroses as *patterns* of behavior. The neuroses are typical shapings of unbalanced behavior for which it is in fact possible to find cultural analogues, since each neurosis is very like a creative, positive, civilizing "symbolic action."

Psychological analogues. In *Totem and Taboo* Freud drew analogies between three kinds of neurosis and three kinds of nonneurotic activity, namely between obsessions and religious ritual, between paranoia and philosophy, between hysteria and mimetic art.[12] In the

---

[8] See the Introduction to Melville's *Pierre* (New York, 1949).

[9] Freud, "Dostoevsky and Parricide" (1928), *Collected Papers*, V, 222–242.

[10] Freud, "The Theme of the Three Caskets" (1913), *Collected Papers*, IV, 244–256. This essay observes and analyzes the parallel between the choice of caskets and the choice Lear makes between his three daughters.

[11] Freud, "Those Wrecked with Success," *Collected Papers*, IV, 323–341. This forms part of a longer essay entitled "Some Character-Types Met with in Psycho-analytic Work" (1915). The earlier part of this essay deals with Shakespeare's *Richard III*.

[12] "In one way the neuroses show a striking and far-reaching correspondence with the great social productions of art, religion and philosophy, while again they seem like distortions of them. We may say that hysteria is a caricature of an artistic creation, a compulsion neurosis, a caricature of a religion, and a paranoiac delusion, a caricature of a philosophic system. In the last analysis this deviation goes back to the fact that the neuroses are asocial formations; they seek to accomplish by private means what arose in society through collective labour. . . . Genetically the asocial nature of the neurosis springs from its original tendency to flee from a dissatisfying reality to a more pleasureable world of phantasy. This real world which neurotics shun is dominated by

last of these—the analogue that would appear to concern us, since we are talking about art—the fundamental point of similarity was the mimetic, miming, identifying, gesturing process that was found common to both art and hysteria. The hysteric acts out his fears and desires for sexual contact, by what is called "conversion," that is, by a kind of mimetic gesturing. Other points of similarity existed, but were subordinate to this primary mimetic function. We know, however, that not all art is mimetic, and the question is therefore left

---

the society of human beings and by the institutions created by them; the estrangement from reality is at the same time a withdrawal from human companionship" (Freud, *Totem and Taboo*, in *Basic Writings*, 863–864).

The collocation of art and hysteria will be less surprising if one makes one or two prior conditions: (1) Freud was aware of the fact that "psychological" novels split up their characters into separate daemons, but he did not pursue this line of thought ("Relation of the Poet to Day-dreaming," in *Collected Papers*, IV). Instead Freud saw art clustered around the mimetic center, a center to which our art traditionally comes back, after flights into mannerism of either the mythopoeic or the allegorical kind. (2) Hysteria must be understood in its *outgoing*, extroverted character: the hysteric, in normal conditions, is a markedly outgoing person, who seeks intimate contact—one might say, erotic contact—with others. It is this impulse to come into intimate knowledge and contact which characterizes the mimetic mode also, the mode which Freud equated with "art." The chief ground for making art the analogue of hysteria is therefore the common fact of *identification*. To make his dramas and fictions the poet "identifies" with other real or imaginary people, imitating their actions and passions. In hysteria identification "enables patients to express in their symptoms not only their own experiences but those of a large number of other people; it enables them, as it were, to suffer on behalf of a whole crowd of people and to act all the parts in a play single-handed. I shall be told that this is not more than the familiar hysterical imitation, the capacity of hysterics to imitate any symptoms in other people that have struck their attention—sympathy, as it were, intensified to the point of reproduction. . . . Identification is not simple imitation but *assimilation* on the basis of a similar aetiological pretension; it expresses a resemblance and is derived from a common element which remains in the unconscious" (*The Interpretation of Dreams*, 149–150).

As to Freud's equation (through parody) of compulsion and religion, there is nothing to prevent us from saying that allegory is the most religious of the modes, obeying, as it does, the commands of the Superego, believing in Sin, portraying atonements through ritual. That it can also be philosophical only speaks for the proximity of paranoia and compulsion.

open as to what may be, if any, the correct analogy to the non-mimetic arts of myth and allegory.

Psychoanalytic evidence suggested plentifully that myth had a correlate in the dream, with its extreme degrees of "condensation," [13] "displacement," [14] "negation," [15] "timelessness," [16] and character of

[13] Cf. Freud, *Interpretation*, 279–305.

[14] Cf. Freud, *Interpretation*, 305–310. Frye, *Anatomy*, 188: "In literary criticism the myth is normally the metaphorical key to the displacement of romance." "The central principle of displacement is that what can be metaphorically identified in a myth can only be linked in romance by some form of simile: analogy, significant association, incidental accompanying imagery, and the like. In a myth we can have a sun-god or a tree-god; in a romance we may have a person who is significantly associated with the sun or trees. In more realistic modes the association becomes less significant and more a matter of incidental, even coincidental or accidental, imagery" (*Anatomy*, 137). This notion of displacement follows from the original Freudian idea that by symbolic changes of referent one makes a dangerous, antisocial, or vicious thought acceptable.

[15] Cf. Freud, *Interpretation*, 310–339. Also Freud, *Collected Papers*, IV, 184–191. See also, Freud's article, "Negation" (1925), in the *Collected Papers*, V, 181–183. "Affirmation, as being a substitute for union, belongs to Eros; while negation, the derivative of expulsion, belongs to the instinct ·of destruction" (185). Frye calls *negation* "demonic modulation" (*Anatomy*, 156–157). Its clearest examples are to be found in Gnosticism, on which see, specifically, Hans Jonas, *The Gnostic Religion*, ch. iii, "Gnostic Imagery and Symbolic Language," 48–100.

De Rougemont, in *Love in the Western World*, 162, gives a list of negations current in the rhetoric of courtly love, where the ambivalence of feeling issues in the classic formulations: "To die of not being able to die," "The struggle of love in which it is needful to be defeated," "Love's dart that wounds but does not kill," "The sweet cautery," etc. In a way Freud's term "negation" names the process by which, unconsciously, the mind selects terms to express its ambivalence. Extreme dualism must cause symbolic antiphrases. One gets the impression sometimes that the most powerful satirists are dualists, users of "negation," to the point that they become naïve gnostics. They, like Gnostics, hover on an edge of extreme asceticism which can drop off absolutely into an extreme libertinism. See Jonas, also Huizinga, *Waning of the Middle Ages*, 109. Huizinga's conception of the waning is that it mingled the extremes of brutality and moral chaos on the one hand, and ornamental refinement and rigid cosmology on the other.

[16] Freud, "The Unconscious," in *Collected Papers*, IV, 119. See also, on the timelessness of mythical thought, Mircea Eliade, *The Myth of the Eternal*

"wish fulfillment," [17] and psychoanalysts like Karl Abraham, Géza Róheim, and Otto Rank were quick to collect from folklore the necessary materials to bear out this analogy between dream and myth. The so-called "true symbols" of the dream (what we would call "Freudian symbols") were indeed found to be present in a wide variety of mythological vocabularies.[18] So far so good—myth has its

---

Return. Eliade studies in detail the way in which "archaic man tolerates 'history' with difficulty, and attempts periodically to abolish it." That would be, in Freud's terms, a regression to the time scheme of the dream. Eliade maintains that in order for primitive man to remain in this "paradise of archetypes" (his timeless world), he must periodically get rid of his sense of "sin," and thus he creates rituals of exorcism. These rituals are the compulsive technique by which the sense of guilt is kept out of consciousness, or else reduced in psychic intensity. Cf. Benjamin Lee Whorf, "Time, Space and Language," in *Culture in Crisis: A Study of the Hopi Indians*, ed. Laura Thompson (New York, 1950), 152 ff.

[17] Cf. Freud, *Interpretation*, ch. iii, and ch. vii, sec. C, for a more technical account of wish fulfillment. Also, "Formulations regarding the Two Principles," *Collected Papers*, IV.

[18] See Géza Róheim, *The Eternal Ones of the Dream* (New York, 1945), 248: "The laws that govern the use of symbols for the purpose of allegory are one of the future tasks of psychoanalytic anthropology. Perhaps my meaning is not quite clear. When I say a symbol, I mean a symbol with an unconscious content (a 'mythical' symbol); in this case, the water-rainbow-snake as representing the combined parent concept. *By allegory I mean something the natives have no reason to repress*, such as the snake representing rain, clouds, water. The use of symbols as allegories is thus an indicator of man's unconscious in relation to environment. The first aim attained is therefore to project an internal strain, but the second function is to minimize environmental dangers by equating them with infantile situations, with dangers that were dangers only in the past." See also Otto Rank, *Art and Artist*, "Myth and Metaphor," 207–235; *The Myth of the Birth of the Hero and Other Writings*, ed. Philip Freund (New York, 1959) (this edition includes chapters from *Art and Artist*).

Ernest Jones, for example, in his essay, "The Theory of Symbolism" (1916), *British Journal of Psychology*, IX (1918), 181. (Cassirer resisted the cross-over between psychoanalysis and the theory of myth.) See Karl Abraham, *Traum und Mythus* (Vienna, 1909). Jung and his followers have inspired innumerable mythic interpretations of literary works, e.g., Maud Bodkin's *Archetypal Patterns in Poetry*, not to mention some of Frye's most important work. For a general, and typical, account of myth, see Warren and Wellek, *Theory of Literature*, 195 ff. "Myth" has come to mean many things, sometimes implying

correlate in dream. But we still have the other type of literature, the allegorical, for which to find an exploratory analogue. It will be apparent that if we hit upon the correct formula, we shall be saying something new about the form of allegories, in the broadest sense of their inner dynamics.

The analogue to allegory. Let us suppose then that the proper analogue to allegory is the *compulsive syndrome,* which Freud himself had made parallel to religious behavior.[19] One condition must be laid down: that we are not talking about the compulsive behavior of authors as men; we are talking about literary products which have this form, a form we can discern regardless of its causes, a form which for our purposes exists as a thing in itself. In each of the five areas we have mapped out—agency, imagery, action, causality, and theme—there should be some psychoanalytic clarification of the true nature of allegory.

Agency: obsessional anxiety. The typical agent in an allegorical fiction has been seen as a daemon, for whom freedom of active choice

---

fixed rituals, sometimes fluid dream images, sometimes implying a story, sometimes implying the breakdown of story. Its classic, and primary Greek sense is "a fable," "a story," "a legend." Frye uses it in a somewhat special way in his article, "Myth as Information," *Hudson Review,* Summer, 1954: "The formal principle is a conceptual myth, a structure of ambiguous and emotionally charged ideas or sense data. Myths in this sense are readily translatable. They are, in fact, the communicable ideogrammatic structures of literature" (234–235). Here "myth" equals Aristotle's *dianoia* and strongly suggests an allegorical framework or, better, a *cosmic* framework. The term is protean, whatever else we say of it.

[19] The major Freudian document on obsession-compulsion is the "Notes on a Case of Obsessional Neurosis," *Collected Papers,* III. See his later *The Problem of Anxiety* (1926) (Standard ed., XX). The work of Karl Abraham is important for the relation between melancholia and obsessive behavior. Stekel's two-volume *Compulsion and Doubt* contains a wide variety of case studies, reported in detail. From it one can gain a picture of the breadth of the problem of compulsion. For a general treatment in summary form, see Bertram D. Lewin, "Obsessional Neuroses," in *Psychoanalysis Today,* ed. Sandor Lorand (London, 1948). Professor J. W. Beach's *Obsessive Images,* published posthumously, is a discerning account of a number of key images that recur in modern literature, Beach argued, with the frequency of obsessions.

hardly exists. This appears to have a major correlate in the theory of compulsive behavior, where it is observed that the mind is suddenly obsessed by an idea over which it has no control, which as it were "possesses" the mind. The commonest experience of the compulsive neurotic is that he is suddenly disturbed by impulses that have no apparent rational meaning, and thence are seen as arbitrary and external "commands." It is this foreignness that is emphasized by psychoanalysts.

An obsession is an idea or desire which forces itself persistently into the patient's mind in what he experiences as an irrational fashion. A compulsion is an act actually carried out, which similarly forces itself upon the patient. Obsessive ideas and compulsive acts are often closely linked: for instance, the obsession that there may be dangerous germs on one's hands leads to the compulsion of handwashing. Minor obsessions and compulsions are familiar in everyone's experience. We keep wondering whether we turned off the gas burner, or we knock on wood after mentioning our good fortune. These everyday phenomena resemble neurotic obsessions and compulsions to the extent that they are sensed as irrational. We know they are foolish, but they seem to have a little push of their own and it is easier to let them have their way. In neurotic obsessions and compulsions, this quality is greatly magnified. The ideas and acts are like foreign bodies, forcing themselves upon the patient yet experienced as no part of the self. Moreover . . . if the patient tries to stop his obsessive ruminations or his compulsive rituals, he is plunged into an attack of anxiety.[20]

This anxiety is precisely the quality of the actions performed by the daemonic character, since he is always determined to get to some goal, to reach home, to reach the Celestial City. Fear of not reaching that goal is even greater than fear of the particular terrors along the way. On the other hand, it is characteristic of allegorical plots that they preserve, on some level of literal meaning, a highly ordered

[20] R. W. White, *The Abnormal Personality* (New York, 1948), 291 (copyright © 1956, The Ronald Press Co.). White gives a good summary of the syndrome. For an extended account see Otto Fenichel, *The Psychoanalytic Theory of the Neuroses* (New York, 1945), ch. xiv, "Obsession and Compulsion."

sequence of events, which suggests that the anxiety does not usually break through the unbroken *surface* of compulsive fictions. The anxiety is kept in bounds by the rigid sequence of events leading to the winning of the quest.[21] The well-known stubbornness, conscientiousness, and idealism of the compulsive neurotic come through in fictional works as the undeviating, totally committed, absolutist ethics of characters like the creative thinkers in Hawthorne, the Christians of Bunyan, the Knights and Ladies of Spenser, the eternally fixed immortal souls of *The Divine Comedy*. The perfect instance of a compulsive character working in the pursuit of high cultural aims, and therefore transcending the bounds of neurosis, while still retaining the formative character type implied by the neurosis, would be Aeneas. Virgil's hero does not deviate from the destined path, and it is only natural that during the middle ages the *Aeneid* be given an allegorical reading. Aeneas is the original "Displaced person," as Eliot has said, implying his alienation from a home toward which he always gravitates, and for which he is compelled to create a substitute. As our theory will show, Aeneas also manages to avoid an accusation of hostility to his fellow man, under the guise of his preordained "destiny." The characteristic aggressions of the compulsive are here serving the "higher" ends of a cultural dream, as with later Christian heroes they serve the Christian concept of a fated Providential destiny, but this should not deter us from perceiving the latent hostility, which is only covered up by a surface appearance of gentlemanly calm, or calm gentleness of bearing. This so-called "withdrawal of affect" is a main characteristic of the neurosis, and in literature it clearly sets the systematic, unfeeling tone of allegories, where real violence is inherent in the well-ordered meaning.[22] Sometimes, to be sure, open violence appears in allegory, as in the struggles of the early *psychomachia*. The excessive violence

[21] Cf. Fenichel, *Psychoanalytic Theory,* 284.

[22] *Ibid.,* 304. This defensive behavior has been characterized as an "armoring" of the body, when it makes the muscles tense and rigid. See Wilhelm Reich, *Character Analysis* (New York, 1961), 39–77, 158–179.

in Spenser would be a good case, because Spenser's poem fully accepts the fact that violence, aggression, and hate are primary problems even in the Faery world.[23]

Above all, the agency suggested by the analogue with compulsion neurosis will be an agency of psychic *possession*. As if he became a daemon, the compulsive character (it is apparent we are not talking about the author here) becomes singled down to a narrow one-track function—a kind of narrowing that is both the strength and the weakness of the compulsive, since on the one hand it enables him to work hard and long at single, difficult tasks, but on the other may prevent him from discovering flexible paths, new short cuts.

Image: the idée fixe. With imagery our parallel implies much the same sort of narrowing process. It is found with obsessional behavior that the daemonic impulse to perform some irrational act is very soon displaced onto some associatively remote item of imagery. The impulse to kill a loved one is accepted into consciousness by the neurotic mind, because this irrational impulse is attached to some object which is only indirectly associated with that loved person. The typical impulse of this sort becomes frozen into an *idée fixe*, it becomes a compulsion, that is to say, we have the same process in compulsive behaviors that we have already noticed in the case of allegorical imagery: it is often a kind of frozen agency. The tendency of agents to become images, which allowed agents to represent the "cosmic" order of allegories, has in psychoanalysis an equivalent in the process of "encapsulation," or "isolation," as it is called.[24]

---

[23] See White, *Abnormal Personality*, 293: "The patient knows that his obsessions and compulsions are inside him; he does not use projection and attribute them to external forces. Yet they feel to him like foreign bodies, not part of the tissue of the self. They intrude themselves from unknown parts of his mind."

[24] See Freud, "A Case of Obsessional Neurosis," 377–378. Fenichel, *Psychoanalytic Theory*, 288: "Thinking in compulsive categories represents a caricature of logical thinking: logical thinking too, is based on a kind of isolation. But the logical isolation serves the purpose of objectivity, the compulsive isolation that of defense. . . . Isolation, it has been mentioned, is related to the ancient taboo of touching. Numerous compulsive systems regulate the modes in

The antisocial impulse that plagues the patient at the same time cries out for an antidote, which it finds in a mental process by which the patient denies his own connection with that impulse. He surrounds it with symbolic barriers. If it were an impulse to dirty himself, he would set aside just one particular moment of the day when it would be all right (*noa*) to do so, and at all other times would steadfastly resist any such temptation.[25] The impulse becomes a little island of desire to which certain recurrent images will be attached, and in time those images will be an adequate substitute (by metonymy) for the impulse. This means that the compulsive syndrome employs ornament in the sense of *kosmos*, partly because the fetishistic detail that fascinates the compulsive is a gemlike talisman, bounded by very strict lines, and partly because each detail is integrated into a highly systematic order of acts, known as the "compulsive ritual."[26]

---

which objects should be or must not be touched. . . . 'Clean' things must not communicate with 'dirty' ones . . . Isolation frequently separates constituents of a whole from one another, where the noncompulsive person would only be aware of the whole and not of the constituents. Compulsion neurotics, therefore, frequently experience sums instead of unities, and many compulsive character traits are best designated as 'inhibition in the experiencing of *gestalten.*' "

[25] Sometimes the ritual is represented by what Fenichel discovered in one of his patients, a compulsive disorder, a rigid avoidance of any order in any form —the effect Sterne was trying to convey in *Tristram Shandy;* this is a main aim of the literature of "stream of consciousness," where the paradoxical order-disorder relationship makes for a crucial problem as to *intention.* Frequently the compulsive neurotic displays a division of his world into an ordered and a disordered half; in the one all is neatness, in the other all chaos. A classic instance would be the dress and manners of Erik Satie, divided into public and private appearance. "It is the paragon of punctuality who in many instances is surprisingly unpunctual, the cleanest person who is in some curious respect astonishingly dirty" (Fenichel, *Psychoanalytic Theory,* 280).

[26] See F. W. J. Hemmings' *Emile Zola,* ch. iii, "Blueprint for a Life's Work," a discussion of Zola's *manie de perfection,* and his indebtedness to the *Traité de l'hérédité naturelle* of Prosper Lucas, a convenient, powerful pseudoscientific system of "election"; Zola's concept of heredity, derived from Lucas, became a magical one; Zola was not fooled into considering himself a true scientist (41). Instead he created characters who "all suffer from being too completely at the mercy of the fatality that overwhelms them, too passive in the current of

Action: compulsive rituals. Compulsive behavior is highly orderly; it is supersystematic; it is excessively scrupulous, even when no particularly unusual "ritual" is performed. Of the compulsive neurotic White says: "Orderliness may become the demon in his life, committing him to an endless task of straightening, arranging, recording, and filing." [27] The form in which this cleaning-up goes on is two-

---

physiological necessity that sweeps them along. . . . *Thérèse Raquin* and *Madeleine Férat* are just fate-tragedies in which the mysterious 'laws of physiology' take the place of the ancestral curse that powers certain dramas of the German Romantics, or of the Erinyes that hunt the protagonist of a Greek tragedy. The two novels have many of the incidental characteristics of such productions" (30).

On the side of the creator, we have evidence of Zola's quite consciously exercised "encyclopedic instinct": he himself admitted "I always try, as we say, to bite off more than I can chew. When I attack a subject, *I would like to force the whole universe into it. Hence my torments, in this desire for the enormous and for totality which is never satisfied*" (my italics). These constitute a perfect criterion for the sublime, and therefore, to my mind, of what is essentially allegorical during the period following the post-Renaissance weakening of Christian scriptural norms. There is a nice corroboration of the idea that in Zola a compulsive "collector's mania" found its perfect literary exponent, in that he was himself, as Hemmings put it, "the junk-shop dealer's natural victim"—"There was that in Zola which made hugeness and comprehensiveness come more naturally than daintiness and selection. He had the collector's instinct and the architect's brain.

"The two things were symbolized in his house at Médan. . . . Inside, the visitor was bewildered by an indescribable medley of miscellaneous pieces of furniture and *objets d'art*, for Zola was the junk-shop dealer's natural victim; contemporary prints of the interior of the house show well this concentration of bric-a-brac. Outside the house the builders were seldom idle, adding and elaborating under Zola's personal direction. Médan was *Les Rougon-Macquart* edited in bricks and mortar and upholstery" (36). In terms of the "collector's mania" Rabelais had earlier made a cosmic satire on scholasticism.

[27] White, *Abnormal Personality*, 292. E. M. W. Tillyard makes this a crucial point, on which he must defend allegory. "Indeed what appears to aim at a very hampering rigidity may actually result in the elusive and ambiguous and iridescent. If all three or four senses are not maintained throughout but come and go, there must be a transfer from complex to simpler scales of allegory and back again; and such acts of transfer will themselves become the habit of mind, the contrary of the ancient Greek, that refuses to stick to one fixed humanistic centre of reference and varies its abode from earth to heaven. This

fold: it can either involve *symmetrical* grouping of items or *ritualistic* grouping of items. There is likely to be one part of the day in which the neurotic expresses a whole series of aggressive, hostile acts; he may do this symbolically and not overtly. Then, in exact opposition to these aggressions, he will pass the rest of the day in "undoing" the antisocial impulses, by accumulating a series of exactly parallel equal-and-opposite "good deeds." [28] "Orderliness, rituals, cleanliness, propitiatory acts, self-imposed duties, and punishments all testify to the patient's need to counteract and set right his antisocial tendencies." [29] This psychomachia naturally displays a seesaw motion, and its form is highly symmetrical.

At the same time the patient acts according to the classical symptomatic pattern of the compulsion neurosis, namely the ritual. Such a ritual would, for example, be a series of rearrangements of some precise number of objects in a room: the objects would first be given one order, then given a second order, then a third, then a fourth, and so on, until the patient felt he had gone through a ritual that was long enough, precise enough, and rigid enough to be a proper expiation for some kind of impurity. Compulsive rituals have an infinite number of kinds of materials. Almost any object, any image, any word or words, any icon will do for this purpose, since what makes something a ritual is not a particular substance, but a particular order and repetition of parts. The compulsive performs his rituals in order to allay anxiety; he counts sheep, or counts the squares on the ceiling or the posts in a fence—not once, but several times, and with each new count of the total he becomes less sure than before, because while statistically he might be said to be approaching certainty, the very fact that he has found himself recounting the total suggests *to him* that there may have been an error. Thus in these rituals there is an

---

habit of mind lasted, though in less spiritual form, to Spenser, whose *Faerie Queene* constantly varies in the amount of attention the allegorical meaning required" (*Poetry Direct and Oblique* [London, 1945], 144).

[28] See Fenichel, *Psychoanalytic Theory*, 288 ff., and White, *Abnormal Personality*, 294.

[29] White, *Abnormal Personality*, 292.

element of rumination, and if the form of allegories is reduced finally to a "progress" form, we must keep in mind that this progress does not truly advance. Allegory progresses with an "apparent motion," making the circular movements of the Wheel of Fortune. *Plus ça change, plus c'est la même chose.*

It follows from the ruminant character of such ritual behavior that there will always be new rituals added onto the existing sequences. This proliferation of ritual suggests what actually occurs all the time in allegory, where either the progress is turned aside in a "digression," or else there are double, triple, and quadruple plots all going at once with Gothic exuberance. The encyclopedic allegory like the *Confessio Amantis* or the *Passetyme of Pleasure*[30] has a certain economy, it is true, but it is an economy of riches, where no limit beyond sheer endurance is ever invoked by the poet. The classic criterion of brevity has no place here, except as an arbitrary imposition as in a poem like "The Phoenix and the Turtle," or "The Dialogue of Self and Soul" of Marvell, where one feels a definite constraint and a search for the most desiccated form possible. This form is a naming of parts, since compulsive rumination seeks the stability of feeling that is conferred by the verbal spell itself.

Causality: magical practices. In *Totem and Taboo* Freud pointed out that obsessional behavior required the use of contagious magic,

---

[30] Lewis, *Allegory of Love*, 280–281: "Perhaps Hawes himself would have been neither able nor willing to throw much light on the deeper obscurities of his poem. He loves darkness and strangeness, 'fatall fictions,' as he says, and 'clowdy figures' for their own sake; he is a dreamer and a mutterer, dazed by the unruly content of his own imagination, a poet (in his way) as possessed as Blake. It is at once his strength and his weakness that he writes under a kind of compulsion. Hence the prolixity and frequent *longeurs* of his narrative, but hence also the memorable pictures, whether homely or fantastic, which sometimes start up and render this dreariness almost a 'visionary dreariness.'" If one had to find a parallel, in psychoanalytic theory, for the sudden visions of Hawes, it would surely be those strange outbursts which Freud calls "deliria" —a hybrid symptom in this case. See "Notes on a Case of Obsessional Neurosis," *Collected Papers*, III, 358. "Delirium" here has the original meaning of the plough jumping out of the furrow.

since it is by a contagion from one sign to the next that the ritual acquires its efficacy. The *magic of names*,[31] which more than any other linguistic phenomenon dominates the allegorical work, is likewise an essential ingredient in the neurosis. Names are felt to be adequate substitutes for things, even better than adequate since it is easier to manipulate names than things. Rather than accumulate a large number of objects associated with the person one wished to curse or bless, one could more readily find names that might be applied to him—the Catholic custom of giving a number of Christian names to the child is a nonprimitive instance of "verbal icons." In allegory we have numerous instances of "number symbolism," [32] which is perhaps the purest form ever taken by the magic of names, but the belief that icons of any kind can have the "power of the

[31] Cf. Fenichel, *Psychoanalytic Theory*, 295–296, and 300 ff. Also Freud, *Totem and Taboo*, in *Basic Writings*, 849–851. Otto Jespersen, in *Mankind, Nation and Individual* (London, 1946), 169, says: "We shall never thoroughly understand the nature of language, if we take as our starting point the sober attitude of the scientifically trained man of today, who regards the words he uses as a means for communication, or further developing thought. To children and savages a word is something very different. To them there is something magical or mystical in a name."

[32] See Vincent F. Hopper, *Medieval Number Symbolism: Its Sources, Meaning and Influence on Thought and Expression* (New York, 1938), especially 90 ff., on the relation between number symbolism and astrology, with its implied control over human action; on the connection between this symbolism and the body-image, see n. 30, page 17: Francesco Sizzi, arguing against Galileo's discovery of more than 7 planets: "There are 7 windows in the head, 2 nostrils, 2 eyes, 2 ears, and a mouth; so in the heavens there are 2 favorable stars, 2 unpropitious, 2 luminaries, and Mercury alone undecided and indifferent." Curtius' Excurses XV and XVI in *European Literature and the Latin Middle Ages*, "Numerical Composition," and "Numerical Apothegms," were written independently of Hopper's work. Recently A. Kent Hieatt has performed a remarkable numerological exegesis: *Short Time's Endless Monument: the Symbolism of the Numbers in Edmund Spenser's Epithalamion* (New York, 1960); see also the amplifying essay, Hieatt, "The Daughters of Horus: Order in the Stanzas of *Epithalamion*," in *Form and Convention in the Poetry of Edmund Spenser*, ed. William Nelson (English Institute Essays; New York and London, 1961), 103–121. Our problem with such exegesis, insofar as we are twentieth-century readers, lies in the difficulty of taking numbers magically.

word" is no doubt at the base of the naturalistic type of allegorical fiction. Such fiction builds a whole world out of documentary detail, which at first appears intended solely to inform the reader, but which on second view appears intended to control the reader.

> The creation of this replica of the real world makes it possible to calculate and act out in advance in this "model world" before real action is taken. . . . Words and worded concepts are shadows of things, constructed for the purpose of bringing order through trial action into the chaos of real things. The macrocosm of real things outside is reflected in the microcosm of thing-representatives inside. The thing-representatives have the characteristics of the things, but lack the character of "seriousness" which the things have; and they are "possessions"; that is, they are mastered by the ego; they are an attempt to endow the things with "ego quality" for the purpose of achieving mastery over them. He who knows a word for a thing, masters the thing. This is the core of the "magic of names," which plays such an important part in magic in general. It is represented in the old fairy tale of Rumpelstilzchen, in which the demon loses his power once his name is known.[33]

I have insisted that virtue, the positive ideal of moral allegory, needs to be given its original sense of "power," and moral fables need then to be reinterpreted as having chiefly to do with polarities of strength and weakness, confidence and fear, certainty and doubt, rather than with some ideal constellation of Christian graces and fallen states.

The highly ordered sequence of events in the typical fable likewise has at first a deceptive, seemingly scientific order. Yet, as Fenichel observes, "Compulsive systematizing, performed not for the purpose of mastering reality, but rather in order to deny certain aspects of it, falsifying reality, is a caricature of science." This is precisely the caricature that Swift deliberately employed in the third book of *Gulliver's Travels*, and which occurs with somewhat less irony in some of the less sophisticated science fiction of today, where an elaborate jargon of technical performance lards the text of

---

[33] Fenichel, *Psychoanalytic Theory*, 295 (by permission W. W. Norton & Co.).

otherwise bald romances. This presumably might be the pseudo science of Fletcher's *The Purple Island*, where quaint learning takes the place of the kind of speculation and real anatomical work being in fact done in the very same period by William Harvey. Harvey, like Phineas Fletcher, somehow believes in the old imagery likening the state to a human body, but he keeps this belief for his dedication to the king, and thus keeps his text free for science and empirical observation, for "the purpose of mastering reality." On the contrary a Phineas Fletcher is not so much trying to pass on sound knowledge as to fix knowledge in compartments that will not change, that will become fixed images instead of testable hypothetical constructs. It is natural for such a poet to flee "from the macrocosm of things to the microcosm of words." Nothing is more remarkable than the iconographic complexity of some allegorical systems, yet this ingenuity can be accounted for in terms of a belief that runs concurrent with the magic of names, the so-called "omnipotence of words," which is explained as a sort of superabstract withdrawal into a verbal universe.

Compulsive thinking is not only abstract, it is also *general*, directed toward systematization and categorization; it is theoretical instead of real. The patients are interested in maps and illustration rather than in countries and things. . . . The overvaluation of intellect often makes compulsion neurotics develop their intellect very highly. However, the high intelligence shows archaic features and is full of magic and superstition. Their ego shows a cleavage, one part being logical, another magical. The defensive mechanism of isolation makes the maintenance of such a cleavage possible.[34]

Nowhere is this mixture of logic and superstition clearer than in the allegorical use of oracles, which is often accompanied by the creation of a "double" who can foresee the future (thus the magical mirror of a Merlin). And this oracular mentality also characterizes the compulsive.

[34] *Ibid.*, 296–297.

Patients consult oracles, make bets with God, fear the magical effect of the words of others, act as if they believe in ghosts, demons, and especially in a very malicious sage, and yet otherwise are intelligent persons, completely aware of the absurdity of these ideas.[35]

Psychoanalysis takes a skeptical attitude toward this absurdity, but it must be understood that the main stream of religious allegory is, from the analyst's point of view, closely akin to a mentally dangerous belief in oracles. The main stream is prophetic. Scriptural exegesis interprets Holy Writ in historical terms, as being capable of foretelling the future and explaining the past and present, by assuming that the prophets were divinely inspired through voices from God or his angels. The method absolutely requires a belief in daemonic agency and inspiration. The psychoanalyst therefore differs from the exegete in the values he places upon the truth of oracular messages and occult signs. The findings of the psychoanalyst are borne out further by the uses to which oracles are put in the poetry of the ancient world, where they authorize given lines of conduct.

Consulting an oracle, in principle, means either forcing permission or forgiveness for something ordinarily prohibited or an attempt to shift the responsibility for the things about which one feels guilty onto God. The oracle is asked for a divine permission, which may act as a counterweight against conscience.[36]

[35] *Ibid.*, 302.

[36] *Ibid.*, 270. Also, the classic statement of ambivalence, Freud, "Notes on a Case of Obsessional Neurosis," *Collected Papers*, III, 374: "The other conflict, that between love and hatred, strikes us more strangely. We know that incipient love is often perceived as hatred, and that love, if it is denied satisfaction, may easily be partly converted into hatred, and poets tell us that in the more tempestuous stages of love the two opposed feelings may subsist side by side for a while as though in rivalry with each other. But the chronic coexistence of love and hatred, both directed towards the same person and both of the highest degree of intensity, cannot fail to astonish us. We should have expected that the passionate love would have long ago conquered the hatred or been devoured by it. And in fact such a protracted survival of two opposites is only possible under quite peculiar psychological conditions and with the co-operation of the state of affairs in the unconscious. The love has not succeeded in extinguishing the hatred but only in driving it down into the

297

This counterweighting of conscience implies the strong temptations that characterize the compulsive moral life. The compulsive personality is both attracted and repelled at once by the objects of desire.

Theme: ambivalence in "antithetical primal words." Psychoanalysts seem to agree that at the heart of the compulsion neurosis there is a high degree of ambivalence, which in turn is bound to accompany any extreme development of the superego, or conscience. The ritual of atonement arises out of the need to break the bonds of the ambivalence. Stekel's "bipolarity of thinking," which would in older parlance have been called "moral dualism," though the latter implies too conscious a process, is of course endlessly complicated by the merging of the polar opposites. This merging would appear to be a logical impossibility. But psychologically it is quite possible, and proceeds by the means of displacement and "negation," by which is meant that in the unconscious and generally in neurotic behavior anything can come to mean its opposite. As with "antithetical primal words" like the Latin *altus*, which means both *high* and *deep*, an image in a compulsive ritual can hold two contrary significances.[37]

Such double meanings are essential to any tabooed object, which will always mean both the most desirable (holy) and repulsive (dreadful) thing the mind can conceive. The best case of this in psychoanalytic findings will be probably the ambivalent valuation of *money*. It is found that money is both the finest and richest object on the one hand, and the dirtiest, lowest object on the other. (This is institutionalized in Christian teachings about the virtue of poverty, teachings which are couched in ambiguous language, since the good Christian is exhorted to lay up "riches" in heaven, if not on earth.)

---

unconscious; and in the unconscious the hatred, safe from the danger of being destroyed by the operations of consciousness, is able to persist and even to grow. In such circumstances the conscious love attains as a rule, by way of reaction, an especially high degree of intensity, so as to be strong enough for the perpetual task of keeping its opponent under repression."

[37] Stekel, *Compulsion and Doubt*, translator's Introduction, sec. iii, 10–23, on "mechanisms." Cf. Freud, Antithetical Sense of Primal Words" (1910).

This kind of ambivalence appears clearly in Orwell's novel, *Keep the Aspidistra Flying*.

The money-stink, everywhere the money-stink. He stole a glance at the Nancy [*sic*]. . . . The skin at the back of his neck was as silky-smooth as the inside of a shell. You can't have a skin like that under five hundred a year. A sort of charm he had, a glamour, like all moneyed people. Money and charm; who shall separate them? [38]

The money is contaminated, as befits a tabooed object, and while it is richly desirable, it is also deadly to the touch, with a sort of poisonous magical "charm."

This double cathexis has been reduced at times to its better-known form, moral dualism, and there it seems easier to relate to the traditions of allegorical literature. In treating compulsive neurotics, the psychoanalyst is concerned chiefly with the therapeutic transference of a dangerous authoritarianism.[39] The therapy must destroy the hold of some authoritarian figure, since this particular neurosis has its source in the period of strictest parental disciplining, the toilet-training period, when the child is first learning to control his own excretory processes, and thence (by generalization) to control him-

[38] See the commentary on this passage in Anthony West, *Principles and Persuasions* (New York, 1957). The chapter on Orwell appeared originally in *The New Yorker*. On mixed attitudes toward money and property, see J. C. Flugel, *Man, Morals and Society*, 295–297. This work is of considerable importance to the study of conscience, since it analyzes the "projections of the super-ego." Flugel, furthermore, has written another work relevant to the study of *kosmos* and allegory, *The Psychology of Clothes* (London, 1930), in which see especially ch. ii, "Decoration—Purposive Aspects." Cf. Baudelaire, "The Painter of Modern Life," especially sec. ii, "In Praise of Cosmetics."

[39] See Adorno, Frenkel-Brunswik, Levinson, and Sanford, *The Authoritarian Personality* (New York, 1950), where Elsa Frenkel-Brunswik develops her notion of "intolerance of ambiguity." See also Abraham and Edith Luchins, *Rigidity of Behavior* (Eugene, Ore., 1959), for a complete review of the literature on "einstellung" (set), including summaries of various psychoanalytic positions (ch. i). Two figures, it seems to me, emerge as having primary importance in this field, Wilhelm Reich, author of *Character Analysis*, and Heinz Werner, author of *Comparative Psychology*. Their approaches to the problem of rigid behavior are obviously quite different.

self in all areas where parental authority has set a standard of behavior.[40] The "authoritarian personality," so-called, which closely parallels the compulsive personality, has simply (or not so simply) achieved an "automatization of conscience." When trying to account for the large number of automatized, robotlike characters of moral fable we should examine the degree to which, therefore, there is inherent in their actions some fixed image of conflicting emotions, since the parental figure and the parental command are bound to elicit such emotions. Part II of *Faust* is a major allegorical expression of the mixed attitude toward the Mother.[41] The noticeably less mimetic quality of this second part seems to result from the need to give a more rigid organization to the analysis of the problem of authority; whereas the first part in fact could concern itself with the power of love, Goethe's sequel is concerned with the love of power.

We can finally ascribe the analytic character of major allegory to the generalized effects of ambivalence of emotion.

[40] Cf. Fenichel, *Psychoanalytic Theory*, 278–284.

[41] *Faust.*   Then, quick, let these be told!
   Mephistopheles.
      Loth am I now high mystery to unfold:
      Goddesses dwell, in solitude, sublime,
      Enthroned beyond the world of place or time;
      Even to speak of them dismays the bold.
      These are the Mothers.
   Faust.   Mothers?
   Mephistopheles.   Stand you daunted?
   Faust.   The Mothers! The Mothers—sound with wonder haunted.
   Mephistopheles.
      True, goddesses unknown to mortal mind,
      And named indeed with dread among our kind.

The second part of *Faust* ends with a double image of the Woman, first, that of the burial scene in Act V, where the jaws of Hell appear to be identified with the "terrible mother," and, second, in the final scene of redemption, where Woman becomes a virgin goddess, represented by the penitents, including the penitent Gretchen, and by the Mater Gloriosa. The attitude toward Woman is then highly ambivalent, as in Part I, where there is a constant suggestion that Gretchen is both Faust's lover and his "mother." (I have used Philip Wayne's translation, Penguin ed., Baltimore, 1959.)

Moral conflict, if radical and stubborn, results in a division, an inflexible dualism, in all branches of feeling and thought, which so influences the sufferer's apperceptions, that every significant object becomes ambivalent to him, that is, it both attracts and repels him, being composed, as he sees it, of two contrary elements, one good and one evil, which cannot be reconciled or blended. He discovers in due time a radical defect in every person who has appealed to him and begins hating what he has loved, though unconsciously he continues loving the object of his hate. Thus no whole-hearted embracement of anyone is possible, and the constructive tendency toward synthesis and integration is perpetually obstructed.[42]

In conclusion, it is apparent that psychoanalytic theory has brought us to our final point about *theme*, that allegory always demonstrates a degree of inner conflict, which we call "ambivalence." Psychoanalysis has also described the other major characteristics already stressed: the daemonic agency (the compulsive believes in daemonic possession); the cosmic imagery (he believes that metonymic signs "contain" or "encapsulate" his large-scale problems); the magical causality (he believes in contagious magic, in the "magic of names," and in oracular destiny); the ritualized action (he performs compulsive rituals, in either arcane or mundane forms); and finally the ambivalent thematic structure (he is constantly ruminating about his own desires, suffering extreme temptation). When we say that the compulsive "believes" in these various illusions, we are implying that he *acts* according to his beliefs, so that his behavior can be studied as a pattern in itself. No biographical information is required to see that a man is a cripple, if you watch him walk; similarly, no such information is required to show that a given action is compulsively ordered. The analyst simply has to inspect the rhythm of the action. Thus it is with literary criticism. No psychobiography of authors is required, though it can become a useful control, when the works they create correspond to known patterns. Only the pattern itself needs to be considered in this rather

[42] Henry Murray, ed., Introduction to Melville's *Pierre*, xv.

idealized criticism. If one wanted to go further and write psycho-biography, one could, but the personal history of the author's life and character is not a requisite of a psychoanalytic criticism, however interesting it may be on its own merits, as long as that criticism remains focused on the formal properties of works.

The use of the analogy. Looking back over the points of analogy between the compulsive syndrome and allegorical literature, we discern a number of similarities, of both form and content. But it may be asked, what is the use of the analogy? We can answer that such comparisons refer allegory, as a mode of communication, back to some kind of essential behavior, which we find in the skeletal structure of the compulsive ritual. Further, while compulsive behavior is often a form of physical human action (the rite consists of actual body movements, for example), it is even more profoundly a form of "symbolic action," and therefore can be properly compared to the "symbolic action" known as allegory. It becomes possible to predict what is going to happen in allegories. With our analogy in hand we learn to look afresh at the mode. In both cases, therefore, we find an authoritarian sort of behavior, rigid, anxious, fatalistic; the hero of an allegorical epic will be presented to us doing things the way a compulsive person does things, regularly, meticulously, blindly. In both cases there is great play for magical influence, psychic possession, taboo restrictions. In both cases we shall expect events to be isolated from each other into highly episodic forms, thereby "encapsulating" particular moments of contagion and beatitude. The compulsive pattern of behavior often shows a use of oracular omens, which are felt to be binding, and this provides the overall sublime pattern for a prophetic literature, where the hero is compelled ever onward and is held on his path by these predestinating omens and oracles. In both cases we meet a language of taboo, of "antithetical primal words," in which the single term contains diametrically opposed meanings, allowing for paradoxes and ironies at the heart of allegories. The presence of paradox is not always apparent, and inexpert authors may be unaware of its availability. But the great allegories show no lack of irony. The paradoxes of taboo combine with the other major traits of compulsive behavior to give allegory a function in the rendering of a large part of our psychic life. As such it is bound to have widespread interest, and partly conscious understanding, even among readers who are not schooled in the particular niceties of iconography. We are, after all, all of us compulsive in some way or other.

7

Value and Intention:

The Limits of Allegory

THE value of allegory, called into question both by the Romantic critics who follow Goethe and by the New Critics,[1] cannot be determined apart from a consideration of its function. Critics have not always sought positively for the things allegory does well. One gets the impression, furthermore, that when they attack such a protean procedure as this, they are doing so in order to praise some other procedure they prefer.

Since allegory implies a dominance of theme over action and image, and therefore, as Frye has observed, "explicitly indicates the relationship of his [the poet's] images to examples and precepts," the mode necessarily exerts a high degree of control over the way any reader must approach any given work. The author's whole technique "tries to indicate how a commentary on him should proceed." [2] Frye has ingeniously argued that "the commenting critic is often

[1] A typical case would be the remarks on allegory in Cleanth Brooks and R. P. Warren, *Understanding Poetry* (rev. ed., New York, 1950), 274–278.
[2] Frye, *Anatomy*, 90.

prejudiced against allegory without knowing the real reason, which is that continuous allegory prescribes the direction of his commentary, and so restricts its freedom." [3] Thus, for example, Frye's own commentary on Blake, in *Fearful Symmetry*, might prejudice the reader against Blake, since at the very moment it demonstrates the richness of thought in Blake, it also cuts down on the number of readings (or the type of readings) the reader is now able to bring to the poet. This argument finds support in my own parallel argument that the form of allegories is ritualized and their whole character compulsive.

The step from the *compulsive* to the *compulsory* is but short, and in fact the two terms differ only in referring to the different degrees of consciousness that may be involved in forced actions. Compulsive behavior is organized on an enforced basis without much consciousness of the motivations behind the behavior, whereas compulsory behavior is manifestly controlled from the outside in a material way, by some external authority, such as a policeman directing traffic. Since allegorical works present an aesthetic surface which implies an authoritative, thematic, "correct" reading, and which attempts to eliminate other possible readings, they deliberately restrict the freedom of the reader. The Elizabethan rhetoricians cautioned the allegorist on the one hand against overly obscure and enigmatic figures, and on the other against frivolous obscene figures, suggesting that a point could be reached where free fantasy and wit might vitiate the proper authoritarian, doctrinaire function of the mode. The implication of these warnings seems to be that, since allegory cannot help but instruct, it must be made to instruct clearly, giving continual "object lessons" in the manner of old-fashioned schoolteaching. The mode appears not only to restrict the reader's freedom, but further to restrict itself, in scope of moral attitude and degree of enigma.

Allegory as a violation of the criterion of disinterestedness. Thematic function is the chief characteristic by which readers know and

[3] *Ibid.*

judge the value of allegories. Frequently didactic in aim, allegories raise questions of value *directly*, by asserting certain propositions as good and others as bad. Typically, a poem like *The Faerie Queene* constitutes an art that breaks the Kantian rule of disinterestedness.[4] Spenser continually affirms rules of conduct and powers of soul he would label "virtuous." The reader is forced into an attitude either of acceptance or rebellion, and for this reason there is room for more than a merely aesthetic dislike of the mode; we can include among critical dislikes of allegory the strong reservation that particular allegories may in fact be teaching wrong things. It is hard for the disinterested critic to maintain "a steady advance toward undiscriminating catholicity," [5] when the literature in his path is itself highly discriminating, in the sense of prejudiced. Frye makes

[4] Thus, Kant argues that "the beautiful is that which apart from concepts is represented as the object of a universal satisfaction" (*Critique of Aesthetic Judgment*, 55, quoted by Knox, *Aesthetic Theories of Kant, Hegel and Schopenhauer* [London, 1958], 28). Knox further quotes Baumgarten to the effect that "Ideas which can be distinctly conceived, and which are adequate and perfect, are not sensuous and, consequently, not poetical. Since clear or vivid ideas are poetical, but distinct ideas are not, it is only confused [i.e. sensuous] but vivid ideas which are poetical." See Baumgarten, *Reflections on Poetry*, tr. and ed. K. Aschenbrenner and W. B. Holther (Berkeley, 1954). This doctrine can be traced back to the Aristotelian notion that *art* must deal with the variable and with matters of "choice," i.e., with matters over which one "deliberates." Aristotle, *Nicomachean Ethics*, llllb: "Deliberation is concerned with things that happen in a certain way for the most part, but in which the event is obscure, and with things in which it is indeterminate. We call in others to aid us in deliberation on important questions, distrusting ourselves as not being equal to deciding." This might be the case with an allegorical obscurity, it is true, and to that extent allegory could constitute an art. But to the extent that its matter is "ideas which can be distinctly conceived," it is not art, as Aristotle or Kant understand that term, the artistic function being the creation of beautiful objects. On the variable, and the variable nature of the true matter of art, see Aristotle, *Nicomachean Ethics*, 1140a. "Art," it is understood here, means simply, "the skill involved in making something," or perhaps "the skill involved in doing something well that needs to be deliberated about." For Kant "art" already implies an *aesthetic* function to the exclusion of other "well-done" activities.

[5] This is a main theme of the "Polemical Introduction" to Frye's *Anatomy*.

"catholicity" a virtue of good criticism, not of ethical behavior outside the literary domain, but even so the question should be raised whether allegory can ever properly be judged according to a standard of beauty. The argument of Chapter 5 suggested that it could not thus be judged, since it is a sublime modality. That is, applying the Kantian requirement of disinterestedness to allegory and then finding it wanting, would be an error, in that the sublime is by definition never disinterested. The sublime is not a medium for tragedy or comedy, both of which tend not to judge the hero, nor to reward him with "poetic justice," but rather tend to show him for what he is, failing or triumphing over evil.

"Poetic justice": the teleological control of intention. "Poetic justice" requires the deliberate, calculated, moralistic violation of natural probabilities at the end of a literary work. The phrase implies an imposed *moralitas*, which, with its "I told you so" tone, hints at the arbitrary nature of any fiction that ends thus. For "poetic justice" to fit the conclusion of an action the poet must, of course, doctor the action so that it conforms to theme and precept. Given a rather narrow view of allegory, one can agree with Elder Olson, when he says, "the allegorical incident happens, not because it is necessary or probable in the light of other events, but because a certain doctrinal subject must have a certain doctrinal predicate; its order in the action is determined not by the action as action, but by the action as doctrine." [6] This seems to be a harsh assessment of dependence on doctrine, but it is evidently correct in its emphasis on compulsory actions. Even so, before we assume that Olson's quite typical view is the last word and that allegory is lessened in aesthetic value through its doctrinal rigidity, we must nevertheless inquire into the techniques by which poets vary and control their intentional, purposive structures. It will appear that while allegorical intention is usually under a high degree of authorial control, means are available whereby the controlling rigors are softened or the simplifying ef-

[6] "William Empson, Contemporary Criticism, and Poetic Diction," in Olson's *Critics and Criticism,* ed. R. S. Crane (abr. ed., Chicago, 1957), 46.

fects of control are counteracted by various devices of complication, chief of which is an ironical gaze turned in upon the work itself. These counterdevices seem to increase the variability, and hence the aesthetic value, of allegory.

Self-criticism of intention. The devices of control are often obvious enough. Fables and riddles and even longer works provide either a running commentary or a "moral" at the end. These signposts state the aim of the work. They explicitly draw attention to the secondary meaning which the work is intended to convey. An animal fable is likely to conclude, not with a self-contained moment of action in which a natural climax is reached (the mouse getting to shore, the fox getting caught, the dove escaping the hawk) but rather with a sententious, externally applied *moralitas*, usually in the form of a proverbial phrase or motto. When we are dealing with "everyman's metaphor," [7] as in Aesop's *Fables*, the moral appears to be a clear and unequivocal statement of the allegorical sense, and we come to expect such aids toward clear interpretation. But what do we make of the ironic morals used by James Thurber, in his *Fables for Our Time;* they are at least as enigmatic as their accompanying allegories.

When we shift from the culturally standard, nominally unequivocal kinds of fable to the allegory that runs *de travers*, taking the moral saws of its own period as dubious, not to say specious, meanwhile enjoying an ironic freedom from accepted moral norms (e.g.,

[7] The epithet is Coleridge's, appearing in *Misc. Crit.*, 29: "It may indeed be justly said, that in a fable no allegoric agent or image should be used which has not had some paramount quality universally attributed to it beforehand, while in an allegory the resemblance may have been presented for the first time by the writer. This is the true cause why animals, the heathen gods, and trees, the properties of which are recalled by their very names, are almost the only proper *dramatis personae* of a fable. A bear, a fox, a tiger, a lion, Diana, an oak, a willow, are every man's metaphor for clumsiness, cunning, ferocious or magnanimous courage, chastity, unbendingness, and flexibility, and it would be a safe rule that what would not be at once and generally intelligible in a metaphor may be introduced in an allegory, but ought not to be in a fable. This, however, is one of the conditions of a good fable rather than a definition of a fable generally, and fortunately the difficulty of defining a thing or term is almost always in an inverse proportion to the necessity."

Swift, Kafka), we have then before us a much less obvious kind of control of intention. Kafka seems to be teasing his readers into a state of iconographic uncertainty, while Swift's *A Tale of a Tub* moves through a series of upheld and then rejected proposals of intention, such that the first account the reader gets of the author's purpose is completely obliterated by the time it has been replaced several times over. Each "preface" and each "digression" of the *Tale* marks a fresh redefinition of intent, and with each new phase the satire shifts its base of reference. With such a work Swift is in fact playing on the methods of satire itself, perhaps as Shakespeare plays in *Hamlet* on the methods of dramaturgy, in the midst of dramatizing an action. As *Hamlet* presents at least one "play within a play," so *A Tale of a Tub* presents at least one "satire within a satire."

This is not an uncommon procedure. Art works of all kinds may criticize their own "kind," by directing irony at the method they happen to employ. (Thus Shakespeare often makes fun of imagistic brilliance and rhetorical display.) Thus the romantic epic in which the author introduces a mocking persona who laughs at the marvels of the genre itself is using irony to complicate its intention. When Swift mocks digression itself, he is complicating the satirical purposes of *A Tale of a Tub*. He is making a parody out of a satire. The result is an art form that has more vigor, more color, more truth, than a work which lacked this self-criticism.

Even so, it would be an error to assume that inwardly directed "ironic contemplation" always confers strength upon literary works. Although irony exists to check excess of sentiment, even irony itself may become a sentiment and then will require to be checked by some further irony, or by some other counterforce. Parodistic works are often too ironical; they attack their objects too tenaciously, and the reader wearies of the attack. Whereas irony usually complicates intention, in any overlong parody it begins again to be an oversimplification. Bad parody always ends by striking the reader as sticking too close to the vices to be parodied, and this clinging irony is felt to be unfair even to the object under criticism.

309

Occasionally an author frees himself from the irony with which he began a given work. He checks the irony by a relaxation of his original satiric intent. Fielding's *Shamela* is pure parody, and profits by its extreme economy. It is not allowed to go on for very long. On the other hand *Joseph Andrews* during its earlier pages parodies Richardson's *Pamela*, but Fielding gradually works loose from his first aim, which was, as with *Shamela*, to ridicule Pamela's false piety, and *Joseph Andrews* is allowed to take its own course toward a freely developing picaresque action. This is also what happened, it would seem, in Fielding's model, *Don Quixote*. Both the Fielding and the Cervantes illustrate a mixture, or a shift, of intention. This same shift is likely to occur whenever the degree of irony present in a given kind of narration is suddenly, or even gradually, allowed to change.

The case of *Joseph Andrews* is unlike that of the fables of an enigmatic allegorist like Dante, whose obscurity lies *in the particular allegorical intention* at any given moment. Fielding is not being obscure and enigmatic about the meaning of his story; he is gradually shifting from one sort of fiction to another, from an allegorical to a more or less mimetic sort of writing. If this is so, it is clear that there are two major problems here.

First we need to be aware that allegory teems with cases where the particular meaning of the work is not immediately obvious, where the intention of the work is to shroud abstract ideas under a cover of dimly understandable imagery, as in the mystical and doctrinal passages of *The Divine Comedy*, or the deliberate obscurities of the troubadour poetry known as *trobar clus*.[8] This enigmatic

---

[8] On *trobar clus*, Maurice Valency, *In Praise of Love*, 125–130: "The best of *trobar clus* is characterized by a parabolic quality, the result of a studied ambiguity which implies a reserve of meaning beyond the comprehension of the average intelligence. The poem communicates a feeling that more is meant than meets the eye, and what meets the eye is by no means certain. We are thus aware of penumbral significances which may or may not have been intended, as well as of a general exasperating breakdown of communication. Such poetry teases the mind into poetic activity on its own account. It elicits an

art thrives because its "difficult ornament" arouses the reader's curiosity. It therefore deliberately tries to be obscure. In the same way the occasional poet, wishing to praise but not to embarrass, or to damn but not appear scurrilous, will hide the identity of the true objects of his poem—real people, since this is occasional poetry—and once again a particular "intention" may be said to be deliberately obscured. But this does not mean that we have any doubt as to the *kind* of search for intention that is involved. The search consists in

---

athletic response which is in pleasant contrast with the more passive pleasure of easy poetry, and thus brings about an enhanced participation on the part of the listener or the reader, who has a feeling, if he succeeds in penetrating the poet's meaning, of greater intimacy than less exclusive types of poetry can afford. Of those who practiced the closed style among the troubadours, none was able to compose a masterpiece of the magnitude of Donne's 'A Nocturnal Upon S. Lucie's Day,' but the seventeenth century poet's relation to his predecessors in the closed style is unmistakable.

"In one direction, inevitably, this sort of poetry bordered upon allegory. It was noted quite early in the development of the chanson that any sort of aspiration could be expressed 'in semblance of love.' The lady of the song could be easily taken, for example, to connote the Blessed Virgin; in time it became possible to address in '*sembianza d'amore*' whatever was conceived of as the object of desire—the Ideal, Wisdom, Justice, Beauty, Glory, or Salvation. Not many of the troubadours were in any sense scholars, but in the Middle Ages love and the symbolic method were equally inescapable. Between the allegorical methods of scriptural interpretation transmitted through Augustine and applied with the greatest freedom by the doctors of the church, and the methods for the interpretation of secular matter illustrated by Dante in the *Convivio,* and later by Ficino and Pico, the most obvious relation exists. The type of *sovrasenso* which Bruno extracted from the love-sonnets of *Gli Eroici Furori* was the natural outcome of this line of thought, and this extraordinary work is, of course, by no means an isolated example of the allegorical exegesis of love-poetry in the time of the Renaissance" (copyright 1958; quoted by permission of The Macmillan Company).

To this I would only add that the criteria of *trobar clus,* its methods and intention parallel those of *the sublime,* as I have interpreted that concept. The Longinean stress on struggle, stimulus, "athletic response" is all here, and when we turn to the more intimate art implied by the theory of the picturesque, we have the analogue to Valency's "greater intimacy." The materials of the poetry may differ from age to age, but between their intention "the most obvious relation exists," even down to Price's criterion that "the effect of the picturesque is curiosity." "All such deep coves and hollows, as are

an identification of personae, and at no time is there any doubt that the procedure is allegorical. The same goes for those earliest of English allegorical poems, the Old English riddles, and in general we may say that the enigmatic, emblematic, occasional, or occult traditions of allegorical poetry elicit only particular doubts as to the intentions of specific symbols. (Does this monkey symbolize wisdom or trickery? Does this dove belong to Venus, or Noah's Ark? Is this amethyst a talisman against drunkenness? Does this opal signify bad luck?)

But second there are works where it is by no means clear that we have a warranty for any allegorical interpretation at all. There are works where, although emblematic devices appear from time to time, they do not predominate, nor do they override mimetic countermovements. These works, where it is not even clear that we have an allegorical intention throughout, are more important to the theory of allegory than those others, where there might be particular questions of intent. They provide us with a second more general question. They raise a doubt as to the boundaries between allegory and other modalities of literature.

Loosening the boundaries of the mode. Allegory is never present as a pure modality.[9] The characteristics I have singled out are rarely introduced in absolute extremes: there is rarely an extreme of the

---

usually found in this style of scenery, invite the eye to penetrate into their recesses, yet keep its curiosity alive and unsatisfied" (*On the Picturesque*, 114). This suggests, further, that a comparative study should be made of the idea of the court of love, and the "improved" landscape of eighteenth-century theory. On this point, see Frank E. Manuel, *The Eighteenth Century Confronts the Gods* (Cambridge, Mass., 1959), ch. i, "The New Views of Pagan Religion," and ch. ii, "The English Deists," sec. 3, "A Psychopathology of Enthusiasm," and ch. iii, "The Birth of the Gods," sec. 4, "President de Brosses; In Memory of the little Fetish," and ch. v, "The New Allegorism," *passim.*

[9] Isaac Disraeli, *Amenities of Literature* (London, 1859), in the chapter "Allegory," calls this the "art in which one thing is related, and another understood," but he goes on to say this view is "too narrow to comprehend the multiform shapes which allegory assumes, either in the subtility or the grossness of its nature."

daemonic, of the "cosmic," of "isolation," of contagious magic, of emotive ambivalence; there are only degrees of these characteristics. Over and above my own set of distinguishing characteristics there is the main traditional criterion, the double meaning, and even here there are degrees of allegory. The common case is that observed by Dante, namely, *polysemous* textures whereby ambiguity is loosely maintained.[10] No one who has sought strictly for the fourfold medieval scheme of allegory, literal, allegorical, tropological, and anagogical levels,[11] will question the difficulty of knowing exactly where one level predominates over another, where one begins and another leaves off. This difficulty reaches an extreme in the study of romance forms, since most romances are read primarily for the adventure, and the fast-moving story is often sufficiently glittering to keep attention away from any underlying allegorical message.

Whereas in romance the story is mainly what seduces the reader away from the allegorical message, imagery also may seduce the reader away from an allegorical reading. The allegorical image, the kosmos, may revert to a "merely" ornamental function. We see this reversion occurring whenever critics begin to emphasize the "illustrative" and "visual" character of poems like *The Faerie Queene* or *The Purple Island*. In the nineteenth century critics encourage the view that Spenser was a poetic sensualist, delighting in his rich tapestries and brilliant processions for their own sake and not for any supposed emblematic intention they might have. The very idea that there is a typically "Spenserian" style of poetry, rich in image, slow-moving, digressively labyrinthine, derives from a refusal to take allegory seriously. Hazlitt, for example, would have the reader dismiss

---

[10] In the letter to Can Grande, Dante employs this term, as subsuming all others that might be applied to his method. He is anxious to be treated as a poet, not a theologian.

[11] It is not often noticed that the fourfold scheme of levels, which becomes a semantic puzzle for students of medieval exegesis, and for students of Dante especially, is a translation into semantic terms of the fourfold Aristotelian scheme of *causes*. Yet we get the correspondence: literal—material; allegorical—formal; tropological—efficient; anagogical—final.

Spenser's main interest, his iconography. Even the eighteenth-century notion that Spenser is "Gothic" opens the door to an only partially allegorical reading, since "Gothic" is next door to the grotesque, the mannered, the shocking, a literature whose aim is surface excitement and thrills, but not exactly an allegorical message. This same decline of strict traditional allegorism occurs, I have argued, in those arts of landscape known as picturesque and sublime, where the "cosmic" detail of a daemonic landscape is likely to be felt by many readers to lack any message beyond prettiness or sententious pomp.[12] But the picturesque, as Price understood it, and the sublime as Kant and Schiller understood it, have a strong underlying allegorical intention, and both kinds of art—defined chiefly by their having forms of "infinite" magnitude—tend to elicit ideal conceptions in the beholder's mind. With such arts we reach the most tenuous sort of symbolic control over the reader; the reader of the sublime odes of Collins or Gray might very well not be aware that their's was poetry with double meanings, since on the one hand their landscapes could appear self-sufficient natural descriptions, and on the other their use of personified abstractions could seem to be but a highly charged poetry of statement. Yet is this poetry any less paradigmatic in essence? The question can be answered intelligently only if we allow for degrees of allegorical intention. Just because kosmos decays into the "merely decorative" does not mean that it has totally lost its relevance to the structure of a universe.[13]

[12] This proposition should be tested with a poem like Thomson's *The Seasons*, keeping in mind Thomson's other major allegorical works, *Liberty* and *The Castle of Indolence*.

[13] Thus, critics insisting on the decorative, sensuous aspects of Spenser and Shelley are presumably unwilling to accept the cosmic consequences of belief in their poetry. The idea of "mere ornament" then becomes a method of averting serious thought about the problem of belief. In a debased form, this avoidance leads to the cult of a "pure" art or else of "art for art's sake"—a manifestly illogical or, at best, paradoxical, position, since art is defined in terms of aesthetic criteria, i.e., public values raised to a pitch of discrimination. The tendency to see "mere ornament" appears partially developed in the Gothic reading of Spenser and Tasso, in the eighteenth century. But the idea

Rather we may suspect that readers who insist on the *merely* decorative are refusing, with that very gesture, an ideological commitment to the universe implied by the ornaments they are thus depriving of allegorical function. To insist that a poet use "poetic diction" is to deny his humanistic importance.

With the picturesque and sublime it is not easy to distinguish the abstract aims of the art from its function as an exploration of the wonders of natural beauty, which the eighteenth century saw, while it rejected the ugliness of urban life. When, we may ask, does the impulse to enjoy nature become an Idea, an abstract and theoretical aim embodied by the sublime or picturesque art, and when does it fall short of ideal abstraction and become actual nature worship? (We must distinguish between poetical mountaineers and real mountaineers.) Other arts also show a conflict of intention of this kind. For example, the present thesis maintains that the naturalist novel— most readers call it "realistic"—is allegorical because its heroes are daemonically simplified and lack power to choose their destiny, because the imagery is always "cosmic," because there is usually at the base of such works a dualistic conflict, as a result of which the novels abound in dramatizations of taboo. The total effect of the usual naturalist novel is to suggest that powerful thematic conceptions govern the action. This means that a movement toward abstractness in imagery and action is bound to affect the reader, counteracting the very "realism" which the novelist seems to be seeking. So far so good—there is no need to find any invariant relation of either "abstraction" or "realism" with some supposed essence of allegory. But there is still a degree of simple realism in naturalist fiction, while the authors of such "scientific novels" at least appear to have thought they were only *representing a world* with the greatest possible ac-

---

of Gothic itself is infused with strong emotive valuations, and the term "Gothic" takes on meanings stronger and more threatening than it would have had, had it remained a term in the history of art. We remember here that "danger" means *control*, as it would, for example, in Chaucer; and that the terror of the Gothic novel is a species of control over the characters, and thus of the readers.

curacy. It does not matter if they did not see the inner dynamics of such a representation, if they did not see how abstract such a compulsive documentation must be, and as a result how thematically their works were intended. Here is one case at least where allegorical intention is always open to change or frustration, as the simple result of any naturalism breaking free of its message. Suppose that Upton Sinclair had decided that his hero Jurgis could *not* be helped by social legislation, which would constitute a denial of message.[14] At such a moment the allegorical purpose that typically characterizes such works would have been replaced by a more mimetic intention. Jurgis would have become the typical hero of a mimetic drama, a tragedy.

With certain kinds of satire there appears to be another sort of conflict as to the purity of allegorical intention. An author like Swift is able to make fun of the very devices by which his satire proceeds on its obsessive course, most notably in *A Tale of a Tub* and *A Modest Proposal*, but also in *Gulliver*, where he is at pains to complicate the perspective we get on the visited lands, by making Gulliver himself a complex figure, a growing character rather than a type. This self-criticism of satire is its own strongest weapon, since in this way it is protected from the charge of excessive bitterness and strictness—one does not trust a man whose irony systematically negates all that is happening in the real world, but one will take a good deal from a man who makes sport of his own methods. This same freedom of the satirist appears again with Byron, and later with modern practitioners of the Menippean Satire, Čapek and Zamiatin in *The War of the Newts* and *We,* and with the *New Yorker* satires of White, Thurber, and Perelman. When these authors make fun of

---

[14] Upton Sinclair, *The Jungle* (New York, 1960), 177: "Jurgis could see all the truth now—could see himself, through the whole long course of events, the victim of ravenous vultures that had torn into his vitals and devoured him; of fiends that had racked and tortured him, mocking him, meantime, jeering in his face. Ah, God, the horror of it, the monstrous, hideous, demoniacal wickedness of it.'" And on and on in the same vein—to indicate the Gothic and diabolically picturesque aspects of the naturalist tradition.

their own symbolic procedures, we are led to read them less strictly, and this amounts to a reduction of the degree of allegory their works convey. Their messages diminish in value, while their realism, their verve, their delight in life itself, regardless of any more remote meanings, is bound to increase.

Predominance of commentary over literal surface. So far I have been considering ways in which the literal surface of certain kinds of allegories is freed of the usual allegorical intention, so that the work is no longer felt to be strongly iconographic; that is, its literal surface tends to be taken in a completely literal way. The literal surface then becomes sufficient unto itself, and the reader senses his own freedom from iconographic control. But there is also the common situation in which the poet gives extended commentaries on his own symbolism, as Dante, Langland, and Bunyan do. Several methods of commentary are possible. The author may speak *in propria persona*, in a preface published with the work he is explaining, or at a later time when questioned by his critics. This authorial explication is common in modern times. An instance would be the following commentary which William Golding made on his most important book, *Lord of the Flies.*

The theme is an attempt to trace the defects of society back to the defects of human nature. The moral is that the shape of a society must depend on the ethical nature of the individual and not on any political system however apparently logical or respectable. The whole book is symbolic in nature except the rescue in the end where adult life appears, dignified and capable, but in reality enmeshed in the same evil as the symbolic life of the children on the island. The officer, having interrupted a man-hunt, prepares to take the children off the island in a cruiser which will presently be hunting its enemy in the same implacable way. And who will rescue the adult and his cruiser? [15]

Golding not only describes the thematic content of his fable. He goes further and describes its symbolic method. Standing completely

[15] William Golding, *Lord of the Flies* (Capricorn ed., New York, 1959), the author quoted by E. L. Epstein in a critical note appended to the novel.

outside the work, writing in his own person, he can perhaps make this methodological criticism more readily than if he were employing a persona within the fiction. The latter method is the one used by Spenser and Dante, and perhaps by most allegorists. Dante introduces a character "Dante," who has many obvious identifications with the man himself, who, however, both experiences the vision of the Other World and comments upon it, as he comes to understand it. This "Dante" gradually changes, by learning more and more, and by being gradually purified, during the ascent through Purgatory and Paradise. Whereas in the Inferno he had been an observer of what was essentially alien to him, the afterlife of the damned (in spite of his sharing such sins as rage and pride), he comes slowly to be a participant instead of an observer. This means in effect that "Dante" the commentator becomes less objective as he rises; the poet has suggested this very strongly in the "Paradiso," where the light of the angelic powers is always more blinding than the traveler can tolerate. In short, the commentator is slowly pushed aside, while the mystic participant takes his place. This would in itself be a sufficiently complex development to mark off *The Divine Comedy* as a special case, but there is yet another complication of persona. "Dante" has two guides, Virgil and Beatrice, so that the commentary has a secondary speaker at all times. More precisely, Virgil and Beatrice are the primary commentators, and their fellow traveler, "Dante," is secondary. They after all understand more fully than he what the vision means, and they guide the analysis of intention just as they guide "Dante." Beyond this use of two guides, the poet has also allowed minor characters throughout the poem to explain who they are and what they are doing. In sum, *The Divine Comedy* shows the most elaborate rhetorical control of intention that can be found in any allegorical work.

Spenser's use of the narrator as persona is much less complicated. He refers to "himself" as "I," and this pronominal designation is only varied when he refers to himself under the pastoral name of Colin Clout, in Book VI. As Colin Clout, however, he never steps into the foreground very openly; the poem asks, teasingly: "Who knows not Colin Clout?" With Spenser generally one senses that the "I" of the poem is an agency whose function is dependent more upon the needs of the poem than on anything Spenser himself may have felt, although in the complaint against Burleigh in the Proem to Book IV, he comes close to the kind of self-revelation that Dante achieved continuously in *The Divine Comedy*.

The intention of *The Faerie Queene* is not very sharply revealed by the narrator's persona. It may be that the aim of the epic as a whole is more clearly revealed by Spenser's use of simile, as Harry Berger has suggested,[16] than by any direct commentary of the "I" of the poem. Spenser, unlike Dante, shows no sign of letting the commentary engulf the action. Spenser is sparing at all times in his explanations. He is far less doctrinal in his digressions than Dante or Langland or Bunyan, all of whom are likely to drop the story while they quote from relevant authorities.

Genre and the engulfing of action. Certain allegorical genres tend naturally toward this engulfing of action. The encyclopedic epic, of which Jean de Meung's continuation of *The Romance of the Rose* would be a good case, attempts to relate a sufficiently large number of facts or opinions or doctrines, such that little room is left for a story. In this sense Dante was only admitting his kinship to encyclopedic epic, when in his letter to Can Grande he said that his own method was "digressive." The digressions of allegory tend usually to be expository, though they may take the form of subplots, as they do in most romances. A second allegorical genre that loses itself in commentary is the anatomy, of which Boethius' *Consolation of Philosophy* would be the most widely read example during the great ages of allegory. Here the personified abstraction, Philosophy, has only the most limited power of action; instead, she talks to the incarcerated Boethius, who listens and asks questions. The same proliferation of the expository occurs with such abundance in Burton's *Anatomy of Melancholy* that the reader is bound to forget that this

[16] Harry Berger, Jr., *The Allegorical Temper*, 122 ff.

is in essence an allegorical fiction, whose chief persona, Democritus Junior, is the hero. Swift beats the devil at his own game by attacking the attacker; commentary tries to engulf the fable of Peter, Jack, and Martin in the *Tale*, but the effect is kept satirical, and manages to undercut the ponderous method characteristic of the anatomy. In *Tristram Shandy*, as in Rabelais, the commentary is allowed to expand into burlesque of itself, and to assume a new visionary, or fantastic, function.

All these works share the prosaic tendencies of the "debate," and like it their dramatic structure undergoes severe strain. One or two other forms are obviously open to the inroads of excessive intentional control, the utopia and the imaginary voyage, which are akin to each other in presenting the vision of an unfamiliar imaginary world. In these genres the author is allowed great freedom to expatiate on what he thinks is morally or politically significant about this brave new world, and if, like Samuel Butler, he has much to say in this vein, his utopia will seem at first glance to be a series of dramatically framed essays. A certain amount of the material in *Erewhon* is developed directly out of essays which Butler had previously written in reply to Darwinian views on evolution.[17] A travelogue form saves the utopia from freezing solid into expository statement: it is natural for the traveler in a strange country to be amazed at wonders, to require explanations of what he sees from the natives, and to give embroidered explanations to those "back home" when he returns. But even this can easily become a worn-out device.

"Treatise poems" like Cowper's *The Task* probably mark the extreme limit reached by the usurping commentary; in these poems commentary has become the whole body of the work, and what is left over is of minor import. But this may be the same as saying that the poet acts as his own interpreter and here treats *all* his images, all the things his traveler sees, as kosmoi. What for us is plain exposi-

[17] See Basil Willey, *Darwin and Butler* (New York, 1960), 49–50, on the use of personified agents in Darwinian theory, and 67–72, on the development of human limbs as "machines," in *Erewhon*, chs. xxiii and xxiv.

tion of ideas and journalistic fact is for the poet a highly charged ornamental poetry. By some such process the Wordsworthian narrative poem develops its vigorous, visionary inner nature. With such works one can assume that the need to expose a body of doctrine, or give a certain kind of personally validated information, is far greater than the need to create an autonomous imagery; the treatise poem and the Wordsworthian narrative are but slightly veiled essays in verse, although the latter moves toward a psychological portraiture of the author's persona.

The intentional shift from allegory to myth. If allegory recedes into the background of works whose literal surface becomes a self-sufficient, nakedly adequate, "realistic" fiction, and if it recedes when commentary takes over the figurative level, it can also recede into insignificance when the allegory becomes mythical and dreamlike. Such a moment would be the passage of *The Faerie Queene* where Spenser describes the eternal return of life in the Gardens of Adonis, or when he penetrates the mysteries of the Temple of Isis in Book V, moments that require of the reader an acceptance of overwhelming paradox, since these moments create an ultimately inexplicable knot of imagery and action. Ultimately the reader has to give a mythical account of the Gardens and the Temple, yet their resistance to rationalization does not imply a lack of signifying power. It is the peculiar character of true myth, we may say, to enforce acceptance of a totally ambivalent imagery, whereas true allegory would achieve a rigid displacement of one aspect of the ambivalence, by arguing that either death *or* life predominated in the Gardens, either justice and clemency *or* injustice and draconian rigor predominated in the Temple of Isis. But such displacement does not occur at these moments of Spenser's poem. Rather he maintains an equality between the polar opposites of the ambivalent attitudes and almost insists that they must be joined, the apocalypse being thus gained in a moment of total consciousness. It has been felt with increasing surety in recent years that Spenser's aim was not simply to write allegory; he is too concerned with mystery and with the rationally inexplicable aspect of an eternal destiny. If we choose to call the Gardens and the Temple (and other scenes comparable to them) "anagogy," in the manner of medieval exegesis, this is an acceptable term to apply, since anagogy implies a mythic, visionary structure that goes beyond the poetry of strict correspondences which we normally call "allegory." If, furthermore, we were to call the modern allegory of Kafka "anagogical," instead of "mythical," we would only be applying the same language in a modern context. It is always difficult, with both Spenser and Kafka alike, to fix the border between allegory and myth, a difficulty to which criticism of both authors will testify. The same difficulty exists in an even more aggravated form with Blake. The recent work of Harold Bloom has again raised the problem of distinguishing myth and allegory, and Bloom has concluded that the visionary poetry of Shelley and of the Romantics in general is a mythopoeic poetry.[18] If there is in fact a poetry of "unmediated vision," it is surely found in that borderland where one passes from allegory into myth, from allegory into what Goethe would have called "symbol." But the borderlines are not capable of clear delineation, except to say that in the case of allegory there is no intention of ultimate paradox, whereas in myth and "symbol" the poet refuses to admit that reason or perception provide the highest wisdom.

Allegorical simplicity of intention: its purposive drive. With allegory the problem of intention seems far simpler than with either a mimetic art, where nature suffices of itself to please and "entertain" the audience, or a mythic art, where some question arises about the existential certainties of common experience and where a higher reality is pressed upon the reader in the form of some cardinal, underlying question about existence itself. Allegory does not possess a Kantian "disinterest." [19] Allegory does not accept doubt; its enigmas

---

[18] Bloom, *Shelley's Mythmaking* (New Haven, 1959). See Bibliography.

[19] "Taste is the faculty of judging of an object or a method of representing it by an entirely disinterested satisfaction or dissatisfaction. The object of such satisfaction is called beautiful" (*Critique of Judgment*, I, 5). See the discussion of this "purposiveness without purpose," in Israel Knox, *The Aesthetic Theories of Kant, Hegel and Schopenhauer*, 11–53.

show instead an obsessive battling with doubt. It does not accept the world of experience and the senses; it thrives on their overthrow, replacing them with ideas. In these ways allegory departs from mimesis and myth, and its intention in either case seems to be a matter of clearly rationalized "allegorical levels of meaning." These levels are the double aim of the aesthetic surface; they are its intention, and its ritualized form is intended to elicit from the reader some sort of exegetical response. Whereas a simple story may remain inscrutable to the sophisticated reader, and a myth inscrutable to any reader at all, the correspondences of allegory are open to any who have a decoder's skill. In this way, oddly enough, allegorical intention is in general a simple matter. But since mythic and mimetic moments are always possible in the midst of a fable, we find that exegetical problems can always arise as to the specific intention of any particular work.

We can now clarify the sense in which the reader can be said to be unfree, that is, interested. He is not allowed to take up any attitude he chooses but is told by the author's devices of intentional control just how he shall interpret what is before him. He is told, perhaps rather indirectly, what commentary to make on the text. This argument would locate the freedom and the lack of freedom, not in the work, but in the reader's response to the work—psychologically a sound position.[20] On the other hand I think it critically convenient to assume that whatever inhibits the reader's freedom is something in the work, and we can therefore often speak as if the lack of freedom were somehow inherent in the work. Whether by form or by some limitation of content, the poet makes a constricted work of art, which in turn imposes its own constriction upon the reader. If it seemed necessary to speak of allegory as a type of "symbolic action," then we might wish to say that the lack of freedom is not in any

[20] Gombrich calls this, "shifting something of the load of creation to the beholder," though he is thinking chiefly of mimetic art. His criterion applies better to the sublime. See, on Gombrich, Peter McKellar's *Imagination and Thinking* (New York, 1957), 142. Also, E. H. Gombrich, *Art and Illusion: A Study in the Psychology of Pictorial Representation* (New York, 1960).

important way *in* the work. In that case what matters is the way an allegory gets a person to act rather rigidly, *after* he has read the work, rather than during the period when his reading experience is going on. If an allegory is propagandistic, as, for example, it typically has become in Russian letters, it may get the reader to act with the group, and this solidarity of reader and political group is something that exists outside any work of literature.

Intentional control in political allegory. It is chiefly in the area of political allegory that the thematic function of an "Aesop language" can be justified. For while we may suspect the modern Russian art of "socialist realism," [21] which reinforces the *status quo* without any

---

[21] The Soviet brand of allegory recalls the ideal Platonic art, as described in *The Republic*, where any politically unhealthy images are banned, all healthy ones encouraged.

For an official interpretation of "socialist realism" and its consequences, see Mao Tse-tung, *Problems of Art and Literature* (New York, 1953). This and other similar works show that the usual Soviet search for a "typical" character ends by reinstating the old "copy theory" of imitation, a sort of neo-medieval "figural realism," without the medieval religious structure to make it (Platonically) "real." Thus Mao says: "You can educate the masses only by representing them," and we ask who "they" are. We find that Mao has decided to represent the brave young people according to a revolutionary theory, and not just as they ("they" being a statistical average at best) or any one of them might be. Literature is above all useful to the State: "We are the revolutionary utilitarians of the proletariat."

Material on this subject is rapidly accumulating. Among available original sources is the Stalinist Andrei Zhdanov's *Essays on Literature, Philosophy and Music* (New York, 1950), where the educational function of Soviet literature is defined: "to maintain our cadres, to teach and educate them" (35–37). The pseudonymous Abraham Tertz, *On Socialist Realism*, tr. George Dennis (New York, 1960), attacked the Stalinist doctrines and showed its anti-esthetic consequences. Speaking of "the positive hero" and the "strictly hierarchical distribution of the other roles in plot and in language," Tertz wrote: "Beginning with the 1930's, the passion for solemnity imposes itself [on Soviet literature], and a pompous simplicity of style, the hallmark of classicism [in the special Soviet sense] becomes fashionable. We call our state 'the Power'; the mujik 'cultivator of the bread'; the soldier, 'the warrior'; the sword, 'saber.' We capitalize a great number of words. Allegorical figures and personified abstractions invade our literature, and we speak with slow solemnity and grandiose gestures" (83–84). This book had to be smuggled out of the Soviet Union.

For the background to this literature see: Harold Swayze, *Political Control*

critical flexibility, we respect the very same propagandistic method when it is turned *against* inflexible governmental censorship. Communist Russia and China have praised the art of the "typical," by which they understand an art of stereotypes, in which the West is villainous, the East virtuous. But when the artist produces "types" who are deviations from the party line, there is much to be said for their method, and the method in itself begins to seem more desirable than before. We cannot then condemn allegory as an instrument of universal conformity, until we have admitted that it is also the chief weapon of satire.

As a cosmic instrument allegory is open to the same objections that can be raised against a Tolstoyan aesthetic, that it attempts a spurious unity of all men. We cannot maintain that a classic (tragic or comic) art is the highest kind if we accept the late Tolstoyan position.

Christian Art, that is, the Art of our time, must be catholic in the direct sense of that word—that is, universal—and so must unite all men. There are but two kinds of sensations which unite all men—the sensations which arise from the recognition of man's filial relation to God and of the brotherhood of men, and the simplest vital sensations which are accessible to all men without exception, such as the sensations of joy, meekness, spirit, alacrity, calm, etc. It is only these two kinds of sensations that form the subject of the Art of our time, which is good according to its contents.[22]

"Even a joke," I. A. Richards remarked, "is for Tolstoy only a joke so long as all men may share in it, a truly revolutionary amendment.

_____

of Literature in the U.S.S.R. 1946–59 (Cambridge, Mass., 1962); E. J. Simmons, *Through the Glass of Soviet Literature: Views of Russian Society* (New York, 1953), "Introduction: Soviet Literature and Controls," 3–27; Simmons, *Russian Literature and Soviet Ideology* (New York, 1958); N. A. Gorchakov, *The Theatre in Soviet Russia*, tr. Edgar Lehrman (New York, 1957); Jules Monnerot, *The Sociology and Psychology of Communism*, tr. Jane Degras and Richard Rees (Boston, 1953), especially the chapter, "Projections of the Sacred"; R. W. Mathewson, *The Positive Hero in Russian Literature* (New York, 1958).

[22] Tolstoy, *What is Art?* quoted by I. A. Richards, *Principles of Literary Criticism* (1925; reprinted New York, 1952), 65. See also Orwell's essay "Tolstoy, Lear and the Fool."

The sharing is more important than the merriment." [23] From this position Tolstoy chooses *Uncle Tom's Cabin* over *King Lear*, his own *Resurrection* over *War and Peace*. He demands fixed hierarchies, cosmic unity, and, notably, a "withdrawal of affect," a calmness and meekness one suspects to be quite utopian. The net effect of this totalitarian world view is to praise an anesthetic art.

Because the critic fears a Tolstoyan aesthetic of uniformity, which the allegorical mode perfectly fits, since it is always "cosmic" in imagery and in overall order, he may fall into the very error which allegory itself is supposed to foster. He may prejudge, one way or the other, the restriction of freedom implied by a cosmic imagery and order. He may assume that rigid social orders and attitudes are entirely bad. But there are times when, to be useful, fictions need to be purposively controlled as they are in allegory. These are times when censorship is extreme, or when authoritarian government, either secular or sacred, assumes full control of the means of public communication. No matter how strict a censoring procedure is invoked by a repressive government, some sort of allegorical subterfuge is possible. Kenneth Burke has aptly described this situation.

In our highly mobile world of today, the usual equivalent of the catacombs is exile. Exile or silence seem to be the only choices open to writers who, born and trained in the ways of liberalism, are suddenly compelled to meet situations of absolute dictatorship wholly alien to their training. Bred to one situation, with their methods formed by it, they find a totally alien situation abruptly forced upon them. Thus, even in remaining at home, they would be living in a kind of exile, a world with new deprivations and without new promises to match.

But I can imagine there gradually arising, among a younger generation of writers bred to the new situation, a new language of deployments and maneuvers, with sly sallies that have an implied weighting far in excess of their surface meanings. In short, I am suggesting that no political structure, if continued long enough for people to master its ways, is capable of preventing forms of expression that tug at the limits of patronage. A patronage may affect the conditions of expression, but cannot

[23] Richards, *Principles*, 65.

prevent this pressure against its limits. Even under the censorship of the Czar, for instance, there were circumlocutions, known to all informed readers, that referred to the day when the Czar would be deposed. Nor were these any less known to the censors than to the readers. They were allowed in part, perhaps, as a way of revealing to government agents those particular authors who might, by thus expressing their attitudes, provide the agents with valuable "leads" into more serious forms of conspiracy.[24]

Bertram Wolfe has described how this "language of deployments and maneuvers" enabled Lenin "to fight Russian imperialism in wartime by a statistical, theoretical analysis of the German variety. Still later Bukharin was to employ the same device to circumvent a more vigilant and ruthless censorship when he wrote a pamphlet attacking the Vatican, in which his criticisms of Loyola and the 'corpse-like obedience and discipline of the Jesuits' implied his criticism of the Stalin regime." [25] One tends to think of this literature as being not exactly literature, and to assume that its methods have no relevance to aesthetics properly speaking. But Burke is willing to tolerate an "art" which speaks through an "Aesop-language," and whose main aim is political subversion—of a defensible kind, since the powers to be subverted are denying political liberties.

One could even imagine the emergence of a particular aesthetic school, in which not one single thought or image was "subversive" on its face, yet functioned as a *Bundschuh*. Nazis in Poland, for instance, wear white sox, harmless enough in themselves, yet significant enough as to enrage a Polish patriot—and so there may be subtler aspects of a style, functioning like the white sox in Poland, even stylistic ways of wearing anti-white-sox in Hitler's Germany. So with "travel literature" like that of Tacitus, who wrote under conditions of dictatorship, and attacked the local political situation by an ambiguous device, in presenting an ideali-

---

[24] *Philosophy of Literary Form* (Vintage ed., New York, 1957), 198 ff.
[25] Bertram Wolfe, *Three Who Made a Revolution* (Boston, 1955), 23. On a similar persecution of the Jewish priests which occurred during the great period of *midrashic* interpretation, see the *Encyclopedia of Religion and Ethics*, ed. James Hastings, VIII, 627b–628a.

zation of Germany that implied a criticism of Rome? . . . Utopias have regularly arisen in this way, as strategies for criticizing the *status quo* with immunity. And we might even say that the conditions are "more favorable" to satire under censorship than under liberalism, for the most inventive satire arises when the artist is seeking simultaneously to take risks and escape punishment for his boldness, and is never quite certain himself whether he will be acclaimed or punished. In proportion as you remove these conditions of danger, by liberalization, satire becomes arbitrary and effete, attracting writers of far less spirit and scantier resources.[26]

This subversive style, sometimes satirical, sometimes utopian, always seemingly innocuous, preserves freedom against tyranny. Allegory presumably thrives on political censorship. The early stages of Soviet rule witnessed a flourishing of satire, because there were obvious abuses in both the left-over old regime and the rising new regime. But when the Soviets were fully established, it required a very delicate hand to avoid complete suppression. Thus Ilf and Petrov survived Stalinist days,[27] but Meyerhold did not. When Meyerhold's invective turned upon the new regime, having previously demolished the old regime, he was himself suspected by the new rulers, and stamped out because he failed to be sufficiently indirect.

Puttenham: the Elizabethan subversive. Elizabethan rhetoric presents us with a full account of the subversive functions of allegory. George Puttenham argues in *The Arte of English Poesie* (1589) that allegory is "the chief ringleader and captain of all other figures, either in the poetic or oratory science," an assertion which follows from the Elizabethans' hierarchical conception of the universe. He further argues that allegory is the deceptive, subversive "figure of false semblaunt." [28] He asserts that the courtier will "never or very seldome thrive or prosper in the world" if he cannot put allegory to

[26] *Philosophy of Literary Form*, 199.

[27] Maurice Friedberg's Introduction to Ilf and Petrov, *The Twelve Chairs*, tr. John H. C. Richardson (New York, 1961). On Meyerhold, see Gorchakov's *Theatre in Soviet Russia*.

[28] Note that False Semblance is one of the main characters in Jean de Meung's

use, that is, if he cannot speak deceptively and equivocally.[29] Puttenham quotes the old proverb, *Qui nescit dissimulare nescit regnare*. Again and again, as he runs down the list of subdivisions—riddles (*aenigma*), proverbs (*paremia*),[30] the "drie mocke" (*ironia*), the "bitter taunt" (*sarcasmus*), the "merry scoffe, or civil jest" (*asteismus*), the "fleering frump" (*micterismus*), the "broad floute" (*antiphrasis*), the "privie nippe" (*charientismus*), "the loud lier, otherwise called the overreacher" (*hyperbole*), the "figure of ambage" (*periphrasis*), the "figure of quick conceit" (*synecdoche*)—Puttenham maintains that all these figures are used for the express purpose of dissembling, and they appear therefore to be instances of a generalized irony. Sometimes, as with *enigma*, the dissembling is politic in a very mannered way, since there one can indulge in off-color and even quite obscene conceits, by a method of "covert and dark speeches." In most cases the dissembling character of the particular device is obvious, and where we might tend to overlook the duplicity, Puttenham puts it clearly before us.

---

continuation of *The Romance of the Rose*. Puttenham, *The Arte of English Poesie*, III, vii, 154: "As figures be the instruments of ornament in every language, so be they also in a sorte abuses or rather trespasses in speach, because they passe the ordinary limits of common utterance, and be occupied of purpose to deceive the eare and also the minde, drawing it from plainnesse and simplicitie to a certain doublenesse, whereby our talke is the more guilefull and abusing, for what else is your *Metaphore* but an inversion of sense by transport; your *allegorie* by a duplicitie of meaning or dissimulation under covert and darke intendments: one while speaking obscurely and in riddle called *Aenigma*: another while by common proverbe or adage called *Paremia*: then by merry scoffe called *Ironia*; then by bitter tawnt called *Sarcasmus*: then by periphrase or circumlocution when all might be said in a word or two: then by incredible comparison giving credit, as by your *Hyperbole*; and many other ways seeking to inveigle and appassionate the mind."

[29] On allegory, see Puttenham, *Arte of English Poesie*, Book III, ch. xviii, 186–196.

[30] Origen, in his commentary on *The Song of Songs*: "The word pro-verb denotes that one thing is openly said, and another is inwardly meant." The standard English example is the proverbs of John Heywood, but the idea of the proverbial being an allegorical mode appears early, with the idea of "sentence" in Chaucer and Gower, suggesting our word "sententious."

329

Then ye have the figure *Periphrasis*, holding somewhat of the dissembler, by reason of a secret intent not appearing by the words, as when we go about the bush, and will not in one or a few words expresse that thing which we desire to have knowne, but to chose rather to do it by many words.[31]

In short, though allegory may be intended to reveal, it does so only after veiling a delayed message which it would rather keep from any very ready or facile interpretation.

While one can justify the Puttenham aesthetic on the Augustinian basis that whatever is acquired with difficulty is more highly valued, and one can invoke the standard Renaissance belief in this view, that is not Puttenham's view. Instead he is thinking chiefly of the "courtier," that type of Proteus who rides the waves of courtly fortune and favor and escapes drowning only by the highest skill in the political maneuver.[32] To survive under the strain of this maneuvering requires a rhetorician's ability always to calculate the attitude, and then to meet the attitude, of one's audience. Anxiety is here as else-

---

[31] Puttenham, *Arte of English Poesie*, 193. Cf. Dickens, *Little Dorrit*, and the Department of Circumlocution, which is analogous to the miasmic fog in *Bleak House*, the image of the Chancery labyrinth.

[32] "When symbols have become attached to a status position over a long period of time, the symbols themselves take on such value that whoever learns to attach them to his own cause rises to power. Ecclesiastic rank affects devout worshipers because the hierarchy of rank ends in God, and, as the communicant kneels, he kneels not to the priest but to his God." "But, if the problem for those in superior status positions is how to safeguard the purity of their symbols and yet, at the same time, not make such symbols so exclusive that they cannot easily be understood, the problem for those in inferior status positions is how to be sure that they are using symbols which identify them with those in power. For the inferior, just like the superior, must be sure that his communications are being heard across the many gaps in social space. The more separate we are in space and time, the more problematic our communications become. To keep any symbol glamorous, we must keep it strange. This is done by making it exclusive, by limiting its applications so that it cannot be used in a familiar manner and hence become subject to contempt. We limit the use of any symbol by making it difficult to use except by those who are superior to us in rank" (Duncan, *Language and Literature in Society* [University of Chicago Press, 1953], 123 and 126).

where the dominant feeling accompanying allegorical procedures.

One can politically justify the "figure of false semblaunt" when the *status quo* is being maintained by censorship from above, since at such times the mode allows the writer to attack. Presumably, from another point of view one can justify the cosmic defense of the *status quo*, if that reigning situation is seemingly valid. If one feels that revolution is dangerous, one can only applaud the way in which allegories sometimes thematically underwrite current proprieties. This is presumably the aim of the Pseudo-Dionysian and Thomist scheme that gives *The Divine Comedy* its cosmic scope and form, and this very aim would disturb the Luther who attacked Dionysius in his *Pagan Servitude of the Church*. Dante seeks to use the visions implied by Pseudo-Dionysian and Thomist theology "to remove those living in this life from a state of misery and to lead them to a state of happiness." He is not attacking, so much as creating a system of enlightenment; and his hope that the image of the afterlife will change the view men take of this life is based on a belief that whatever political animosities we may feel or may cause, we still have our souls to consider, and such a consideration is ultimately the only important one. Dante has a positive aim throughout the *Comedy*, and in spite of the superior attitude he seems to us to have assumed, he is mainly concerned to be exact in the demonstration of God's Providence.

Accommodation and syncretism. Halfway between the attack and the defense of the *status quo* there is an art which acts an intermediary part.[33] This preeminently would be pastoral, in the Empsonian sense,

---

[33] On the plane of theological conflicts, cf. Anders Nygren, *Agape and Eros,* 320: "In general, it may be observed that allegorism and syncretism readily go hand in hand—for obvious reasons. Allegorism is arbitrary, and can make anything mean anything; contours are obliterated and different motifs run easily into one another."

See also H. J. Paton, *The Modern Predicament: A Study in the Philosophy of Religion* (London and New York, 1955), for an Anglican view, the chapter on "The Way of Allegory": "Nevertheless until breaking-point is reached, there may be effective continuity in a faith which finds very different intellectual interpretations at different stages of its development" (123). Allegory in this view can become a means of transition from one world-view to an-

an art of class mobility as well as of class conflicts. A sort of social syncretism works here,[34] the equivalent of that major allegorical process by which two rival religions may join hands under an amalgamated dogma. As such, allegory is the instrument of accommodation and compromise. It may be that without this use of the mode literature would lack an important means of cultural survival, since from the compromise between two world views, as for example in Spenser, there may arise a new and truly unified sensibility and method. This may be the basis on which Milton comes to depend so heavily on Spenser; the compromise between medieval morality and Renaissance humanism works itself out in *The Faerie Queene*, at least to the point where it can be assumed by Milton. In the same way Bunyan makes a compromise between a realistic fiction, which presages the novelistic techniques of Defoe, and an abstract thematic art deriving from the Bible and the Moralities, which give to Defoe a model for serious thematic understructure. By the time the later author comes to write, the compromise has settled to a natural complexity, which might even be called an "organic form."

This is to suggest that no easy criticism can be made of the cosmic function of allegory, even though one suspects the mode of lending itself too readily to a restriction of freedom—since on the one hand we have seen how it can turn toward satire and need not be the

---

other, by which the old faith is retained. St. Augustine would be a good instance of the believer for whom allegory was a mediating mechanism at the moment of dogmatic transition (as in the *Confessions*, Bk. V, ch. xiv, and Bk. VI, ch. iv). By taking Bishop Ambrose allegorically, Augustine could absorb and accept what he otherwise must have rejected.

Comparetti argues against the idea that this was hypocritical. "Nor must one think any the worse, as one is easily tempted to do, of either religion for its recourse to this expedient, as if it were the result of cold calculation or a deliberate 'pious fraud.' It is the instinctive and honest resource of men whose minds are dominated at one and the same time by two contradictory influences of equal power, from neither of which are they able to free themselves" (*Vergil in the Middle Ages*, tr. E. F. M. Benecke [London, 1895]), 105–106.

[34] "The moral level is the social level for it is by virtue of its archetypes or myths that the work of art becomes the focus of the community" (Frye, "Levels of Meaning in Literature," *Kenyon Review*, Spring, 1950, 259.

bonded servant of the *status quo*, which it may attack, while on the other hand it can serve as a basis for new cultural growth.

The syncretic function of allegory has a similar counterpart in the deployment of a daemonic agency. Not only does the mode unify disparate cosmic views in compromise relations, but it enables any given religion to people the air with intermediate spirits, the daemons. A monotheism requires such agents to exist because it needs to have objects of heretical worship; it needs the petty, schismatic little gods which are created by popular superstition and fancy.[35] These fractionations of the One become proper objects of attack, since they are the cause of schisms within the orthodox belief. In attacking heresies, orthodox Christianity attacks all those beliefs that tend to

[35] From Plutarch's dissertation "On Superstition" one gets a glimpse of the attitudes of a pagan, polytheistic world, faced with the narrowing of the scope of its belief and disbelief to a Single, One God; and, incidentally, one sees the ambivalence elicited by the Sacred Object. "But what sort of things the superstitious think about the gods—imagining them to be furious, faithless, fickle, revengeful, cruel, covetous; from all which it necessarily follows that the superstitious man both hates and fears the gods: for how can he do otherwise, when he believes that the greatest evils have happened to him through their doing, and will happen to him again? Hating the gods and fearing them, he is their enemy, and though he may reverence and do obeisance, and sacrifice, and keep vigils in their temples, it is not to be wondered at, for people bow down before tyrants and pay court to them, and erect their statues in gold, but hate in silence all the time they are offering sacrifice to them" (in *Plutarch's Morals,* tr. King, 272). "The atheist *thinks* there are no gods, the superstitious man *wishes* there were none" (272). Earlier in this dissertation Plutarch comments on the belief in the corporal embodiment of Virtue and Vice, and this too, he argues, is a superstition. "On the other hand, one man fancies that Virtue and Vice are a body: a disgraceful blunder, perhaps, but not worth crying for or lamenting over: but whatever are such maxims and opinions as this,

> 'Poor Virtue! Thou wert then a name, but I
> Pursued thee as a Truth,

and cast aside injustice, the cause of wealth, and intemperance the real source of all happiness'—*these* sentiments, indeed, we ought both to pity and be angry with." Plutarch concludes: "Atheism is Reason deceived, Superstition a passion arising out of false reasoning." This suggests very strongly the concept of heresy as "bad theology."

split up the essentially unified notions of the single all-powerful, all-good deity. And orthodoxy requires an opposition, something to fight against. If from monotheism we turn to polytheism, it is obvious that there is immediately a place for daemonic agents, since the "many gods" are partners in a great daemonic conspiracy to replace any single, or even dualistic, order of things. All sorts of Manichaean thinking are at home in the daemonic universe, and allegory in general has a Manichaean appearance for that reason.

If daemonic agents are necessarily going to appear in religious warfare between orthodoxy and heterodoxy, they are likewise going to occur quite naturally whenever the orthodox Christian (and orthodox member of any religion, one is tempted to say) tries to "work out" the true bases of his belief. He is orthodox, but he must try himself to find out whether he can reject the daemonic powers that beset orthodoxy. A Redcrosse knight knows what he ought to believe, and that he ought to reject vain fancies wrought upon him during sleep, but he has still to learn the habits of piety. He has to meet the wiles of Archimago and Duessa, both of whom serve a fractionating function in the poem, in fact creating daemons to trick the protagonists into false theology. The same fight against the daemonic population of the air occurs throughout Bunyan and Defoe, where once again the orthodox believer is exploring the bases of a religion that ought not to permit any but a secondary role to daemons.

The psychological orientation in *Robinson Crusoe* and especially in the *Serious Reflections of Robinson Crusoe*,[36] where Defoe gives his own allegorical commentary on the book, puts daemonic agency in a curious light. For while Robinson Crusoe seems to believe entirely in the reality of daemonic agency, he also tries to explain it away in terms of psychology and medicine. He points out that his visions were no doubt due to his debilitated physical and mental condition, and he clearly states that during much of his stay on the island he was too anxious and upset to think properly of the true, sublime

[36] Defoe, *Serious Reflections of Robinson Crusoe*, III, esp. ch. i, "Of Solitude."

334

objects of religious contemplation. Defoe's work here bridges the gap between theology and psychology, which is to be expected, given his discursive treatises, *An Essay on the History and Reality of Apparitions*, *A System of Magic*, and *The Political History of the Devil*.

Modern psychological allegory accepts daemonic agency in full force and gives a simulacrum of scientific explanation for it. Popular works like *The Snake Pit* are richly ornamented by all sorts of daemonic agencies, and yet the attempt is finally made to explain these away. Somehow the effect of explaining away is not much different here from what it would be if we were reading in an orthodox religious context, since the latter always shows the ultimate defeat of the Devil and his minions—a defeat not unlike the psychiatric triumph over complexes, fixations, traumas, and repressed aggressions. There is some justification for this image of the daemonic, since, as Freud himself admitted, the theories of classical psychoanalysis are "dualistic'" and Platonic,[37] and therefore will tend to produce images of a daemonic sort. Sometimes popular versions of psychoanalysis push the dualism very far; Hubbard's "Dianetics" is patently a kind of allegory and is full of gremlins and bogies as well as good spirits.[38] Edward Glover's attack on Jung accuses him of being an allegorist for the same reason, namely that Jung has given material existence to theoretical constructs and has reified the ideal.[39] So there is no lack of an allegorical bias in a good deal of psychoanalytic thinking. Both the science and the art, after all, have their origin in some kind of *psychomachia*.

---

[37] Freud, *Beyond the Pleasure Principle*, tr. James Strachey (London, 1950), 72: "Our views have from the very first been dualistic, and today they are even more definitely dualistic than before."

[38] L. Ronald Hubbard, *Dianetics* (New York, 1950). Most faith healers use a highly ornamental jargon, so that their message is obscurely prophetic of cure, without any semblance of empirical truth to be affirmed or denied. The ornamental diction of certain authors seems to act as a verbal tranquilizer, and this is especially true if the jargon is vaguely scientific-sounding.

[39] Glover, *Freud or Jung?* (London, 1950).

Yet we sometimes justify allegory aesthetically for just this very reason, since it so closely parallels the most influential of all psychological movements, psychoanalysis. True psychoanalytic theory, as the Freudians see it, avoids allegory because it always recurs to the behavioral and developmental theory of what human beings actually do and what they have actually experienced. But just a short step away from this scientific method there is a quasi-scientific method which smacks of magic and suggests, in books like *The Snake Pit*, a sort of elegant pseudoscience which accommodates science to our impressionistic notions of mind.

Science fiction: open space for the daemonic intermediary. Psychological allegory is not the only area of literature where the daemonic agent has free reign in modern times. Science fiction gives him even freer play. Not only do the science fiction writers use robots and all sorts of automated devices, but they turn human beings into automata, thus creating a "scientific" equivalent of the old religious intermediate agents, the "messengers" between heaven and earth. The cosmos has expanded and scientific materialism is rampant, but still the agency is of that controlled, predestined, narrowed kind we have described as daemonic.[40] This can be seen for example in the

[40] Burton's psychology of motives and his type of fantasy suggest modern science fiction; he is delighted by the prospect of space travel, since it will open new fields to the speculative mind and will join past, present and future in one vast cosmic vision.

"I would have a convenient place to go down with Orpheus, Ulysses, Hercules, Lucian's Menippus, at St. Patrick's Purgatory, at Trophonius' den, Hecla in Iceland, Aetna in Sicily, to descend and see what is done in the bowels of the earth; do stones and metals grow there still? how come fir trees to be digged out from tops of hills, as in our mosses and marshes all over Europe" and so on. Burton did not confine his speculations to the center of the earth, but looked also outward. "Kepler (I confess) will by no means admit of Brunus' infinite worlds, or that the fixed stars should be so many Suns, with their compassing Planets, yet the said Kepler, betwixt jest and earnest in his Perspectives, Lunar Geography, and his Dream besides his Dissertation with the Sidereal Messenger [of Galileo], seems in part to agree with this, and partly to contradict. For the Planets, he yields them to be inhabited, he doubts of the Stars: and so doth Tycho in his Astronomical Epistles, out of a consideration of their vastity and greatness, break out into some such like speeches, that he will never believe those great and huge bodies were made to no other

very witty and exciting tales of Robert Sheckley, who not only creates daemons for his dramatis personae, but gives them the required hierarchic order, as in his book *The Status Civilization*.[41] A more restrained science fiction characterizes the work of Huxley and of other modern utopian satirists, but in them also the machine triumphs, whether actually or ironically, and this leads to a daemonic agency that is the perfect image of a way of life which, though we may deny its likelihood, is still possible for a future world in which automation becomes increasingly more prevalent.

The cult of power: a role for daemons. Daemonic agency is usually introduced as a way of expressing a human wish for great power, whether for good or evil purposes. The satanic mind seeks power through diabolical agencies, the messianic mind through angelic agencies, and both are daemonic. Dante presents us with the whole range, from diabolic to angelic, from satanic to seraphic. His *Comedy* is the single most extensive treatment of power as a kind of good or evil daemonic influence. During modern times there is a tendency to emphasize only the satanic character of the daemonic; Hawthorne, for example, is mainly concerned with the powers that induce a state of sin and guilt. Samuel Butler, in his attack on Darwin, creates a world of evolutionary change where science sees only a malignant, thoughtless, daemonically controlled change. He makes the limbs of the body into parts of machines, in *Erewhon*, and in his *Life and Habit* he compares the man of science to a "medicine-man, augur,

---

use than this that we perceive, to illuminate the earth, a point insensible, in respect of the whole. But who shall dwell in these vast bodies, Earths, Worlds, if they be inhabited? rational creatures? as Kepler demands, or have they souls to be saved? or do they inhabit a better part of the World than we do. Are we or they Lords of the World? And how are all things made for man? It is a difficult knot to untie: 'tis hard to determine; this only he proves, that we are in the best place, best World, nearest the heart of the Sun" (*Anatomy of Melancholy*, 412). This kind of scientific fantasy is not without precedent; it occurs first perhaps in Lucian; it appears in *The Travels of Sir John Mandeville*, important as one of the first English printed books, and a work of immense popularity.

[41] New York, 1960. See also Walter M. Miller, *A Canticle for Leibowitz* (New York, 1959; Bantam ed., New York, 1961).

priest," a controller of human thought, "requiring to be well
watched by those who value freedom." [42] This is the modern scientist
who crowds the pages of science fiction. He has a remote-controlled
genius which seems "mad" or not, depending on one's private views
of what constitutes progress. He is less likely to be good than bad and
is less likely to preserve than to subvert human freedom, as Butler
suggested. His type is perhaps established by the Satan of *Paradise
Lost*, that philosophical venturer through space. Opposed to his "pioneer character" is the totally conservative character of the hero of
the Christian battle to achieve grace, and also the hero of the pagan
battle for tragic integrity—neither of the latter types seek progress
or self-improvement, neither of them seeks power in any material
sense.

The search for pure power, which is at the heart of all allegorical
quests, goes on in spite of its fundamental irrationality. Through the
creation of stories in which characters have the freedom from reality
which only daemons can possess, the allegorist devises systems of a
questionable order. In a world where might is always right, and
where ethics are always converted to terms of expediency and utility,
there is no place for the "reality principle." There is no place for
either comedy, which solves problems communally, or tragedy,
which resolves by the death or exclusion of the hero from the community. There is rationalization rather than rationale.[43] Allegory
seems often to be more orderly than any other mode of literature. In

[42] Butler, *Life and Habit* (London and New York, 1910), 41.

[43] "Allegory might also be said to constitute the bone, muscle and nerves of
serious medieval literature. The medieval mind, inhabiting a more intelligible
world than ours, saw everywhere correspondences between sets of facts and
ideas that to us seem unrelated. . . . We shall escape from it (the habit of allegory, reading allegory into books, which goes back to before Plato) only
. . . when the rationalism of the later 17th century bores through things
mysterious with a cold hard stare" (Bush, *Mythology and the Renaissance
Tradition*, 15). Officially this is a fair statement, but allegory had other strings
to its bow, the sublime being one of them, and it is a real question as to just
how the medieval world was "a more intelligible world than ours," unless
"intelligible" implies scholasticism.

fact it appeals to that *excess* of reason which constitutes—and here I am taking a deliberately extreme view—the modern form of authoritarian lunacy, the guilty conscience demanding a self-flagellation that in turn requires sadistic infliction of pain on all about the flagellator. The "reason" behind the allegorist's destruction of evil, which he accomplishes by sending a daemonically empowered agent of death against the camp of the evildoers, is an overordered reason, no way balancing the claims of abstraction and experience. The expression of utopian good and utopian evil (Sir Thomas More vs. George Orwell) provides no solid grounding in experience. Instead it requires us to accept a spurious rationality growing out of its own ruminations. It furthermore makes a strong appeal to the irrational in ourselves, since empathy with the daemonic character confers the daemon's power upon the reader. Propagandistic literature appropriates this empathy for its major weapon. Whether one can accept this "calling of the tune" depends on one's personal attitudes, or on one's need to survive in an alien culture by an accommodation to that culture.

Some modern allegorists have mocked this implicit notion that daemonic power is good, which is a belief, finally, that might is right. In their mockery they disturb intention in the ways we have seen. Capek, in his *War with the Newts,* and his *R.U.R.,* created daemonic agents out of a plasmic substance and in both cases showed the vicious nature of a society based on the employment of these daemonic agents. He showed that the lower-than-animal newts and the higher-than-human robots were incapable of being held under human control and were therefore ultimately destructive, although immediately most profitable to their owners. In the Čapek brothers' *The Insect Play,* as in so many fables of modern life, the hero is reduced to a subhuman level. Orwell took animals and, by conferring on them the daemonic powers which normally would be exerted only by human beings, showed them so inadequate in their decisions and valuations that ultimately they pull their world to ruins. True, the animals are "types" of human behavior, but by their restriction of character they become so *narrowly* human that they do not have what we usually· call "character." Orwell's animals are possessed, and their power to organize into a communist state on their little farm belies an incapacity which, were they humans, we would call a failure to value the objects for which social organization exists. This mockery of automatized powers goes even further in *1984*, where the tone is generally more pessimistic. Kafka needs only to be mentioned, to remind us that the exercise of power in modern times has struck the allegorist in an ironic light, since Kafka always presents us with the most strongly ambivalent image of power. We never know whether his heroes love or hate their gaolers, love or hate their bosses—though we suspect the balance will finally tip down on the side of hate. When we turn from the allegory of Orwell and Kafka to that of William Golding, we get an even deeper mockery of human power, personified as it is in the vicious characters of the shipwrecked children in *Lord of the Flies*. So deeply does Golding fear the human ability to exercise sheer power that he ends his fable on a note of absolute pessimism, since the grownups who rescue the children from their island kingdom are themselves engaged in the very war of which the children have been building up the fundamental paradigm.

It is in this way that allegory becomes what Frye has called "anti-allegorical," by which he means ironical. He sees this trend occurring with increasing force as we approach modern times; he sees in it an aspect of the general ironic (we might more accurately call it the meiotic) trend of Western literature.[44] It seems unwise, however much we may agree with this analysis of a general "downward" trend, to label the ironic as "anti-allegorical," since allegory is itself a form of *ironia*, and has traditionally been thus classified by rhetoricians. (Or, perhaps *ironia* is a type of allegory.) In any case, what happens is not that allegory ceases to be used in modern times—there never was more of it being produced. Rather, the work that is produced takes a negative view of its precepts; it says, automatism is

[44] Frye, *Anatomy*, 91–92.

bad, whereas a medieval allegory is likely to imply that the automatic response against the Christian "sins" is always good. Now it becomes fashionable to distrust even good impulses, when they are conditioned reflexes. The modern author takes an extremely negative attitude toward Big Brother, the Boss, the Emperor, and the like. But he still expresses this attitude through the medium of indirect, iconographic speech. In short, for Frye's term "anti-allegorical" the critic should substitute the more accurate "anti-affirmative," or even *kakodaemonic;* evil-daemoned. This revision of terminology does not, however, negate the main point Frye was making, namely, that the modern allegorist tempers what had traditionally been the optimistic view of human perfectibility (whether called "anagogy" or "progress"). Furthermore, if this is the case, there is major evidence that allegory is not so much written *in* a fog of compulsion as it is written *about* the fog of compulsion. The detachment of satirists and ironical pessimists has a curative virtue in it, and seems to justify allegory aesthetically by balancing its daemonology with a degree of skepticism as to the good of sheer power.

Magic and the enlargement of thought. There is equally a defense of allegory possible when one turns to its magical character. Even in our world there is still a place for wonder, perhaps even a greater place than ever, as the circle of the unknown contracts. If allegory keeps alive that curiosity from which philosophy springs, it is performing a major function. That it should and can do so is apparent from the aesthetic of the sublime with which I have already dealt. The sublime (and Shelley's *Defence* echoes this presupposition in his view of the highest kind of poetry) is intended to arouse the torpid mind. True, a Shelley is likely to think of the older allegory as dull and uninspiring, and of Spenser as a secondary author. But this is perhaps a personal rivalry, since he owes some of his deeper skills to Spenser. His view in general accords with the standard view of what is sublime (which would include much of Spenser): "But poetry acts in a diviner manner. It awakens and enlarges the mind itself by rendering it the receptacle of a thousand unapprehended combinations of thought." [45] True, Shelley follows Blake in praising the poetry of sensuous awareness, but his primary concern is with the enlargement of the mind, as his own poetry continually demonstrates. It speaks of the body and of nature, but it addresses itself to the intellect. It is above all a magical poetry and invokes magic quite directly most of the time. Here the aesthetic justification rests on the eliciting of awe, that special ambivalence of fear and attraction which we feel toward whatever is sacred or taboo.

By developing a poetry in which tabooed objects have a central place, the allegorist draws on our most primitive responses. Since these objects have magical significance, they are never simply perceived or quietly apprehended by the rational mind. But they do get us to think more intensely and to worry more profoundly, which perhaps gives a high value to the medium in which they are conveyed. It is surprising that the New Critics, with all their praise of paradox, did not take to allegory. It after all contains ambivalence and expresses anxiety. They appear to have defined the mode too narrowly, equating it with what Frye has called "naïve allegory." In detail their attacks made allegory into a case of mixed metaphor, which as Frye observes, is the radical of naïve allegory.[46] Even assuming this impoverished definition of the concept, the New Critics seem in a weak position, since ambivalence is still at the heart of naïve allegory—a "disguised form of discursive writing"—for the good reason that such writing *assumes* the ambivalence, and forgets about it. Naïve allegory flourishes where pioneer, or highly competitive, social conditions pertain, and those are conditions where sheer survival is at stake, and there is no place for dialectical subtleties. Even there, however, ambivalent attitudes appear about the roots of the fiction. Even an art as patently "naïve" as magazine advertising shows that the public is being offered objects of desire that are more than

[45] *The Defence of Poetry*, as quoted by I. A. Richards, in *Principles of Literary Criticism*, 67.
[46] Frye, *Anatomy*, 90. Frye notes the importance of naïve allegory in pedagogy, advertising, etc., where an immediate, schematic appeal is necessary.

simple objects of desire; they are objects toward which the public entertains highly mixed attitudes, objects which are both taboo and desirable. Advertising does not escape the old Christian problem about the value of the pursuit of Mammon.

Defensive ritual: the "lower" function. The response to ambivalence is of course what counts, since mixed attitudes in themselves are natural in all human thought. We cannot escape ambivalence, but we can respond differently to situations which arouse this state of feeling. Here also there is an aesthetic rationale for the allegorical mode.[47]

Ritual is its characteristic allegorical way of showing the human response to ambivalence. Under "ritual" I subsume all those devices of symmetry and balance which allegory carries to such extremes.[48] It has to be clearly understood that there are other ways of responding to the intense simultaneous mixture of love and hate. One can respond by a hysterical outburst of rage or affection, which are likely to bring on tears and violent outcries. One can respond by a gradual cooling off, under the control of the intellect, but at the same time without the distinct coldness and detachment that marks compulsive behavior. One can lapse into daydream and free fantasy, and then we have something which might be called a "mythical" symbolic response. The allegorist responds otherwise, as I have argued. He creates a ritual which by virtue of its very repetition and symmetry "carries off" the threat of ambivalent feelings, and shows this same

[47] On the general problem of artistic and other types of sublimating behavior, see J. C. Flugel, *Studies in Feeling and Desire* (London, 1955); also Edward Glover, "Sublimation, Substitution and Social Anxiety," *International Journal of Psychoanalysis*, XII (1931). The term was, I believe, introduced by Ernest Jones; see his "Theory of Symbolism," reprinted in *Papers on Psychoanalysis*. See also the bibliography of psychoanalytic treatments of the function of art as a response to the environment, in Jones, *Life and Work of Sigmund Freud*, III, 521–522.

[48] Frye, *Anatomy*, 105–110, uses the term "ritual" more loosely than I— quite rightly, given his aims. I am consistently thinking of the pattern of the *compulsive* ritual, not any repetitious act at all, but only this specific type and function of ritual.

process of displacement occurring in the fiction. The central characteristic of the compulsive response to ambivalence is the ordered ritual which gives to this particular behavior its form. Its effect is to allow a degree of certainty in a world of flux. By making lists (naturalism), by creating complicated "double plots" (pastoral), by building "summation schemes" and antithetical polarities in "debate" (*psychomachia*), the allegorist slows and regulates the pace of the existence his fiction represents. He furthermore keeps the threatening ambivalence from taking up any focal point other than those defined by the strictest polar frame of reference. The tendency toward polarization may not always operate in practice, but underneath surface complications and subtleties one can always discern a subtending structure which opposes the powers of darkness to the powers of light.

The aesthetic of mimesis, which gives highest praise to "high mimetic" actions, whether tragic or epic, and then immediately below them praises the comic forms, does not allow an equally high place to actions where variability in action and character are restricted by ritual. The "dramatic temperament of nature" does not authorize such a nondramatic order of events, and for this reason the Aristotelian aesthetic (as best we can guess at it) does not give the highest place to "dramas" where the action must be concluded by arbitrary thematic devices such as the *deus ex machina*. Richards has given the best rationale for this valuation of modes.

It is essential to recognize that in the full tragic experience there is no suppression. The mind does not shy away from anything, it does not protect itself with any illusion, it stands uncomforted, unintimidated, alone and self-reliant. The test of its success is whether it can face what is before it and respond to it without any of the innumerable subterfuges by which it ordinarily dodges the full development of experience. Suppressions and sublimations alike are devices by which we endeavour to avoid issues which might bewilder us. The essence of Tragedy is that it forces us to live for a moment without them. When we succeed we find, as usual, that there is no difficulty. The difficulty came from the suppressions and sublimations.[49]

Much the same validation can be given for comedy, in the fullest sense of that term, by which we imply that, facing all the bafflements, pains and embarrassments of experience, the hero is shown coming to terms and achieving a successful return to society. But no such avoidance of "subterfuge" can be asserted of allegory. The art of subterfuge par excellence, it needs to be justified as an art proper to those moments when nothing but subterfuge will work, as in a political state where dictatorial censorship prevails. That it appears an inferior mode simply casts an inferior cultural value on the ages when it is the only possible artistic mode, as indeed it becomes the major mode during highly religious epochs, or politically totalitarian epochs, which perhaps defy such neat labeling, but which still perhaps could be isolated to a degree. One might claim that the religious defense of the self against fears of death and evil is weaker than the tragic, realistic, nontranscendental confrontation of that fear, and therefore that a disguising or spiritualistic art is of lower order than a mimetic art. These values are certainly capable of dispute.

On the other hand, there is no virtue in totally denying the need for defense when the personal ego or the popular culture are under hopelessly powerful attack. When ritual constitutes the only available means of mental survival, and when furthermore physical survival is being threatened, this secret mental survival is better than none at all.[50] To argue otherwise would be to attack the very founda-

[49] Richards, *Principles of Literary Criticism*, 246. This, significantly, forms part of the chapter on imagination.

[50] Honig, *Dark Conceit*, 53: "From the beginning, allegory has offered the rational consciousness a way of regulating imaginative materials that otherwise appear confounded by contradictions and bristling with destructive implications. In allegory the irrational becomes viable through a corporative method that may be called differentiation: the narrative builds up the sense of the distinctions to be drawn among the 'levels of meaning' and between the accidental and purposeful, the explicit and the implicit, and so on. The irra-

tions of religious belief. Even taking a less grim view of defense, if we should happen to find allegory playful, then there also is a healthy substitutive function. Certain intricacies in emblematic art, its surrealistic complications, can give the same pleasure as a child's game. Ritual of that fanciful sort takes relaxation and restoration for its goal.

Visionary ritual: the "higher" function. The function of ritual, as I have been describing it, has been psychologically defensive, that is, allegorical rituals resemble rituals in the compulsive syndrome of behavior, since in both cases the *form* of the symbolizing seems to alleviate the tensions which are called "ambivalence." The very high degree of emotive ambivalence in allegorical literature cannot be denied; it is sometimes even synonymous with the names of authors —Swift, Bunyan, Melville, Kafka. But to view the ritual forms evolved by these authors merely in the light of psychoneurosis would be, among other failures, to go against the principles of Freud, to whom we owe this sort of psychoanalytic approach. He never once said, nor in any way implied, that the work of art was a neurotic product—he merely showed the formal similarities of art works and neurotic behavior patterns and then argued that the origins of daydreaming fantasies and art works could be identical. The aesthetic skills, what Freud called "the essential *ars poetica*," appeared to him an "innermost secret" known only to the artist, and although Freud discerned therein a technique of disguise, whereby the artist made his private, perhaps shameful, daydreams into publicly acceptable

---

tional is thereby given an authentic, undiminished force which otherwise— according to law, custom, dogma—would be distorted or obscured. The constant layering of meaning in the narrative proves to be decisive in creating the whole effect which the literary work can have upon us. When one thinks of the great mythopoeic works like the Bible, *Oedipus Rex,* and the Homeric poems, harnessed as they have been by extensive commentary, it is striking that the interpreters have focused their efforts on domesticating the irregular and forbidding insights which, if taken literally, would be destructive of the very code on which society is built."

forms, he still maintained that the artist's skills were those of a crafts-man who "bribes us by the offer of a purely formal, that is, aesthetic, pleasure in the presentation of his fantasies." [51] He saw a quite posi-tive activity, not a simply defensive preservation of private fantasies. This was furthermore the case when he noted the similarity between the compulsive neurosis and certain religious ceremonies, a similarity which also concerns us whenever we have an art that might be called either compulsive or religious.

Disregarding Freud's general attack on religious world views, we can see he would have accepted a distinction between the compulsion neurosis and that religious activity which appeared to him to be a travesty of the neurosis. "One might venture to regard the obsessional neurosis as a pathological counterpart to the formation of a religion, to describe this neurosis as a private religious system, and religion as a universal obsessional neurosis." [52] The neurosis, being "patho-logical," involves "ceremonies" of a quite lower order than those employed in a religious observance, even though formally the cere-monial action is similarly shaped in both cases. This is a matter of judgment and evaluation and brings us very quickly to the area of ultimate values and rival philosophies of life. But even without taking any stand on the relative values of neurotic symptoms and religious symptoms, we can see that our allegorical literature provides some "higher" and "lower" instances of ritual behavior. I have already sug-gested that when the author has presented his readers with situations of acute emotional ambivalence, there may be a need to alleviate that tension, a need shared equally by author and reader, and the alle-gorical ritual (e.g., a monotonously paratactic order of sentences) does in fact alleviate any such tension. But there is possibly a higher kind of ritual, or rather a higher effect of ritual. Besides being a defense mechanism, it can be a means to a positive moment of exu-

[51] "The Relation of the Poet to Day-Dreaming" (1908), in *Collected Papers*, IV, 183.

[52] Freud, "Obsessive Acts and Religious Practices" (1907), in *Collected Papers*, II, ed. Joan Riviere (London, 1950), 34.

berance and delight. Such in fact is what I mean by "visionary ritual."

Many traditional allegories belong to a class which might be called a genre, namely "vision." One thinks immediately of the allegorical figures in Aeneas' descent to the underworld, in the vision of Piers Plowman, in *The Divine Comedy*,[53] and in Don Quixote's descent into the Cave of Montesinos, where the poet presents a fabled story as it might be experienced in a dream. The stock beginning of a late medieval allegory is likely to be the hero's awakening into a dream vision. The vision may not be psychologically defined; it may consist rather in the hero's being presented as somehow in isolation from the everyday world, in such a way that he apprehends all about him with an unfamiliar clarity and freshness. It follows from the use of the *hortus conclusus*, for example, that whatever transpires within the garden will have the character of a dream vision, since the garden is cut off from the world of waking reality. Stephen Hawes, author of the early sixteenth-century *Passetyme of Pleasure*, gets this effect of unreality and visionary freedom by insisting on the ease with which the hero moves: "Forth then I walked without impediment/ Into a medowe both gaye and glorious." Bunyan too parallels the primitive notion of mankind that in dreams the soul walks forth with complete freedom, coursing through the wide ranges of the earth, only to return into the body before dawn and the hour of waking. Thus he begins *The Holy War:* "In my travels, as I walked through many regions and countries, it was my chance to happen into that famous continent of Universe; a very large and spacious country it is." We are made to feel how very small it is, on the contrary—precisely the effect of the "enclosed garden"—which we feel even more strongly at the start of *The Pilgrim's Progress*, where Bunyan

[53] See Curtius, *European Literature*, 214 ff.: Giovanni del Virgilio was able to call Dante "Theologos Dantes." Coming in the tradition of so-called "mythical theology," in which pagan and Christian fables could be combined, the poet was able to write a visionary poetry which adumbrated a providential scheme of history.

uses the classic device: "I laid me down in that place to sleep, and, behold, I dreamed a dream."

This dream beginning becomes a standard device; as a cliché it does not retain much metaphoric validity at the present time. But a far deeper visionary tendency does seem to persist in allegorical literature and seems furthermore to be the outcome, or perhaps the collateral, of its ritualistic forms. First of all allegory has an ideal character, a freedom to play with completely mental constructs, which appear, when they are embodied in a story, to allow the same detachment from reality that we find in our dreams. The very idea of a cosmic ordering of images suggests that here we have philosophical or scientific systems crying out to be comprehended all at once in the simultaneous vision of the dream. The dream detaches itself from conscious contacts with reality and allegorical visions likewise detach themselves from the everyday world as we perceive it, even, as I have argued, when the allegory is "naturalistic." But the allegorical vision differs crucially from the dream in that it is organized ritualistically, thus conforming rather to the "waking dreams" of the compulsive or obsessional personality. Often it comes at the climax of a ritual build-up, like the scene when the curtain goes up after several minutes of a Rossini crescendo.

The Christian archetype of all such visions would be the *The Revelation of St. John the Divine*, where, along with the wildest exuberance of fantasy, we are given an orderly, ornate catalogue of visionary objects. Like a vast liturgical drama, *The Revelation* unfolds. Following such a pattern, Christian poets could develop visions which might be less concerned with "the last things," but which still would retain the hierarchical character of *The Revelation*. There is a tendency for the unveiling of the process of revelation to become a rite, a metonymic listing of participants. This tendency is apparent in Dante or Spenser, for whom the allegorical pageant is a major device; while allegorical pageants themselves, whether staged publicly for triumphal entries of monarchs into late medieval and

Renaissance cities or staged in the private theatres of the masque, are full testimony to the vigor of the tradition in which ritual and vision are copartners. Whenever the poet is of lesser stature than a Jonson, a Spenser, or a Dante, the listing becomes more obvious; witness Hawes' *Passetyme of Pleasure*, with its ritual presentation of the traditional parts of wisdom, or witness the more obviously cosmic ritual used by Palingenius to organize *The Zodiacke of Life*,[54] where each book is governed by a particular sign of the zodiac.

Going one step further, we find that central to most such rituals there are special moments of particular exuberance, particular intensity, particular vision, and these moments involve what we have called "symbols of the center." To recall the main criterion: from the spatial point of view such a symbol, as Eliade has described it, would be a temple or indeed any sacred place to which the hero is drawn and in which he receives his initiation into the vision of his true destiny.[55] Spenser, perhaps following Virgil, uses his symbols of

[54] Miss Tuve, in her edition of Googe's translation of Palingenius, notes the paradox "that this is most typically a book of the Renaissance by virtue of the mediaeval character of most of its proposed solutions. The problem of evil, posed again and again, is teased through all the familiar arguments: of contingency, of refinement through suffering, of stoic disregard, of Christian redefinition of the good, of Plotinian optimism in the statement of the concept of the scale of being, of a linked order of causes with the devil as the basest, of a dualistic conception of vile body and heavenly soul, 'two so farre contrary things . . . compact in one' (Scorpius, 144). The reality of evil seems to be asserted in passages of a terror and power which may have ranged their author with writers accused of the Manichaean heresy. No Marston or Nashe could outdo the lashing savagery of detail, or the bitterness with which he tells men to go build them churches and rattle out hymns to ask for the lengthening of their flea-bitten lives (Virgo, Capricornus). Yet all this is as it is in those later authors, a scourge of villainy; and man, not God, is the villain" (*The Zodiacke of Life* [reprinted in facsimile, New York, 1947], xxi).

[55] In the eyes of William Blake "the last Judgment is not Fable or Allegory, but Vision. Fable or Allegory are a totally distinct and inferior kind of Poetry. Vision or Imagination is a Representation of what Eternally exists, Really and Unchangeably. Fable or Allegory is Form'd by the Daughters of Memory. Imagination is surrounded by the daughters of Inspiration, who in the aggregate are call'd Jerusalem. Fable is Allegory, but what Critics call The Fable, is Vision itself. The Hebrew Bible & the Gospel of Jesus are not Al-

the center—the House of Holiness, the House of Alma, the Gardens of Adonis—for a special visionary effect which depends upon the positioning of the hero's arrival at the "center." Spenser seems to place his symbolic centers after the mid-point in any given book of *The Faerie Queene* in order that he may increase the power of the hero during the second half of each book, with the result that the hero is readied for a final, greatest of all challenges, usually a final culminating battle with the forces of evil. Each book then appears to be a double incline of mounting challenge to the hero, each ascent being surmounted by a triumph, the first potential, over the self, the second, actual and magnificent, over Satan's minions.

Parallel cases in Dante would be the vision of the Church Triumphant at the end of the "Purgatorio," which marks a potential victory of Christ, as compared with the vision of the multifoliate rose at the end of the "Paradiso," whereby we are to understand an ultimate, eternal, yet actual total victory of Love. The vision, furthermore, is not always visual. It appears that any temporal moment of particular intensity can serve as a symbol of the center, or, putting it another way, just as space is "sacred space" in the Temple, so time is "sacred time" in the Temple, while we can sometimes be shown a moment of sacred time without any of the spatial trappings that go to make up a proper temple. Interpreted somewhat freely, these notions allow a wide variety of things and experiences to possess the qualities of holiness. In *Don Quixote*, for example, the whole story is a texture of visions (and debunking countervisions), but certain places—crossroads and above all, inns—are sacred for Don Quixote, since in them time stands still and his mind runs where it will, although these places would not ordinarily be assumed to have anything sacred about them. Unlike such humble, ordinary places, the Cave of Montesinos would represent a mysterious dream world, as in a comic way would Sancho's Island of Barataria. If we are to understand the higher func-

---

legory, but Eternal Vision or Imagination of All that Exists. Note here that Fable or Allegory is seldom without some Vision" (*Complete Writings*, 604–605).

tion of ritual, we must preserve some freedom of interpretation, to allow authors like Cervantes their own favorite forms of visionary place and time.

Melville provides another instance of an unfamiliar scene providing the backdrop and an unfamiliar moment, the occasion, of an ultimate vision. The final encounter of Ahab with the White Whale is the apocalyptic vision of the war between two daemonic powers, and as such it links Melville's romance to the main tradition established by *The Revelation of St. John the Divine*. Immediately before his final encounter, Ahab himself, by a minute act, establishes one of those temporal moments of heightened intensity which I have likened to the Symbol of the Center.[56] Indeed in the passage that follows we have a pattern for the way such symbolic centers may be created within the bounds of a novelistic literature, by means of an ornamental diction.

Slowly crossing the deck from the scuttle, Ahab leaned over the side, and watched how his shadow in the water sank and sank to his gaze, the more and the more he strove to pierce the profundity. But the lovely aromas in that enchanted air did at last seem to dispel, for a moment, the cankerous thing in his soul. That glad, happy air, that winsome sky, did at last stroke and caress him; the stepmother world, so long cruel—forbidding—now threw affectionate arms round his stubborn neck, and did seem to joyously sob over him, as if over one, that however wilful and erring, she could yet find it in her heart to save and to bless. From beneath his slouched hat Ahab dropped a tear into the sea; nor did all the Pacific contain such wealth as that one wee drop.

Starbuck saw the old man; saw him, how he heavily leaned over the side; and he seemed to hear in his own true heart the measureless sobbing that stole out of the centre of the serenity around. Careful not to touch him, or be noticed by him, he yet drew near to him, and stood there.

What follows gives us an ever deeper vision of the total meaning of Ahab's quest; he becomes Adam, "staggering beneath the piled cen-

[56] I have chosen the concluding passages of ch. cxxxii, "The Symphony."

turies since Paradise." In a moment that recalls the *Urne-Buriall* of Sir Thomas Browne, Ahab expresses the fate of man as a kind of endless depredation of time, a simultaneous stilling and moving.

"By heaven, man, we are turned round and round in this world, like yonder windlass, and Fate is the handspike. And all the time, lo! that smiling sky, and this unsounded sea! Look! see yon Albacore! who put it into him to chase and fang that flying-fish? Where do murderers go, man? Who's to doom, when the judge himself is dragged to the bar? But it is a mild, mild wind, and a mild looking sky; and the air smells now, as if it blew from a faraway meadow; they have been making hay somewhere under the slopes of the Andes, Starbuck, and the mowers are sleeping among the new-mown hay. Sleeping? Aye, toil we how we may, we all sleep at last on the field. Sleep? Aye, and rust amid greenness; as last year's scythes flung down, and left in the half-cut swaths—Starbuck!"

It is toward this kind of moment, as toward moments like the descent to the Underworld, or the drowning of Palinurus in the *Aeneid*, that all the great allegories move, and if we do not seek conventional imagery only, we shall even find such moments where we would hardly expect them, in so-called "naturalistic" works. After all, even *Moby Dick* has great stretches of the purest naturalism, in documentation of the whaling life. With such authors as Melville, Cervantes before him, and Kafka after him, the critic must preserve some freedom of interpretation and not fit these authors into schemes with which they were doubtless familiar, but which they very likely avoided in order to go beyond the purely didactic. There is no absolute necessity for the author of an allegory to choose his cosmic language from one perfect sacred vocabulary—many such vocabularies are available. Similarly the author is free to place his apocalyptic "center" wherever he wishes in the hero's quest, although difference of position will determine the hero's fate differently. A hero who is immediately initiated into his Order of Knighthood (a Don Quixote) may have a more consistently daemonic power, from the start, than a hero who must wait to the end, like Lucius in *The Golden Ass*.[57] Spenser's method of centering his symbols of the center in each book allows his heroes to take on special powers halfway through their careers, and the second half of each book then gains a new interest. The vision in these cases coincides with an access of power, since what the hero sees constitutes an initiation.[58]

Finally, perhaps more important than the intermediary moments of vision, chiefly initiatory moments, are those final moments of vision which climax most major allegorical works, like the one in *Moby Dick*, and which constitute the highest function to be accorded the allegorical mode. After the eschatological vision of the forces of destruction, *The Revelation* reveals to us the river of the water of life, the tree of life, and the ultimate triumph of the Spirit and of the Christian Truth. As Frye has shown, these sublime triumphs of the Divine Being are expressed by material elements which become traditional apocalyptic images: the evildoers (dogs, sorcerers, whoremongers, murderers, idolaters, liars) are kept outside the walls of the Heavenly City, while within a marriage of Christ and the Church is to be consummated.[59] The final apocalyptic vision promises to man-

[57] It could be argued that the Circean transformation of Lucius into the ass is itself a daemonic metamorphosis, as a result of which he is brutalized. But that is exactly what Apuleius wants to avoid saying; rather he keeps showing us what it is to be a human being, having once lost the status of a human being. The metamorphosis allows a fresh definition of a particularly human person, the hero of the book. On the conversion of Lucius Apuleius, see A. D. Nock, *Conversion*, ch. ix, "The Conversion of Lucius." Also, on the "reforming" of the soul, through religious conversion and illumination, see Gerhart B. Ladner, *The Idea of Reform: Its Impact on Christian Thought and Action in the Age of the Fathers* (Cambridge, Mass., 1959), especially sec. 4 of ch. v, where Ladner relates the concept of spiritual reform—we might more often call it "rebirth"—to the flowing of time. He is discussing the views of Augustine in the *Confessions*.

[58] Compare in Malory the difference between Lancelot and Galahad, when each wishes for the vision of the Grail. An initiation is not possible to all men, as Lancelot's example shows.

[59] See Frye, *Anatomy of Criticism*, the section on apocalyptic imagery in the "Theory of Myths"; also Frye, "New Directions from Old," in *Myth and Mythmaking*, ed. Henry Murray (New York, 1960), 124-125, on the *locus*

kind an eternal fruitfulness. It shows a triumph of love and creation, following the destructive war with evil, following the confession of sins and the saying of a creed. Even assuming a final cosmic catastrophe, the triumph of an antichrist, or a millenarian destruction of the political order, as in *1984*, or a purely mechanical destruction of the world—such as abounds in modern science fiction—the final apocalyptic vision has the same culminating character.[60] It seems to be the mirror of an ultimate hope or, rather, an ultimate wish fulfillment, whether for life or death. As such, allegory would seem capable of exchanging its endless ritual form for a kind of closed climactic form.

The visionary moment is felt to be a climactic expansion of imagery, action, and thought, such that we feel we have emerged from the bondage of the liturgical rite into the pure insight of contemplation. Such is the final vision in Eliot's *Ash Wednesday*, such the repose and absolute certainty of "Death by Water" and "The Fire Sermon" in *The Waste Land*. Such, above all, are the "timeless" movements of the *Four Quartets*. Ritual alters its pace, exchanges preparatory steps for a final consummation, or rather for a higher order of truth. The argument of the present book suggests that the exchange is a radical one, and once allegory becomes truly apocalyptic it ceases to be mere allegory and comes instead to share in the higher order of mysterious language, which we may perhaps call mythical language.[61] But this may only be a semantic distinc-

---

amoenus: "a place of perpetually temperate climate from which the seeds of vegetable life in the world below proceed, and to which they return." The Gardens of Adonis in Spenser are the most important case; but Dante employs a *locus amoenus* in *Purgatorio*, Canto XXVIII; and presumably all such uses look back to a primitive archetype such as the Garden of Eden.

[60] Major examples of the catastrophic vision would be the plays of Samuel Becket. Becket presents catastrophe as a gradual grinding down and slowing to a dead stop. He is obsessed with the isolation of the people he portrays; indeed that isolation is his great theme, as it is of Bertolt Brecht.

[61] I have several times suggested that myth and allegory are two different stages of a single archetypal story-telling process. Myth seems to me to correspond generally to dream, allegory to rationalization and compulsive think-

tion, since the sublime magnitude of major allegory does seem to elicit the same ecstasis and enthusiasm that characterize the full re-

ing. Allegory seems usually to follow upon myth, in that the story it pulls apart into separate levels must have once been a unity. (An artist might nonetheless attempt a reversal of this process; perhaps Ezra Pound is such a case; perhaps Eliot succeeded at precisely this enterprise.) We might seek evidence of the analytic-synthetic polarity in the difference between the mythical and the allegorical type of *hero*. We have said, following Frye, that the heroes of myth are truly gods, those of allegory (Frye's "romance") are either daemons or daemonically empowered humans. The former have all power, the latter only a conditional power, as they frequently have only a "conditional immortality"—e.g., the heel of Achilles, the magic bolt of Talus, the earth-bound strength of Antaeus. The difference between mythic and allegorical heroes comes out nowhere more strongly than in their sexual character.

Thus Eliade, in *Myths, Dreams and Mysteries*, tr. Philip Mairet (London, 1960), 174-176, the section on "Androgyny and Wholeness," remarks: "We do know, in fact, that a certain number of the Supreme Beings of the archaic peoples were androgynes. But the phenomenon of divine androgyny is very complex: it signifies more than the co-existence—or rather coalescence—of the sexes in the divine being. Androgyny is an archaic and universal formula for the expression of *wholeness*, the co-existence of the contraries, or *coincidentia oppositorum*. More than a state of sexual completeness and autarchy, androgyny symbolizes the perfection of a primordial non-conditioned state." We can explain in these terms the emergence of heroes and perhaps even more, of heroines, in *The Faerie Queene*, from a state of allegorical significance to a state of mythical significance. The tendency in Spenser is for all major characters to move toward androgyny, the most notable instance being Spenser's most richly developed character, Britomart. Similarly with Amoret—for her, Spenser actually used the image of Hermaphrodite in the first edition of his poem, ending Bk. III with it; he later dropped the stanzas to make a smoother and more continuous transition into Bk. IV, which was published in the second edition.

Eliade goes so far as to define divinity in terms of the androgyne: "But androgyny extends even to divinities who are pre-eminently masculine, or feminine. This means that androgyny has become a general formula signifying *autonomy, strength, wholeness;* to say of a divinity that it is androgynous is as much as to say it is the ultimate being, the ultimate reality." Surely mythology indicates the approximate truth of this statement. The characteristic device of allegory is to split this original wholeness into fundamental divisions which in turn perhaps become archetypes, but which, like the two sexually halved creatures in Aristophanes' myth of Eros, are continually seeking to be reunited. Allegory gives us Macbeth and Lady Macbeth. Its heroes are not men and women; they are divided androgynes.

sponse to the apocalyptic, as either Dante or Blake will show. That increasing sense of wonder which pervades Dante's ascent through his universe, the verbal ecstasy that pervades the songs of a Blake or a Christopher Smart, seems in fact to be the natural response to visions that may easily be called "mythic," "apocalyptic," or "final" —but which might equally be called "allegorical." The final vision of the Mystic Rose in *The Divine Comedy* is certainly from a semantic point of view an allegory, as is the vision of the Graces or any other such vision in Spenser, or the vision of the end of the world, whether it be *The Revelation of St. John the Divine,* or ironic modern equivalents like *The City of Dreadful Night, The Waste Land, Brave New World,* or *The Castle.* (Whenever in these ultimate visions the poetry revolves around a metaphoric equation of the physical, political, or spiritual universe with the human organism, it appears that the final apocalyptic vision is taking its imagery from the simplest, most familiar source, namely the human body, the body of bodies. The body image need not be very obvious; it is not always as clear as it is in Blake's *Jerusalem,* where the landscape becomes a face, torso, limbs, and so on.) [62] The distinction

[62] Blake's *Jerusalem* (*Complete Writings,* 745) for example ends with the earth-body coalescence:

And every Man stood Fourfold; each Four Faces had: One to the West,
One toward the East, One to the South, One to the North, the Horses Fourfold.
And the dim Chaos brighten'd beneath, above, around: Eyed as the Peacock,
According to the Human Nerves of Sensation, the Four Rivers of the Water of Life.

South stood the Nerves of the Eye; East, in Rivers of Bliss, the Nerves of the
Expansive Nostrils; West flow'd the Parent Sense, the Tongue; North stood
The labyrinthine Ear; Circumscribing & Circumcising the excrementitious
Husk & Covering, into Vacuum evaporating, revealing the lineaments of Man,
Driving outward the Body of Death in an Eternal Death & Resurrection,
Awaking it to Life among the Flowers of Beulah, rejoicing in Unity

between a semantic and metaphysical order of things may be necessary if we are to pierce through all the confusion as to what is
"mythical" and what is "allegorical" in the apocalyptic and prophetic
traditions; the semantic character of these traditions would seem to
be allegorical, while their metaphysical character would seem to be
mythical. In much the same way a dream is metaphysically a myth,
but semantically, when we interpret it, we take it to be allegory. By
stressing the metaphysical nature of certain intense moments of allegorical literature, we do in fact also stress absolute value, since
these are the very moments that would seem to be of higher importance to humanity.

To say that a given work is allegorical is therefore not to say anything about its value, since allegory is only a mode of symbolizing.
But to observe the analytic function of a work, or a satirical function, seems a positive evaluation. And to observe the apocalyptic
function of some allegories surely is to suggest they are endowed
with some sort of final significance, a value they possess even if
perchance they do not communicate with many readers. The
prophetic tradition of allegory and *figura* does not require its

---

In the Four Senses, in the Outline, the Circumference & Form, for ever
In Forgiveness of Sins which is Self Annihilation; it is the Covenant of
Jehovah.

This daring use of the body-image as a cosmic "creature" is not original with
Blake, nor is it confined solely to the poetry of vision. One expects it in the
latter; one is at first surprised to find it the basis of the seemingly more
prosaic topographical poems of the Elizabethans, e.g., Drayton's *Polyolbion*.
To make sense or derive much pleasure from such rambling poetry is an unlikely accomplishment, unless one sees that Drayton is turning England into
"the world's body," and therefore constantly and in endless reiteration using
metaphors which equate the countryside with the limbs and organs of the
body. The poetic imagery has a parallel, and a gloss, on the title-page of
Polyolbion, where England, the goddess, is shown wearing a gown that contains the map of England, the island. Beginning with such a gloss, one can
explicate the poem as one of the great Elizabethan cosmic visions—whose like
is to be found, perhaps, only in such a master moment as the Marriage of the
Thames and the Medway in *The Faerie Queene*. We are enabled to "en-
vision" the England of Drayton and in that sense remove any taint of prosiness.

ultimate truths to be popular, or even commonly known. Prophecies usually have their select prophets, who see and expound a mystery. One might, from that point of view, give Blake's prophetic poems a higher value than his songs, on the ground that communication is not relevant to absolute truth, and the latter is what his visions are intended to yield, if only to a small and select group of readers. Further, one would have always to be willing to allow that such visionary truth follows from *one's own* willingness to accept a given set of doctrines, in Blake's case certain Christian doctrines.

Whether this limiting condition is a grave weakness of allegory is a matter for aestheticians to decide; in the meantime one can see how it might involve a narrowing of the circle of readers who might be expected to participate in or enjoy the mere poetry of the work. The poetic excellences of Blake will be lost on those who happily admit they "simply don't know what it's all about." The same limitation seems also to apply to all other major allegorists, including Dante, in despite of Auerbach's beautiful defense of Dante's mimesis in the recently translated *Dante, Poet of the Secular World*. Obscurity appears to be a price necessarily paid for the lack of a universal, common doctrinal background. If readers do not share this background with the author, they may still be impressed by the ornaments of the vision, as "mere ornaments," but these will not for such readers have the cosmic reference of true allegorical language. Clearly, however, the appeal may remain strong, in either case, with either naïve or sophisticated readers.

Afterword

IT is difficult to make a final summary statement at the end of a work such as this. In the nature of the case there are further problems yet to be studied, detailed discriminations to be made. Perhaps this is the proper aim of theory, to encourage a state of readiness for special devices by which given literary works conform to the large-scale patterns set forth. Individual style and individual creativity are always possible for the allegorist, and this freedom is a major reason why, in spite of the analogy drawn between allegory and compulsion, it would be wrong to call this mode "inhibited" or "neurotic." Rather, it is best to allow works in this mode a more positive function. In a word, I suspect they are the monuments to our ideals.[1] They do not mimetically show us the human beings who need these ideals, but they examine the philosophic, theological, or moral

---

[1] This much neglected concept of monumentality is the subject of essays by Siegfried Giedion, *Architecture, You and Me: The Diary of a Development* (Cambridge, Mass., 1958). The term rightly suggests both special size, the sublime magnitude, and special function, the official art that supports tradition or the Establishment. Monuments are made with ulterior, not inherent purposes. Yeats would be a problematic figure in this regard, since his final rejection of the iconography of *A Vision* may be a rejection of ulterior purposes. Perhaps it is fairer to say that Yeats simply goes beyond his early and middle period of allegorical poetry. "The Circus Animals' Desertion" could well be called an allegory, and it is late, so that he never fully escapes the mode. His Byzantium poems are openly monumental.

premises on which we act, and then they confront us with the perfection of certain ideals, the depravity of others. Furthermore, allegories frequently suggest that even the ideals of the evil-minded
could be valid, were it not that a humane world view or some physical necessity prevents this conversion to evil. Sometimes, indeed, an
allegorist will go out of his way to create the monuments of evil
and the rationality of madness, as Spenser does in Book V of *The
Faerie Queene*, where he shows that Radigund, the absolute antag-
onist of the good, has her own laws, her own rights, her own feelings,
and her own ideals.

The effect of monumentality remains constant, even in the vision
of evil. Some predominant cultural ideal needs to be memorialized or
publicly praised, and when the Renaissance poets make what they
call "history" their model of moral instruction, they look to conflicts
from which they can extract a "triumph"; they single out those
moments of heroic behavior that can rightly become the monuments to a cultural ideal.[2] They necessarily neglect all moments in
past history that are ignoble, or ordinary—one sure minor sign that
Shakespeare is not primarily an allegorist is the degree to which
common people enter his history plays as individuals, since there

---

[2] Huizinga has described the charismatic power of certain monumental
iconographies, "historical ideals of life," such as the image of chivalry, the
image of the nation-state, the image of a *pax romana*. He defines the term as a
type of cultural projection: "Hence a historical life-ideal may be defined as
any concept of excellence man projects into the past," and these are increasingly nonmythical as time goes on (*Men and Ideas: History, the Middle Ages,
the Renaissance*, tr. by J. S. Holmes and Hans van Marle [New York, 1959],
"History," 17–158).

See the comments on the bridge of Emerson's *Concord Hymn*, in the ingenious essay by Paul Goodman, "Notes on a Remark of Seami," *Utopian
Essays and Practical Proposals*, 130–137. This essay presents a theory of poetic
and dramatic monuments, starting with Seami the Noh playwright's remark,
"If there is a celebrated place or ancient monument in the neighbourhood,
[mention of it] is inserted with the best effect somewhere near the end of the
third part of the Development." Goodman himself has written *Stop-Light:
5 Dance Poems* (Harrington Park, N.J., 1941), in the manner of the Noh plays
with an essay on Noh by the author.

we might expect an allegorist to play up the purely heroic act, and there, if anywhere, a possibility for this monumentality exists. By the same token, when Shakespeare's history plays are presenting the allegory of a providential history—England's ideal temporal destiny—he is exactly at his most monumental.

There is, of course, some difficulty in deciding whether the term "monumental" should be given an iconographic or a dimensional meaning. I seem to be taking it chiefly in the former sense, but clearly the allegorical works of tradition are often of sublime grandeur, and we are directly assaulted by their magnitude. That a sort of inverse grandeur is possible has appeared from our discussion of the picturesque, a modality where the overall form becomes less significant than the agitated surface texture, which in turn seems obsessional, daemonic, and highly inwrought. There seems to be no escape from the immediate iconographic assault of these formal properties. In a recent account of a picture of the Virgin in the illuminated *Shaftesbury Psalter*, D. W. Robertson has used the term "monumental" to denote a hierophany resulting from mainly formal properties.

In illumination the natural articulation of the human figure is sacrificed for the sake of balanced line and symmetrically arranged surfaces. The Virgin achieves an "hieratic" or "monumental" appearance by virtue of the stringency with which a geometrical pattern is imposed upon her figure. . . . This geometrical symmetry which subordinates the parts to an artificially ordered whole, is a step toward the abstract realm of the invisible, which is also governed by an artificial order. Elsewhere, the same kind of order falls on monsters as well as saints, but this is as it should be, since, as we have seen, all are a part of the beauty of the Divine Order.[3]

Defined in terms of rigidity, "isolation," and hypersymmetry, as well as of sublime or picturesque magnitude, the allegory of even such minor forms as the riddle and the emblem poem seems to be "hieratic" and "monumental." These minor forms have a special

[3] *A Preface to Chaucer*, 148–149.

importance in that they are frequently popular in appeal. From the earliest times riddles and emblems have been the media of familiar inherited knowledge and maxims of conduct. They employ those proverbial iconographies we know best, in former times the woodcuts that could be profitably reproduced even when their outlines were worn down by hundreds of impressions, in recent times the advertising cuts that become even more familiar through endless reproduction in the popular magazines, on television, on billboards. We have today an odd situation in which we make traditions almost overnight by continued, oversimplified, oppressive reiteration of stock images, whether on television or by some other means of popular propaganda. Yet it seems important to the modern emblematist that he help create these traditions and that in turn he derive from them the values on which to base his romances.[4] Our "Hollywood" ideals are akin to those with which a large manufacturer might like to associate his product; our consumer goods are necessarily tied in with typical romantic symbols of status, symbols that have their counterpart, though with greater degrees of sobriety, in the older iconographies.[5] A world like ours, in which theological

---

[4] This process resembles the transmutation of agency into imagery, which was described in Chapters i and ii above. A "stock response" requires the fixation of a normally labile response, and this fixation requires activity to be stilled into inactivity, emotion which is ongoing to be stopped, and replaced by the fixed idea. Any monument likewise stills the flow of time at a specific historical moment. Statues appear to turn agency into imagery, and thus a play like *The Winter's Tale* and an opera like *Don Giovanni* seem essentially to involve the analysis of the concepts of time, motion and history (memory, the *memento mori*, the memorial). Triumphal arches and columns in antiquity told a stylized, abstracted history of those they honored. Petrarch's *Triumphs* are doubly effective representations of the time-flow, because each succeeding *Triumph* of the six shows the defeat of a previous victor (each a dimension of experience), until only Eternity is left victorious, beyond experience.

[5] Fitzgerald and West both parodied or actually used the iconography of the "Hollywood" ideal, the former in *Tender Is the Night*, *The Last Tycoon*, and a number of stories, the latter in *Miss Lonelyhearts* and *The Day of the Locust*.

values are doubtful, cannot hope to represent the goods of existence, whether material or spiritual, in the higher terms of metaphysics, and there is therefore a falling off in dignity in modern allegory. Frye, as I have noted, has said we are in an "anti-allegorical" phase. Surely to the extent that glory is not the ideal of the writer, we are in such a phase. Legendary heroes are created with difficulty.[6] There

[6] See E. R. Curtius, "The Poetry of Jorge Guillén," tr. R. W. Flint, *Hudson Review*, VII (Summer, 1954), 222–223: "According to Aristotle, all poetry from the beginning is either praise or blame. Goethe also defined poetry as the 'human Hymn of Praise to which Godhead might gladly listen' ('Lobgesang der Menschheit, dem die Gottheit so gern zuhören mag'). The literature of the last hundred years has exploited blame in all its varieties more than praise. Everything that twenty or thirty Naturalisms, Expressionisms and Existentialisms of all countries and continents have gathered as material for the reproach of mankind, life and being, can, in effect, be collected under the neutral concept of blame. The sum of these utterances represents the upshot of the European nihilism which Nietzsche diagnosed. 'You will either destroy your reverence—or yourselves.' Modern literature has fulfilled its historical mission in destroying all reverence."

Even the recent popular recreation of a legend, the film, *Lawrence of Arabia*, shows the difficulty of making a true romantic hero. Were Euhemerus alive today, he might say, "This is how it begins," but would note the ironies in Lawrence's story. The living and near-living legend were of Lawrence's own making, a fact nowhere more apparent than in chs. xcix, c, ciii, of the *Seven Pillars of Wisdom*. These chapters with certain others spell out the iconographic intention, not only of Lawrence's book, but even more profoundly, of the life he planned and lived out during the Arab Revolt. He begins with a disability: "The epic mode was alien to me, as to my generation," and one way or another he tries to construct a romantic epic, of which the *Seven Pillars of Wisdom* is the title. To give but one instance of his abstract romance-form, let me quote from ch. xcix. Lawrence is describing the peace council of the Arab chiefs at Jefer, where the unity and the purpose of the Revolt were finally in doubt—but where Prince Feisal, the prophet politician, as ever, played the iconographic role of inspired leader:

"Feisal brought nationality to their minds in a phrase, which set them thinking of Arab history and language. . . . Another phrase showed them the spirit of Feisal, their fellow and leader, sacrificing everything for the national freedom; and then silence again, while they imagined him day and night in his tent, teaching, preaching, ordering and making friends: and they felt something of the idea behind this pictured man sitting there iconically, drained of desires, ambitions, weakness, faults; so rich a personality enslaved by an abstraction,

is nowadays a sort of inverse glory, however, a cherished moral depravity which we impose on our alienated heroes to connect them with our times. A typical hero, Winston Smith, like Orwell himself, seems to glory in his own weakness. William Golding's Pincher Martin is strong only one degree above absolute inability to move, and the author revels in the impossible struggle.

According to the older view of allegory, this inversion of monumentality has destroyed the mode itself, but such a conclusion does not follow from the theory I have outlined. This theory maintains rather that a reader can seek the "dark conceit" in any iconographic vocabulary. Consider the films: there has been no lack of allegory in recent cinema. The current masters of the film have all attempted works in the "higher" category of visionary ritual: witness De Sica's *Miracle in Milan*, Clément's *Forbidden Games*, his *Gervaise*, Bergman's *The Seventh Seal*, *The Virgin Spring*, *Through a Glass Darkly*, and *The Magician*, Fellini's *La Strada*, *La Dolce Vita*, and *The Temptation of Dr. Antonio*, Buñuel's *Viridiana*, Antonioni's *L'Avventura* and *La Notte*, Alain Resnais's *Last Year at Marienbad* [7] —while the films written by Marguerite Duras, *Hiroshima Mon*

made one-eyed, one armed, with the one sense and purpose, to live or die in its service.

"Of course it was a picture-man not flesh and blood, but nevertheless true, for his individuality had yielded its third dimension to the idea, had surrendered the world's wealth and artifices. Feisal was hidden in his tent, veiled to remain our leader: while in reality he was nationality's best servant, its tool, not its owner. Yet in the tented twilight nothing seemed more noble."

Of such figures allegories are made, and when the man is an actual man like Lawrence, his legend, like that of Feisal, is *figura* and he himself "a personality enslaved by an abstraction." Yet finally he abandons his abstraction, and therein lies the irony of acting within history.

[7] Resnais, the director has said: "We can imagine *Marienbad* is a documentary about a statue, with interpretive take-offs on the gestures and the return, each time, to the gestures themselves, just as they stand, frozen in sculpture. Imagine a documentary that would succeed, with a statue of two people, by uniting a series of views taken from diverse angles and with the help of diverse camera movements, in telling this way a whole story. And at the end you would see that you had come back to the point of departure, the statue itself" (*New York Film Bulletin*, III, no. 2).

Amour and above all *Une Aussi Longue Absence* (*The Long Ab-sence*),[8] follow along in a major surrealist tradition of film making that clearly is iconographic, taking over a procedure established by artists like Clair, Cocteau, and Buñuel. Finally, Eisenstein established the use in Russian films of a historically based "figural realism." (In this he belonged to a much larger movement in Russian art. In the twentieth century Russian artists are creating monuments to a revolutionary change, from political chaos to political cosmos; and in the choice of subject as well as in form socialist realism provides the closest modern analogue to medieval religious monumentality.) Film makers, like writers, reflect the continuing need for the emblematic mode. Like the writers, film makers find their subjects in the highly charged fields of political and social allegiance; they have often worked in overtly programmatic political or social movements. De Sica and Fellini have found their subjects in the economic injustices

[8] This great film, pushed out of the limelight by a relatively minor work, Bourguignon's *Les Dimanches et Cybèle*, has an immensely complex, perfectly ordered, endlessly suggestive texture and form. Based on the myth of Cybele, like *Les Dimanches* also, *Une Aussi Longue Absence* shows the consummate skill of its director, Henri Colpi; it also shows the profound resources of a genuine myth, that of the "terrible mother," Cybele. Journalistic critics seem in this instance to have shown the impossibility of appreciating a work of "difficult ornament" under the pressure of a newspaper deadline. They also showed the truth of Anton Ehrenzweig's theory of "dazzle detail," that misleading device by which the detective story writer usually diverts his reader's attention from the "true" meaning of the story. Here also there seems to have been a remarkable inability on the part of journalists simply to look at what was before their eyes. This resistance may be the unavoidable result of the ornament used. Any "difficult" film like *Une Aussi Longue Absence* needs to be seen several times, pondered, discussed at length, referred to its literary and historical origins. Mere presence in the theatre is not enough. See Ehrenzweig, *Psychoanalysis of Artistic Vision and Hearing*, 43-44, 134. Speaking of the "superimposition of several plots or polyphony of plots," Ehrenzweig shows that by such means "the reader can never concentrate"; his attention is constantly diverted, while he is led gradually to the "last minute logical satisfaction" which is the peculiar pleasure of a certain kind of riddle. "It is no mean achievement," he remarks, "to keep a story ambiguous so that several series of clues are kept running simultaneously."

sharply isolated by a socially conscious postwar Communist view, Bergman in the austere religio-sexual concerns of a typically North-European introspection (in this he is perhaps influenced by Carl Dreyer), Clément in the opposition to war and to social disorder; Antonioni and certain New Wave directors mingle the sexual motif with the social; the screen writer Marguerite Duras mingles sexual motifs with the theme of world harmony and world progress. What matters here is not the precise degree to which all these artists are "allegorical," but rather that they may be called allegorical at all. It is important for the scholar of medieval literature to be aware that he is not working in a historical vacuum. He is working in a continuing tradition that has never at any time died, that will last as long as the artist is capable of categorizing and yet at the same time remains capable of doubt and anxiety and hope.

"That art is a mediocre art which demands from us an effort of reflection in order that we may be in a position to apprehend its images." [9] Thus the critic Ramón Fernández once spoke of George Meredith's ornamental style. The account of allegory I have presented does not suggest mediocrity, and yet I have emphasized the "effort of reflection" it demands. Fernández would say I had proved precisely his view and had made this mode appear less valuable than dream or mimesis. Perhaps I have done so. Values are at stake here. Let us grant the fundamental problem.

The potential weaknesses of the mode are by now clear enough. They may be summed up in the one word "anesthesia." The reader can be anesthetized by the ritual order of enigma and romance. There is further a weakness inherent in the sublime and picturesque tendencies of the mode, namely a diffusion of inner coherence, since the typical allegory threatens never to end. The magnitude of the encyclopedic poem is controlled arbitrarily, which is to say it has no inherent limit. We need not be doctrinaire neo-Aristotelians to see

[9] "On Philosophical Criticism," in *Messages*, tr. by Montgomery Belgion (London, 1927), 8.

the aesthetic virtues of the maintenance of "proper magnitude," which allegories tend to violate. Their sublime magnitude disallows true organic form.

The strengths of the mode are equally clear. It allows for instruction, for rationalizing, for categorizing and codifying, for casting spells and expressing unbidden compulsions, for Spenser's "pleasing analysis," and, since aesthetic pleasure is a virtue also, for romantic storytelling, for satirical complications, and for sheer ornamental display. To conclude, allegories are the natural mirrors of ideology.

The Illustrations

COMPLEMENTARY to the text of this book, the selection of pictures exemplifies some major stylistic elements of allegorical painting. The selection is intended to illuminate the theory of literary allegory I have presented, an aim justified because there has always been a tendency among critics to refer fable and parable to analogous visual counterparts and justified further because I have shown that ritualized, iconographic stories tend toward points of fixation, their agents being transformed into static images. (The analogous process in painting is that whereby the imagery takes on so-called "literary" meanings.) Paintings need not employ traditional arcane emblems to be iconographic. The iconography can include familiar "odds and ends," which are not in themselves allegorical. The represented elements do not, as individual items, introduce the allegorical enigma; rather their ordering, especially discontinuity in their relations, creates the enigma.

The selection is presented without regard for strict historical continuity, the pictures being arranged in seven groups, each designed to emphasize a major parallel with literary theory. Moreover, in every picture is to be found that element of allegory which subsumes all the others, namely, isolation of parts—the use of encapsulated visual units within a larger frame so as to produce a studied discontinuity within the whole. This "isolation" is a direct consequence of ornamental imagery (Group I), daemonic abstraction (Group II), and an overall surrealism (Group VII). Collateral to such a style is the use of sublime and picturesque landscape (Groups III, IV, and V) and of monumental forms and ritual repetitions (Groups IV and VI).

In the notes to the paintings there will be found a brief commentary on the formal elements for which each picture was chosen, with occasional notes on iconographic content as well. Particular comments are grouped under the general headings, I–VII, but a degree of cross reference within the total number should be assumed. Here the form and placement of emblems matters more than their specific provenance. Unlike the art historian, who would be interested in the ancient religious origins of an emblem, I wish primarily to show the inherently surreal form of the paintings, as a key to the process by which they convey an allegorical message.

The reader may wish to know something of the context from which the selection of pictures is drawn. No such group of thirty-two illustrations can pretend to be comprehensive, and I would like therefore to note a number of excellent examples which are left out.

Medieval book illuminations, church decorations, domestic and public tapestries are all repositories of daemonic devices and magical impresas. Much medieval Western art, like Byzantine art, is ritualized, daemonic, and ornamental to a degree that immediately bears out my theory of allegory. Alchemical and theosophical art is devoted to the rendering of magic symbols in visual form, as in the tarot cards; the total number of illustrations from this source would be almost inexhaustible. But while certain medieval religious images are perhaps even too conventional, certain magical devices are too eccentric to provide a standard group.

In choosing among the great pictorial allegorists, I have tended to favor works which are not often reproduced; for that reason I have necessarily omitted many well-known allegorists: e.g., Ambrogio Lorenzetti, Piero di Cosimo, Giovanni Bellini, Perugino, Mantegna, Botticelli, Titian, and Veronese. Bosch, Brueghel, Goya,

. Peter Blume. *Elemosina* (1933). (Collection, The Museum of Modern Art, New York, gift of Mrs. John D. Rockefeller, Jr.)

2. Carlo Crivelli (*ca.* 1435–*ca.* 1493).
Saint George. (The Metropolitan Museum
of Art, Rogers Fund, 1905.)

3. Rembrandt van Rijn (1606–1669). *Bellona*. (The Metropolitan Museum of Art, Michael Friedsam Collection, 1931.)

4. Girolamo dai Libri (1474–1555). Detail of *Madonna and Child with Sa*
(The Metropolitan Museum of Art, Fletcher Fund, 1920.)

5. Lorenzo Costa (*ca.* 1460–1535). *Saint Lucy.* (The Metropolitan Museum of Art, Theodore M. Davis Collection, bequest of Theodore M. Davis, 1915.)

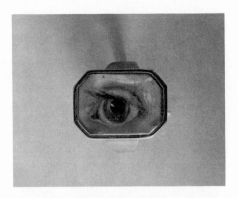

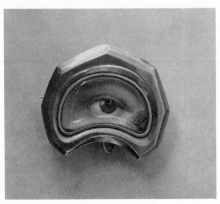

6. British artist, unknown (eighteenth century). Three water colors on ivory, each entitled *Miniature of an Eye*. (The Metropolitan Museum of Art, gift of Mr. and Mrs. John W. Starr, 1954.)

Odilon Redon (1840–1916). *The Eye like a Strange Balloon Moves towards Infinity,* Plate I from *To Edgar Poe,* 1882.   (Collection, The Museum of Modern Art, New York, gift of Peter H. Deitsch.)

8. Albrecht Dürer (1471–1528). *Nemesis*. (Prints Division, New York Public Library.)

Giovanni Battista Tiepolo (1696–1770). *Juno and Selene.* (The Metropolitan Museum of Art, gift of Lillian S. Timken, 1951.)

10. Jean Léon Gérôme (1824–1904). *Pygmalion and Galatea*. (The Metropolitan Museum of Art, gift of Louis C. Raegner, 1927.)

11. Gustave Moreau (1826–1898). *Oedipus and the Sphinx.*
(The Metropolitan Museum of Art, bequest of William B.
Herriman, 1921.)

12. Max Ernst. *Napoleon in the Wilderness* (1941). (Collection, The Museum
of Modern Art, New York.)

13. Max Ernst. *Nature at Daybreak* (1938). (Collection, The Museum of Modern Art, New York.)

14. Nicolas Poussin (1594–1665). *The Blind Orion Searching for the Rising Sun.* (The Metropolitan Museum of Art, Fletcher Fund, 1924.)

15. Thomas Cole (1801–1848). *The Titan's Goblet*. (The Metropolitan Museum of Art, gift of Samuel Avery, Jr., 1904.)

16. Thomas Cole (1801–1848). *The Course of Empire: I—Savage State or Commencement of Empire.* (Courtesy of the New-York Historical Society, New York City.)

17. *The Course of Empire: II—Arcadian or Pastoral State.* (Courtesy of the New-York Historical Society, New York City.)

18. *The Course of Empire: III—Consummation of Empire.* (Courtesy of the New-York Historical Society, New York City.)

19. *The Course of Empire: IV—Destruction.* (Courtesy of the New-York Historical Society, New York City.)

20. *The Course of Empire: V—Desolation.* (Courtesy of the New-York Historical Society, New York City.)

21. Peter Blume. *The Eternal City* (1937). (Collection, The Museum of Modern Art, New York, Mrs. Simon Guggenheim Fund.)

22. Albrecht Dürer (1471–1528). *Triumphal Arch*. (Prints Division, New York Public Library.)

23. Erastus Salisbury Field (1805–1900). *Historical Monument of the American Republic.* (The Morgan Wesson Memorial Collection, Museum of Fine Arts, Springfield, Massachusetts.)

24. Giovanni Paolo Pannini (1691–1765). *Ancient Rome.* (The Metropolitan Museum of Art, Gwynne M. Andrews Fund, 1952.)

25. Giovanni Paolo Pannini. *Renaissance Rome.* (The Metropolitan Museum of Art, Gwynne M. Andrews Fund, 1952.)

26. Lorenzo Monaco (*ca.* 1370–1425). *Pietà*. (Galleria Accademia,
Florence.)

27. Italian artist, unknown (fourteenth century). *Madonna della Misericordia* (statue in polychrome wood). (Museo Nazionale, Florence.)

28.   Carlo Crivelli (*ca.* 1435–*ca.* 1493).   *Madonna and Child.*   (The Metropolitan Museum of Art, Jules S. Bache Collection, 1949.)

PVS·KAROLI·CRIVELLI·VENETI

29. Girolamo dai Libri (1474–1555). *Madonna and Child with Saints* (Catherine, Leonard, Augustine, Apollonia). (The Metropolitan Museum of Art, Fletcher Fund, 1920.)

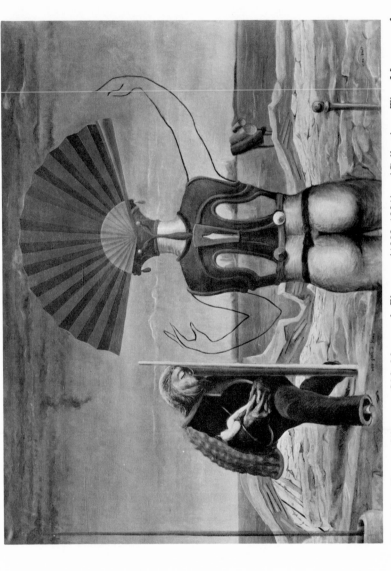

30. Max Ernst. *Woman, Old Man and Flower* (1923–1924). (Collection, The Museum of Modern Art, New York.)

31. Paul Delvaux. *Phases of the Moon* (1939). (Collection, The Museum of Modern Art, New York.)

32. Giorgio de Chirico. *The Great Metaphysician* (1917). (Collection, The Museum of Modern Art, New York.)

and Rousseau also all have been concerned with the daemonic. Dali, perhaps the best-known surrealist of our century, may well occur to the reader, since in both his practice and theoretical writings he has insisted on the obsessional, iconographic nature of surrealist art. In lieu of such a well-known figure I have stressed the work of Max Ernst. Yet another type of allegorical imagery often reproduced in monographs (those of Panofsky, Seznec, Wind, Praz, and others) is found in the Renaissance emblem books.

Certain celebrated allegorical occasions would be represented in a comprehensive history of the visual mode: conflicts of virtues and vices, triumphal processions and festivals in the Renaissance masques, temptation scenes like the portrayals of St. Anthony, topical cartoons and caricatures of political and social intent.

A number of special cases, relevant to a larger display of visual allegory, are worth mentioning. Giuseppe Arcimboldo (ca. 1530–1593) painted fantastic allegorical heads and daemonic landscapes—*paysages moralisés*—which have opened the way to several modern artists, particularly the American "magic realists." The development of operatic and dramatic decor, especially in the masques (e.g., those of Inigo Jones), at once supports a theory stressing the ritual side of emblematic expression; similarly the costuming and caricaturing of the *commedia dell'arte*, as shown in the etchings of Jacques Callot (1592–1635), demonstrate the functioning of the grotesque in this mode. Beside the highly ornamental art of Moreau, here represented by the relatively austere *Oedipus and the Sphinx*, one might set the landscape scenes of that late master of the picturesque, Rudolphe Bresdin. Finally, beside the work of the surrealists one might set the work of Fuseli, Blake, and a number of Pre-Raphaelites who experimented in depicting dream experience and its links with the documentary style of "magic realism."

These are the great riches of art from which the thirty-two illustrative pictures are drawn. This selection, I believe, will give a sharp idea of the same devices that I have been following in literary works.

I. *Kosmos*

1. Peter Blume. *Elemosina* (1933).
2. Carlo Crivelli (*ca.* 1435–*ca.* 1493). *Saint George.*
3. Rembrandt van Rijn (1606–1669). *Bellona.*
4. Girolamo dai Libri (1474–1555). Detail of *Madonna and Child with Saints.*
5. Lorenzo Costa (*ca.* 1460–1535). *Saint Lucy.*
6. British artist, unknown (eighteenth century). Three water colors on ivory, each entitled *Miniature of an Eye.*
7. Odilon Redon (1840–1916). *The Eye like a Strange Balloon Moves towards Infinity*, Plate I from *To Edgar Poe*, 1882.

This set of pictures emphasizes the use of kosmos, or allegorical ornament. *Elemosina* (Plate 1), Blume's sketch for *The Eternal City* (see also Plate 21) shows the Christ with his identifying crown of thorns and crucifix; but the painter takes kosmos further and drapes the suffering Christ with various emblems: rings, watches, opera glasses, swords, and hearts. These and another common feature of military decoration, the epaulet, are used to make an ornamental enclosure around the seated figure. These kosmoi encapsulate what vain man believes to be his power.

In Plates 2 and 3 the artists use fantastic armor, presumably possessed of magic powers, to clothe and protect the human body. The lion faces (Plate 2) imply that this is St. George the dragon-slayer; the Gorgon's head on Bellona's shield (Plate 3) that she is the goddess of war.

A different use of kosmos occurs in two details (Plate 4) from Dai Libri's *Madonna and Child with Saints* (see also Plate 29), where the robes of St. Leonard and St. Augustine are both decorated with talismanic pictures of other sacred figures, e.g., St. Veronica on Augustine's robe. St. Veronica in turn is shown carrying her emblematic handkerchief or towel, on which appears the picture of

Christ. This picture within a picture intensifies the magical effect of the ornamental process.

Costa's St. Lucy holding her own eyes (Plate 5) further extends the use of iconographic decoration. The magic baubles that are her eyes allude to her self-immolation, and thus contain her saintliness. Here, as in Del Cossa's *Saint Lucy* (see Ferguson, *Signs and Symbols in Christian Art*, Plate 79), the ornament is projected outside the human body. Redon's treatment of the eye (Plate 7) is cosmic in the usual sense. He draws the "eye of the universe," a macrocosmic eye. The eighteenth-century miniaturists had used the same emblem for talismanic adornments in the form of a ring or broaches that could be pinned on a dress (Plate 6).

II. *Daemonic Agents*

8. Albrecht Dürer (1471–1528). *Nemesis.*
9. Giovanni Battista Tiepolo (1696–1770). *Juno and Selene.*
10. Jean Léon Gérôme (1824–1904). *Pygmalion and Galatea.*
11. Gustave Moreau (1826–1898). *Oedipus and the Sphinx.*
12. Max Ernst. *Napoleon in the Wilderness* (1941).
13. Max Ernst. *Nature at Daybreak* (1938).

These six pictures all show the kind of daemonic agency that characterizes allegorical literature. Dürer shows Nemesis standing on the world over which she exercises fatal influence. She carries the emblems of her power. In Plate 9 the moon goddess Selene is identified by the "man in the moon," whom she supports. The picture displays the conflict between two daemonic forces, the Queen of Heaven and her changeful subject, Selene. Plate 10 employs a daemonic metamorphosis—the statue of Galatea is becoming possessed of life, while Eros (whom Plato had cited as the perfect case of a *daimon*) is shown causing the magical event. Moreau (Plate 11) develops another mythological subject into an allegory by actually showing a daemon, the Sphinx whose human half is contaminated by

373

the nonhuman power of its bestial lower part. The human half can also be seen as growing out of the body of Oedipus. The snake and the fantastic heads decorating the chalice are secondary magic agencies. In Plate 12 transmutations of human into vegetable (Napoleon and the woman become treelike forms) and mechanical into animal (the musical horn becomes a marvelous beast) show two sources of "daemonic modulation" (Frye, *Anatomy*, 156–157) that are common in Max Ernst's paintings. Here he furthermore depicts a sea monster whose tail is metamorphosed into a flower. His *Nature at Daybreak* (Plate 13) shows the most extreme daemonizing of nature. Several hierarchic levels of being emerge from the dense texture of foliage: claws and snouts of vermin, the head of a bird, monstrous jaws and other mouthlike features, the leg of a human being. These, like the daemonic figures in the other pictures in this group, all show considerable ornamental intricacy.

III. *Titanic Power in the Sublime*

14. Nicolas Poussin (1594–1665). *The Blind Orion Searching for the Rising Sun.*
15. Thomas Cole (1801–1848). *The Titan's Goblet.*

These two paintings depict what eighteenth-century theorists would call sublime landscapes. Such landscapes symbolize extreme cosmic power (see Burke, *Inquiry*, II, 5). As a result they provide an appropriate setting for the particular allegories presented here. The physical strength of the giant Orion is limited by the fault of his blindness. Poussin contrasts this force with the puny strength of the man who nevertheless, not being blind, has the power to guide the elemental force on whose shoulders he stands. Artemis, whom Orion had challenged in athletic contest, watches from a distant cloud.

The pictorial effect of joining a sublime landscape with an allegorical subject becomes more obvious in *The Titan's Goblet.*

Here the emblem of titanic force, the giant's goblet, grows out of the landscape itself. Cole depicts minute temples, dwellings, sailing vessels, a lake, all supported by the goblet, emphasizing its colossal size. (On such minutiae see Burke, *Inquiry*, II, 7.) As an example of enigma in this picture, consider the concepts of time held by man and the giant. On the rim of the goblet is a flourishing civilization, totally developed, presumably, since the Titan last took a sip.

IV. *Thomas Cole: The Sublime and the Picturesque*

16. Thomas Cole (1801–1848). *The Course of Empire: I—Savage State or Commencement of Empire.*
17. *The Course of Empire: II—Arcadian or Pastoral State.*
18. *The Course of Empire: III—Consummation of Empire.*
19. *The Course of Empire: IV—Destruction.*
20. *The Course of Empire: V—Desolation.*

This series constitutes a cycle and therefore the ritual recurrence of "the course of empire." In depicting the cyclical phases Cole has deployed all the techniques of both sublime and picturesque art. He begins with a scene of untamed nature (Plate 16), where man is a barbarous hunter whose power over his environment is minimal. The cloud formations and the giant rock in the background suggest the immensity of nature, the relative weakness of man. Plate 17, *Arcadian State,* shows a picturesque scene of farmers, shepherds, shepherdesses, children at play, and combines these with two other examples of nascent civilization, the philosopher drawing geometric designs in the sand and the Druidic temple at the center of the painting. The theme of cultural development is thus established in the actions portrayed. These actions are paralleled by a change from a sublime to a picturesque landscape. Yet this general softening of the landscape from a terrifying, hostile environment to one that is ordered, grazed, and trimmed, does not go so far as to diminish wholly the sublime authority of the towering mountains.

375

It is essential to the idea of cultural development that we see the terrain undergoing change without losing the identifying marks of sameness. Cole establishes this sameness by using the giant rock a second time. The rock becomes an identifying device, and it will be found to reappear in all five pictures, though always from a slightly different point of view. Since it does not change throughout the cycle, it may also represent "unchanging nature," contrasted with the rise and fall of the human construct.

Consummation of Empire (Plate 18) marks the triumphal high point of the cycle. Here the sublime in nature is replaced, with the sole exception of the rock, by the sublime human artifact. Burke's *Inquiry* cites columned façades, great causeways, and magnificent displays of power, and these monuments all appear in this apotheosis of the imperial venture. Nature has been decorated by man, while he has erected statues of his gods (the daemons of empire) and has ornamented his own constructions with drapery, plants, and monstrous fountains.

Perhaps the most perfectly sublime of the five paintings, *Destruction* (Plate 19), represents immense powers equal to those required to build the city. Terror and astonishment of the kind Cole imagines here are the first cause of the sublime cited by Burke (*Inquiry*, II, 1 and 2). Throughout the cycle Cole has shown the daemonizing of religion, and here he treats the destruction of the city as an iconoclastic, savage assault. In *Desolation* (Plate 20) uncontrolled nature reasserts itself. Man is totally absent; only the relics of his past, ruined and decaying, remain. These ruined monuments are decorated by a mantle of vegetation. The cycle has come to an end.

This last painting serves to illustrate a special problem raised by Price. In *Desolation* the sublime modality gives way to a special type of picturesque: not that of the "improvers," which Price attacked and which was one aspect of the *Arcadian State*, but Price's "roughness," "deformity," and decay. He notes that scenes of ruin and dissolution are picturesque, since their textural intricacy and daemonic forms produce an ambivalent pleasure in the beholder. Vines and shrubbery are ornamental to look at, but they are also threatening, inasmuch as they seem destined to encroach finally on human works. They reassert daemonic nature, the essence of Price's conception.

V. *A Modern Allegory*

21. Peter Blume. *The Eternal City* (1937).

Blume employs all the devices exemplified in the foregoing illustrations. His Christ, imprisoned in a shrine (see Plate 1), is highly ornamental—the microcosmos of the whole design. His Mussolini is a green-faced devil with a dragon's tail, a "machine" in the form of a jack-in-the-box. Fragments of statuary suggest daemonic mutations of human beings, while the bandaged leg of the beggar woman, left foreground, makes her look partially statuesque. The far background shows sublime mountains, while the foreground and center show picturesque ruins. Blume has contracted the whole cycle of the course of empire into one single canvas. A. H. Barr (*What Is Modern Painting?* [New York, 1946], 39) observes that this work is prophetic; it could be analyzed in terms of "visionary ritual."

VI. *Allegorical Monuments*

22. Albrecht Dürer (1471–1528). *Triumphal Arch.*
23. Erastus Salisbury Field (1805–1900). *Historical Monument of the American Republic.*
24. Giovanni Paolo Pannini (1691–1765). *Ancient Rome.*
25. Giovanni Paolo Pannini. *Renaissance Rome.*

Of the *Triumphal Arch* of Maximilian I (Plate 22), Panofsky has said, "The iconography of this fantastic structure employs all known devices of glorification, from the simple recording of historical events to cryptic emblematic allusions" (*Albrecht Dürer*, 176–177).

The Arch is about three meters high, allowing innumerable very meticulous kosmoi a niche in its ritualized mosaic of patterns. The symmetrically placed "windows" show us scenes of German and Roman history, heraldic coats of arms, daemonic birds, beasts, and plants, relief statues of men, written commentaries on the allegory of the whole, a genealogy and apotheosis of the Emperor. Everywhere we find magical "doubling." All these devices are also apparent in Field's *Historical Monument* (Plate 23), though more grandiosely presented. Field's daemonic agencies reflect an advance in technology: between the tops of the towers he has steam locomotives running on steel bridges.

As the rhetorical device of hierarchical ranking, allegory often shows us ideal monuments—the status symbols—of a culture. These appear in Pannini's two interiors (Plates 24–25), where each decorative panel that clothes the wall, and each piece of sculpture, is a specific monument to past glory. The walls are, as it were, punctured by windows through which we see memorial images of an idealized past. In another sense the salon is a fantastic museum where the artist has collected the Pantheon, the Colosseum, the Laocoön group, the Dying Gaul, and so on, of ancient Rome—Michelangelo's Moses, the Bernini fountains and statues, the St. Peter's, of Renaissance and baroque Rome. Pannini's scheme, by isolating each image in a segmented architectural fabric, makes an ornate ritual out of the catalogue. This is more than a pictorial guidebook; each monument has magical efficacy, each is a kratophany. Ritual furthermore appears in the symmetrical "doubling" of the two periods of time: The ancient and Renaissance salons are back to back in an isomorphic parallel, suggesting the magical or fatalistic destiny of the Eternal City. The first two could be followed by a third, *Modern Rome*.

VII. *Surrealism in Old and New Allegories*

26. Lorenzo Monaco (*ca.* 1370–1425). *Pietà*.
27. Italian artist, unknown (fourteenth century). *Madonna della Misericordia*.

28. Carlo Crivelli (*ca.* 1435–*ca.* 1493). *Madonna and Child.*
29. Girolamo dai Libri (1474–1555). *Madonna and Child with Saints.*
30. Max Ernst. *Woman, Old Man and Flower* (1923–1924).
31. Paul Delvaux. *Phases of the Moon* (1939).
32. Giorgio de Chirico. *The Great Metaphysician* (1917).

The term "surrealism" denotes a school of twentieth-century painters whose manifestos and whose practice indicate an approximate definition of the term: it implies obsessional and dream imagery, unexpected even shocking collocations of heterogeneous objects, psychological emblems (usually Freudian), hyperdefinite draftsmanship, distortions of perspective—with all these working together to produce enigmatic combinations of materials. Above all, discontinuity and unnatural groupings seem to characterize surreal art. Objects quite "real" in themselves become "nonreal," i.e., surreal, by virtue of their mutual interrelations, or rather, through their apparent lack of rational interrelation when combined within single frames. This deliberately enigmatic, teasing, strange style is to be found, as this brief selection indicates, in early allegories as well.

Lorenzo Monaco's *Pietà* (Plate 26) collects in one picture a large number of fantastically dismembered, isolated, and encapsulated items, all of which are emblems of the Passion. The clarity of demarcation produces a "magic realism." The wood statue of the Madonna della Misericordia (Plate 27), though conventional in iconography, displays extreme disproportion of scale. The bizarre cloak of the Madonna is a hierarchical system, its surrealistic "little people" born of the theological idea that they are helpless children protected by the enfolding skirts of the Madonna. This same "absurdity" appears in the oversize fly (an emblem of mortality) in Plate 28. Here the fruit, emblematic of peace, favor, and fertility, has an excessive clarity and massiveness. In Plate 29 the religious allegory is so traditional that one fails to note how fantastic is the collection of pictorial elements. The landscape, the peacock, the symmetrical shape of the olive tree, the accoutrements of the saints, the pictures on their vestments (see Plate 4)—all these could only be "real" to those of us who are habituated to Christian iconography. Since we are habituated, we normally fail to notice how unnatural is the scene presented.

Because his iconography is unfamiliar, Ernst's *Woman, Old Man and Flower* (Plate 30) must force the viewer to accept a shocking discontinuity of elements. Daemonic mutations, baffling transparencies, nightmarish shapes make up this typically surreal modern painting. The "flower" is a statuesque mannequin whose armored vest and arms are windows onto the landscape. Like Delvaux, Ernst aims at enigma. Delvaux's women in *Phases of the Moon* (Plate 31) are oblivious of their nakedness, as are the two men—the ritual unfolds in a trance. Delvaux combines fantasy with meticulous naturalistic rendering of detail, a combination which is more or less synonymous with surrealism. The same obsessional fantasy predominates in De Chirico's *The Great Metaphysician* (Plate 32), where the buildings have mysterious façades, and the allegorical "machine" in the foreground, an Arcimboldesque statue, is a "composed" body made of concretized ideas. Extreme isolation of parts forces us to ask: What is the metaphysic represented by this allegory? And when we answer the riddle, we do so in terms of the elements thus isolated.

Bibliography

THIS bibliography lists the editions used, not always showing the date and place of initial publication. It is not intended as a complete, or even approximately complete, bibliography of books, articles, and other texts pertaining to the study of allegory.

Abraham, Karl. *Traum und Mythus.* Vienna, 1909.

Abrams, M. H. *The Mirror and the Lamp: Romantic Theory and the Critical Tradition.* New York, 1953.

Adams, Robert M. *Strains of Discord: Studies in Literary Openness.* Ithaca, 1958.

Adorno, T. W., E. Frenkel-Brunswik, *et al. The Authoritarian Personality.* New York, 1950.

Aichinger, Ilse. *The Bound Man and Other Stories.* Tr. by Eric Mosbacher. New York, 1956.

Alanus de Insulis (Alain de Lille). *The Complaint of Nature (De Planctu Naturae).* Tr. by Douglas Moffat. ("Yale Studies in English Literature," XXXVI.) New York, 1908.

Alexander, P. J. "The Iconoclastic Council of St. Sophia (815) and Its Definition (*Horos*)," *Dumbarton Oaks Papers,* Number 7. Cambridge, Mass., 1953.

Amis, Kingsley. *New Maps of Hell.* New York, 1960.

Anastos, M. V. "The Ethical Theory of Images Formulated by the Iconoclasts in 754 and 815," *Dumbarton Oaks Papers,* Number 8. Cambridge, Mass., 1954.

BIBLIOGRAPHY

Andrew, S. O. *Syntax and Style in Old English*. Cambridge, 1940.

Aristotle. *The Ethics of Aristotle (The Nicomachean Ethics)*. Tr. by J. A. K. Thomson. Penguin ed., 1958.

———. *The Poetics. (Works,* XI.) Ed. by W. D. Ross; tr. by Ingram Bywater. Oxford, 1924.

———. *The Rhetoric. (Works,* XI.) Ed. by W. D. Ross; tr. by W. R. Roberts. Oxford, 1924.

Athanasius, St. *Life of St. Antony*. Tr. by R. T. Meyer. Westminster, Md., 1950.

Auden, W. H. *The Collected Poetry of W. H. Auden*. New York, 1945.

———. "The Guilty Vicarage: Notes on the Detective Story, by an Addict," in *The Critical Performance*. Ed. by S. E. Hyman. New York, 1956.

Auerbach, Erich. *Dante: Poet of the Secular World*. Tr. by Ralph Manheim. Chicago, 1961.

———. *"Figura,"* in *Scenes from the Drama of European Literature: Six Essays*. New York, 1959.

———. *Mimesis: The Representation of Reality in Western Literature*. Tr. by W. R. Trask. Anchor ed., New York, 1957; originally published Princeton, 1953.

Augustine, St. *The City of God*. Tr. by G. E. McCracken. Loeb Classics ed., Cambridge, Mass., 1957.

Balakian, Anna. *Surrealism: The Road to the Absolute*. New York, 1959.

Baltrusaitis, Jurgis. *Aberrations: Quatre essais sur la légende des formes*. Paris, 1958.

———. *Anamorphoses ou perspectives curieuses*. Paris, 1955.

———. *Le Moyen age fantastique*. Paris, 1955.

Barfield, Owen. *Poetic Diction*. London, 1952.

Bate, W. J. *The Achievement of Samuel Johnson*. New York, 1955.

Baumgarten, A. G. *Reflections on Poetry*. Tr., with the original text, and ed. by Karl Aschenbrenner and W. B. Holther. Berkeley, 1954.

Beach, J. W. *Obsessive Images: Symbolism in Poetry of the 1930's and 1940's*. Minneapolis, 1960.

Beckford, William. *Vathek: An Arabian Tale,* in *Shorter Novels of the Eighteenth Century*. Ed. by Philip Henderson. London, 1956.

Beer, J. B. *Coleridge the Visionary*. London, 1959.

BIBLIOGRAPHY

Bentham, Jeremy. *Handbook of Political Fallacies.* Ed. with a preface by H. A. Larrabee. Baltimore, 1952.

Berger, Harry. *The Allegorical Temper: Vision and Reality in Book II of Spenser's* Faerie Queene. New Haven, 1957.

The Bestiary. Tr. by T. H. White. New York, 1954.

Bezankis, Abraham. "An Introduction to the Problem of Allegory in Literary Criticism." Unpublished Ph.D. dissertation, University of Michigan, 1955.

Black, Max. *Models and Metaphors: Studies in Language and Philosophy.* Ithaca, 1962.

Blair, Hugh. *Lectures on Rhetoric and Belles Lettres.* Edinburgh, 1783.

Blake, William. *Complete Writings.* Ed. by Geoffrey Keynes. London, 1957.

Bloom, Edward. "The Allegorical Principle," *Journal of English Literary History* [hereafter abbreviated as *ELH*], XVIII (1951).

Bloom, Harold. *Blake's Apocalypse.* New York, 1963.

———. *Shelley's Mythmaking.* New Haven, 1959.

Bloomfield, M. W. *The Seven Deadly Sins.* East Lansing, 1952.

Boaden, James, ed. *Memoirs of Mrs. Inchbald: Including Her Familiar Correspondence with the Most Distinguished Persons of Her Time.* London, 1833.

Boccaccio, Giovanni. *Genealogy of the Gods,* Book XIV, sec. 12. Tr. as *Boccaccio on Poetry,* by C. G. Osgood. Princeton, 1930.

Bodkin, Maud. *Archetypal Patterns in Poetry: Psychological Studies of Imagination.* London, 1934; reprinted New York, 1958.

Bodsworth, Fred. *The Strange One.* New York, 1959.

Boethius. *The Consolation of Philosophy.* With an introduction by Irwin Edman. Modern Library ed., New York, 1943.

Boisacq, Emile. *Dictionnaire étymologique de la langue grècque.* Paris and Heidelberg, 1938.

Borges, J. L. "The Fearful Sphere of Pascal," *Noonday 3.* New York, 1960.

Bowra, C. M. *From Virgil to Milton.* London, 1948.

Brecht, Bertolt. *Selected Poems.* Tr. by H. R. Hays. New York, 1959.

Brée, Germaine, and Margaret Guiton. *An Age of Fiction.* New Brunswick, 1957.

Bronson, Bertrand. "Personification Reconsidered," *ELH,* XIV (1947).

383

BIBLIOGRAPHY

Brooke-Rose, Christine. *A Grammar of Metaphor.* London, 1958.

Brooks, Cleanth, and R. P. Warren. *Understanding Poetry.* New York, 1950.

Brower, Reuben. *Alexander Pope: The Poetry of Allusion.* Oxford, 1959.

Browne, Sir Thomas. *The Pseudodoxia Epidemica.* (*Works,* II, III, V.) Ed. by Geoffrey Keynes. London, 1928–1931.

——. *Religio Medici.* Ed. by J.-J. Denonain. Cambridge, 1953.

——. *Urne Buriall and The Garden of Cyrus.* Ed. by John Carter. Cambridge, 1958.

Bruyne, Edgar de. *L'Esthétique du moyen age.* (An abbreviated version of *Etudes d'esthétique médiévale.*) Louvain, 1947.

——. *Etudes d'esthétique médiévale.* Bruges, 1946.

Buchan, John. *A History of English Literature.* New York, 1923.

Buchanan, Scott. *Symbolic Distance in Relation to Analogy and Fiction.* London, 1932.

Bukofzer, Manfred. "Allegory in Baroque Music," *Journal of the Warburg Institute,* III (1939–1940), nos. 1–2.

——. "Speculative Thinking in Mediaeval Music," *Speculum,* XVII (April 1942).

Burke, Edmund. *A Philosophical Inquiry into the Origins of the Sublime and the Beautiful.* World's Classics ed., London, 1906–1907; reprinted 1920 and 1925.

Burke, Kenneth. *The Philosophy of Literary Form: Studies in Symbolic Action.* New York, 1957.

——. *A Rhetoric of Motives.* New York, 1955.

Burckhardt, Jacob. *The Age of Constantine the Great.* Tr. by Moses Hadas. New York, 1949.

——. *The Civilization of the Renaissance in Italy.* Ed. by B. Nelson and N. Trinkhaus; tr. by S. G. C. Middlemore. New York, 1958.

Burnet, John. *Early Greek Philosophy.* New York, 1957.

Burton, Robert. *The Anatomy of Melancholy.* Ed. by Floyd Dell and P. Jordan-Smith. New York, 1927; reprinted 1948.

Bush, Douglas. *Mythology and the Renaissance Tradition in English Poetry.* Minneapolis and London, 1932.

Butler, Samuel. *Life and Habit.* New York, 1910.

Calderón de la Barca. *Four Plays.* Tr. by Edwin Honig. New York, 1961.

Campbell, George. *The Philosophy of Rhetoric.* London, 1776.

BIBLIOGRAPHY

Campbell, Joseph. *The Hero with a Thousand Faces.* New York, 1949.

Campbell, L. B., ed. *The Mirror for Magistrates.* New York, 1960.

Camus, Albert. *L'Exil et le royaume.* Paris, 1957.

Čapek, Karel. *In Praise of Newspapers.* Tr. by M. and R. Weatherall. New York, 1951.

——. *War with the Newts.* Tr. by M. and R. Weatherall. New York, 1959.

——, and Josef Čapek. *R.U.R. and the Insect Play.* Tr. by P. Selver. London, 1961.

Casa, Giovanni della. *Galateo: or, The Book of Manners.* Tr. by R. S. Pine-Coffin. Penguin ed., 1958.

Cassirer, Ernst. *An Essay on Man.* New York, 1953.

——. *The Philosophy of Symbolic Forms.* New Haven, 1955.

Castelli, Enrico, ed. *Christianismo e ragion di stato: L'Umanesimo e il demoniaco nell'arte.* Rome, 1953.

Castiglione, Baldassare. *The Book of the Courtier.* Tr. by C. S. Singleton. New York, 1959.

Chambers, William. *Dissertation on Oriental Gardening* (1772), quoted in A. O. Lovejoy, "The Chinese Origin of a Romanticism," *Essays in the History of Ideas.* New York, 1960.

Chapin, C. F. *Personification in Eighteenth-Century English Poetry.* New York, 1955.

Charney, Maurice. *Shakespeare's Roman Plays: The Function of Imagery in the Drama.* Cambridge, Mass., 1961.

Chastel, André. *Marsile Ficin et l'art.* Paris, 1954.

Chenu, M. D. *La Théologie au douzième siècle.* Paris, 1957.

Cicero, Marcus Tullius. *The Orator (De Oratore).* Ed. and tr. by E. W. Sutton and H. Rackham. Loeb Classics ed., London, 1948.

——. *Rhetorica ad Herennium.* Ed. and tr. by Harry Caplan. Loeb Classics ed., Cambridge, Mass., 1954.

Clark, Kenneth. *The Nude: A Study in Ideal Form.* New York, 1959.

Cochrane, C. N. *Christianity and Classical Culture: A Study of Thought and Action from Augustus to Augustine.* New York, 1957.

Cohen, Morris, and Ernest Nagel. *An Introduction to Logic and Scientific Method.* New York, 1934.

Coleridge, S. T. *Essays and Lectures on Shakespeare and Some Other Old Poets and Dramatists.* Everyman ed., London, 1907.

——. *Miscellaneous Criticism.* Ed. by T. M. Raysor. London, 1936.

——. *The Statesman's Manual.* (*Complete Works*, VI.) Ed. by W. G. T. Shedd. New York, 1875.

Collingwood, R. G. *The Idea of Nature.* New York, 1960.

Comparetti, Domenico. *Vergil in the Middle Ages.* Tr. by E. F. M. Benecke. London, 1895.

Constandse, A. L. *Le Baroque espagnol et Calderón de la Barca.* Amsterdam, 1951.

Cooper, Lane. *Aristotelian Papers.* Ithaca, 1939.

Cornford, F. M. *Origins of Attic Comedy.* Introduction by Theodor Gaster. New York, 1961.

——. *From Religion to Philosophy.* New York, 1957.

——. *The Unwritten Philosophy.* Ed. by W. K. C. Guthrie. Cambridge, 1950.

"Cronaca prima d'anonimo," *Il Tumulto dei Ciompi.* ("Rerum Italicarum Scriptores," XVIII, iii.) Ed. by Gino Scaramella. Bologna, 1934.

Cruttwell, R. W. *Virgil's Mind at Work.* Oxford, 1946.

Cudworth, Ralph. *The True Intellectual System of the Universe* (1678). Ed. with a translation of the notes of J. L. Mosheim, by John Harrison. London, 1845.

Cumont, Franz. *After Life in Roman Paganism* (1922). Tr. by H. D. Irvine. New York, 1959.

——. *Astrology and Religion among the Greeks and Romans* (1912). Tr. by J. B. Baker. New York, 1960.

Curtius, Ernst. *European Literature and the Latin Middle Ages.* Tr. by W. R. Trask. New York, 1953.

——. "The Poetry of Jorge Guillén," *Hudson Review*, Summer, 1954.

Cyprian, St. "The Dress of Virgins," in *The Fathers of the Church*, XXXVI. Tr. and ed. by R. J. Deferrari. New York, 1958.

——. "That Idols Are Not Gods," in *The Fathers of the Church*, XXXVI. Tr. and ed. by R. J. Deferrari. New York, 1958.

——. "On the Unity of the Catholic Church," in *The Library of Christian Classics*, V. London, 1956.

Danby, J. F. *Poets on Fortune's Hill: Studies in Sidney, Shakespeare, Beaumont and Fletcher.* London, 1952.

Daniélou, Jean. "Le Démoniaque et la raison d'état," in *Christianismo e ragion di stato.* Ed. by Enrico Castelli. Rome, 1953.

——. *Philon d'Alexandre.* Paris, 1958.

BIBLIOGRAPHY

——. *Platonisme et théologie mystique: Essai sur la doctrine spirituelle de St. Grégoire de Nysse*. Paris, 1944.

Dante Alighieri. *Eleven Letters*. Tr. by C. S. Latham. Boston and New York, 1892.

D'Arcy, M. C. *The Mind and Heart of Love*. New York, 1947.

Darwin, Erasmus. *The Temple of Nature, or, The Origin of Society*. London, 1803.

Davis, B. E. C. *Edmund Spenser: A Critical Study*. Cambridge, 1933.

Davy, M.-M. *Essai sur la symbolique romane: XII siècle*. Paris, 1955.

Defoe, Daniel. *Serious Reflections of Robinson Crusoe with His Vision of the Angelic World*. London, 1790.

De la Mare, Walter. *Desert Islands and Robinson Crusoe*. London, 1930.

Déonna, Waldemar. *Du Miracle grec au miracle chrétien: Classiques et primitivistes dans l'art*. Basel, 1956.

Dieckmann, Liselotte. "Renaissance Hieroglyphics," *Comparative Literature*, IX (1957), no. 4.

Disraeli, Isaac. *Amenities of Literature*. London, 1859.

Dodds, E. R. *The Greeks and the Irrational*. Berkeley, 1951.

Donatus, Aelius. "On Comedy and Tragedy," in *European Theories of the Drama*. Ed. by Barrett Clark. New York, 1947.

Drayton, Michael. *Works*. Ed. by J. W. Hebel. Oxford, 1931.

Dubos, J. B. *Critical Reflections on Poetry, Painting and Music* (1719). Tr. by Thomas Nugent. London, 1748.

Duncan, H. D. *Language and Literature in Society*. Chicago, 1953.

Durkheim, Emile. *The Elementary Forms of the Religious Life*. Tr. by J. W. Swain. Glencoe, Ill., 1947.

Dvornik, Francis. "The Patriarch Photius and Iconoclasm," *Dumbarton Oaks Papers*, Number 7. Cambridge, Mass., 1953.

Edelstein, Ludwig. "The Golden Chain of Homer," in *Studies in Intellectual History*. Baltimore, 1953.

Egerton, J. E. "King James's Beasts," *History Today*, XII (June, 1962).

Ehrenzweig, Anton. *The Psychoanalysis of Artistic Vision and Hearing*. London, 1953.

Einhard. *The Life of Charlemagne*. Tr. by S. E. Turner, with a foreword by Sidney Painter. Ann Arbor, 1960.

Eliade, Mircea. *Images et symboles*. Paris, 1952. (Tr. as *Images and Symbols* by Philip Mairet, New York, 1961.)

——. *The Myth of the Eternal Return*. Tr. by W. R. Trask. New York, 1954. (Reprinted as *Cosmos and History*, New York, 1959.)

——. *Myths, Dreams and Mysteries*. Tr. by Philip Mairet. London, 1960.

——. *The Sacred and the Profane*. Tr. by W. R. Trask. New York, 1961.

——. *Traité d'histoire des religions*. Paris, 1949. Tr. as *Patterns in Comparative Religion* by Rosemary Sheed. Chicago, 1958.

Elliott, Robert C. *The Power of Satire: Magic, Ritual, Art*. Princeton, 1960.

Elyot, Thomas. *Bibliotheca Eliotae: Eliotes Dictionarie*. Ed. by Thomas Cooper. London, 1559.

Empson, William. *Seven Types of Ambiguity*. London, 1930; reprinted New York, 1955.

——. *Some Versions of Pastoral*. New York, 1960.

——. *The Structure of Complex Words*. London, 1951.

Erlich, Victor. *Russian Formalism*. The Hague, 1955.

Evans, Joan. *Cluniac Art of the Romanesque Period*. Cambridge, 1950.

——. *Magical Jewels of the Middle Ages and the Renaissance, Particularly in England*. Oxford, 1922.

——. *Nature in Design: A Study of Naturalism in Decorative Art from the Bronze Age to the Renaissance*. London, 1933.

——. *Pattern: A Study of Ornament in Western Europe from 1180 to 1900*. Oxford, 1931.

Faral, Edmond. *Les Arts poétiques du XII et du XIII siècle*. Paris, 1924.

Feldman, A. B. "Zola and the Riddle of Sadism," *American Imago*, XIII, 1956.

Fenichel, Otto. *The Psychoanalytic Theory of the Neuroses*. New York, 1945.

Fernández, Ramón. *Messages*. Tr. by Montgomery Belgion. London, 1927.

Fisher, P. F. "Blake's Attacks on the Classical Tradition," *Philological Quarterly*, XL (Jan. 1961).

Fisher, Seymour, and S. E. Cleveland. *Body Image and Personality*. New York, 1958.

Fletcher, J. B. "Some Observations on the Changing Style of *The Faerie Queene*," *Studies in Philology*, XXX (1934).

Fletcher, Phineas. "The Purple Island," in *Poems*, IV. Ed. by Alexander Grosart. London, 1869.

Flores, Angel, and M. J. Benardete, eds. *Cervantes across the Centuries.* New York, 1947.

Flugel, J. C. *Man, Morals and Society.* New York, 1961.

——. *The Psychology of Clothes.* London, 1930.

——. *Studies in Feeling and Desire.* London, 1955.

Fontenrose, Joseph. *Python: A Study of Delphic Myth and Its Origins.* Berkeley and Los Angeles, 1959.

Fowlie, Wallace. "Mallarmé's Island Voyage," *Modern Philology,* XLVII (1950), no. 3.

Francis, W. N. *The Structure of American English.* New York, 1958.

Frank, R. W. "The Art of Reading Medieval Personification Allegory," *ELH,* XX (1953).

Frankfort, Henri. *Ancient Egyptian Religion.* New York, 1948.

——, J. A. Wilson, T. Jakobsen, and W. A. Irwin. *Before Philosophy.* Penguin ed., 1951.

Frazer, J. G. *The Golden Bough.* Abridged ed., New York, 1951.

——. *The New Golden Bough.* Ed. and abridged with notes by Theodor Gaster. New York, 1959.

Freeman, Rosemary. *English Emblem Books.* London, 1948.

Freud, Sigmund. "The Antithetical Sense of Primal Words" (1910), in *Collected Papers,* IV. Ed. by Joan Riviere. London, 1950.

——. *Basic Writings.* Ed. by A. A. Brill. Modern Library ed., New York, 1938.

——. *Beyond the Pleasure Principle.* Tr. by James Strachey. London, 1950.

——. *On Creativity and the Unconscious.* Ed. by Benjamin Nelson. New York, 1958.

——. "Dostoevsky and Parricide" (1928), in *Collected Papers,* V. Ed. by James Strachey. London, 1950.

——. "Formulations Regarding the Two Principles in Mental Functioning" (1911), in *Collected Papers,* IV. Ed. by Joan Riviere. London, 1950.

——. *The Interpretation of Dreams.* Tr. by James Strachey. New York, 1956.

——. "Negation" (1925), in *Collected Papers,* V. Ed. by James Strachey. London, 1950.

——. "Notes on a Case of Obsessional Neurosis" (1909), in *Collected Papers,* III. Tr. by A. and J. Strachey; ed. by Joan Riviere. London, 1950.

——. "Obsessive Acts and Religious Practices" (1907), in *Collected Papers*, II. Ed. by Joan Riviere. London, 1950.

——. *The Problem of Anxiety* (1926), in *Standard Edition of the Complete Psychological Works*, XX. Ed. by James Strachey. London, 1953–1962.

——. *The Psychopathology of Everyday Life* (1901), in *Standard Edition*, VI. London, 1953–1962.

——. "The Relation of the Poet to Day-Dreaming" (1908), in *Collected Papers*, IV. Ed. by Joan Riviere. London, 1950.

——. "Some Character-Types Met with in Psycho-Analytic Work" (1915), in *Collected Papers*, IV. Ed. by Joan Riviere. London, 1950.

——. "The Theme of the Three Caskets" (1913), in *Collected Papers*, IV. Ed. by Joan Riviere. London, 1950.

——. *Totem and Taboo*, in *Basic Writings*. Also in *Standard Edition*, XIII. Ed. and tr. by James Strachey. London, 1953–1962.

——. "The Unconscious" (1915), in *Collected Papers*, IV. Ed. by Joan Riviere. London, 1950.

Frye, Northrop. *Anatomy of Criticism: Four Essays*. Princeton, 1957.

——. *Fearful Symmetry: A Study of William Blake*. Princeton, 1947.

——. "Levels of Meaning in Literature," *Kenyon Review*, Spring, 1950.

——. "Myth as Information," *Hudson Review*, Summer, 1954.

——. "New Directions from Old," in *Myth and Mythmaking*. Ed. by Henry Murray. New York, 1960.

——. "Notes for a Commentary on *Milton*," in *The Divine Vision*. Ed. by V. de Sola Pinto. London, 1957.

——. "The Typology of *Paradise Regained*," *Modern Philology*, LIII.

Gascoigne, George. *The Steele Glas*, in *English Reprints, George Gascoigne, Esquire*. Ed. by Edward Arber. London, 1869.

Gelli, G. B. *Circe*. Tr. by Tom Brown; ed. with an introduction by R. M. Adams. Ithaca, 1963.

Giedion, Siegfried. *Architecture, You and Me: The Diary of a Development*. Cambridge, Mass., 1958.

Gierke, Otto. *Political Theories of the Middle Age*. Tr. by F. W. Maitland. Boston, 1959.

Givry, Grillot de. *A Pictorial Anthology of Witchcraft, Magic, and Alchemy*. Tr. by J. C. Locke. New Hyde Park, N.Y., 1958.

Glover, Edward. *Freud or Jung?* London, 1950.

——. "Sublimation, Substitution and Social Anxiety," *International Journal of Psychoanalysis*, XII (1931).

Goethe, J. W. *Faust: Part II.* Tr. by Philip Wayne. Penguin ed., Baltimore, 1959.

Golding, William. *Lord of the Flies.* New York, 1959.

——. *Pincher Martin.* London, 1956.

Gombrich, E. H. *Art and Illusion: A Study in the Psychology of Pictorial Representation.* New York, 1960.

Goodman, Paul. "Notes on a Remark of Seami," *Kenyon Review*, XX (1958), no. 4. (Also in *Utopian Essays and Practical Proposals*, New York, 1962.)

——. "The Real Dream," *Midstream*, V (1959), no. 1.

——. *Stop-Light: 5 Dance Poems.* Harrington Park, N.J., 1941.

——. *The Structure of Literature.* Chicago, 1954.

Gorchakov, N. A. *The Theatre in Soviet Russia.* Tr. by Edgar Lehrman. New York, 1957.

Grant, R. M. *The Letter and the Spirit.* London, 1957.

Grierson, H. J. C. *Cross Currents in English Literature of the Seventeenth Century.* London, 1929.

Grube, G. M. A. *Plato's Thought.* London, 1935; reprinted Boston, 1958.

Guthrie, W. K. C. *In the Beginning.* Ithaca, 1959.

Haarhof, T. J. *The Stranger at the Gate.* Oxford, 1948.

Hamilton, A. C. *The Structure of Allegory in* The Faerie Queene. Oxford, 1961.

Hanson, R. P. C. *Allegory and Event.* London, 1959.

Harington, John. *A New Discourse of a Stale Subject, called the Metamorphosis of Ajax.* Ed. by E. S. Donno. New York, 1962.

Hartman, Geoffrey. *The Unmediated Vision: An Interpretation of Wordsworth, Hopkins, Rilke, and Valéry.* New Haven, 1954.

Hastings, James. *Encyclopedia of Religion and Ethics.* New York, 1916.

Hawes, Stephen. *The Pastime* [original: *Passetyme*] *of Pleasure.* Ed. by W. E. Mead. London, 1928.

Hawthorne, Nathaniel. *Short Stories.* Ed. by Newton Arvin. New York, 1955.

Hazlitt, William. "On Chaucer and Spenser," in *Lectures on the English Poets.* (*Complete Works*, V.) Ed. by A. R. Waller and A. Glover.

London, 1902. (Also in *Hazlitt on English Literature*, ed. by Jacob Zeitlin, Oxford, 1913.)

Heinle, E. C. "The Eighteenth Century Allegorical Essay." Unpublished Ph.D. dissertation, Columbia University, 1957.

Hemmings, F. W. J. *Emile Zola*. Oxford, 1953.

Henryson, Robert. *Poems and Fables*. Ed. by H. H. Wood. Edinburgh and London, 1958.

Hesiod. *The Homeric Hymns and Homerica*. Tr. by H. G. Evelyn-White. Loeb Classics ed., London, 1929.

Hesse, Hermann. *The Journey to the East*. Tr. by Hilda Rosner. New York, 1957.

Hieatt, A. K. "The Daughters of Horus: Order in the Stanzas of *Epithalamion*," in *Form and Convention in the Poetry of Edmund Spenser*. (English Institute Essays.) Ed. by William Nelson. New York, 1961.

——. *Short Time's Endless Monument: The Symbolism of the Numbers in Edmund Spenser's* Epithalamion. New York, 1960.

Hinks, Roger. *Myth and Allegory in Ancient Art*. London, 1939.

Hirn, Yrjö. *The Sacred Shrine*. London, 1958.

Hobsbawm, E. S. *Social Bandits and Primitive Rebels*. Glencoe, Ill., 1959.

Holt, E. G. *A Documentary History of Art*. New York, 1957.

Homer. *The Iliad*. Tr. by Richmond Lattimore. Chicago, 1957.

Honig, Edwin. "Calderón's Strange Mercy Play," *Massachusetts Review*, III (Autumn 1961).

——. *Dark Conceit: The Making of Allegory*. Evanston, 1959.

Hopper, V. F. *Medieval Number Symbolism: Its Sources, Meaning and Influence on Thought and Expression*. New York, 1938.

Hoyle, Fred. *Astronomy*. New York, 1962.

——. *The Black Cloud*. New York, 1957.

Hubbard, L. R. *Dianetics*. New York, 1950.

Hugh of St. Victor. *Soliloquy on the Earnest Money of the Soul*. Tr. with an introduction by Kevin Herbert. Milwaukee, 1956.

Hughes, John. *An Essay on Allegorical Poetry*. London, 1715.

Hugnet, Georges. *Fantastic Art Dada Surrealism*. Ed. by A. H. Barr. New York, 1936.

Huizinga, Johan. *Men and Ideas: History, the Middle Ages, the Renaissance*. Tr. by J. S. Holmes and Hans van Marle, with an introduction by B. F. Hoselitz. New York, 1959.

——. *The Waning of the Middle Ages.* Tr. by F. Hopman. New York, 1954.

Huppé, Bernard. *Doctrine and Poetry.* Albany, 1959.

Hurd, Richard. *An Introduction to the Study of the Prophecies concerning the Christian Church, and, in Particular, concerning the Church of Papal Rome, in Twelve Sermons.* London, 1772.

Ilf and Petrov. *The Twelve Chairs.* Tr. by J. H. C. Richardson. Introduction by Maurice Friedberg. New York, 1961.

Inge, W. R. *Mysticism in Religion.* London, 1948.

Isidore of Seville. *Etymologies (Etymologiarum Sive Originum).* Ed. by W. M. Lindsay. Oxford, 1911.

Izutsu, Toshihiko. *Language and Magic: Studies in the Magical Function of Speech.* Tokyo, 1956.

Jacobi, Jolande. *Complex/Archetype/Symbol.* Tr. by Ralph Manheim. New York, 1959.

Jacquot, Jean, ed. *Les Fêtes de la Renaissance.* Paris, 1956.

Jakobson, Roman. "The Cardinal Dichotomy in Language," in *Language: An Enquiry into Its Meaning and Function.* Ed. by R. N. Anshen. New York, 1957.

James, Henry. "Emile Zola," in *The Future of the Novel.* Ed. by Leon Edel. New York, 1956.

——. "Flaubert's *Temptation of St. Anthony*," in *Literary Reviews and Essays.* Ed. by Albert Mordell. New York, 1957.

Jankélevitch, Vladimir. *L'Ironie ou la bonne conscience.* Paris, 1950.

Janson, H. W. *Apes and Ape Lore in the Middle Ages and the Renaissance.* London, 1952.

Jean, Marcel. *The History of Surrealist Painting.* Tr. by S. W. Taylor. New York, 1960.

Jespersen, Otto. *Mankind, Nation and Individual.* London, 1946.

Johnson, F. R. *Astronomical Thought in Renaissance England.* Baltimore, 1937.

Johnson, Samuel. "The Life of Milton," *Works,* II. Ed. by Arthur Murphy. New York, 1843.

Jonas, Hans. *The Gnostic Religion: The Message of the Alien God and the Beginnings of Christianity.* Boston, 1958.

Jones, Ernest. *Hamlet and Oedipus.* New York, 1955.

——. *The Life and Work of Sigmund Freud.* New York, 1957.

——. "The Theory of Symbolism," *British Journal of Psychology*, IX. (Reprinted in *Papers on Psychoanalysis*, 5th ed., London, 1948.)

Jones, H. S. V. "Spenser's Defence of Lord Grey," *University of Illinois Studies in Language and Literature*, V. Urbana, 1919.

Jung, Carl. "The Archetypes of the Collective Unconscious," in *Collected Works*, IX. New York, 1953–1961.

——. "The Paradigm of the Unicorn," in *Collected Works*, XII. New York, 1953–1961.

——, and Karl Kerenyi, *Essays on a Science of Mythology*. Tr. by R. F. C. Hull. New York, 1949.

Juret, A. *Dictionnaire étymologique grec et latin*. Mâcon, 1942.

Kafka, Franz. *The Great Wall of China: Stories and Reflections*. Tr. by Willa and Edwin Muir. New York, 1948.

——. *Parables*. Tr. by Willa and Edwin Muir. New York, 1947.

——. "In the Penal Colony," in *The Penal Colony: Stories and Short Pieces*. Tr. by Willa and Edwin Muir. New York, 1961.

Kant, Immanuel. *The Critique of Aesthetic Judgment*. Tr. and ed. by J. C. Meredith. Oxford, 1911.

Kantorowicz, Ernst. *The King's Two Bodies*. Princeton, 1957.

Katzellenbogen, Adolf. *Allegories of the Virtues and Vices in Mediaeval Art*. London, 1939.

Ker, W. P. *Epic and Romance: Essays on Medieval Literature*. London, 1896; reprinted New York, 1957.

Kirkman, Francis. *The Counterfeit Lady Unveiled and Other Criminal Fiction of Seventeenth Century England*. Ed. by Spiro Peterson. New York, 1961.

Kitzinger, Ernst. "The Cult of Images in the Age before Iconoclasm," *Dumbarton Oaks Papers*, Number 8. Cambridge, Mass., 1954.

Knox, Israel. *Aesthetic Theories of Kant, Hegel and Schopenhauer*. London, 1958.

Knox, Ronald. *Enthusiasm: A Chapter in the History of Religion with Special Reference to the XVIIth and XVIIIth Centuries*. Oxford, 1950.

Körner, Stephan. *Conceptual Thinking: A Logical Analysis*. Cambridge, 1955.

Kolb, G. J. "Johnson's 'Dissertation on Flying' and John Wilkins' *Mathematical Magic*," *Modern Philology*, XLVII (1949), no. 1.

Krappe, A. H. *La Genèse des mythes*. Paris, 1952.

Kroner, Richard. *Speculation in Pre-Christian Philosophy*. Philadelphia, 1956.

Ladner, G. B. "The Concept of the Image in the Greek Fathers and the Byzantine Iconoclastic Controversy," *Dumbarton Oaks Papers*, Number 7. Cambridge, Mass., 1953

——. *The Idea of Reform: Its Impact on Christian Thought and Action in the Age of the Fathers*. Cambridge, Mass., 1959.

——. "Origin and Significance of the Byzantine Iconoclastic Controversy," *Medieval Studies*, II. New York and London, 1940.

Laistner, M. L. W. *Thought and Letters in Western Europe: A.D. 500 to 900*. Ithaca, 1957.

Lambert, Margaret, and Enid Marx. *English Popular Art*. London, 1951.

Langer, Suzanne. *Philosophy in a New Key*. New York, 1942.

Langland, William. *Piers the Ploughman*. Tr. with an introduction by J. F. Goodridge. Penguin ed., 1959.

Langton, Edward. *Essentials of Demonology*. London, 1949.

Larkin, Oliver W. *Art and Life in America*. New York, 1949.

Legge, M. D. " 'To Speik of Science, Craft, and Sapience' in Medieval Literature," in *Literature and Science*. Oxford, 1955.

Lesser, S. O. *Fiction and the Unconscious*. Boston, 1957.

Lethaby, W. R. *Architecture, Nature and Magic*. London, 1956.

Levi, Carlo. *Of Fear and Freedom*. Tr. by Adolphe Gourevitch. New York, 1950.

Lévy-Bruhl, Lucien. *L'Ame primitive*. Paris, 1927.

——. *Les Fonctions mentales dans les sociétés inférieures*. Paris, 1910.

Lewin, B. D. "Obsessional Neuroses," in *Psychoanalysis Today*. Ed. by Sandor Lorand. London, 1948.

Lewis, C. S. *The Allegory of Love*. Oxford, 1936.

——. *A Preface to Paradise Lost*. London, 1960.

Lewis, Matthew. *The Monk* (1796). New York, 1952.

Lewis, Wyndham. *Time and Western Man*. New York, 1928.

Leyburn, E. D. *Satiric Allegory: Mirror of Man*. New Haven, 1956.

Longinus. *On the Sublime*. Tr. by W. Rhys Roberts. Cambridge, 1907.

Lovejoy, A. O. *Essays in the History of Ideas*. Baltimore, 1948; reprinted New York, 1960.

——. *The Great Chain of Being: A Study of the History of an Idea*. Cambridge, Mass., 1953.

Luchins, Abraham and Edith. *Rigidity of Behavior.* Eugene, Ore., 1959.

Lynn, Kenneth. *The Dream of Success.* Boston, 1955.

MacDonald, George. *Phantastes* (1858). Ed. by Greville MacDonald. Everyman ed., 1916.

McKellar, Peter. *Imagination and Thinking.* New York, 1957.

Mâle, Emile. *The Gothic Image: Religious Art in France of the Thirteenth Century.* Tr. by Dora Nussey. New York, 1958.

Malinowski, Bronislaw. *Magic, Science and Religion.* Boston, 1948.

Mann, Thomas. *Death in Venice and Seven Other Stories.* New York, 1958.

Manuel, F. E. *The Eighteenth Century Confronts the Gods.* Cambridge, Mass., 1959.

Mao Tse-tung. *Problems of Art and Literature.* New York, 1953.

Marcuse, Ludwig. "Freuds Aesthetik," *PMLA,* LXXII (June, 1957).

Marignac, Aloys de. *Imagination et dialectique.* Paris, 1951.

Mathewson, R. W. *The Positive Hero in Russian Literature.* New York, 1958.

Maturin, C. R. *Melmoth the Wanderer* (1820). Ed. with an introduction by W. F. Axton. Lincoln, 1961.

Mazzeo, J. A. *Medieval Cultural Tradition in Dante's Comedy.* Ithaca, 1960.

——. "Metaphysical Poetry and the Poetic of Correspondence," *Journal of the History of Ideas,* XIV (April 1953).

Melville, Herman. *Pierre.* Ed. with an introduction by Henry Murray. New York, 1949.

[Metropolitan Museum of Art.] *Historical Armor: A Picture Book.* New York, 1957.

Miller, W. M. *A Canticle for Leibowitz.* New York, 1959.

Monk, Samuel. *The Sublime: A Study of Critical Theories in XVIII-Century England.* Ann Arbor, 1960.

Monnerot, Jules. *The Sociology and Psychology of Communism.* Tr. by Jane Degras and Richard Rees. Boston, 1953.

Moulinier, Louis. *Le Pur et l'impur dans la pensée des Grecs d'Homère à Aristote.* Paris, 1952.

Mourey, Gabriel. *Le Livre des fêtes françaises.* Paris, 1930.

Mueller, W. R. *John Donne, Preacher.* Princeton, 1962.

Murray, Margaret, ed. *Egyptian Religious Poetry.* London, 1949.

BIBLIOGRAPHY

Murry, J. Middleton. *The Problem of Style*. London, 1960.

Neumann, Erich. *The Great Mother: An Analysis of the Archetype*. Tr. by Ralph Manheim. New York, 1955.

——. *The Origins and History of Consciousness*. Tr. by R. F. C. Hull. New York, 1954.

Newdigate, Bernard, ed. *The Phoenix and Turtle: By William Shakespeare, John Marston, George Chapman, Ben Jonson, and Others*. Oxford, 1937.

Nicolson, Marjorie. *The Breaking of the Circle: Studies in the Effect of the "New Science" upon Seventeenth-Century Poetry*. New York, 1960.

——. *Voyages to the Moon*. New York, 1960.

Nilsson, M. P. *Greek Folk Religion*. Ed. by A. D. Nock. New York, 1961.

——. *Greek Piety*. Tr. by H. J. Rose. Oxford, 1948.

Nock, A. D. *Conversion: The Old and the New in Religion from Alexander the Great to Augustine of Hippo*. London, 1933.

Nohl, Johannes. *The Black Death*. Tr. by C. H. Clarke. New York, 1960.

Nygren, Anders. *Agape and Eros*. Tr. by A. G. Hebert and P. S. Wilson. London, 1933.

O'Brien, G. W. *Renaissance Poetics and the Problem of Power*. Chicago, 1956.

Ogden, C. K. *Bentham's Theory of Fictions*. London, 1932.

——, and I. A. Richards. *The Meaning of Meaning* (1923). 8th (Harvest) ed., New York, 1959.

Olson, Elder. "William Empson, Contemporary Criticism, and Poetic Diction," in *Critics and Criticism*. Ed. by R. S. Crane. Abridged ed., Chicago, 1957.

Origen. *Commentary on* The Song of Songs. Tr. and ed. by R. P. Lawson. Westminster, Md., 1957.

——. *Contra Celsum*. Tr. by Henry Chadwick. Cambridge, 1953.

Otto, Rudolph. *The Idea of the Holy*. Tr. by J. W. Harvey. New York, 1958.

Ovid. *Fasti*. Tr. by H. T. Riley. London, 1890.

Owst, G. R. *Literature and Pulpit in Medieval England*. Cambridge, 1933.

BIBLIOGRAPHY

Palingenius, Marcellus. *The Zodiacke of Life.* Tr. by Barnabe Googe. Ed. in facsimile by Rosemond Tuve. New York, 1947.

Panofsky, Erwin. *Albrecht Dürer.* Princeton, 1948.

——. *Galileo as a Critic of the Fine Arts.* The Hague, 1954.

——. *Meaning in the Visual Arts.* New York, 1955.

——. *Studies in Iconology: Humanistic Themes in the Art of the Renaissance.* New York, 1939; reprinted New York, 1962.

Paracelsus. *Selected Writings.* Ed. by Jolande Jacobi. New York, 1951.

Parker, A. A. *The Allegorical Drama of Calderón.* London, 1943.

Patch, H. R. *The Goddess Fortuna in Medieval Literature.* Cambridge, Mass., 1927.

——. *The Tradition of Boethius: A Study of His Importance in Medieval Culture.* New York, 1935.

Paton, Alan. "The South African Treason Trial," *Atlantic Monthly,* CCV (Jan. 1960).

Paton, H. J. *The Modern Predicament: A Study in the Philosophy of Religion.* London and New York, 1955.

Peacham, Henry. *The Garden of Eloquence* (London, 1593). Ed. in facsimile by W. G. Crane. Gainesville, Fla., 1954.

Pearl. Ed. with an introduction by E. V. Gordon. Oxford, 1953.

Pépin, Jules. *Mythe et allégorie.* Paris, 1958.

Perrow, E. C. "The Last Will and Testament as a Form of Literature," reprinted from *Transactions of the Wisconsin Academy of Sciences, Arts, and Letters,* XVII (Dec. 1913) Part I.

Peter, J. D. *Complaint and Satire in Early English Literature.* Oxford, 1956.

Phillips, Edward. *The New World of English Words* (1658). 4th ed., London, 1678.

Philo Judaeus. *Works.* Tr. and ed. by F. H. Colson and G. H. Whitaker. Loeb Classics ed.; London, 1929.

"The Phoenix," *Early English Christian Poetry.* Tr. by C. W. Kennedy. London, 1952.

Plutarch. "On the Cessation of Oracles," *Plutarch's Morals.* Tr. by C. W. King. London, 1903.

——. *Moralia.* Tr. by W. W. Goodwin. Boston, 1878.

Pohl, Albert, and C. M. Kornbluth. *The Space Merchants.* New York, 1953.

Politzer, Heinz. *Frank Kafka: Parable and Paradox.* Ithaca, 1962.

Porphyrius. *Commentary on Odyssey XIII (Treatise on the Homeric Cave of the Nymphs),* in *Select Works of Porphyry.* Tr. by Thomas Taylor with an appendix explaining the allegory of the wanderings of Ulysses. London, 1823.

Poulet, Georges. *The Interior Distance.* Tr. by Elliott Coleman. Baltimore, 1959.

——. *Studies in Human Time.* Tr. by Elliott Coleman. Baltimore, 1956.

Pound, Ezra. *Personae.* New York, 1926.

Praz, Mario. *The Flaming Heart: Essays on Crashaw, Machiavelli, and Other Studies in the Relations between Italian and English Literature from Chaucer to T. S. Eliot.* New York, 1958.

——. *Studies in Seventeenth Century Imagery.* London, 1939.

Price, Uvedale. *On the Picturesque.* Ed. by Sir Thomas Dick Lauder. London, 1842.

Priestley, Joseph. *A Course of Lectures on Oratory and Criticism.* London, 1777.

Propp, Vladimir. *The Morphology of the Folktale.* Tr. by Laurence Scott. Introduction by Svatava Pirkova-Jacobson. Bloomington, 1958.

Prudentius. *Works.* Tr. and ed. by H. J. Thomson. Loeb Classics ed.; London, 1949.

Pseudo-Dionysius the Areopagite. *On the Divine Names and Mystical Theology.* Tr. by C. E. Rolt. New York, 1940.

——. *Oeuvres complètes du Pseudo-Denys L'Aréopagite.* Tr. by Maurice de Gandillac. Paris, 1943.

Pulver, M. "The Experience of the Pneuma in Philo," in *Spirit and Nature* ("Eranos Yearbooks," Bollingen Series, XXX). New York, 1954.

Puttenham, George. *The Arte of English Poesie* (London, 1589). Ed. by Gladys Willcock and Alice Walker. Cambridge, 1936.

Quintilian. *The Institutes of Oratory.* Tr. by H. E. Butler. Loeb Classics ed., London and Cambridge, Mass., 1953.

Rado, Sandor. *Psychoanalysis of Behavior: Collected Papers.* New York, 1956.

Raglan, Lord. *The Hero.* London, 1936; reprinted New York, 1956.

Rahner, M. "Earth Spirit and Divine Spirit in Patristic Theology," in

BIBLIOGRAPHY

Spirit and Nature ("Eranos Yearbooks," Bollingen Series, XXX). New York, 1954.

Rank, Otto. *Art and Artist: Creative Urge and Personality Development.* New York, 1932.

——. *The Myth of the Birth of the Hero and Other Writings.* Ed. by Philip Freund. New York, 1959.

Rapaport, David, ed. *Organization and Pathology of Thought.* New York, 1951.

Raven, C. E. *Natural Religion and Christian Theology.* Cambridge, 1953.

Réau, Louis. *Iconographie de l'art chrétien.* Paris, 1955–1959.

Reich, Wilhelm. *Character Analysis.* New York, 1961.

Richards, I. A. *The Philosophy of Rhetoric.* London, 1936.

——. *Practical Criticism* (1929). New York, 1956.

——. *Principles of Literary Criticism* (1925). New York, 1952.

——. *Speculative Instruments.* Chicago, 1955.

Ritchie, A. D. *Studies in the History and Methods of the Sciences.* Edinburgh, 1958.

Ritter, Gerhart. *The Corrupting Influence of Power.* Tr. by F. W. Pick. London, 1952.

Robbins, R. H., ed. *Historical Poems of the XIVth and XVth Centuries.* New York, 1959.

Robertson, D. W., Jr. "The Doctrine of Charity in Mediaeval Literary Gardens," *Speculum*, XXVI (1951).

——. *A Preface to Chaucer: Studies in Medieval Perspectives.* Princeton, 1962.

Robinson, H. W. *Inspiration and Revelation in the Old Testament.* Oxford, 1946.

Róheim, Géza. *The Eternal Ones of the Dream.* New York, 1945.

Roques, René. *L'Univers dionysien: Structure hiérarchique du monde selon le Pseudo-Denys.* Paris, 1954.

Rougemont, Denis de. *Love in the Western World.* Tr. by Montgomery Belgion. New York, 1957.

Runes, Dagobert, ed. *Dictionary of Philosophy.* New York, 1942.

Rynell, Alarik. "Parataxis and Hypotaxis as a Criterion of Syntax and Style," *Lunds Univ. Artskrift*, N.F. Avd. 1, XLVIII (1952), no. 3.

Sabbattini, Nicolo. *Manual for Constructing Theatrical Scenes and Machines (Practica di fabricar scene e machine ne' teatri*, Ravenna,

1638), in *The Renaissance Stage: Documents of Serlio, Sabbattini, and Furttenbach.* Tr. by Allardyce Nicoll, J. H. McDowell, and G. R. Kernodle. Ed. by Barnard Hewitt. Coral Gables, Fla., 1958.

Säve-Söderbergh, Torgny. *Pharaohs and Mortals.* Tr. by R. E. Oldenburg. Indianapolis, 1961.

Saintsbury, George. *The Flourishing of Romance and the Rise of Allegory.* New York, 1897.

Sambursky, Samuel. *Physics of the Stoics.* London, 1959.

Saunders, J. W. "The Façade of Morality," in *That Souereign Light: Essays in Honor of Edmund Spenser 1552–1952.* Ed. by W. R. Mueller and D. C. Allen. Baltimore, 1952.

Schiller, Friedrich. "The Sublime," in *Essays Aesthetical and Philosophical.* London, 1882.

——. *Wallenstein: A Historical Drama in Three Parts.* Tr. by C. E. Passage. New York, 1958.

Schneweis, Emil. *Angels and Demons According to Lactantius.* Washington, 1944.

Schwartz-Metterklume, Ludwig. *Der Weltschmertz und die Frau Potter.* Leipzig, 1905.

Sciama, D. W. *The Unity of the Universe.* New York, 1961.

Scott, Geoffrey. *The Architecture of Humanism.* 2d ed., 1924; reprinted, Anchor ed.

Seboek, T. A., ed. *Myth: A Symposium.* Bloomington, 1958.

Segal, C. P. "ΥΨΟΣ and the Problem of Cultural Decline in the *De Sublimitate*," *Harvard Studies in Classical Philology,* LXIV (1959).

Seligmann, Kurt. *The Mirror of Magic.* New York, 1948.

Seznec, Jean. *The Survival of the Pagan Gods.* Tr. by Barbara Sessions. New York, 1953.

Shaftesbury, Anthony Ashley Cooper, 3rd Earl of. *Second Characteristics.* Ed. by Benjamin Rand. Cambridge, 1914.

Shakespeare, William. *Coriolanus,* in *Bell's Shakespeare.* London, 1773.

Sheckley, Robert. *Notions Unlimited.* New York, 1950.

——. *The Status Civilization.* New York, 1960.

——. *Untouched by Human Hands.* New York, 1960.

Shelley, P. B. *Defence of Poetry.* Oxford, 1932.

Sigerist, Henry. *A History of Medicine.* New York, 1951.

Simmons, E. J. *Russian Literature and Soviet Ideology.* New York, 1958.

——. *Through the Glass of Soviet Literature: Views of Russian Society.* New York, 1953.

Simon, Marcel. *Hercule et le Christianisme.* Paris, 1955.

Sinclair, Upton. *The Jungle.* Signet ed.; New York, 1960.

Skinner, John. *Prophecy and Religion: Studies in the Life of Jeremiah.* Cambridge, 1961.

Smith, Henry. *Micro-cosmo-graphia: The Little-Worlds Description, or, The Map of Man.* Tr. by Joshua Sylvester. Grosart ed., privately printed, 1880.

Soby, James Thrall. *Giorgio de Chirico.* New York, 1955.

Solmsen, Friedrich. *Aristotle's System of the Physical World.* Ithaca, 1960.

Soury, Guy. *La Démonologie de Plutarque.* Paris, 1942.

Spink, J. S. "Form and Structure: Cyrano de Bergerac's Atomistic Conception of Metamorphosis," in *Literature and Science.* (Proceedings of the 6th Triennial Congress, Oxford, of the International Federation for Modern Languages and Literatures.) Oxford, 1955.

Spitzer, Leo. *Classical and Christian Ideas of World Harmony.* New York, 1944–1945.

——. *Linguistics and Literary History.* Princeton, 1948.

Steiner, Franz. *Taboo.* London, 1956.

Stekel, Wilhelm. *Compulsion and Doubt.* Tr. by Emil Gutheil. New York, 1949.

Stevens, Wallace. *Collected Poems.* New York, 1954.

Stravinsky, Igor. *The Poetics of Music.* New York, 1956.

Summers, J. H. *George Herbert: His Religion and Art.* Cambridge, Mass., 1954.

Swayze, Harold. *Political Control of Literature in the U.S.S.R. 1946–59.* Cambridge, Mass., 1962.

Temkin, Owsei. "An Historical Analysis of the Concept of Infection," in *Studies in Intellectual History.* Baltimore, 1953.

Tertullian. "On Idolatry," in *The Library of Christian Classics,* V. Tr. and ed. by S. L. Greenslade. London, 1956.

Tertz, Abraham. *On Socialist Realism.* Tr. by George Dennis. New York, 1960.

Thucydides. *The Peloponnesian War.* Tr. by Rex Warner. Penguin ed., 1954.

Tillyard, E. M. W. *Poetry Direct and Oblique*. London, 1945.

Troeltsch, Ernst. *The Social Teaching of the Christian Churches*. Tr. by Olive Wyon. New York, 1960.

Tuve, Rosemond. *Elizabethan and Metaphysical Imagery*. Chicago, 1947.

Tuveson, Ernest. *The Imagination as a Means of Grace: Locke and the Aesthetics of Romanticism*. Berkeley, 1960.

Tylor, E. B. *The Origins of Culture* (1871). New York, 1958.

Tymms, Ralph. *Doubles in Literary Psychology*. Cambridge, 1949.

Tzara, Tristan. *Le Surréalisme et l'après-guerre*. Paris, 1947.

Valency, Maurice. *In Praise of Love: An Introduction to the Love-Poetry of the Renaissance*. New York, 1958.

Vallins, G. H. *The Pattern of English*. Penguin ed., 1957.

Van Ghent, Dorothy. "Clarissa and Emma as Phèdre," *Modern Literary Criticism*. Ed. by Irving Howe. Boston, 1958.

——. *The English Novel*. New York, 1953.

Vernon, M. D. *A Further Study of Visual Perception*. Cambridge, 1954.

Virgil. *The Aeneid*. Tr. by Rolfe Humphries. New York, 1951.

Wagman, F. H. *Magic and Natural Science in German Baroque Literature: A Study in the Prose Forms of the Later 17th Century*. New York, 1942.

Waites, M. C. "Some Aspects of the Ancient Allegorical Debate," *Studies in English and Comparative Literature*. (Radcliffe College Monographs, No. 15.) London and Boston, 1910.

Walker, D. P. *Spiritual and Demonic Magic from Ficino to Campanella*. London, 1958.

Wallerstein, Ruth. *Richard Crashaw: A Study in Style and Poetic Development*. Madison, 1935.

Warner, Rex. *The Cult of Power*. London, 1946.

Warren, Austin, and René Wellek. *Theory of Literature*. New York, 1949.

Warton, Thomas. "Of the Plan and Conduct of the *Fairy Queen*" (1762), in *Spenser's Critics*. Ed. by William Mueller. Syracuse, 1959.

——. "Of Spenser's Allegorical Character" (1762), in *Spenser's Critics*. Ed. by William Mueller. Syracuse, 1959.

Watkins, W. B. C. *Shakespeare and Spenser*. Princeton, 1950.

Watson, C. B. *Shakespeare and the Renaissance Concept of Honor*. Princeton, 1960.

BIBLIOGRAPHY

Webber, Joan. *Contrary Music: The Prose Style of John Donne*. Madison, 1962.

Wellek, René. *A History of Modern Criticism*. New Haven, 1955.

Wells, Henry. *Poetic Imagery*. New York, 1924.

Werner, Heinz. *Comparative Psychology of Mental Development*. Chicago, 1948.

West, Anthony. *Principles and Persuasions*. New York, 1957.

Weston, Jessie, tr. *Romance, Vision and Satire*. Boston, 1911.

White, R. W. *The Abnormal Personality*. New York, 1948.

Whorf, B. L. "Time, Space and Language," in *Culture in Crisis: A Study of the Hopi Indians*. Ed. by Laura Thompson. New York, 1950.

Willey, Basil. *Darwin and Butler*. New York, 1960.

——. *The Seventeenth Century Background*. New York, 1953.

Willi, W. "The History of the Spirit in Antiquity," in *Spirit and Nature* ("Eranos Yearbooks," Bollingen Series, XXX). New York, 1954.

Williams, Charles. *The Greater Trumps*. New York, 1950.

Wilson, R. McL. *The Gnostic Problem: A Study of the Relations between Hellenistic Judaism and the Gnostic Heresy*. London, 1958.

Wilson, Thomas. *The Arte of Rhetorique* (1585). Ed. in facsimile by G. H. Mair. Oxford, 1909.

Wimsatt, W. K., and Cleanth Brooks. *Literary Criticism: A Short History*. New York, 1957.

Wind, Edgar. *Pagan Mysteries in the Renaissance*. London, 1958.

Windsor, H.R.H. the Duke of. *Windsor Revisited*. Cambridge, Mass., 1960.

Wolfe, Bertram. *Three Who Made a Revolution*. Boston, 1955.

Wolfson, H. A. *Philo*. Cambridge, Mass., 1947.

——. *The Philosophy of the Church Fathers*. Cambridge, Mass., 1956.

Worringer, Wilhelm. *Abstraction and Empathy*. Tr. by Michael Bullock. New York, 1953.

Yeats, W. B., ed. *Edmund Spenser*. Edinburgh, 1906.

Zamiatin, Eugene. *We*. Tr. by Gregory Zilboorg. New York, 1959.

Zhdanov, Andrei. *Essays on Literature, Philosophy and Music*. New York, 1950.

Index

INDEX

Dec. 1, 1972
Discussion
(Spenser, Books on Chaucer, Dilemma Paper, J's BF)